Communications in Computer and Information Science 1502

More information about this series at https://link.springer.com/bookseries/7899

Ranjeet Singh Tomar · Shekhar Verma ·
Brijesh Kumar Chaurasia · Vrijendra Singh ·
Jemal Abawajy · Shyam Akashe ·
Pao-Ann Hsiung · Vijay K. Bhargava (Eds.)

Communication, Networks and Computing

Second International Conference, CNC 2020
Gwalior, India, December 29–31, 2020
Revised Selected Papers

Editors
Ranjeet Singh Tomar
ITM University
Gwalior, India

Brijesh Kumar Chaurasia
IIIT Lucknow
Lucknow, India

Jemal Abawajy
Deakin University
Geelong, Australia

Pao-Ann Hsiung
National Chung Cheng University
Chiayi City, Taiwan

Shekhar Verma
IIIT Allahabad
Allahabad, India

Vrijendra Singh
IIIT Allahabad
Allahabad, India

Shyam Akashe
ITM University
Gwalior, India

Vijay K. Bhargava
University of British Columbia
Vancouver, Canada

ISSN 1865-0929 ISSN 1865-0937 (electronic)
Communications in Computer and Information Science
ISBN 978-981-16-8895-9 ISBN 978-981-16-8896-6 (eBook)
https://doi.org/10.1007/978-981-16-8896-6

This Springer imprint is published by the registered company Springer Nature Singapore Pte Ltd.
The registered company address is: 152 Beach Road, #21-01/04 Gateway East, Singapore 189721, Singapore

Preface

The book focuses on communication, networks, and computing to simplify the real-time problems occurring in different domains within these fields. Presently, research is entering a new era of convergence of these domains wherein the established models and techniques are being challenged. New ideas are being proposed and established ideas are being retested. Evaluating the performance of emerging smart technologies, however, poses a huge challenge.

The book includes high-quality papers presented at the International Conference on Communication, Networks, and Computing (CNC 2020), organized by ITM University Gwalior, India. Offering significant insights into this domain for academics and industry alike, the book aims to inspire more researchers to work in the field of "Next Generation Networks for Communication Systems", which was the theme of the conference. This theme covers the exciting new areas of wired and wireless communication systems, high-dimensional data representation and processing, networks and information security, computing techniques for efficient network design, vehicular technology and applications, and electronic circuits for communication systems, which all promise to make the world a better place to live in.

ITM University Gwalior, India, is a multidisciplinary university with an international reputation for the quality of its research and teaching across the academic spectrum. The university has received more than 40 awards and has been ranked in the top category by a number of governmental and other agencies. The university was ranked 32nd in management and 58th in engineering in 2016 by the National Institutional Ranking Framework, MHRD, Government of India. The university is approved by the regulatory bodies required to run courses in engineering, management, pharmacy, commerce, agriculture, architecture, computer applications, teacher education, art and design, physical education, sciences, law, India and South Asia studies, journalism, nursing, etc. It is at the forefront of learning, teaching, and research and the leader in different fields. It seeks to sustain and enhance its excellence as an institution of higher learning through outstanding teaching and the world-class societies it serves.

The ITM School of Engineering and Technology is one of the flagship and leading schools of central and north India. The school is unique in that it tries to assimilate cutting-edge ideas in engineering and technology through a variety of projects in association with industry. In addition, prominent industries directly contribute to the knowledge and skill sets of students through various augmentation programs customized for students of ITM University. A mix of lectures, tutorials, laboratory studies, seminars, and projects are used to develop the conceptual and analytical abilities of students. For the first time in India, ITM University Gwalior has taken the initiative to introduce activity-based continuous assessment (ABCA) and project-based learning (PBL) in order to increase the employability of students.

The CNC 2020 conference was successful in facilitating academics, researchers, and industry professionals to deliberate upon the latest issues, challenges, and advancements in communication, networks, and computing. In total, 102 papers were submitted for six tracks. After a thorough review process, 30 papers were selected for oral presentation during the conference, which are published in the book.

This conference proceedings volume will prove beneficial for academics, researchers, and professionals from industry as it contains valuable information and knowledge on developments in communication, networks, and computing.

November 2021

Ranjeet Singh Tomar
Shekhar Verma
Brijesh Kumar Chaurasia
Vrijendra Singh
Jemal Abawajy
Shyam Akashe
Pao-Ann Hsiung
Vijay K. Bhargava

Organization

Chief Patron

Ramashankar Singh (Founder Chancellor)	ITM University Gwalior, India
Ruchi Singh Chauhan (Chancellor)	ITM University Gwalior, India

Patrons

Kanupriya Singh Rathore (Chairperson)	ITM Universe, Vadodara, India
Ravindra Singh Rathore (Managing Director)	ITM Universe, Vadodara, India
Daulat Singh Chauhan (Pro Chancellor)	ITM University Gwalior, India
Kamalkant Dwivedi (Vice-chancellor)	ITM University Gwalior, India
R. D. Gupta (Advisor to Chancellor)	ITM University Gwalior, India
Omveer Singh (Registrar)	ITM University Gwalior, India

General Chairs

Shekhar Verma	IIIT, Allahabad, India
Ranjeet Singh Tomar	ITM University Gwalior, India
Ramjee Prasad	Aarhus University, Denmark

Program Chairs

Pao Ann Hsiung	National Chung Cheng University, Taiwan
Vijay K. Bhargava	University of British Columbia, Canada
Brijesh Kumar Chaurasia	IIIT Lucknow, India

Technical Committee Chairs

Jemal Abawajy	Deakin University, Australia
Vrijendra Singh	IIIT Allahabad, India
Shyam Akashe	ITM University Gwalior, India

Publications Chairs

Sanjay Jain	ITM University Gwalior, India
Rishi Soni	ITM Gwalior, India

Publicity Chairs

Pallavi Khatri	ITM University Gwalior, India
Shashikant Gupta	ITM University Gwalior, India

Workshop/Tutorial Chairs

Arun Kumar Yadav	ITM University Gwalior, India
Rajendra Singh Kushwah	Digitalkal, India

Hospitality Chairs

Mukesh Kumar Pandey	ITM University Gwalior, India
Keshav Kansana	ITM University, Gwalior, India
Manish Sharma	ITM University, Gwalior, India

Program Committee

Abdul Rahman	Lee Kong Chian Faculty of Engineering & Science, Malaysia
Q. C. Kanhu Kamre	HIT, Zimbabwe
Tendai Padenga	HIT, Zimbabwe
Raj Kumar Buyya	University of Melbourne, Australia
Hairul Azhar	UTAR, Malaysia
Kim Yee Lee	UTAR, Malaysia
Bebo White	Stanford University, USA
Peter Robinson	University of Cambridge, UK
Pradeep K. Khosla	University of California, San Diego, USA
Banmali Rawat	University of Nevada, Reno, USA
Aditya Mathur	Singapore University of Technology and Design, Singapore
Paul Gries	University of Toronto, Canada
David Gries	Cornell University, USA
Akhil Kumar	Pennsylvania State University, USA
Pavel O. V. Seiko	University of Oxford, UK
Pinaki Mazumder	University of Michigan, USA
Pawan Khera	Carnegie Mellon University, USA
Animesh Animesh	McGill University, Canada

Venky Dubey	Bournemouth University, UK
Supriya Chakrabarti	University of Massachusetts, USA
Soumya Kanti Manna	Bournemouth University, UK
Leonard Lye	Memorial University of Newfoundland, Canada
Emili Balaguer	Bournemouth University, UK
Chi-Ling Pan	Chaoyang University of Technology, Taiwan
Sandhya Samarasinghe	Lincoln University, New Zealand
Faisal Khan	Memorial University of Newfoundland, Canada
Gora Chand Mohapatra	Gulf Cooperation Council, UAE
Yizhou Yu	University of Hong Kong, Hong Kong
Rashmi Dravid	University of Northampton, UK
Pao-Ann Hsiung	National Chung Cheng University, Taiwan
Kishor Trivedi	Duke University, USA
Jiyun Li	Donghua University, China
Poonam Yadav	Imperial College London, UK
Sugam Sharma	Iowa State University, USA
A. Mohanty	IIT Kharagpur, India
Saurav Mohanty	Altran, France
Neeti Parashar	Purdue University, USA
Sartaj Sahni	University of Florida, USA
Jai P. Agrawal	Purdue University, USA
S. N. Mishra	Walter Sisulu University, South Africa
Vipin Chaudhary	University at Buffalo, USA
Wu-Yuin Hwang	National Central University, Taiwan
J. R. Nanda	NIC Delhi, India
Y. N. Singh	IIT Kanpur, India
S. D. Joshi	IIT Delhi, India
L. M. Joshi	CSIR-CEERI Pilani, India
Ekram Khan	Aligarh Muslim University, India
N. S. Raghava	Delhi Technological University, India
A. Shivanthu Pillai	DRDO, India
S. S. Pathak	IIT Kharagpur, India
R. K. Ghosh	IIT Kanpur, India
Aditya Jagannathan	IIT Kanpur, India
Aditya Trivedi	ABV-IIITM Gwalior, India
Manish Kumar	IIIT Allahabad, India
Rajat Kumar Singh	IIIT Allahabad, India
R. D. Gupta	ITM University Gwalior, India
B. K. Singh	Institute of Technology & Management Gwalior, India
Yogesh Upadhyay	Jiwaji University Gwalior, India
D. C. Tiwari	Jiwaji University Gwalior, India

Manu Pratap Singh	Dr. B. R. Ambedkar University, India
Rishi Soni	Institute of Technology & Management Gwalior, India
Rajendra Singh Kushwah	Institute of Technology & Management Gwalior, India
Anand Tripathi	Institute of Technology & Management Gwalior, India
Rajeev Chaturvedi	SRCEM Morena, India
Mritunjay Rai	Lovely Professional University, India
Pradheepkumar Singaravelu	IIIT Allahabad, India
Neeraj Shrivastava	Rustamji Institute of Technology, India
Vivekanand Mishra	SVNIT Surat, India
Manjusha Pandey	KIIT University, India
Siddharth Rautarey	KIIT University, India
Dilip Sharma	Ujjain Engineering College, India
Wilfred Godfrey	ABV-IIITM Gwalior, India
U. C. Pati	NIT Rourkela, India
Sumant Kumar Tiwari	BBD University, India
Chandrashekhar Gautam	IIT Kanpur, India
Nafisuddin Ahmad	JUET, India
Abhishek Pandey	IIIT Allahabad, India
A. P. Manu	IIIT Allahabad, India
D. K. Chaturvedi	Dayalbag Educational Institute, India
Sarabjeet Singh Bedi	MJP Rohilkhand University, India
Prem Pal Singh Tomar	Dayalbagh Educational Institute, India
Lalit Awasthi	NIT Hamirpur, India
Rajiv Tripathi	MNNIT Allahabad, India
M. M. Sharma	MANIT Jaipur, India
R. P. Yadav	MNIT Jaipur, India
K. K. Sharma	MNIT Jaipur, India
Mohd. Salim	MNIT Jaipur, India
Shailendra Jain	MANIT Bhopal, India
Indra Vijay Singh	MGM College of Engineering & Technology, India
Ashutosh Sharma	BITS Bhopal, India
Aditya Vidyarthi	BIST Bhopal, India
Akhilesh Upadhyay	SIRT Bhopal, India
Anand Singh Jalal	GLA University Mathura, India
Upasna Singh	DIAT Pune, India
Kapil Govil	ITM University Gwalior, India
Kapil Singh Dhama	St. Andrews Institute of Technology & Management, India

Vinod Jain	IIITDM Jabalpur, India
Matadeen Bansal	IIITDM Jabalpur, India
Jawar Singh	IIITDM Jabalpur, India
Bibhuti Bhuhan Nayak	NIT Rourkela, India
Tripty Singh	Amrita University Coimbatore, India
Durgesh Mishra	Acropolis Institute of Technology & Research, India
Shashi Bhushan Kotwal	Shri Mata Vaishno Devi University, India
Sunit Gupta	Shri Mata Vaishno Devi University, India
Amit Kant Pandit	Shri Mata Vaishno Devi University, India
Jnyana Pati	UC Leuven, Belgium
Ramesh Joshi	Tribhuwan University, Nepal
Swastik Sahu	GITAM Bangalore, India
Ragini Sharma	KIET Ghaziabad, India
Ravi Yadav	TIT Bhopal, India
Neelesh Mishra	RKGIT, India
Praveer Saxena	ITS Ghaziabad, India
Rachna Pathak	Al-Falah University, India
Keshav Mishra	SIRT Bhopal, India
Ranjeet Kumar	IIIT Allahabad, India
Rashmi Tikar	Institute of Technology & Management Gwalior, India
Rinkoo Bhatia	Amity University Gwalior, India
Manoj Niranjan	Rustamji Institute of Technology, India
Ratnesh Pandey	KIIT University, India

Local Organizing Committee

Ratan Kumar Jain	ITM University Gwalior, India
Geetanjali Surange	ITM University Gwalior, India
Shailendra Singh Ojha	ITM University Gwalior, India
Ashish Garg	ITM University Gwalior, India
Bhupendra Dhakad	ITM University Gwalior, India
Mayank Sharma	ITM University Gwalior, India
Abhishek Saxena	ITM University Gwalior, India
Abhishek Tripathi	ITM University Gwalior, India
Upendra Bhushan	ITM University Gwalior, India

Organizing Secretariat

Sadhana Mishra	ITM University Gwalior, India

Contents

Vehicular Technology and Applications

Electronic Circuits for Communication Systems

Wired and Wireless Communication Systems

A Detailed Survey on Classification of Localization Techniques in Wireless Sensor Networks

Goldendeep Kaur[1(✉)], Kiran Jyoti[2], and Prabhat Thakur[3]

[1] Department of Computer Science and Engineering, Guru Nanak Dev Engineering College, Ludhiana 141006, Punjab, India
goldendeep@gndec.ac.in

[2] Department of Information Technology, Guru Nanak Dev Engineering College, Ludhiana 141006, Punjab, India
kiranjyotibains@gndec.ac.in

[3] Centre for Smart Information and Communication Systems, Department of Electrical and Electronics Engineering, University of Johannesburg, Auckland Park Kingsway Campus, Johannesburg 2006, South Africa
prabhatt@ut.ac.za

Abstract. In this global economy, advancements in wireless technology communications have provoked the demand for Wireless Sensor network (WSN). WSN is gaining central attraction today in the scientific community. It consists of plenty of tiny, low-cost devices known as sensors that are capable of collecting and forwarding the data and are being adopted in numerous applications that focus on finding the exact location like tracking of children or pets located in the indoor or outdoor environment, environmental monitoring, biomedical health monitoring. So localization study plays a vital role in our lives today. It is done to locate the coordinates of unknown target nodes that are being placed in the sensor field. This paper is providing a comprehensive review of the classification techniques that are applied to acquire the exact location of the nodes, comparative analysis of the most relevant techniques, and future aspects for the localization algorithms.

Keywords: WSN · GPS · Localization · Range based · Range free

1 Introduction

WSNs nowadays have become a crucial tool for a wide range of applications, including natural resource exploration, tracing of static or dynamic targets, and in areas where it is difficult to reach. A WSN is made up of a variety of sensors that are either homogeneous or heterogeneous [1]. These sensor nodes communicate with one another via a wireless link. Each node includes a restricted memory, a processor unit, a radio transceiver, and a battery for transmission and collects the data such as pressure, temperature, and humidity, do some processing on its own, and then communicate the information to a nearby node, which may be linked to a central system for further

R. S. Tomar et al. (Eds.): CNC 2020, CCIS 1502, pp. 3–17, 2021.
https://doi.org/10.1007/978-981-16-8896-6_1

processing. This primary system is one out of a larger network, allowing the data to be transmitted from one system to another in a network.

There are numerous difficulties involved in the evolution of wireless sensor networks at various stages and levels [2]. For example, the sensor nodes are susceptible to failures. So the network should be fault-tolerant and can resume the functionalities without any disruption [3]. New protocols and paradigms should be established for all the layers of the protocol stack to observe and respond to attacks. Another biggest challenge is the localization, or figuring the position of nodes in the sensor field. This is significant for a variety of reasons. The data accumulated by a sensor node must be attributed to the place from where it was obtained. The collection of various parameters such as temperature and pressure measurements is meaningless if the points of reference from where these values were reported are not known. Moreover, configuring the location of the nodes manually during deployment is not a feasible option [4]. So in almost all the applications, sensor nodes should know their location. This problem of estimating the position and location of the sensor nodes is called localization [5, 6]. Also, the deployment of nodes in a wireless sensor network may not always be static. The nodes may be moving but the problems like energy utilization, connectivity maintenance should be taken care of. So mobility is a significant challenge in dynamic wireless sensor networks is a major concern.

One of the most straightforward methods for obtaining localization position is to use GPS; however, each node must be provided with a GPS receiver capable of accurately providing the sensor nodes with their position [7]. But the high-cost weakness of GPS devices may raise the deployment cost to a point where it becomes infeasible to include it in every node in the network [8]. Moreover, the GPS is not devised to save energy. As a result, GPS devices are ineffective in making the localization problem feasible in wireless sensor networks. Another sensor node requirement is that its size must be very tiny. With the inclusion of a GPS device, it would increase significantly, violating one of the sensor node's fundamental requirements once again. GPS provide accurate positioning in outdoor environments but where there is a weak satellite link available, GPS terminates its functioning as in the case of indoor applications, such as underground parking, supermarkets, or in a dense forest [9, 10].

Due to the aforementioned restrictions, technology such as GPS cannot be utilized to locate sensor nodes in the indoor environment. However, GPS devices can be employed in a small percentage of nodes. These nodes can act as beacon nodes or reference nodes which can help in locating the position of dumb nodes or unknown nodes. The accuracy with which dumb nodes locate themselves is decided by the beacon node's transmission range and density. Various techniques and algorithms have been suggested by different researchers and this is a popular research area right now [11].

The remainder of the paper is categorized as follows: Sect. 2 represents the classification of localization techniques, Sect. 3 represents the localization challenges, Sect. 4 provides the performance metrics for evaluation, Sect. 5 provides the comparative review of the various algorithms, and the last section provides the conclusion and future directions.

2 Classification of Localization Techniques

As determining the sensor node's location is a crucial part of wireless sensor networks. Knowing where the sensor nodes are located helps to process the data more efficiently. The literature review provides a comprehensive description of the localization approaches used to carry out this task. The process comprises of two steps:

The initial step is to map the distance and angle between the beacon nodes and the to-be localized nodes. This step is known as the measurement phase.

The next step is to combine the mapped distances and angles to solve the computations. This step is known as the computational phase.

A. **Measurement Stage**
   The main task is to identify the location of the destined node. The localization methods are broadly divided into two categories namely Target/Source Localization and Node Self Localization as shown in the Fig. 1 [12].

2.1 Target Localization

Target Localization is segregated into two subclasses: Single target Localization and Multiple Target Localization.

- Single Target Localization
  The localization in which there is a single particular node that needs to be localized is known as single target localization.
- Multiple Target Localization
  The localization in which there is more than one particular node that needs to be localized is known as multiple target localization. Multiple targets or nodes are localized at the same time.

2.2 Node Self Localization

In this localization, the unknown nodes determine their positions themselves taking into consideration the locality of beacon nodes. Node Self Localization can be categorized as Range Based and Range Free Localization Techniques based upon the mechanism used for estimating the angle or distance particulars to identify the node position. This data can further be accustomed to find out the sensor node position. When we use the distance measurement as a central approach to identify the node position it is called "Lateration", whereas if the angle is used to locate the place of the sensor node it is called "Angulation". However, Range Free Techniques do not need the distances or angle estimation to the nearest nodes, but they utilize the count of hopes between the node pair as a basis to identify their position in the network. Range Free approaches offer less accuracy as compared to range-based approaches, but due to the hardware limitation of the sensor network devices, range free techniques offer an effective substitute than the costly range-based techniques.

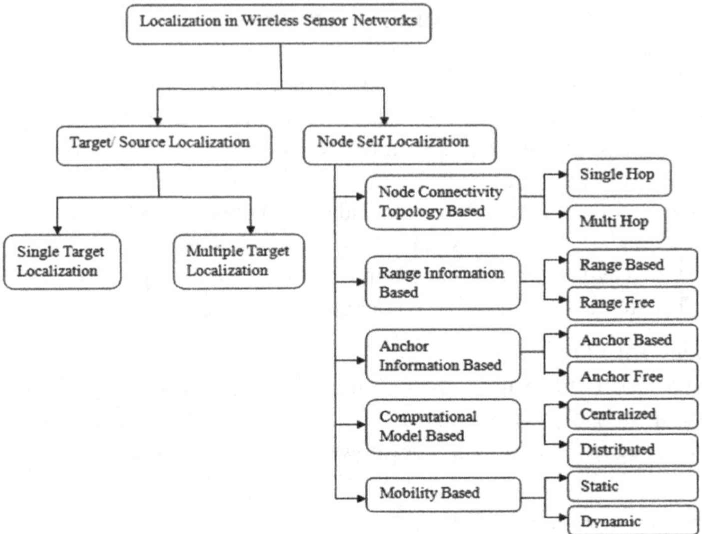

Fig. 1. Classification of localization techniques

2.2.1 Range Based Localization Techniques

As Range Based methods need distance or angle among the nodes to identify the target location, so the first step is calculating the angle or distance. The various methods that are used to calculate this include: Angle of Arrival (AOA), Time of Arrival (TOA), Time Difference of Arrival (TDOA) and Received Signal Strength Indicator (RSSI). The information provided by these methods is then used to find the location using one of the algorithms such as Trilateration, Triangulation, and Multilateration.

The Range Based Methods are as follows:

- Angle of Arrival (AOA)
  The Angle of Arrival method is utilized to compute the angles of the node as observed by the beacon nodes. It estimates the angle in the direction the signals are received at the dumb node. The positioning of at least three beacon nodes in addition to their three angles of arrival is used to identify the unknown node. Directional antennas should be employed on the beacon nodes to measure the angle of arrival. This method offers more accuracy than other methods but the cost of deployment of antennas makes it impractical for localization. Moreover, the rotation of directional antennas on small nodes is complicated and the parts are susceptible to failures [13, 14].
- Time of Arrival (TOA)
  Time of Arrival technique is based upon calculating the time of traveling of signal between the nodes i.e. the time of signal traveling from the beacon node to the target node is calculated and converted into distance using the Eq. (1):

$$d = v * t \text{ where v is the known signal propagation speed} \quad (1)$$

This method can be applied to varying kinds of signals such as RF, Ultrasound, and Infrared [11]. Now for this method to provide accurate measurements, the transmission time of the signal of the sender must be known and the sender and receiver clocks must be synchronized otherwise it will result in an error thereby calculating incorrect distance measurements.

- Time Difference of Arrival (TDOA)
  This technique measures the difference in time of arrival of two signals at the node rather than measuring the time of arrival of the signal. So no synchronization among the dumb node and beacon node clock is required but synchronization is required between the beacon nodes. The difference in the arrival time of two signals transmitting between the dumb node and two nodes is calculated. It uses two kinds of signals, RF and Acoustic [11]. Figure 2 illustrates the concept of TDOA.

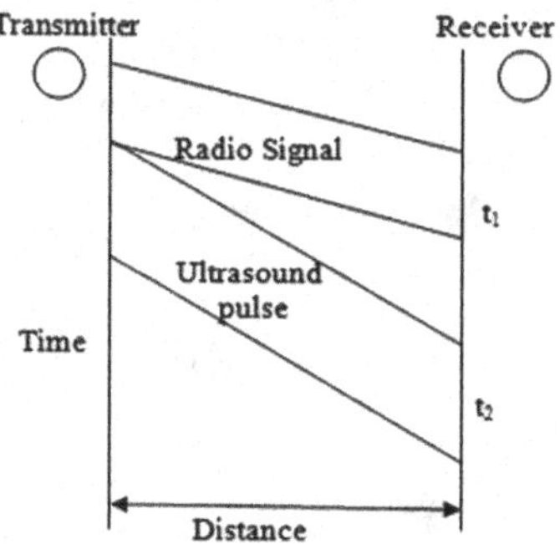

Fig. 2. Time difference of arrival

- Received Signal Strength Indicator (RSSI)
  The Received Signal Strength Indicator relies on the evidence that the signal is attenuated, as it travels the distance which means that the strength of the signal is reduced with distance. It focuses on calculating the power of the received signal knowing the transmitted power of the signal. Based on the strength of the received signal, the distance among the beacon node and unknown node is estimated [7].

B. Computational Stage

The distance estimation or angle estimation provided by the measurement stage is then combined to solve the computations required for identifying the locality of the unknown node. The algorithms that are used for computational analysis are:

- Trilateration

In Trilateration, the distance from three or more beacon nodes whose locations are already known is used to acquire the position of the target node. The coincidence of three consecutive circles determines the location of the target node as shown in the Fig. 3. In 2D space, the minimum of anchor nodes taken into consideration for estimating the target location is three whereas, in 3D space, a minimum of four anchor nodes is required [15] (Fig. 4).

- Multilateration
  In real-world applications, using the Trilateration approach to estimate the node location is not perfect as the inaccurate distance estimations along with the imprecise location of beacon nodes make it tough to identify the exact position. If the circles do not converge at one point, there may be a set of multiple possible solutions. In that case, if there are a great number of beacon nodes, the multilateration can be applied to determine the node's location [16].

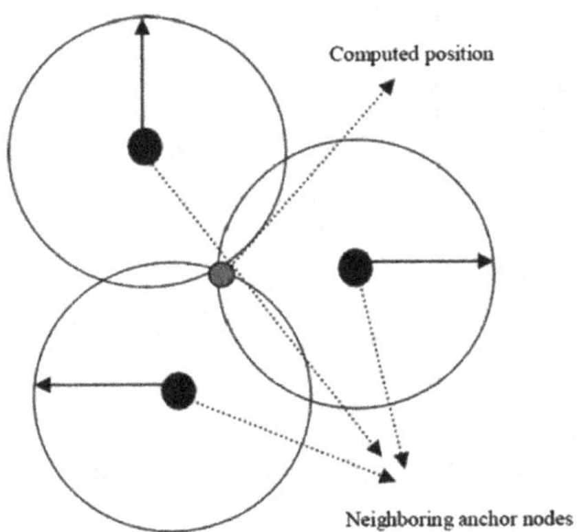

Fig. 3. Trilateration

- Triangulation
  In Triangulation, angle information is used rather than distance information to compute the node location. The unknown node computes its position taking at least beacon nodes and measuring its angle formed with the three beacon nodes available [17].

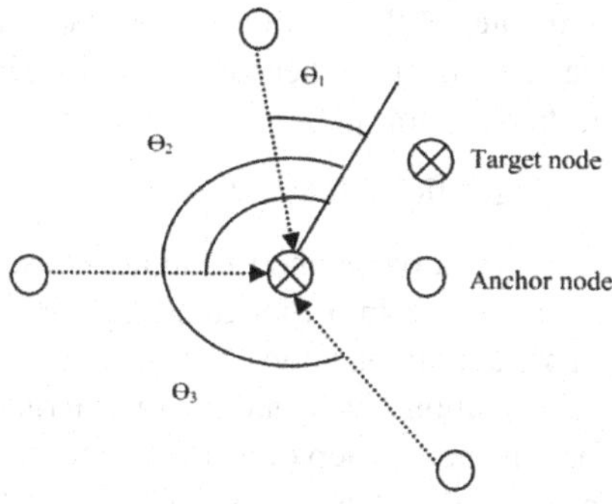

Fig. 4. Triangulation

2.2.2 Range Free Techniques

As Range Free methods do not require any information related to angle or distance. These methods offer the cost-effective solutions as no additional hardware is required. The range free methods rely on the hop count that is in direct proportion to the distance between the nodes [18]. The various range free methods are as follows:

- Centroid Method

This method was developed by Blusu et al. in which they used a minimum of three beacon nodes to estimate the target location by using the Centroid Eq. (2):

$$(X_{est}, Y_{est}) = \left(\frac{X_1 + \ldots + X_n}{N}, \frac{Y_1 + \ldots + Y_n}{N}\right) \tag{2}$$

where X and Y represent the coordinates of the beacon nodes and N is the total count of the beacon nodes.

X_{est}, Y_{est} denotes the coordinates of the unknown node.

- DV-Hop Method

D. Niculescu and B. Nath proposed this DV-Hop method which works on the concept of Distance Vector Routing and measures the distance in terms of count of hops. So initially the hop count parameter is set to one and one beacon node transmits the signal that is broadcasted throughout the network comprising the beacon nodes location. Each receiving node keeps with itself the minimum counter value per beacon node of all the signals it collects and rejects the signals with higher hop count values. These hop count values are increased at every intervening node.

After then this hop count value is converted into a distance value. The mean single-hop distance computed by the beacon node 'i' is given by the Eq. (3):

$$\mathrm{Hopsize_i} = \frac{\sum\sqrt{(x_i - x_j)^2 + (y_i - y_j)^2}}{\sum h_j} \tag{3}$$

where x_j, y_j are the co-ordinates of the locality of the beacon node 'j' and 'h_j' is the hop distance from the beacon node 'j' to beacon node 'i'. This information is then being shared in the sensing field region [21–24].

- Approximate Point in Triangulation Method (APIT)

Approximate Point in Triangulation Method is an area-based method in which the area under investigation is segregated into triangular regions as shown in the Fig. 5. The three beacon nodes that are at only one hop count from the unknown node are used to check the unknown node's position either internal or external the triangular area set up by the beacon nodes. Then the next group of beacon nodes is chosen and the process is repeated. The unknown node identifies its location by contacting the area of the intersection of triangles [20].

- Multi-Dimensional Scaling (MDS)

This technique is a dimensionality reduction technique that is used to plot higher dimensional data into lower dimensional data maintaining the necessary information so that it becomes straightforward to understand. MDS is applied to calculate the node positions such that it matches the distance estimated using Dijkstra's algorithm between every set of nodes and a respective map is generated in such a way the neighboring relationship is maintained as of the original one. At last, these respective locations are converted to fixed coordinates taking into consideration the position of beacon nodes [25–28].

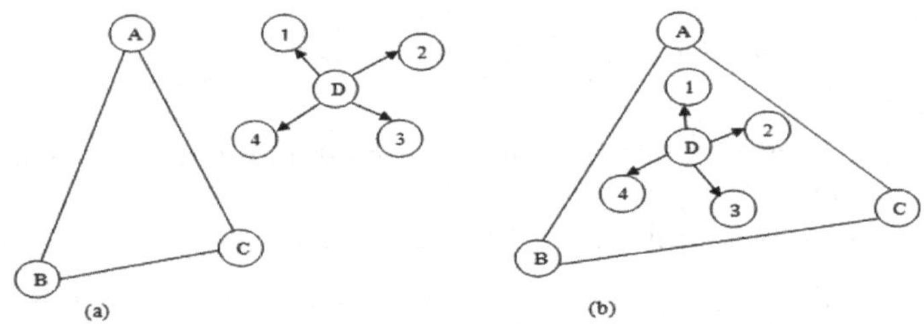

Fig. 5. Approximate point in triangulation

2.2.3 Localization based on Node Connectivity

The localization based on node connectivity comprises of two types: Single-Hop Localization and Multi-Hop Localization. A straightforward link connecting two nearest nodes is called a hop. In Single Hop Localization, every sensor node with an unknown position communicates directly with the anchor node, whereas, in Multi-Hop Localization, every target node or unknown node is more than one hop far from the anchor node [29–32].

2.2.4 Anchor Based or Anchor Free Localization

Localization algorithms are also categorized into Anchor Based and Anchor free techniques. In Anchor based localization, a part of the nodes must be aware of their position either by using GPS embedded in them or manually by the time when they are deployed. The unknown nodes in the network depend upon the anchor node for finding its position whereas, in anchor free localization, no data about the anchor nodes is needed. The nodes are not aware of their pre-configured positions. Every node determines its coordinates by the use of localization techniques available for calculating the distance between them and their nearest nodes [21, 22].

2.2.5 Centralized and Distributed Localization

Depending upon the type of problem the network is handling, the localization can be centralized or distributed. The network which is used for purpose of monitoring requires a centralized approach in which the central processor manages all the computations and the information from all the nodes is gathered at one central place. It provides high accuracy but the only limitation is that all the nodes must transmit their data back to the base station. Conversely, the distributed localization requires the computation to be carried out by the sensor nodes on an individual basis so that they can localize themselves respective to their neighbors [23, 24].

2.2.6 Static and Dynamic Localization

Localization can be divided into static or dynamic depending upon the deployment of the nodes in the region. In Static Localization, the nodes once deployed will not move. Their position is determined when the wireless sensor network is set up. But in dynamic localization, the nodes have mobility. These nodes keep on moving and changing their positions. An extra care is taken off to continuously monitor the position of moving nodes periodically [4, 33–35].

3 Localization Challenges

Localization is an essential need of day-to-day applications. There are numerous challenges involved in the process of localization that needs to be taken care of [1]. These are:

3.1 Power Consumption

The sensor nodes deployed in the region are dependent on the battery life which is limited and non replaceable for carrying out the essential operations such as sensing, data processing and communicating [25].

3.2 Node Mobility

In the case of dynamic localization, the mobile nature of the nodes is a challenging task. Special features should be included that periodically keeps track of the changing positions of the sensor nodes [4, 33].

3.3 Environment

WSNs are often established in rigid and adverse geographical locations. There is a need for strong management techniques for such kinds of environments.

3.4 Accuracy

The difference between the real and calculated position must be as low as possible so that exact results can be attained by making use of available localization techniques [27, 28].

3.5 Fault Tolerance

If there is any failure in the sensor node, the system must be established in such a fault-tolerant way that it keeps on continuing its operations without any kind of interference.

4 Performance Metrics for Localization

Performance metrics are an essential part of the localization used to differentiate the algorithms based on various parameters that best suits the needs of the scenario. As the requirements vary from application to application, so it is crucial to identify which algorithms are to be compared against which parameters. The metrics include:

4.1 Cost

Cost is described with respect to parameters such as power consumed, maximizing the lifetime of the network, minimizing the time to locate a sensor node, and making use of as limited number of anchor nodes as possible. Considering these factors the algorithm that minimizes the cost is the more preferable one.

4.1.1 Anchor to Node Ratio

The anchor to node ratio is defined in terms of the total count of beacon nodes divided by the sum of nodes in the network. This parameter is beneficial while constructing the localization algorithm and is used for measuring the trade-off between the proportion of unknown nodes that are being localized and their accuracy in localization.

4.1.2 Algorithm Complexity

Algorithm Complexity is measured in terms of space and time i.e. how much time the algorithm takes to execute before the estimation of all the nodes' positions and how much space is necessary for computation.

4.1.3 Convergence Time

This is computed against the size of the network i.e. the time an algorithm takes from collecting the related information to finally estimating the locations of nodes in the network. As the size of the network increases, the convergence time of the algorithm should be less.

4.2 Coverage

Coverage refers to the proportion of the nodes in the network which can be localized irrespective of the accuracy. There might be a case in which all the nodes in the network cannot be localized due to certain reasons such as positioning of anchor nodes, the denseness of nodes in the network. To assess the coverage performance, different scenarios need to be considered for positioning of the anchor nodes and modifying the number of nodes.

5 Comparative Analysis of Various Localization Techniques

Based on the analysis done, the pros and cons of the various range based and range free techniques are presented in the Table 1 and 2.

Table 1. Analysis of range based localization techniques

Range based localization techniques		
Technique	Advantages	Disadvantages
Time of Arrival (TOA)	• Provides accurate measurement if synchronized • No multipath effects in the indoor environment	• Difficult to implement • Requires Synchronization between devices • Cost is very high
Time Difference of Arrival (TDOA)	• Does not require synchronization between the base station and target node but only requires synchronization between base stations [29]	• Affected by multipath of signals • Require prior information to remove position ambiguity
Angle of Arrival (AOA)	• Phase coherence need not to be maintained at the receiver side with the time source of any beacon as the required timing information of the transmitter is encoded in the signal	• Additional directional antennas need to be mounted for angle measurement thereby increasing the implementation cost • Multipath effects, non-line of sight propagation of signals which degrades its accuracy • Measurements are susceptible to a range
Received Signal Strength Indicator (RSSI)	• Deployment is easy in comparison to other techniques • No specialized hardware is required • Can be used with several technologies	• Obstacles in the path can cause multipath fading • Lower localization accuracy • Consumes a lot of time in building site survey and labor-intensive as well

Table 2. Analysis of range free localization techniques

Range free localization techniques		
Technique	Advantages	Disadvantages
Centroid method	• Cost-Effective • Energy is conserved	• The denseness of beacon nodes is required in the sensor field • Not convenient for multihop nature networks
DV-Hop method	• No additional hardware is required [19]	• Communication Overhead increases as the node density increases [19] • Accuracy degrades if the deployment of sensor nodes is random
Approximate point in triangulation	• No additional hardware is required • Better scalability as it is distributed and adaptable	• Not able to provide good accuracy because of dependency on the density of anchors
Multidimensional Scaling	• Works effectively with both uniform and irregular networks [30] • Provides better and accurate results	• High communication overhead [31] • Not Scalable [32]

6 Conclusion and Future Scope

Localization is a crucial task in Wireless Sensor Networks. In this paper, the issue of localization is discussed; various localization classification techniques proposed by different researchers have been presented. Firstly the localization methods are grouped based on the measurement techniques. Range Based Methods offer much more accuracy than Range Free Methods. But there is a need for additional hardware in Range Based Methods which in turn increases the cost factor also. Conversely, Range Free Methods provide approximate locations but no additional hardware is required in this thereby reducing the cost. Localization methods are also categorized based on centralized or distributed systems. Centralized algorithms are often regarded as a bad option in the case of mobile sensor nodes due to the various constraints such as energy costs incurred and additional latency. The majority of the applications prefer distributed localization than centralized as they are more comfortable for monitoring. So the development of more distributed techniques would be desirable in localizing sensor nodes. Moreover, the static and dynamic nature of the nodes has also been discussed. The algorithm may work well for static nodes but it is still a challenging task in the case of mobile nodes. Another bigger challenge is localizing a node in 2-D and 3-D scenarios. There are many algorithms that can estimate the location of node in the 2-D scenario but only few are there that can estimate the position in the 3-D scenario. So this paper discusses the fundamentals of all the localization techniques and algorithms for locating sensor nodes and the methods to improve localization as well. A more efficient approach can be developed using a hybrid composition of all these techniques and taking the issues into concern.

References

1. Karl, H., Willig, A.: Protocols and Architectures for Wireless Sensor Networks (2006)
2. Akyildiz, I.F., Wang, X.: A survey on wireless mesh networks. IEEE Commun. Mag. **43**(9), 23–30 (2005). https://doi.org/10.1109/MCOM.2005.1509968
3. Kulaib, A.R., Shubair, R.M., Al-Qutayri, M.A., Ng, J.W.P.: An overview of localization techniques for wireless sensor networks. In: 2011 International Conference on Innovations in Information Technology, IIT 2011, vol. 16, no. 3, pp. 167–172 (2011). https://doi.org/10.1109/INNOVATIONS.2011.5893810
4. Singh, P., Khosla, A., Kumar, A., Khosla, M.: Wireless sensor networks localization and its location optimization using bio inspired localization algorithms: a survey. Int. J. Curr. Eng. Sci. Res. (IJCESR) **4**(10), 74–80 (2017)
5. Singh, B., Sahoo, S.K.: A comparative view on anchor based, range based localization systems using AOA, TOA & RSSI, March 2012 (2017)
6. De Oliveira, H.A.B.F., Nakamura, E.F., Loureiro, A.A.F., Boukerche, A.: Directed position estimation: a recursive localization approach for wireless sensor networks. In: Proceedings of the International Conference on Computer Communications and Networks, ICCCN, vol. 2005, pp. 557–562 (2005). https://doi.org/10.1109/ICCCN.2005.1523938
7. Zhu, X., Feng, Y.: RSSI-based algorithm for indoor localization. Commun. Netw. **05**(02), 37–42 (2013). https://doi.org/10.4236/cn.2013.52b007
8. Cheng, L., Chengdong, W., Zhang, Y., Hao, W., Li, M., Maple, C.: A survey of localization in wireless sensor network. Int. J. Distrib. Sens. Netw. **8**(12), 962523 (2012). https://doi.org/10.1155/2012/962523
9. Mesmoudi, A., Feham, M., Labraoui, N.: Wireless sensor networks localization algorithms: a comprehensive survey. Int. J. Comput. Netw. Commun. **5**(6), 45–64 (2013). https://doi.org/10.5121/ijcnc.2013.5603
10. Huang, H., Gartner, G.: A survey of mobile indoor navigation systems. In: Gartner, G., Ortag, F. (eds.) Cartography in Central and Eastern Europe. Lecture Notes in Geoinformation and Cartography, pp. 305–319. Springer, Heidelberg (2009).https://doi.org/10.1007/978-3-642-03294-3_20
11. Amundson, I., Koutsoukos, X.D.: A survey on localization for mobile wireless sensor networks. In: Fuller, R., Koutsoukos, X.D. (eds.) MELT 2009. LNCS, vol. 5801, pp. 235–254. Springer, Heidelberg (2009). https://doi.org/10.1007/978-3-642-04385-7_16
12. Galstyan, A., Krishnamachari, B., Lerman, K., Pattem, S.: Distributed online localization in sensor networks using a moving target. In: 3rd International Symposium on Information Processing in Sensor Networks, IPSN 2004, May, pp. 61–70 (2004). https://doi.org/10.1145/984622.984632
13. Wang, L., Xu, Q.: GPS-free localization algorithm for wireless sensor networks. Sensors **10** (6), 5899–5926 (2010). https://doi.org/10.3390/s100605899
14. Bishop, A.N., Fidan, B., Anderson, B.D.O., Doğançay, K., Pathirana, P.N.: Optimality analysis of sensor-target localization geometries. Automatica **46**(3), 479–492 (2010). https://doi.org/10.1016/j.automatica.2009.12.003
15. Li, M., Ho, K.S., Hayward, G.: Accurate angle-of-arrival measurement using particle swarm optimization. Wirel. Sens. Netw. **02**(05), 358–364 (2010). https://doi.org/10.4236/wsn.2010.24047
16. Kułakowski, P., Vales-Alonso, J., Egea-López, E., Ludwin, W., García-Haro, J.: Angle-of-arrival localization based on antenna arrays for wireless sensor networks. Comput. Electr. Eng. **36**(6), 1181–1186 (2010). https://doi.org/10.1016/j.compeleceng.2010.03.007

17. Oureiro, A.N.A.F.L., Niversity, F.E.U., Inas, O.F.M.: Localization Systems for Wireless Sensor Networks, pp. 6–12 (December 2007)
18. Zhou, Y., Li, J., Lamont, L.: Multilateration localization in the presence of anchor location uncertainties. In: IEEE Global Communications Conference (GLOBECOM), pp. 309–314 (2012). https://doi.org/10.1109/GLOCOM.2012.6503131
19. Tekdas, O., Isler, V.: Sensor placement for triangulation-based localization. IEEE Trans. Autom. Sci. Eng. **7**(3), 681–685 (2010). https://doi.org/10.1109/TASE.2009.2037135
20. Ahmadi, Y., Neda, N., Ghazizadeh, R.: Range free localization in wireless sensor networks for homogeneous and non-homogeneous environment. IEEE Sens. J. **16**(22), 8018–8026 (2016). https://doi.org/10.1109/JSEN.2016.2606508
21. He, T., Huang, C., Blum, B.M., Stankovic, J.A., Abdelzaher, T.: Range-free localization schemes for large scale sensor networks. In: Proceedings of the Annual International Conference on Mobile Computing and Networking, MOBICOM, pp. 81–95 (2003). https://doi.org/10.1145/938985.938995
22. Kumar, S., Lobiyal, D.K.: An advanced DV-Hop localization algorithm for wireless sensor networks. Wirel. Pers. Commun. **71**(2), 1365–1385 (2013). https://doi.org/10.1007/s11277-012-0880-3
23. Tian, S., Zhang, X., Liu, P., Sun, P., Wang, X.: A RSSI-based DV-hop algorithm for wireless sensor networks, pp. 2555–2558 (2007)
24. Niculescu, D., Nath, B.: Ad hoc positioning system (APS) using AOA. In: Proceedings of the IEEE INFOCOM, vol. 3, pp. 1734–1743 (2003). https://doi.org/10.1109/infcom.2003.1209196
25. Stojkoska, B.R., Davcev, D.: MDS-based algorithm for nodes localization in 3D surface sensor networks. In: SENSORCOMM 2013, July, pp. 608–613 (2013)
26. Shang, Y., Ruml, W.: Improved MDS-based localization (2004)
27. Shang, Y., Ruml, W., Zhang, Y., Fromherz, M.P.J.: Localization from mere connectivity. In: Proceedings of the International Symposium on Mobile Ad Hoc Networking & Computing, pp. 201–212 (2003). https://doi.org/10.1145/778415.778439
28. Shang, Y., Ruml, W., Zhang, Y., Fromherz, M.: Localization from connectivity in sensor networks. IEEE Trans. Parallel Distrib. Syst. **15**(11), 961–974 (2004). https://doi.org/10.1109/TPDS.2004.67
29. Mert, B., Min, L., Weiming, S., Hamada, G.: Localization in cooperative wireless sensor networks: a review. In: Proceedings of the 2009 13th International Conference on Computer Supported Cooperative Work in Design, CSCWD 2009, pp. 438–443 (2009). https://doi.org/10.1109/CSCWD.2009.4968098
30. Wu, L., Meng, M.Q.H., Lin, Z., He, W., Peng, C., Liang, H.: A practical evaluation of radio signal strength for mobile robot localization. In: 2009 IEEE International Conference on Robotics and Biomimetics, ROBIO 2009, pp. 516–522 (2009). https://doi.org/10.1109/ROBIO.2009.5420700
31. Franceschini, F., Galetto, M., Maisano, D., Mastrogiacomo, L.: A review of localization algorithms for distributed wireless sensor networks in manufacturing. Int. J. Comput. Integr. Manuf. **22**(7), 698–716 (2009). https://doi.org/10.1080/09511920601182217
32. Lakafosis, V., Tentzeris, M.M.: From single-to multihop: the status of wireless localization. IEEE Microw. Mag. **10**(7), 34–41 (2009). https://doi.org/10.1109/MMM.2009.934690
33. Singh, P., Khosla, A., Kumar, A., Khosla, M.: 3D localization of moving target nodes using single anchor node in anisotropic wireless sensor networks. AEU Int. J. Electron. Commun. **82**, 543–552 (2017). https://doi.org/10.1016/j.aeue.2017.10.016

34. Roumeliotis, S.I., Bekey, G.A.: Bayesian estimation and Kalman filtering: a unified framework for mobile robot localization. In: Proceedings of International Conference on Robotics and Automation, vol. 3, pp. 2985–2992 (2000). https://doi.org/10.1109/robot.2000.846481
35. Reina, G., Vargas, A., Nagatani, K., Yoshida, K.: Adaptive Kalman filtering for GPS-based mobile robot localization. In: IEEE International Workshop on Safety, Security, and Rescue Robotics, SSRR 2007 (2007). https://doi.org/10.1109/SSRR.2007.4381270

WDM Communication Network with Zero Bit Error Rate

Bhupendra Dhakad(✉), Shailendra Singh Ojha(✉), and Mayank Sharma(✉)

Department of Electronics and Communication Engineering, ITM University, Gwalior, Madhya Pradesh, India
{bhupendradhakad.ece, shailendraojha.ec, mayanksharma.ec}@itmuniversity.ac.in

Abstract. Bandwidth demand is increasing day by day because of the several high bandwidth applications like video transmission, social networking and internet suffering etc. Wavelength division multiplexing (WDM) network obtaining more attention for the requirement of high data rate, bandwidth capacity and upgrading in the existing optical system. WDM technology can also use in bidirectional communication which gives green light to increasing the capacity of the network. When we transmit data through a WDM channel, there is a possibility of error in some bits. Bit error rate (BER) is depends on type of devices which are used in the communication network and the parameter of the network like data rate, length and attenuation constant of optical fiber etc. Bit error rate can be minimize by reducing the data rate, length of optical fiber. WDM communication network can provide zero minimum bit error rate up to certain length of optical fiber. This paper gives the optimum value of 4 channel and 8 channel WDN network parameter for zero bit error rate (BER) up to certain length of optical fiber.

Keywords: BER · OFC · EDFA · WDM

1 Introduction

WDM multiplex number of optical carrier signals into single optical fiber by using different wavelength or color of laser light. WDM system uses multiplexer at transmitter end which join number of optical signal and De multiplexer at the receiver end to split out the joined signals.

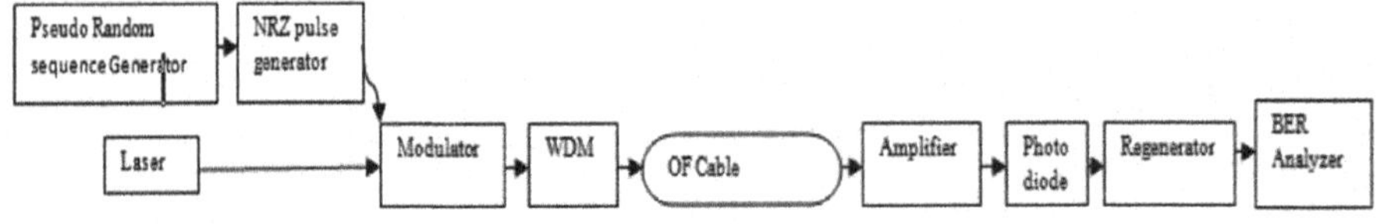

Block diagram of WDM communication network

R. S. Tomar et al. (Eds.): CNC 2020, CCIS 1502, pp. 18–28, 2021.
https://doi.org/10.1007/978-981-16-8896-6_2

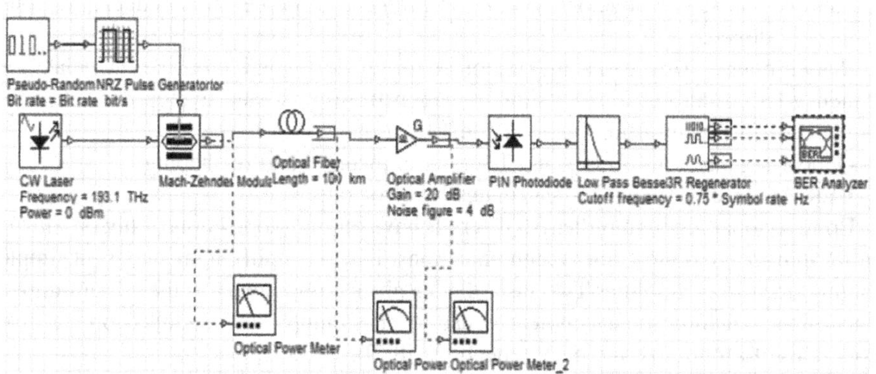

Simulation diagram of signal channel communication network

Optical communication system consist transmitter, channel and receiver. Transmitter is use to decode the massage in to optical signal, channel is use to transmit the [1] signal in to its destination and at destination, receiver encode the optical signal.

Pseudo-Random Bit Sequence Generator - It is use to generate the random binary sequence. c = m − 1/N − 1 is duty cycle, where m is no of ones. N is total no of bits.

NRZ Pulse Generator - Non return to zero is defined as binary sequence. Positive voltage defined for once and negative voltage for zeros. There is no any other neutral or rest condition. NRZ pulse have more energy than return-to-zero (RZ) pulse. Because in RZ pulse have additional rest state. Rise time and fall time 0.05 bit [2, 3].

CW laser-Continuous wave or Continuous waveform (CW) is an electromagnetic wave. It have constant amplitude and frequency almost like a sine wave. Frequency = 193.1, power = 0 dbm, line width = 10 MHz, initial phase 0°.

Mach-Zehnder modulator - This is use for controlling the optical waveform amplitude.

Wavelength-division multiplexing (WDM) is a technology which is use to multiplexes many optical carrier signals onto a single optical fiber cable by using different wavelengths or colors of laser light. This technique can be use for bidirectional communications Bandwidth = 10 GHz, insertion losses 0 db, filter type - bessel [4, 5].

Optical fiber - Optical fiber is a flexible and transparent fiber cable which is made by drawing glass (silica) or plastic. Its diameter is slightly thicker than human hair wavelength = 1550 nm, attenuation constant = .2 db/km.

Optical power meter (OPM) - This device is used measure the optical signal power.

Optical power meter device is use for testing fiber optic systems average power. This measure power in watts and dbm.

Optical amplifier - This device amplifies optical signal without converting the optical signal into electrical signal. gain = 20 db, noise figure 4 db.

PIN diode - PIN diode have undoped intrinsic semiconductor region between p-type and n-type semiconductor region. The p-type and n-type semiconductor regions are heavily doped.

Bessel filter - This gives maximum at group delay and propagation delay for frequency spectrum, but it gives slow transition from pass-band to stop-band. Cut o_ frequency 0.75 Hz, insertion losses = 0 dB [6, 7].

Optical regenerator - This is use for re-amplification and re-shaping.

BER Analyzer - It is use to calculates bit error rate.

Erbium-doped fiber amplifier (EDFA) - It have erbium-doped optical fibers. This is use for long-range optical fiber communications. EDFA amplify light signal. In simple erbium-doped fiber amplifier Two laser diodes gives pump power to the erbium-doped optical fiber. Dichroic fiber couplers is use to give pump light. Pigtailed optical isolators is use to minimize the back-reflections [8, 9].

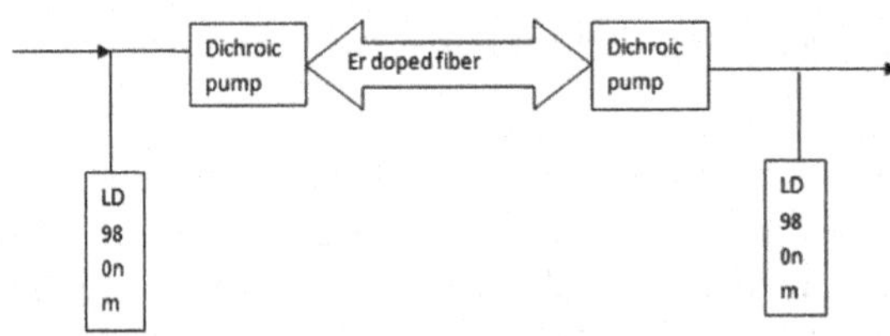

CW laser output is modulated with "Non-Return-to-Zero" (NRZ) sequence in Mach Zender modulator. NRZ is defined as binary code. In NRZ code positive voltage is used denotes ones and negative voltage is use to denotes zeros. In NRZ code there is no neutral condition. Mach-Zehnder modulator is use to control the amplitude of an optical waveform. Then the outputs of the transmitter are multiplexed by wave length division multiplexer and multiplexed signal is transmitted via optical fibre cable. Optical power meters measure the optical signal power in watt or dbm and spectrum analyzer analyze the spectrum. Optical power amplifier amplify the signal in optical domain. Wave length division de multiplexer separates the received signals on the bases of wavelengths of photo detectors. Then the photo detector output becomes input of the Low Pass Bessel Filter. It is a linear analog filter. It have maximum at phase delay. Then the output of this is given to 3-R regenerator it is use to re-amplification and reshaping of the signal. Then the output of 3-R regenerator is given to BER analyzer. It is used to calculate bit error rate [10–15].

1.1 4 Channel WDM Optical Communication Network

In this network 4:1 wavelength division multiplexer and 1:4 de multiplexer is used and all another devices are same with the same parameter.

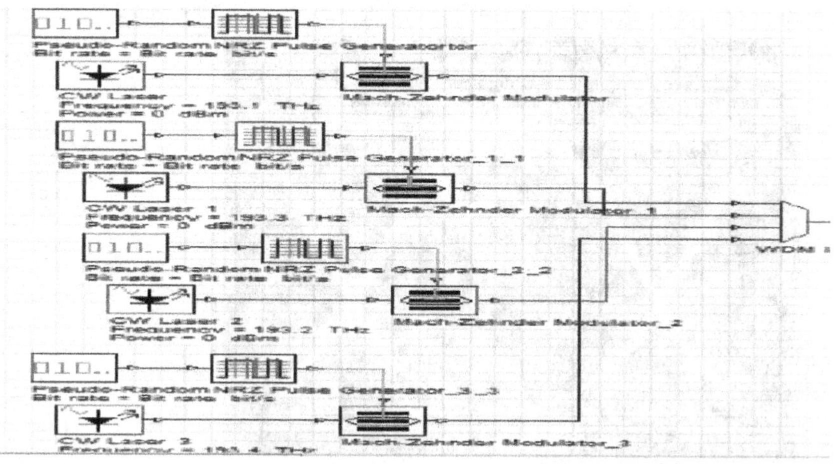

4 channel optical transmitter network

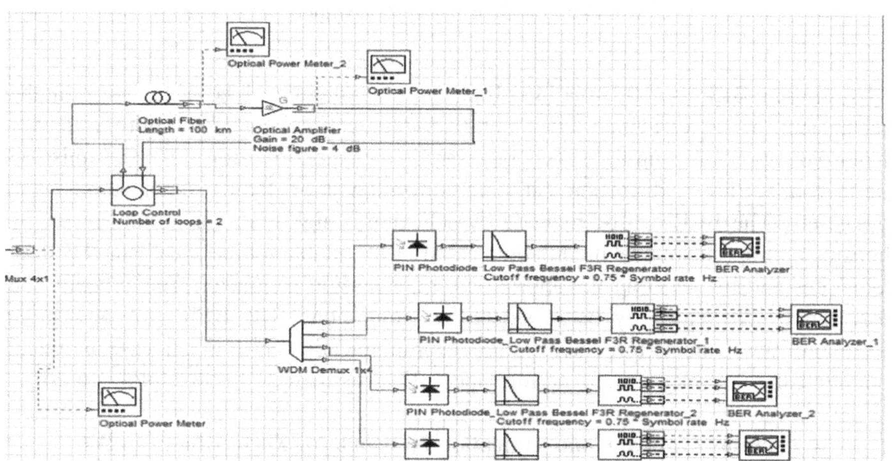

4 channel optical receiver network

Parameter	Value (watt)	Value (dBm)
Total power before transmission	942.765E-6	-0.256
Noise power before transmission	0.00	-100.00
Total power after transmission	9.428E-6	-20.256
Noise power after transmission	0.00	-100.00
Total power after amplifier	1.359E-3	1.333
Noise power after amplifier	396.230E-6	-4.021

Total power and noise power in 4 channel WDM

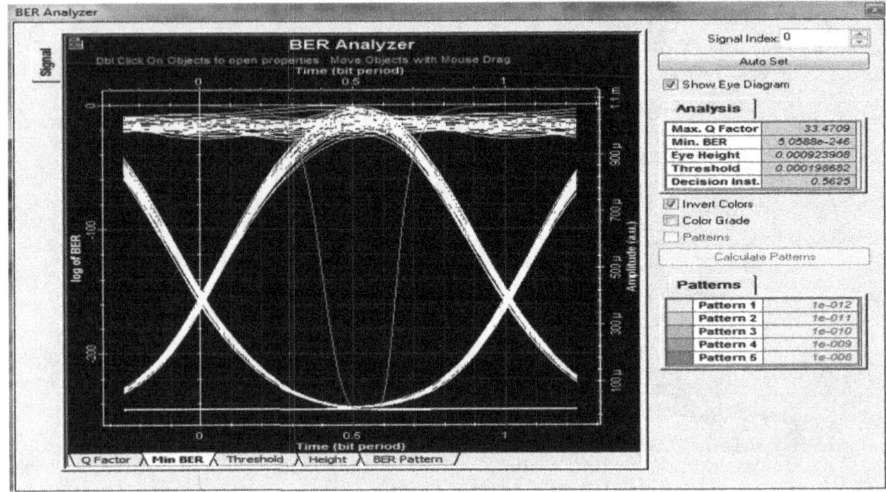

Minimum bit error rate for 4 channel

Minimum BER is 5.0588e−246. It means that there will be 1 bit error in the transmission of 1.44e244 bits. Fiber optic communication networks is able to deliver higher data speeds for multiple users but there is a chances of error in the transmission due to channel noise, distortion, bit synchronization error, fading, attenuation, interference etc. The BER can be reduced by selecting a high massage signal power, by choosing appropriate optical modulation techniques, suitable source and channel coding techniques and by selecting the appropriate transmission parameter. Theoretically the BER can be calculated by using stochastic simulations. The BER plots gives the information about the performance of digital communication networks. In case of optical communication, to measure the performance, BER Vs Received power plot is used.

1.1.1 4 Channel Optical Communication Network for Zero Minimum Bit Error Rate

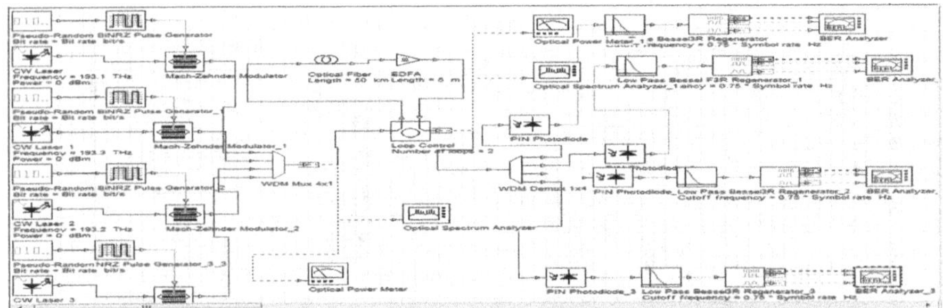

4 channel WDM communication network for zero minimum BER

Parameter for 4 channel wavelength division multiplexing to achieve zero minimum bit error rate for 50 km length of optical Fiber.

Parameter name	Value	Units
Optical fiber length	50	km
Attenuation constant	0.2	db/km
EDFA length	5	m
Bit rate	2.5e+009	bit/s
Time window	51.2e-009	s
Sampling rate	160e+009	Hz
Sequence-length	128	bits
Sample per bit	64	
Guard bit	0	
Symbol-rate	10e+009	symbols/s
Number of sample	8192	

Parameters of 4 channel WDM network

EYE PATTERN-it is also called eye diagram eye diagram measurements are shown in table.

Eye pattern specification	measurement
Eye hight	Additive noise in the signal
Eye overshoot undershoot	Peak distortions
Eye width	Time synchronization and jitter effect
Eye closer	Inter symbols interference

Eye diagram specifications

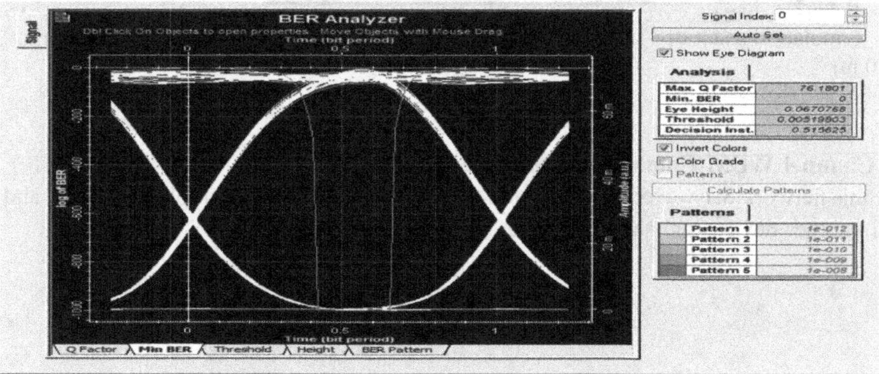

4 channel WDM communication network eye diagram

The simulation result shows zero BER when we have taken above mentioned parameter for optical fiber communication.

1.2 4 Channel Optical Communication Network for ZERO Bit Error Rate Using EDFA (Length 10 m)

If we use EDFA amplifier (length 10 m) then we can achieve zero minimum BER up to 95 km length of optical fiber. Another devices and there parameter are same as specified above.

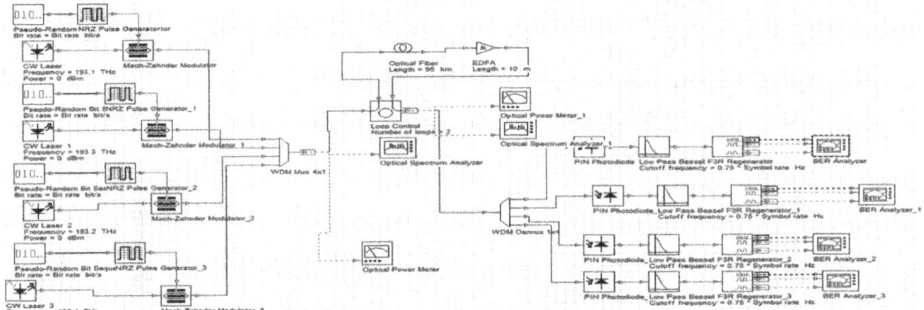

4 channel WDM communication network using EDFA (length 10 m)

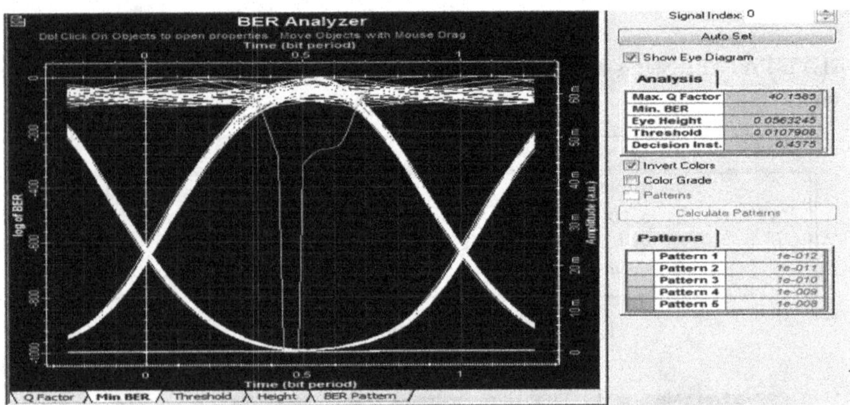

Simulation result of 4 channel WDM communication network using EDFA (length 10 m)

8 Channel WDM Communication Network

In this network 8:1 wavelength division multiplexer and 1:8 de multiplexer is used and all another devices are same with the same parameter.

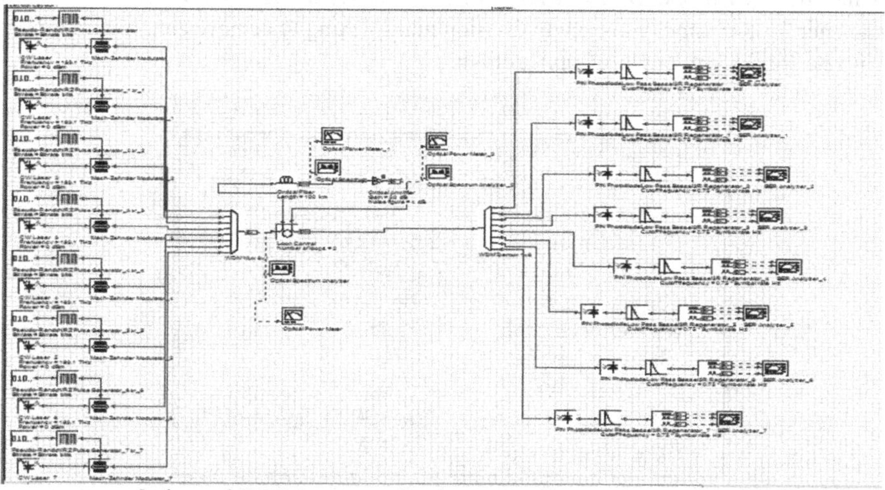

8 channel WDM communication network

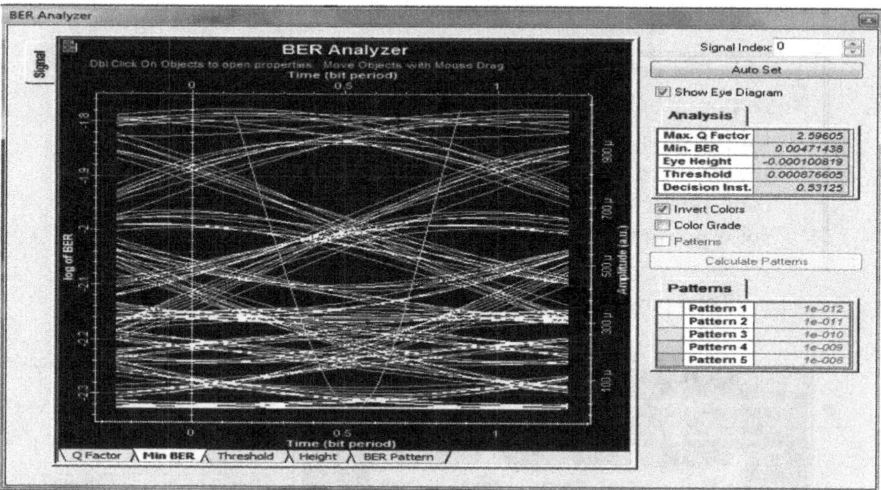

Minimum bit error rate for 8 channel

Parameter	Value (E-6watt)	Value (dBm)
Total power before transmission	411.230	-3.859
Noise power before transmission	0.00	-100.00
Total power after transmission	4.112	-23.859
Noise power after transmission	0.00	-100.00
Total power after amplifier	827.697	0.821
Noise power after amplifier	396.058	-4.022

Total power and noise power in 8 channel WDM

8 Channel Optical Communication Network for ZERO Bit Error Rate

Parameter for 8 channel wavelength division multiplexing to achieve zero minimum bit error rate for 35 km length of optical fiber.

Parameter name	Value	Units
Optical fiber length	35	km
Attenuation constant	0.2	db/km
EDFA length	15	m
Bit rate	2.5e+009	bit/s
Time window	51.2e-009	s
Sampling rate	160e+009	Hz
Sequence-length	128	bits
Sample per bit	64	
Guard bit	0	
Symbol-rate	10e+009	symbols/s
Number of sample	8192	

Parameters of 8 channel WDM network

Parameter	Value (watt)	Value (dBm)
Total power before transmission	461.867 E-6	-3.355
Noise power before transmission	0.00	-100.00
Total power after transmission	92.154 E-6	-10.355
Noise power after transmission	0.00	-100.00
Total power after amplifier	40.376 E-3	16.061
Noise power after amplifier	650.805 E-6	-1.812

Total power and noise power in 8 channel WDM

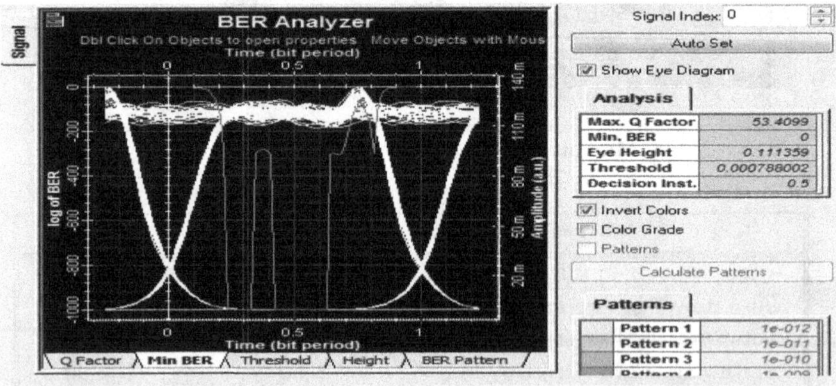

8 channel WDM network simulation result and eye diagram Minimum BER is 0.0 bit per sec.

2 Conclusion

Wave length spacing and bit error rate are inversely proportional to each other because we use same devices with same parameter in 4 channel and 8 channel WDM communication network then we found in 4 channel the minimum bit error rate is 5.0588e −246 and in 8 channel the minimum bit error rate is 0.0047. In case of 8 channel bit error rate is higher then 4 channel. Bit error rate is increases when we increases optical fiber length because in 4 channel WDM communication network we use 100 km length of optical fiber and that gives bit error rate is 5.0588e−246 when we reduces the optical fiber length up to 50 km then we achieve minimum bit error rate is zero If we increase length of EDFA amplifier then we can achieve zero bit error rate for long length of optical fiber because in chapter 8 in case of "4 channel WDM communication network for zero minimum bit error rate" we use EDFA with length 5 m then we achieve zero bit error rate up 50 km. when we use EDFA with 10 m then we achieve zero BER up to 95 km. Bit rate is inversely proportional to bit error rate it means if we reduce bit rate then we can achieve zero BER for large distance. Attenuation constant is depends on bending angle of optical fiber. If reduce attenuation constant then we can achieve zero bit error rate comparatively long optical fiber.

References

1. Babu, P., Singh, M.K., Pal, S.: Optimization of a single-channel optical communication system and an 8-channel WDM system using EDFA. In: Rakesh, P.K., Sharma, A.K., Singh, I. (eds.) Advances in Engineering Design. LNME, pp. 453–464. Springer, Singapore (2021). https://doi.org/10.1007/978-981-33-4018-3_42
2. Sekh, M.A., Rahim, M., Begam, A.: Design of EDFA based 16 channel WDM system using counter directional high pump power. J. Opt. Commun. (2021)
3. Kaur, P., Bhatia, K.S., Kaur, H.: Performance analysis of 16 channel WDM system with 4 OADM. J. Opt. Commun. **36**(2), 169–173 (2015). https://doi.org/10.1515/joc-2014-0056
4. Verma, D., Meena, S.: Flattening the gain in 16 channel EDFA-WDM system by gain flattening filter. In: 2014 International Conference on Computational Intelligence and Communication Networks. IEEE (2014)
5. Kaur, K., Singh, K.: Analysis of numerical aperture dependence in L-band 16-channel WDM optical communication system. Int. J. Eng. Res. Ind. Appl. **4**, 50–57 (2014)
6. Ivaniga, T., Ivaniga, P.: Comparison of the optical amplifiers EDFA and SOA based on the BER and Q-factor in C-band. Adv. Opt. Technol. **2017**, 1–9 (2017). https://doi.org/10.1155/2017/9053582
7. Ivaniga, T., Ovsenk, L., Turn, J.: The four-channel WDM system using semiconductor optical amplifier. In: 26th Conference Radioelektronika 2016, 19–20 April, Koice, Slovak Republic. IEEE (2016). ISBN 978-1-5090-1674-7/16
8. Maharjan, R., Lavrinovica, I., Supe, A.: Minimization of FWM effect in nonlinear optical fiber using variable channel spacing technique. In: 2016 Advances in Wireless and Optical Communications (RTUWO) (2016)
9. Siddiqua, A., Ansari, A., Fundole, A.M., Jamadar, R.: 8-channel wavelength division multiplexing (WDM) with zero BER. In: IEEE International Conference on Recent Trends in Electronics Information Communication Technology, India, 20–21 May 2016 (2016)

10. Shah, A., Mankodi, P.: Analysis and simulation on gain flattening filter of an erbium doped fiber amplifier for multi-channel WDM system. In: 2017 International Conference on Wireless Communications, Signal Processing and Networking (WiSPNET) (2017)
11. Shanker, R., Srivastava, P., Bhattacharya, M.: Performance analysis of 16-Channel 80-Gbps optical fiber communication system. In: 2016 International Conference on Computational Techniques in Information and Communication Technologies (ICCTICT) (2016)
12. Lian, Y., et al.: Ultralow bending-loss trench-assisted single-mode optical fibers. IEEE Photonics Technol. Lett. **29**(3), 346–349 (2017)
13. Chen, T., Xie, Z., Li, Z.-H., Zhou, Y.-M., Guo, H.-Y.: Study on the monotonicity of bending loss of polymer optical fiber. J. Lightwave Technol. **33**(10), 2032–2037 (2015). https://doi.org/10.1109/JLT.2015.2396633
14. Ceballos-Herrera, D.E., Gutierrez-Castrejon, R., Alvarez-Chavez, J.A.: Stimulated Raman Scattering and Four-Wave Mixing Effects on Crosstalk of Multicore Fibers. IEEE Photonics Technol. Lett. **30**(1), 63–66 (2018). https://doi.org/10.1109/LPT.2017.2774501
15. Badhon, A.I., Prapty, H.A., Amin, K.B., Hossain, M.A.: Analysis of coupling coefficient and crosstalk in a homogenous multicore optical fiber. In: International Conference on Advanced Communications Technology, ICACT 2018 (2018)

Theoretical Understanding of Circular Polarization: Case Study of Superstrate-Inspired Monopole Antenna for RF Energy Harvesting Applications

Bikash Ranjan Behera(✉), Priya Ranjan Meher, and Sanjeev Kumar Mishra

Department of Electronics and Telecommunication Engineering, International Institute of Information Technology Bhubaneswar, Bhubaneswar 751003, Odisha, India
c117004@iiit-bh.ac.in

Abstract. In this article, superstrate-inspired monopole antenna with broadband circular polarization & directional pattern is investigated. The proposed antenna offers impedance bandwidth (IBW) of 117.9% (1.81–6.88 GHz) and 3-dB axial bandwidth (ARBW) of 32.22% (4.04–5.59 GHz). So, the outcome of proposed antenna is due to its geometrical occurrences. Initially, a linearly polarized (LP) circular-shaped monopole antenna with partial ground plane is designed at the stage-1. For LP-CP, partial ground plane is transformed into asymmetrical stair-cased partial ground plane (stage-2). Addition of PEC superstrate demonstrates broadband CP and directional pattern (stage-3). The proposed antenna finds its application in RF energy harvesting. Prior to simulation and measurement of S_{11}, the detailed theoretical analogy about circular polarization is persuaded.

Keywords: Broadband · Circular polarization (CP) · Monopole antenna · PEC superstrate · Linear polarization (LP) · RF energy harvesting

1 Introduction

With applicability, RF energy harvesting using electromagnetic spectrum has become significant [1–5]. However, implementation in 1–7 GHz is limited [6, 7]. In [6, 8–10], although monopole antennas cover 1–7 GHz, but non-existence of CP; fails to support its creditability for RF energy harvesting systems. In [11–18], CP is achieved due to asymmetrical stair-cased ground [11], metasurfaces [12, 13], AMCs [14] and DRAs [15–18]. A rectangular-shaped monopole antenna is investigated, but axial bandwidth is <5% [11]. When metasurfaces is included, axial bandwidth of 10% [12] and 18.5% [13] are reported. A rise in 3-dB axial bandwidth was observed. Monopole antennas with artificial magnetic conductor (AMC) are investigated; where, −10 dB impedance bandwidth is controlled for the desired band with axial bandwidth of 18.69% [14].

R. S. Tomar et al. (Eds.): CNC 2020, CCIS 1502, pp. 29–44, 2021.
https://doi.org/10.1007/978-981-16-8896-6_3

To demonstrate more about CP, a number of cases of DRAs were reported; where, 3-dB axial bandwidth was improved to 21.5% with the utilization of trapezoidal DR excited by inclined slot [15]. The fractal concept was introduced in DRA [16], but its axial bandwidth could reach upto 14.01% [17]. So, modification of antenna geometry with stair-shaped DR excited using change in feeding mechanism with 22% ARBW [18]. Prior, tradeoffs like broadband circular polarization, better realized gain (>5.5 dBic) was not achieved in [8–19]. To highlight the suitability for RF energy harvesting system, analogy in terms of required performance indices are given in Table 1.

Table 1. Examination of broadband CP-CSMA with existing antennas [8–18]

Ref.	Type of antenna	−10 dBIm. BW (%)	3-dB AR. BW (%)	CP realized Gain average	Geometrical execution
[8]	Monopole	~167%	–	–	LP
[9]	Monopole	~154%	–	–	LP
[10]	Monopole	152%	–	–	LP
[11]	Monopole	CDMA/GSM	<5.1%	3.5–4.1 dBic	Simple
[12]	Monopole	16%	10%	5.5 dBic	Multi-layered
[13]	Monopole	33.7%	18.5%	5.8 dBic	Multi-layered
[14]	Monopole	34.3%	18.69%	~5.1 dBic	Multi-layered
[15]	DRA	28.1%	22.6%	~5.2 dBic	Complex
[16]	DRA-Array	33.1%	12.4%	≥9 dBic	Complex
[17]	DRA	35.59%	14.01%	3.1 dBic	Complex
[18]	DRA	37%	22%	5.5 dBic	Complex
Proposed	**Monopole**	**117.9%**	**32.22%**	**5.68 dBic**	**Simple**

Besides, none of the referred papers in the same area-of-interest has persuaded the theoretical analogy about circular polarization. Hence, a generic solution is proposed in the form of a multi-layered CP CSMA loaded with PEC superstrate for achieving these tradeoffs [2].

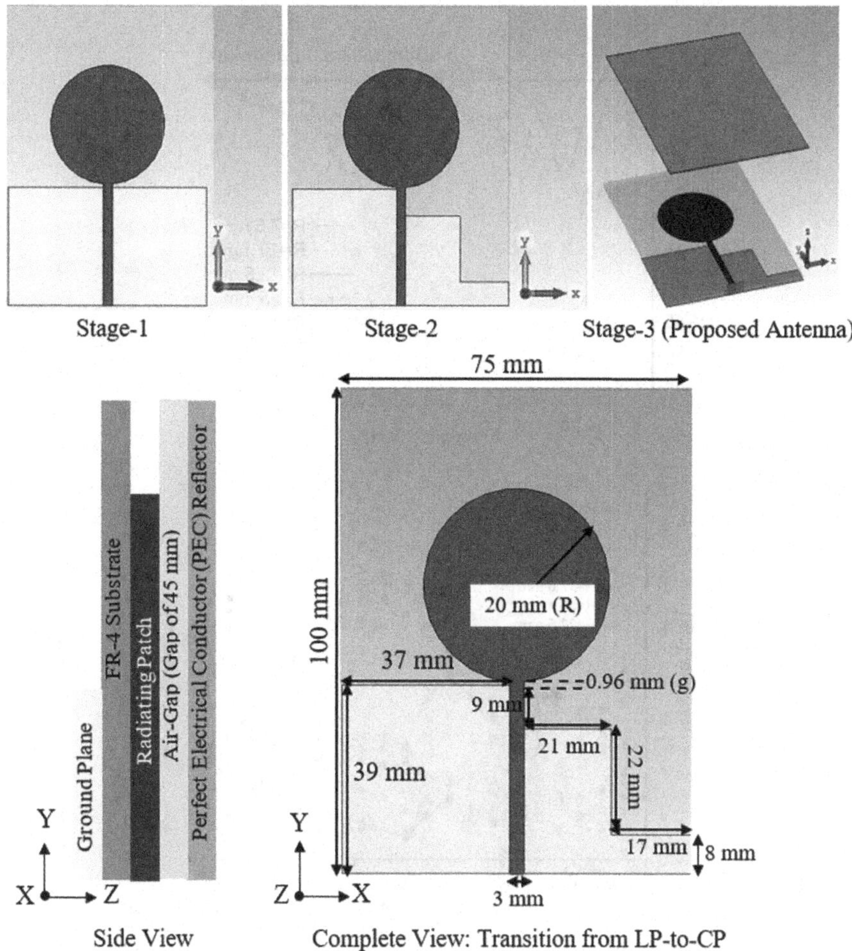

Fig. 1. The evolution and schematic geometry of CP-CSMA loaded with PEC superstrate.

2 Antenna Design and Geometry

Figure 1 shows complete evolution from stage-1 to stage-3 printed on the FR-4 substrate ($\varepsilon_r = 4.4$, tan $\delta = 0.018$). It features about $\lambda/4$ printed circularly-shaped linearly polarized monopole antenna (CSMA) with the partial ground plane (stage-1). Further, partial ground plane is converted to asymmetrical stair-cased partial ground plane; persuaded for existence of horizontal (*x*) and vertical (*y*) field components, needed for circular polarization (stage-2). Then, PEC superstrate is placed on top of radiator at height of 45 mm. As a result of, broadband circular polarization along with directional pattern is achieved (stage-3). In Fig. 1, optimized dimension of CP-CSMA structure (stage-3) is also shown.

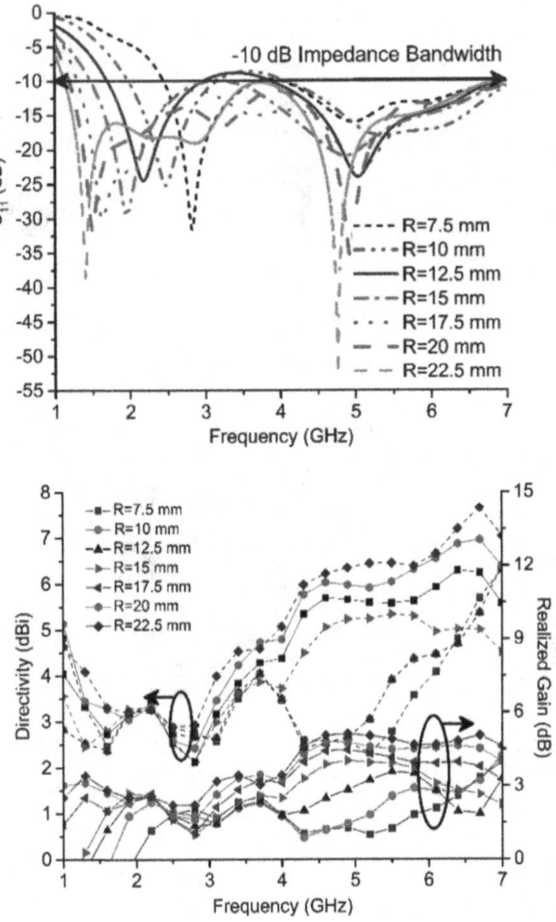

Fig. 2. The effect of variables [(f_L) and R] on the impedance bandwidth, directivity and realized gain of the proposed CSMA at stage-1.

Coming to the physical insight, 'functionality of CSMA' is dependent on the lower resonant frequency (f_L). f_L depends upon radius of circularly shaped monopole (R) and gap (g). Besides, gap (g) has crucial role to play in overall impedance matching. Such correlation of the geometrical sequences is theoretically observed. Primitive findings involve dependency of factors, 'R', along with its impact upon the parameters: −10 dB impedance bandwidth, realized gain and directivity. Figure 2 is highlighting the analogy of various parameters and its impact on the behaviour of CSMA at stage-1.

- With increase in radius (R), there is downwards shifting of impedance (i.e. due to decrease in inductance). Thus, a slight decrease in resonant frequency (f_L), leads to an increase in impedance bandwidth.
- Realized gain shift towards lowest resonating frequency (f_L), with slight increase in radius (R).
- As radius (R) increases, directivity increases marginally. As a result, realized gain bandwidth also increases significantly.

3 Simulation Results with an Appeal to Circular Polarization

Figure 3 shows simulated responses from stage-1-to-stage-3 of proposed CP-CSMA. The performance index of various stages is given as: stage-1 (CSMA + partial ground plane) with impedance bandwidth of 1.2–~7 GHz; stage-2 (CSMA + asymmetrical stair-cased partial ground plane) with the impedance bandwidth of 1.1–6.8 GHz and axial bandwidth of 4.65–5.37 GHz & finally, at stage-3 (CSMA + asymmetrical stair-cased partial ground plane + PEC superstrate) with the impedance bandwidth of 1.81–6.88 GHz and axial bandwidth of 4.04–5.54 GHz. With the scenario of stage-2, there is transition from LP-to-CP with wideband axial ARBW. The geometrical sequences of CSMA + asymmetrical stair-cased partial ground plane is quite responsible for the generation of horizontal (x) + vertical (y) field components, needed for CP generation. At stage-3, broadband CP is attained. Intuition lies with geometrical inclusion of PEC superstrate. The radiated waves from CSMA and PEC superstrate resulted out in the directional property. The exhibition of radiation pattern is one of the most needed key factors in deciding "the amount of power conversion (RF-input to DC-output)" in RF energy harvesting.

Coming to the context of circular polarization, theoretical interpretation is derived and is backed by the surface current distribution [$\boldsymbol{J}_{surface}$], electric-field pattern [$\boldsymbol{E}_{field}$], with the theoretical context of plane-waves and study of normalized radiation pattern. The 1st primitive approach of analyzing circular polarization (CP) is through the study of surface current distribution [$\boldsymbol{J}_{surface}$ A/m]. In stage-1, surface currents evenly cancel at horizontal edges of the partial ground plane (i.e. oppositely directed), indicating the presence of only vertical field components at the monopole arm. In stage-2, due to the presence of asymmetrical stair-cased partial ground plane, it persuaded for existence of horizontal and vertical field components required for the generation of a circularly polarized wave. The detailed analogy in this case is shown in Fig. 4. The 1st approach confirms the existence of circular polarization (CP) in the proposed antenna. In next section, analogy about identification of the nature of CP (LHCP/RHCP) is presented.

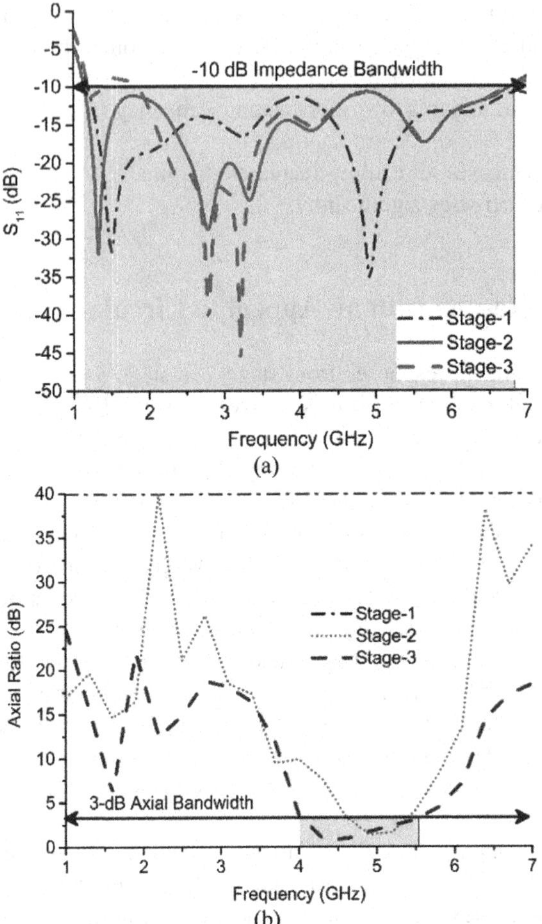

Fig. 3. S_{11} and Axial characteristics of proposed CP-CSMA loaded with PEC (perfect electrical conductor) superstrate. (a) S_{11} v/s frequency traits and (b) axial ratio (AR) v/s frequency traits.

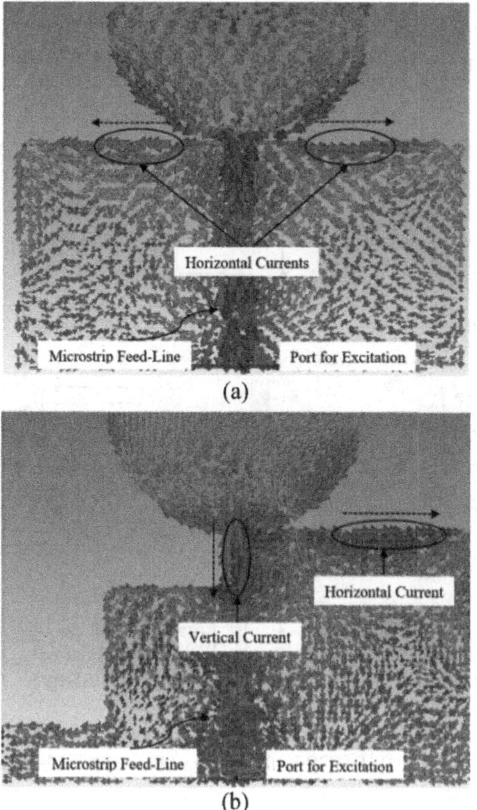

Fig. 4. The surface current distribution of (a) stage-1 (LP) and (b) stage-2 (CP) of the proposed CSMA at $f = 5$ GHz.

The 2nd primitive approach of analyzing circular polarization is the study of E-field pattern through electric field distribution by using EM solver. It relates with finding the nature of CP (RHCP/LHCP). So, it is considered as 'RHCP antenna'; due to the movement of electric fields in the clockwise (CW) direction with - z-axis (outward), as the direction of propagation at $f = 5$ GHz. As a result of which, two field components i.e. horizontal (x) and vertical (y) field components, identified in 1st approach, rotates with the phase difference of 90°. Figure 5 demonstrates orthogonal change in electric-field pattern, when phase changes from 0° to 90°. Prior to it, maximum magnitude of electric fields moves in the clockwise direction from 90° to 180°, 180° to 270° and 270° to 360°. In addition to that, it opened implicit way for identifying nature of circular polarization (CP). Now, coming to the scenario of understanding simulation aspects of CP in CST-MWS (EM solver) (seen in Fig. 5), through theoretical context.

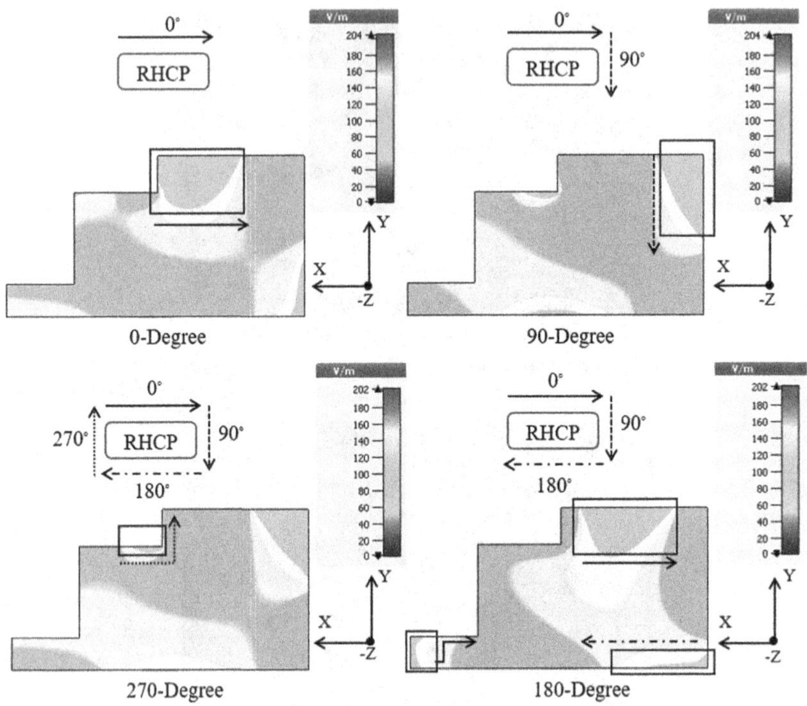

Fig. 5. Electric field distribution of stage-2 of the proposed CSMA at f = 5 GHz for time-varying phases [ωt = 0° to 360°]. RHCP is the nature of circular polarization (CP) at stage-2.

Let us consider that, x and y are linearly polarized waves with complex amplitudes E_x and E_y. Since E_x and E_y components are varying with space and time; then the total electric fields can be represented as:

$$\vec{E}(z) = (E_x\hat{x} + E_y\hat{y})\, e^{j\beta z} \tag{1}$$

Then, the total electric fields can be represented in terms of amplitudes and phases:

$$\vec{E}(z,t) = (E_{x_0}e^{jwt}\hat{x} + E_{y_0}e^{jwt}\hat{y})\, e^{j\beta z} \tag{2}$$

$$= E_{x_0}e^{j(wt+\beta z)}\hat{x} + E_{y_0}e^{j(wt+\beta z)}\hat{y} \tag{3}$$

Considering the time dependence and taking only the real part of Eq. (3), we get,

$$\vec{E}(z,t) = E_{x_0}\cos(wt+\beta z)\hat{x} + E_{y_0}\cos(wt+\beta z)\hat{y} \tag{4}$$

The final representation of electric fields for 'RHCP' is interpreted with consideration of:

$$E_{x_0} = E_0 e^{j.0} = E_0 \text{ and } E_{y_0} = E_0 e^{\frac{j\pi}{2}} \tag{*}$$

Putting the requisite values of (*) in Eq. (4) we get,

$$\begin{aligned}\vec{E}_{RHCP}(z,t) &= E_0\cos(wt+\beta z)\hat{x} + E_0 e^{\frac{j\pi}{2}}\cos(wt+\beta z)\hat{y}\\ &= E_0\cos(wt+\beta z)\hat{x} + E_0 j\cos(wt+\beta z)\hat{y}\\ &= E_0\cos(wt+\beta z)\hat{x} + E_0\cos(wt+\beta z+\frac{\pi}{2})\hat{y}\end{aligned} \tag{5}$$

At $z = 0$,

$$\vec{E}_{RHCP}(0,t) = E_0\cos(wt)\hat{x} + E_0\cos(wt+\frac{\pi}{2})\hat{y} \tag{6}$$

The 3rd primitive approach of analyzing circular polarization is through the study of radiation pattern. Its 1st sub-approach deals with maximum realized gain from 3D radiation pattern. The 2nd sub-approach is related to relative power from the cartesian plot of radiation pattern [3]. Both of them are considered at CP frequencies: 4.7 GHz, 5 GHz and 5.3 GHz. The relevant outcomes of sub-approach-I & sub-approach-II are shown in Table 2 and 3 with reference to Fig. 6 and 7 respectively. Proposed broadband CP-CSMA (stage-2/3) exhibits RHCP in broadside direction (ϕ = 0°, θ = 0° and ϕ = 90°, θ = 0°). Stage-2 offers stronger RHCP than LHCP by 27 dB, 19 dB, 15 dB at 4.7 GHz, 5 GHz and 5.3 GHz respectively. Dominancy of CP components is evaluated by using the formulae in [3]. Its corresponding outcomes are shown in Fig. 7 and Table 3.

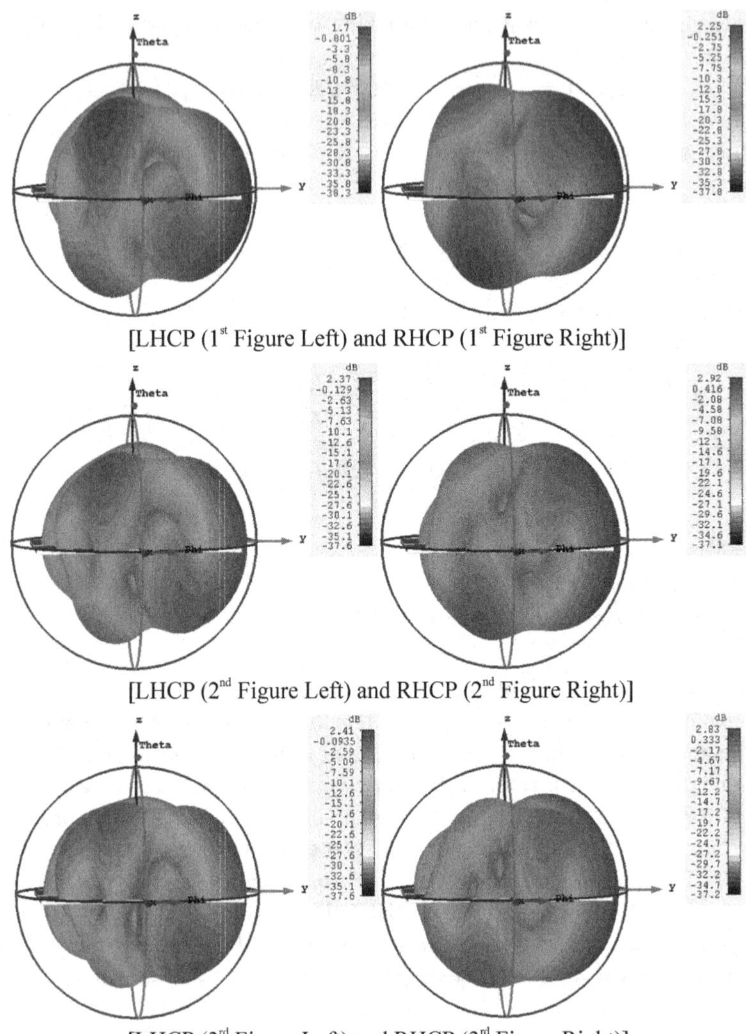

[LHCP (1st Figure Left) and RHCP (1st Figure Right)]

[LHCP (2nd Figure Left) and RHCP (2nd Figure Right)]

[LHCP (3rd Figure Left) and RHCP (3rd Figure Right)]

Fig. 6. Max^{m} realized gain from 3D radiation at stage-2.

Table 2. Sub approach-I

Frequency	LHCP	RHCP	Dominant
4.7 GHz	1.71 dBic	2.25 dBic	RHCP
5 GHz	2.37 dBic	2.92 dBic	RHCP
5.3 GHz	2.41 dBic	2.83 dBic	RHCP

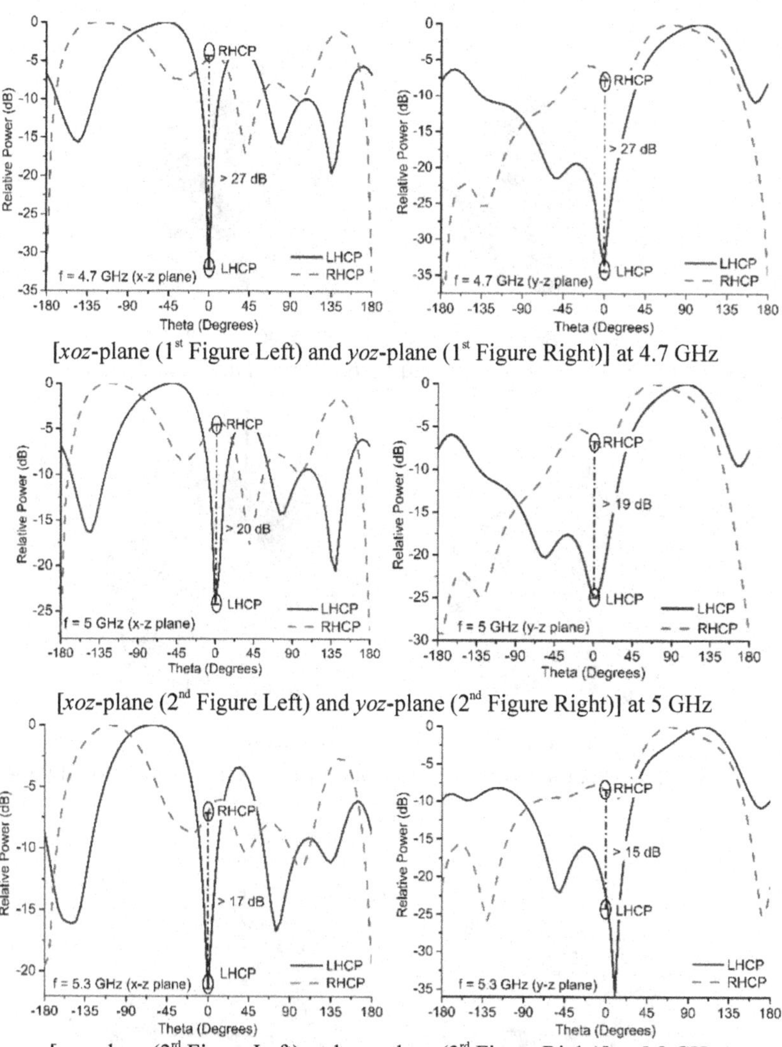

[*xoz*-plane (1st Figure Left) and *yoz*-plane (1st Figure Right)] at 4.7 GHz

[*xoz*-plane (2nd Figure Left) and *yoz*-plane (2nd Figure Right)] at 5 GHz

[*xoz*-plane (3rd Figure Left) and *yoz*-plane (3rd Figure Right)] at 5.3 GHz

Fig. 7. The relative power from radiation pattern of CP-CSMA at stage-2 for usable CP frequencies.

Table 3. Sub approach-II

Frequency	Dominant (LHCP/RHCP) $\|P_{LHCP}-P_{RHCP}\|$ [2]
4.7 GHz	RHCP is dominant to LHCP by >27 dB/>27 dB
5 GHz	RHCP is dominant to LHCP by >20 dB/>19 dB
5.3 GHz	RHCP is dominant to LHCP by >17 dB/>15 dB

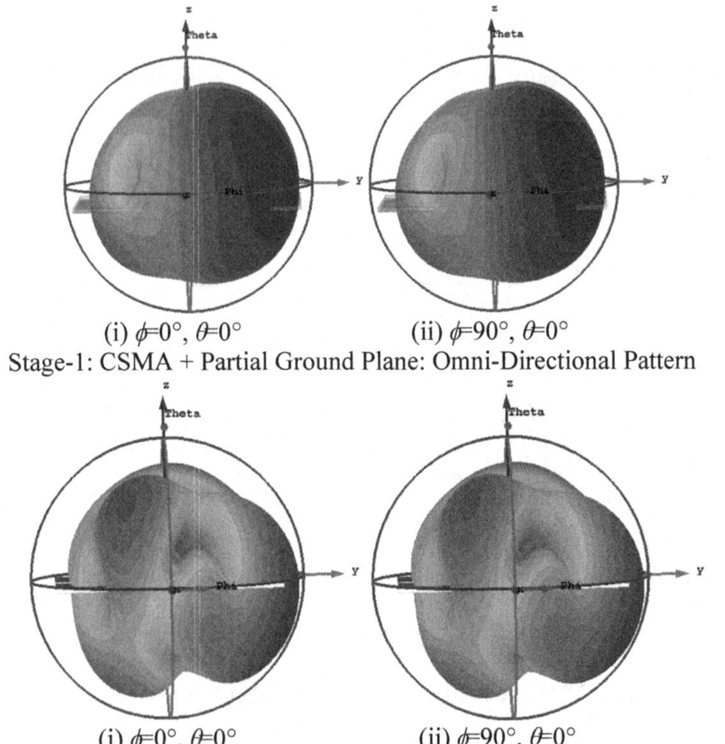

(i) ϕ=0°, θ=0° (ii) ϕ=90°, θ=0°

Stage-1: CSMA + Partial Ground Plane: Omni-Directional Pattern

(i) ϕ=0°, θ=0° (ii) ϕ=90°, θ=0°

Stage-2: CSMA + Asymmetrical Partial Ground Plane: Omni-Directional Pattern

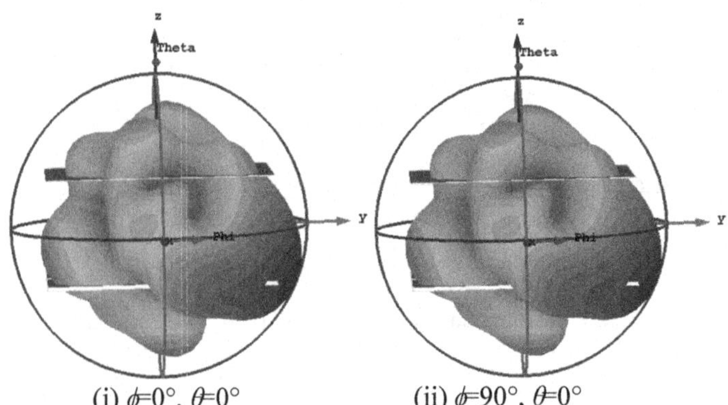

(i) ϕ=0°, θ=0° (ii) ϕ=90°, θ=0°

Stage-3: CSMA + Asymmetrical Partial Ground Plane + PEC (Perfect Electrical Conductor [PEC]) Superstrate: Directional Pattern

Fig. 8. The translational study of incorporation of PEC superstrate: transition of omni-directional radiation to directional radiation pattern [stage-1 to 3].

In broadside direction ($\phi = 0°$, $\theta = 0°$ and $\phi = 90°$, $\theta = 0°$), CP-CSMA loaded with PEC superstrate, showed excellent RHCP radiation. On a similar note, there is a significant improvement of 3-dB axial bandwidth (nearly 2.08 times) from 720 MHz (stage-2) to 1.5 GHz (stage-3), proving importance of PEC superstrate for CP; especially looking at the needs of RF energy harvesting systems. Radiated waves from CSMA and PEC superstrate resulted in exhibition of directional property [20]. Detailed analogy in this prospective (i.e. the transition from omni-directional to directional pattern) is shown in Fig. 8. Attainment of directional pattern is termed as one of the key parameters that decides 'amount of power conversion' (RF signals as input to DC voltage as output) [2, 21]. For supporting the CSMA & PEC superstrate, FOAM is used, at the time of practical realization. To study its impact on 3-dB axial bandwidth, parametric study of $h_{air\text{-}gap}$ is persuaded from 20-to-70 mm. Their corresponding outcomes are shown in Fig. 9.

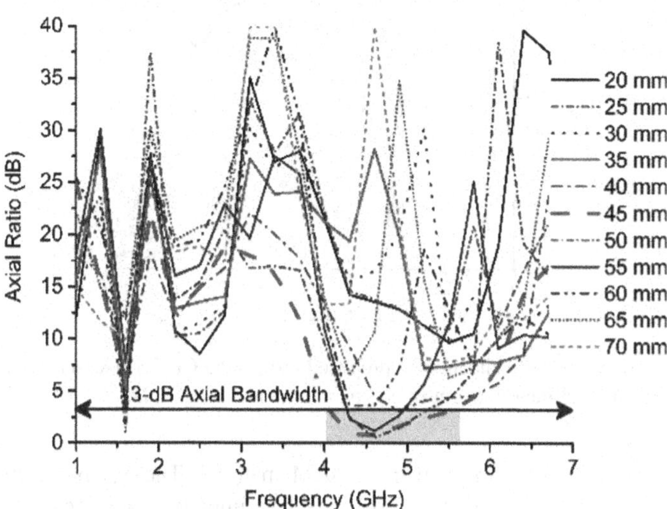

Fig. 9. Translational study of PEC superstrate: consideration of 3-dB axial bandwidth for broadband CP-CSMA [stage-3].

4 Fabrication and Its Experimental Validation

The fabrication and characterization of CP-CSMA loaded with PEC superstrate is persuaded and is shown in Fig. 10. The proposed antenna prototype was fabricated on FR-4 substrate by using PCB prototyping technology. The PEC superstrate is made of copper-clad material of thickness 0.2 mm. Then, CP-CSMA and PEC superstrate are

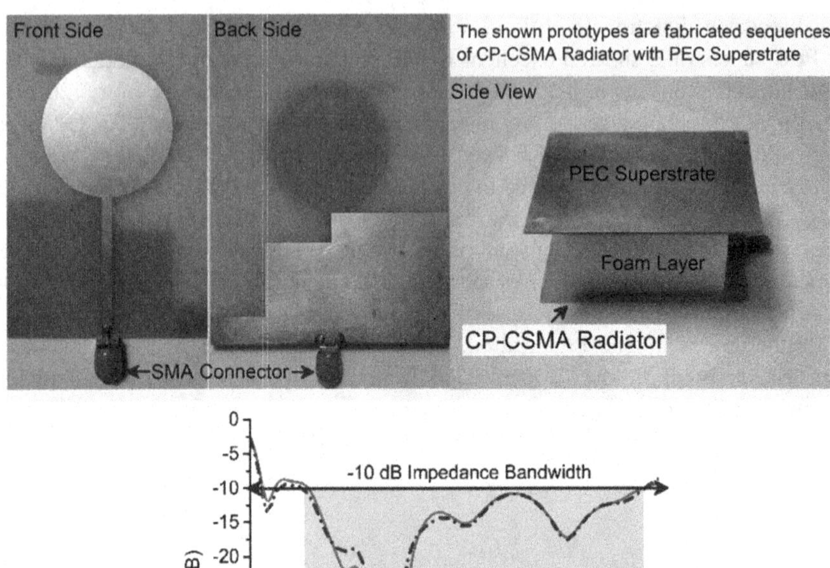

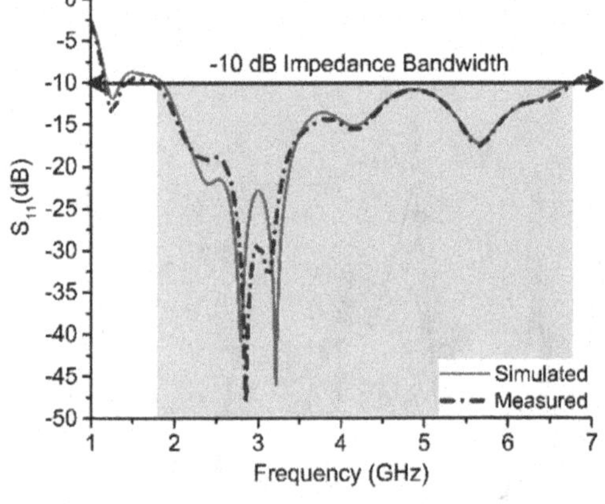

Fig. 10. The fabrication and validation of proposed broadband CP-CSMA [stage-3]. It includes fabricated prototype and measurement of S_{11} parameter by using VNA.

supported at $h_{air\text{-}gap}$ = 45 mm by using FOAM material. The S_{11} parameter is measured by Agilent VNA (model: N5247A). The simulated and measured −10-dB impedance bandwidth is 117.9% (1.81–6.88 GHz) & 117% (1.8–6.88 GHz). An average simulated gain of 5.54 dBi with antenna efficiency of 75%. It shows better performance, when compared with the existing antennas [8–18]. Besides, the outcomes of different stages are shown in Table 4.

Table 4. Examination of CP-CSMA

Parameters	Stage-1	Stage-2	Stage-3 (Proposed)	Stage-3 (Measured)
Type	Partial Ground	Asymmetrical Ground	Asymmetrical Ground + Perfect Electrical Conductor Superstrate	
S_{11}	1.2-7 GHz	1.1-6.8 GHz	1.81-6.88 GHz	1.8-6.88 GHz
Impedance BW (%)	141.4%	144.3%	117.9%	117%
Axial Ratio	--------	4.65-5.37 GHz	4.04-5.54 GHz	
Axial BW (%)	--------	14.1%	32.22%	
CP Gain^{average}	--------	4.62 dBic	5.68 dBic	
Antenna Directivity (f=5 GHz)	5.89 dBi	6.07 dBi	7.3 dBi	Not Measured
AR Beamwidth (f=5 GHz)	--------	62°	84°	
Pattern	Omni-Direc^n	Omni-Direc^n	Directional	

5 Conclusion

Here, multi-layered printed monopole antenna with broadband CP trait is proposed. Due to its geometrical sequences, it offers IBW of 117.9% (1.81–6.88 GHz) & ARBW of 32.22% (4.04–5.54 GHz). Average realized gain of 5.54 dBi and antenna efficiency of 75% is observed. With the physical insights about CP-CSMA, theoretical intuition about CP is derived, backed by surface current distribution, electric-field pattern with context of plane-wave and radiation pattern, with due consideration of frequency of operation i.e. utilization of RF signals (1.8 to 7 GHz as LP antenna & 4 to 5.5 GHz as CP antenna) and attainment of directional pattern.

References

1. Behera, B.R., Meher, P.R., Mishra, S.K.: Microwave antennas—an intrinsic part of RF energy harvesting systems: a contingent study about its design methodologies and state-of-art technologies in current scenario. Int. J. RF Microw. Comput. Aided Eng. **30**(5), e22148 (2020)
2. Divakaran, S.K., Krishna, D.D., Nasimuddin, N.: RF energy harvesting systems: an overview and design issues. Int. J. RF Microw. Comput. Aided Eng. **29**(1), 1–15 (2019)
3. Toh, B.Y., Cahill, R., Fusco, V.F.: Understanding and measuring circular polarization. IEEE Trans. Educ. **46**(3), 313–318 (2003)
4. Liang, J., Chiau, C.C., Chen, X., Parini, C.G.: Study of a printed circular disc monopole antenna for UWB systems. IEEE Trans. Antennas Propag. **53**(11), 3500–3504 (2005)

5. Mishra, S.K., Gupta, R.K., Vaidya, A., Mukherjee, J.: A compact dual-band fork-shaped monopole antenna for Bluetooth and UWB applications. IEEE Antennas Wirel. Propag. Lett. **10**, 627–630 (2011)
6. Ray, K.P.: Design aspects of printed monopole antennas for ultra-wide band applications. Int. J. Antennas Propag. **2008**, 1–8 (2008)
7. Behera, B.R., Meher, P.R., Mishra, S.K.: Compact and efficient printed monopole antenna with broadband circular polarization. In: 2019 IEEE 6th International Conference on Signal Processing and Integrated Networks (SPIN), Noida, India, pp. 1147–1152 (2019)
8. Mathur, M., Agrawal, A., Singh, G., Bhatnagar, S.K.: A compact coplanar waveguide fed wideband monopole antenna for RF energy harvesting applications. Prog. Electromagnet. Res. M. **63**, 175–184 (2018)
9. Dastranj, A.: Very small planar broadband monopole antenna with hybrid trapezoidal-elliptical radiator. IET Microw. Antennas Propag. **11**(4), 542–547 (2017)
10. Elsheakh, D.M., Abdallah, E.A.: Ultra-wide-bandwidth (UWB) microstrip monopole antenna using split ring resonator (SRR) structure. Int. J. Microw. Wirel. Technol. **10**(1), 123–132 (2018)
11. Ghosh, S., Chakrabarty, A.: Dual band circularly polarized monopole antenna design for RF energy harvesting. IETE J. Res. **62**(1), 9–16 (2016)
12. Yue, T., Jiang, Z.H., Werner, D.H.: Compact, wideband antennas enabled by interdigitated capacitor-loaded metasurfaces. IEEE Trans. Antennas Propag. **64**(5), 1595–1606 (2016)
13. Wu, Z., Li, L., Li, Y., Chen, X.: Metasurface superstrate antenna with wideband circular polarization for satellite communication application. IEEE Antennas Wirel. Propag. Lett. **15**, 374–377 (2016)
14. Chen, Q., Zhang, H., Yang, L.-C., Zhang, X.-F., Zeng, Y.-C.: Wideband and low axial ratio circularly polarized antenna using AMC-based structure polarization rotation reflective surface. Int. J. Microw. Wirel. Technol. **10**(9), 1058–1064 (2018)
15. Pan, Y., Leung, K.W.: Wideband circularly polarized trapezoidal dielectric resonator antenna. IEEE Antennas Wirel. Propag. Lett. **9**, 588–591 (2010)
16. Lin, J.-H., Shen, W.-H., Shi, Z.-D., Zhong, S.-S.: Circularly polarized dielectric resonator antenna arrays with fractal cross-slot-coupled DRA elements. Int. J. Antennas Propag. **2017**, 1–11 (2017)
17. Altaf, A., Yang, Y., Lee, K., Hwang, K.C.: Circularly polarized Spidron fractal dielectric resonator antenna. IEEE Antennas Wirel. Propag. Lett. **14**, 1806–1809 (2015)
18. Fakhte, S., Oraizi, H., Karimian, R., Fakhte, R.: A new wideband circularly polarized stair-shaped dielectric resonator antenna. IEEE Trans. Antennas Propag. **63**(4), 1828–1832 (2015)
19. Kumar, R., Thummaluru, S.R., Chaudhary, R.K.: Improvements in Wi-MAX reception: a new dual-mode wideband circularly polarized dielectric resonator antenna. IEEE Antennas Propag. Mag. **61**(1), 41–49 (2019)
20. Chen, Q., et al.: Wideband and low axial ratio circularly polarized antenna using AMC-based structure polarization rotation reflective surface. Int. J. Microw. Wirel. Technol. **10**(9), 1058–1064 (2018)
21. Nintanavongsa, P., Muncuk, U., Lewis, D.R., Chowdhury, K.R.: Design optimization and implementation for RF energy harvesting circuits. IEEE J. Emerg. Sel. Top. Circ. Syst. **2**(1), 24–33 (2012)

Design and Implementation of LoRa Based Automation Device

Pranay Sisodia(✉), Neha Arora, and Jitendra Singh Jadon

Department of Electronics and Telecommunication,
Amity School of Enginnering and Technology, Amity University,
Sector-125, Noida 201303, UP, India
{narora2, jsjadon}@amity.edu

Abstract. In recent times, the dependency on automation devices are increasing rapidly. From healthcare, home appliances to large scale industries, automations are emerging. This research is based on automation particularly in Agricultural scenarios. The research is to provide a simpler communication model with less or no dependency on cellular or any other communication network. Here, LoRa™ i.e. the long range communication model is used which is based on LoRaWAN™. The low-cost and open IoT gateway using RPI 3B & end devices with ARa-02 LoRa has been proposed for both robust and simple deployment. As in rural areas the connectivity with internet is a major issue. This system will definitely help in solving the problem. The post processing features of the development such as interfacing of gateway with cloud and as well as future integration and functionalities have also been suggested.

Keywords: LPWAN · A Ra-02 · Low-power IoT · Low-cost IoT · LoRa

1 Introduction

IoT has clearly increased adeptness through computerization & optimization, the deployment of such Technology in an enormous scale is as yet kept down by specialized difficulties, for example, short correspondence separations. Utilizing the 3G/4G/LTE communication framework is still much costlier and not vitality proficient for autonomous gadgets that must operate on battery for a considerable time. In recent times various technology is being considered for WSN (Wireless sensors Network). Smart cities framework can in the end be acknowledged with such short-range interchanges where high hub thickness with controlling office can be accomplished, it can barely be summed up for the vast part of reconnaissance applications that should be sent in isolated or countryside conditions [12].

Ongoing regulation systems where the protracted diffusion separation (a few kilometers even in NLOS conditions) can be accomplished without hand-off hubs enormously lessens the unpredictability of arrangement and information assortment [1].

R. S. Tomar et al. (Eds.): CNC 2020, CCIS 1502, pp. 45–54, 2021.
https://doi.org/10.1007/978-981-16-8896-6_4

Model have an upper hand as compared to other communications model such as:

1. There is no dependency on cellular network for connectivity
2. Cost is less as compared to other as well as maintenance cost is much less;
3. Can provide long range communication (Fig. 1).

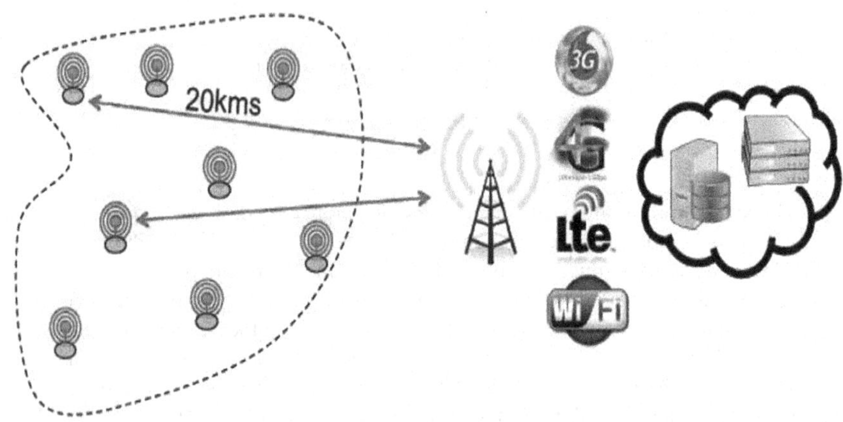

Fig. 1. Extraordinary long-range application

Sigfox™ is one such technology used as a low power and for long distance communication. However, due to its restriction and operator base support, it cannot be developed in an Ad-Hoc manner [10]. Here the LoRa™ technology designed and developed by Semtech™ radio can be utilized. The recent development of LoRaWAN™, has customization capabilities and can be developed further and deployed in Ad-Hoc fashion. The work proposed in this paper is based on Semtech's LoRa Module. We presented here, The low-cost LoRa Gateway & software for designing ad-hoc LoRa IoT automation device based on Agricultural farming in particular, where we defined the End Node and the Gateway [7].

The paper is composed as pursues. Section 2 consist of Literature analysis for Semtech's LoRa. Further LoRa LPWAN i.e. Low power wide area network and its architecture is defined. Section 3 consists of the detail description of designing of the cost effective LoRa gateway and End nodes, we further discuss the connectivity of the gateway with or without internet access. Later in Sect. 4 paper is concluded.

2 LPWAN and LoRa Transmission

2.1 LoRa-A Semtech's Development

The long range technology also known as LoRa is developed by Semtech™. This Semtech's new technology works on "spread spectrum" where regularity and time are two spreaded feature of data, increases the range as well give robustness to the system. Here the receiver's sensitivity is ranges from −137 dBm in 868 MHz and −148 dBm in 433 MHz. here in India the 433 MHz band is the unlicensed spectrum band, hence the 433 MHz LoRa module will be in use. In communication the throughput and the range of the module is indeed depend on some parameters which are SF-Spreading Factor, BW-Bandwidth, CR-Code Rate [6]. The coding Rate or the CR is used for correction and error detections, here the coding rate is inversely proportional to overhead ratio of the coding rate for instance CR = 2(2 + CR) the overhead ratio is 1.15 for CR equals to Unity. Then comes the Spreading Factor (SF), SF lies between 6 to 12 marks where the Spreading factor is Inversely Proportional to transmission speed but proportional to Noise immunity and range. At last BW is the physical bandwidth, higher the bandwidth then higher will be the speed of transmission, Table 1 shows all the LoRa parameters and there transmitted bytes, 255B payload is the greatest throughput appeared in the last section with a. Modes 4 to 6 give very fascinating trade-offs to longer range, higher information rate and invulnerability to obstructions [7].

Table 1. LoRa Modes in comparison to payload size.

LoRa mode	BW	CR	SF	time on air in second for payload size of 5 bytes	55 bytes	105 bytes	155 Bytes	205 Bytes	255 Bytes	max thr. for 255B in bps
1	125	4/5	12	0.95846	2.59686	4.23526	5.87366	7.51206	9.15046	223
2	250	4/5	12	0.47923	1.21651	1.87187	2.52723	3.26451	3.91987	520
3	125	4/5	10	0.28058	0.69018	1.09978	1.50938	1.91898	2.32858	876
4	500	4/5	12	0.23962	0.60826	0.93594	1.26362	1.63226	1.95994	1041
5	250	4/5	10	0.14029	0.34509	0.54989	0.75469	0.95949	1.16429	1752
6	500	4/5	11	0.11981	0.30413	0.50893	0.69325	0.87757	1.06189	1921
7	250	4/5	9	0.07014	0.18278	0.29542	0.40806	0.5207	0.63334	3221
8	500	4/5	9	0.03507	0.09139	0.14771	0.20403	0.26035	0.31667	6442
9	500	4/5	8	0.01754	0.05082	0.08154	0.11482	0.14554	0.17882	11408
10	500	4/5	7	0.00877	0.02797	0.04589	0.06381	0.08301	0.10093	20212

For example, in India, electromagnetic Radio transmissions in 433 MHz ISM Band utilized by Semtech's LoRa innovation comes under the Short Range Devices. The report "ETPI EN75-220-1" has particular guidelines for a device to come under the SRD classification, especially for the one which are on radio movement [11].

Here 2% duty cycle which is about 72 s/h in a normal scenario are constrained to the transmitters. the total transmission time has a duty limit however just about half, that is about 1% duty cycle is also large enough to complies with the need of applications and devices to communicate.

2.2 LoRa LPWAN Network Disposition and Architecture

The LoRa Network works on the gateway centric approach as seen in various other technologies Here, the end node communicate to the gateway end sends the data [12]. Here the designing is based on automation device particular to an agricultural farm. hence the nodes setup across the farm collects the data and send it to the gateway placed somewhere outside the farm, keeping in mind the range of system is around

20 km theoretically and 12 km practically. this whole clusters of end nodes and a gateway is the LoRa LPWAN network deployment, following LPWAN, the alliance has come up with LoRaWAN™ for wider and much greater deployment [3]. Further, cloud integration can provide much greater and robust framework to the network, which in term provide real time updates (Fig. 2).

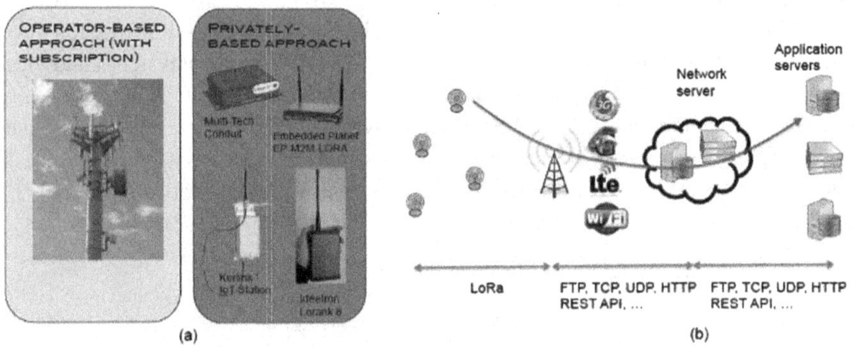

Fig. 2. (a) gateway; (b) LPWAN architecture

The complete setup shows the LoRaWAN™ architecture and depicts the scenarios for deployment and what all a low cost LoRa centric gateway can do, here some features:

(i) The gateway can run without internet connection, however with internet enabled, the gateway can send the data to the cloud [4].
(ii) The Gateway running on low cost and low powered supply with the help of PoE (Power over Ethernet).

3 Economical LoRa Gateway and Devices

3.1 Inexpensive/Low-Cost LoRa Gateway

The sole purpose of the Paper is to design and implement a low cost LoRa Communication system where the LoRa gateway is the key device. The commercial LoRa gateway costs much higher and is consider way too costly for implementation. Whereas in developing countries such as India Bangladesh, and African Sahara where agricultural is the main wheel of the GDP, such costly device has no use [8].

The proposed LoRa Gateway works on Raspberry pi 3B which is powered with a PoE (Power over Ethernet) adapter. The RPI 3B is a very good option as the board had in built Wi-Fi, Ethernet support and the Raspbian OS is very much welcoming for modification The PoE adapter is further connected to voltage regulator which then feed the power supply to the board using micro USB cable. For the communication part the gateway uses Ai Thinker™ Ra-02 SX12768 LoRa radio module [9] with 2.4 GHz

Radio Antenna, we further conducted test with other radio module such asthe Ebyte™ E32 SX1276. Most of the radio module does not required much modification, but there are quite some in this project for further reduction of power consumption by the module we have changed the SF and the modes of working for the best suitable trade-off with range and power consumption, here data rate is not a factor as the data packet transmit in IoT scenarios are very small. The whole setup is then encapsulated inside a waterproof case which in terms provide the whole system rigidness and robustness. The recent development conducted by TheThingNetwork™ where the organization despite everything targets huge scope, open and multi-reason systems remains particularly same. The overall cost of the gateway including the casing is about 7000 INR which 7 times cheaper than the commercial gateways [14] (Fig. 3).

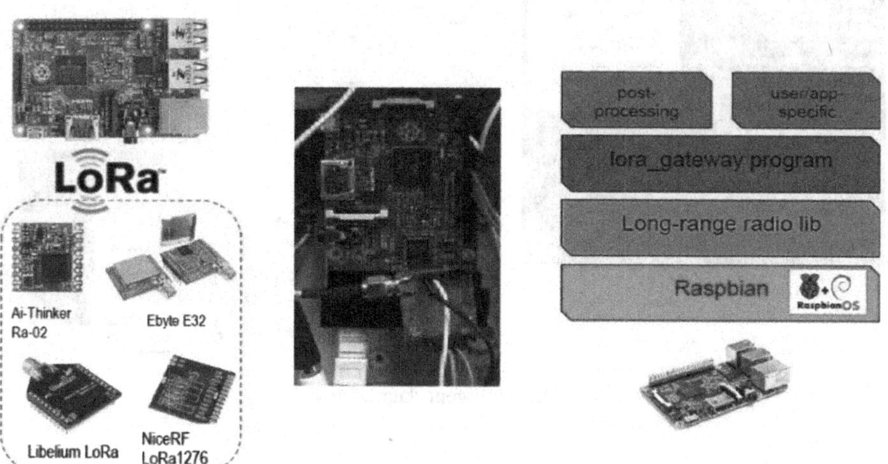

Fig. 3. Proposed gateway architecture.

The key feature of the proposed low cost LoRa gateway running with RPI 3B and Ai Thinker™ Ra-02 LoRa radio module:

(a) The Raspberry RPI 3B operates on Basic Raspbian OS
(b) The Long range library is well defined with conventions to the Ai Thinker Ra-02 LoRa Module [9].
(c) There are lot of integration in LoRa Gateway program which not only runs the gateway without internet and can update the security patches of Raspbian OS automatically.

Various custom libraries are also added to the LoRa gateway program for integration with various IoT fields such as healthcare, home appliances, industrial automation, etc.

The proposed LoRa gateway is tested in scenarios with lot many attributes for example testing with DHT11 Sensors. As well as power consumption monitoring is also done and conducted successfully where the device on transmitting or receiving the data packets consumes about 450 mA power and goes to deep sleep mode, when inactive [15].

3.2 Cloud Integration and Post-Processing

The LoRa gateway program as shown in Fig. 4a is the waking call for the gateway where the libraries after deep sleep cycle runs, here all the libraries introduced to the gateway runs and gather information. Here the Intelligent data analysis comes. The data received is filtered and processed. Post processing the data is stored in the gateway's MongoDB and further send to the cloud server for real time update [5].

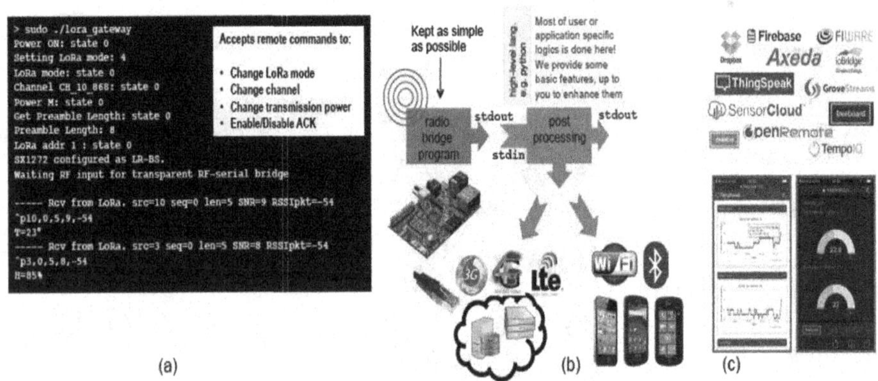

Fig. 4. Intelligent data analysis

The Fig. 4b shows advance data processing using Unix gateway processing as shown in orange bar. Here the higher level language such as python makes it easier to process the algorithm. This design is very common in gateway centric environment however, the system here is intelligent enough to analysis the data and eliminate garbage using the garbage collection algorithm. This in term solve the problem of Big data and etc. in addition to that all these libraries are written in python hence are very light and does not required much RAM of the RPI.

Further the Cloud Integration is shown in Fig. 4c it is a simple process of integrating cloud with the gateway however a running internet connection is required which can enabled with the help PoE adapter which in terms not only provide Ethernet connectivity but also provide the power supply to the RPI board. This helps in reducing the cost and size of the setup. For cloud various providers can be used, for this project ThingSpeak™ [5] is used, further SensorCloud™, GrooveStream™ or FiWare™ can also be used.

This design obviously from the elevated level post-handling highlights. By utilizing elevated level dialects for post-handling, running and modifying information the executives undertakings should be possible shortly.

3.3 Independent of Internet – Gateway

The proposed gateway can also be run independently without internet connection. This is also a key feature of the proposed gateway. In remote areas particularly in an agricultural fields where internet connectivity is zero or minimum, this proposed feature comes in handy. The data can be accessed by a simple laptop by connecting to the RPI Wi-Fi hotspot which is enabled by default and then connecting to user interface of the gateway by 192.168.200.1. Other gateway settings can also be accessed using the same URL. Figure 5 shows other methods of accessing gateway using Bluetooth is under development and the android software is in beta phase [13].

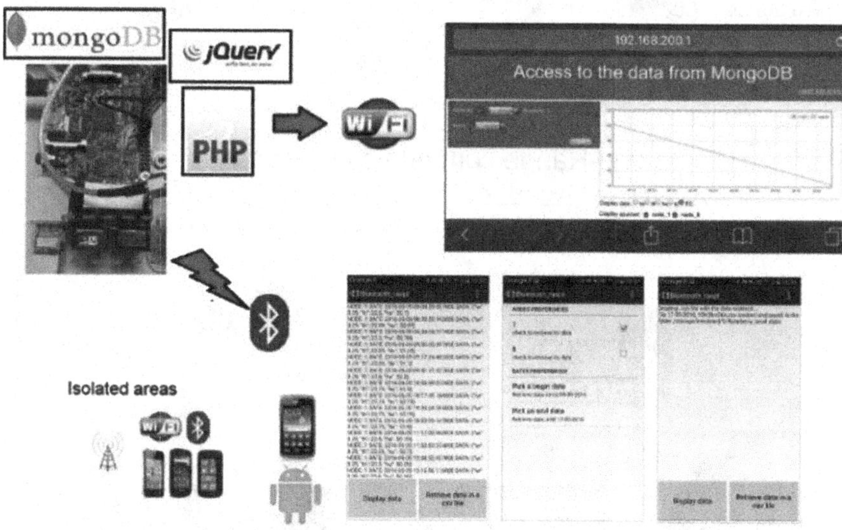

Fig. 5. Independent LoRa gateway

3.4 Inexpensive LoRa Nodes

Arduino board's Inexpensive and simple-to-program features [1]. These are plainly significant issues to consider with regards to developing nations, with the extra reality that because of their prosperity, they can be gained and obtained effectively around the world. Different board that can be utilized relying upon the application and the organization requirements. The Arduino Pro Nano, which come in a small structure and is accessible in a 3.3 v and 8 MHz rendition for low power utilization, has all the earmarks of being the advancement leading body of decision for giving a conventional stage to detecting and long transmission, [8] see Fig. 6.

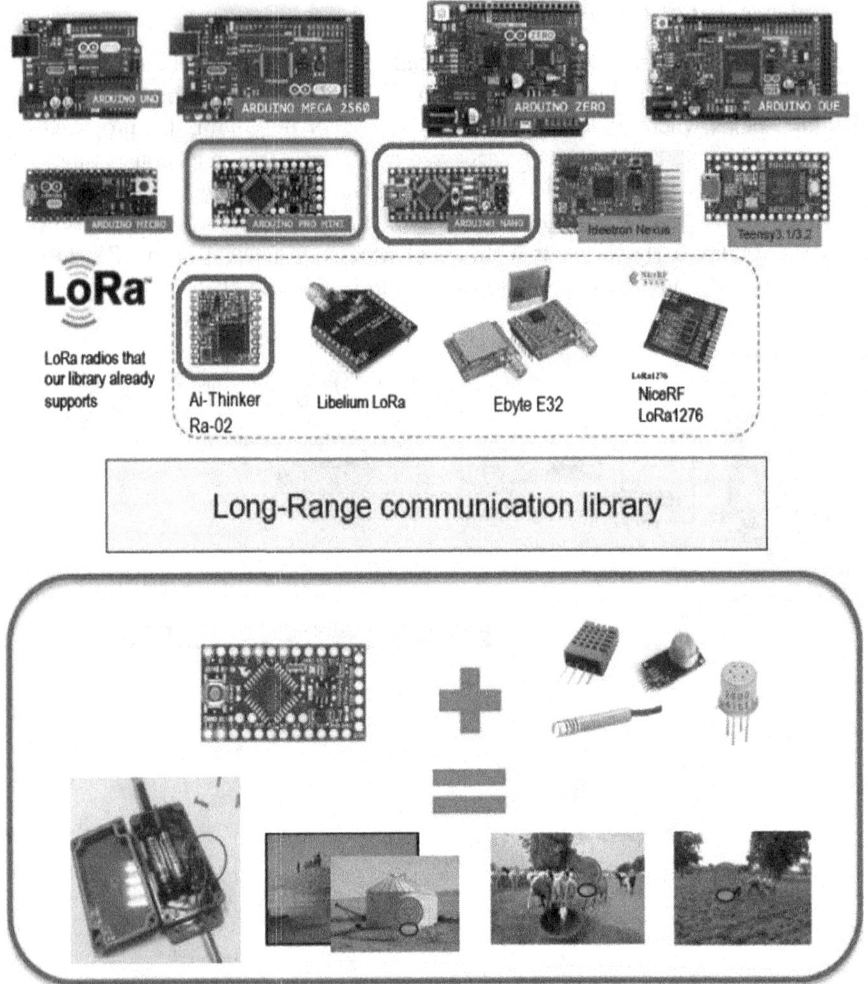

Fig. 6. LoRa end-device

Here for the End Node implementation, Arduino Nano is used which cost around 300 INR. These board are good enough to achieve the objectives. All the libraries implemented in the board is developed using python similar to the proposed gateway [2]. However some of the deep sleep libraries are open source and are available for further customization. These deep sleep libraries plays an important role for achieving a robust end node, consuming very low power.

Further the deep sleep mode is defined as follows, for very less-power applications, deep-sleep mode comes handy while using the small 3.3 V boards such as Arduino Nano or Pro min [8]. Here with a duty-cycle of 1 sample every 30 min, the board can run for 6 months, consuming about 14 mA in deep sleep mode and 93 mA when active and sending, which represents about 4 s of activity time.

The end node further runs on AA batteries with Ai-Thinker Ra-02 Sx1278 radio module and 2.4 GHz antenna. The complete setup is then encapsulated in waterproof box for rigidness and robustness. Hence the device can run for a long period without any attention.

4 Conclusion

Report introduced most significant issues that should be tended to when considering sending IoT arrangements: (a) Longer reach for provincial access, (b) Cost of gear and organizations and (c) Limit dependence to prohibitive structures and give neighborhood association models.

The report is inherited with post processing of the device and its connection with different cloud platform. Examples include DropboxTM, FirebaseTM, ThingSpeakTM, freeboardTM, etc. Further, the report also illustrated the working of the device without internet connection using inbuilt Wi-Fi of the RPI. Here, the low-cost gateway runs on MongoDBTM NoSQL database and a web server with PHP/jQuery to display received data in graphs.

The report portrays the minimal expense and open IoT stages for Long distance application that resolved these issues. Guided for little to medium size arrangement circumstances the stage also helps energetic task and customization by pariahs.

In outcome to that the planning of the minimal expense LoRa entryway and end gadgets is finished with some alteration in the libraries according to the chip set utilized. The passage is likewise tried in different conditions with a DHT22 sensor to screen the temperature and moistness level inside the case. The total framework is currently prepared for additional adjustment and future robotization execution.

Acknowledgments. Aryan Saini contributed to this work by writing the initial specifications and codes for the deep sleep cycle used in the LoRa End Node.

References

1. http://www.cookinghacks.com/documentation/tutorials/extreme-range-lora-sx1278-moduleshield-arduino-raspberry-pi-intel-galileo. Accessed 13 Jan 2018
2. Libelium: Extreme range links: LoRa 868/433mhz SX1278 LoRa module for Arduino, Raspberry PI and Intel Galileo (2018, revised)
3. Raza, U., Kulkarni, P., Sooriyabandara, M.: Low power wide area networks: an overview. IEEE Commun. Surv. Tutor. **19**, 855–873 (2017)
4. Pham, C., Ferrero, F., Diop, M., Lizzi, L., Dieng, O., Thiaré, O.: Low-cost antenna technology for LPWAN IoT in rural applications. In: 2017 7th IEEE International Workshop on Advances in Sensors and Interfaces (IWASI), pp. 121–126. IEEE (2017)
5. TheThingNetwork. http://thethingsnetwork.org/. Accessed 13 Jan 2016
6. Petajajarvi, J., Mikhaylov, K., Roivainen, A., Hanninen, T., Pettissalo, M.: On the coverage of LPWANs: range evaluation and channel attenuation model for LoRa technology. In: 14th International Conference on ITS Telecommunications (ITST), Copenhagen, 2015, pp. 55–59 (2015). https://doi.org/10.1109/ITST.2015.7377400

7. Kim, D.Y., Kim, S.: LoRaWAN technology for internet of things. J. Platform Technol. **3**(1), 3–8 (2015)
8. Zennaro, M., Bagula, A.: IoT for development (IOT4D). In: IEEE IoT Newsletter, 14 July 2015 (2015)
9. Basics, LoRa Modulation. AN1200. 22, Revision 2 (2015)
10. Miorandi, D., et al.: Internet of things: vision, applications and research challenges. Ad Hoc Netw. **10**, 1497–1516 (2012)
11. ETSI: Electromagnetic compatibility and radio spectrum matters (ERM); short range devices (SRD); radio equipment to be used in the 25 MHz to 1000 MHz frequency range with power levels ranging up to 500 MW; part 1 (2012)
12. Uckelmann, D., Harrison, M., Michahelles, F. (eds.): Architecting the Internet of Things. Springer, Heidelberg (2011). https://doi.org/10.1007/978-3-642-19157-2
13. Bachir, A., Dohler, M., Watteyne, T., Leung, K.K.: MAC essentials for wireless sensor networks. IEEE Commun. Surv. Tutor. **12**(2), 222–248 (2010)
14. Dutta, P., Dawson-Haggerty, S., Chen, Y., Liang, C.-J.M., Terzis, A.: Design and evaluation of a versatile and efficient receiver-initiated link layer for low-power wireless. In: Proceedings of the 8th ACM Conference on Embedded Networked Sensor Systems, SenSys 2010, New York, NY, USA, 2010, pp. 1–14. ACM (2010)
15. Hill, J.L.: System Architecture for Wireless Sensor Networks, Ph.D. Thesis, University of California, Berkley (2003)

High Dimensional Data Representation and Processing

Setting up Hadoop Environment and Running MapReduce Job for Teaching BDA in Universities – An Experience

Deepali Bajaj[1(✉)], Urmil Bharti[1], Anita Goel[2], and S. C. Gupta[3]

[1] Department of Computer Science, Shaheed Rajguru College of Applied Sciences for Women, University of Delhi, Delhi, India
{deepali.bajaj,urmil.bharti}@rajguru.du.ac.in

[2] Department of Computer Science, Dyal Singh College, University of Delhi, Delhi, India
goel.anita@gmail.com

[3] Department of Computer Science, Indian Institute of Technology Delhi (IIT), Delhi, India
scgupta@cse.iitd.ac.in

Abstract. Apache Hadoop is a collection of open source software libraries for processing and analysis of big data. Hadoop is popular for its flexible and scalable architecture that stores and processes big data on commodity hardware machines and allows distributed processing on clusters of nodes. The demand for trained data analytics professionals has resulted in the incorporation of big data analytics in University curriculum. As a result, there is a need to set up a Hadoop environment in University labs, for teaching big data analytics. Though, detailed information for setting a multi-machine Hadoop is readily available, however, several additional configurations are required for setting up a cluster and for running a big data application. This paper discusses the experiences and challenges faced during the setup of a multi-node Hadoop cluster and running of MapReduce jobs. It presents system settings and working memory configurations that are required to be done for Hadoop and for running an application. This will benefit the academia for setting up a Hadoop cluster and to run data analytics applications on it.

Keywords: Hadoop · YARN · MapReduce · HDFS · Hadoop memory configurations · BDA

1 Introduction

Big Data Analytics (BDA) is a method of collecting, organizing and analyzing large and heterogeneous data sets called Big Data. Advanced analytic techniques, like machine learning, data mining, predictive analytics and statistics are applied to find the hidden patterns, market trends, hidden correlation, customer preferences and other useful results which help institutions to make more learned business conclusions [1]. To run BDA applications, a framework capable to capture, store, process and analyze gigantic volumes of disparate data is required [2]. Apache Hadoop is one of the most popular platforms for developing and running BDA applications.

R. S. Tomar et al. (Eds.): CNC 2020, CCIS 1502, pp. 57–71, 2021.
https://doi.org/10.1007/978-981-16-8896-6_5

Apache Hadoop is an open-source library of software components that is used for storing and processing of voluminous datasets, using distributed computing. Hadoop clusters are built from low cost widely available hardware machines [3]. A Hadoop cluster is flexible to scale from a single node to thousands of commodity machines. Apache Hadoop is presently utilized by many technology giants like Twitter, Google, LinkedIn, Yahoo, AOL, Facebook, EBay [4] and many more to process large volume of data. Over the years, it has become the central store for big data in several industries.

In Hadoop, MapReduce is a simple programming framework that makes use of parallel and distributed algorithms for processing extremely large datasets on a cluster of machines. Hadoop Distributed File System (HDFS) along with MapReduce is used for handling BDA applications [5]. With the growing popularity of Hadoop for BDA, and to meet increasing demand for trained analytics professionals, the Universities have started including it in their course curriculum [6, 7].

There are several options available to get Hadoop and its ecosystem software components - 1) virtualized Hadoop architecture 2) Hadoop cluster in Docker 3) Physical Hadoop cluster setup.

1. ***Virtualizing Hadoop Cluster:*** Programmers may use virtualization techniques for hosting Hadoop-based applications in a virtual environment [31]. This architecture utilizes Direct Attached Storage (DAS) for storing its data. It is easier to set up and manage the virtualized Hadoop clusters, but they may not handle the same level of functionality, complexity and fault tolerance as compared to real physical cluster architecture. So, the virtual Hadoop environment is not a serious business environment for big data applications [32].
2. ***Hadoop Cluster in Docker:*** This option allows programmers to create Hadoop clusters on their own machines using Docker container platform [29]. Hadoop Docker image contains Hadoop code, bundled with all other environments, dependencies and libraries. But, dockerization will run Hadoop at application level not at operating system level. This leads to two levels of file system abstraction to physical disk - initially at Docker and then at HDFS. This makes applications to execute a little slower in Docker containers [30].
3. ***Physical Hadoop Cluster setup:*** This option uses commodity hardware machines to create a physical cluster. Here, Hadoop runs at the operating system level, so it achieves a faster execution environment for big data analytics applications. In this paper, we'll use this approach to create a Hadoop cluster.

Amazon Web Services (AWS) has also come up with Amazon Elastic MapReduce (EMR) which is a cloud based tool for processing and analysis of big data [34]. But EMR is paid service so the users have to pay not only for EMR service but also for EC2 Instance types supported by EMR. These services are billed per second, with a minimum of one minute duration. So these cloud based services does not reap cost benefits when it comes to teach BDA in universities. So, we argue that Hadoop clusters can be created in universities using the experiences we have described in this paper.

Although, there exist several sources like [8–11, 14] for Hadoop installation and execution of MapReduce jobs but Hadoop could not be installed successfully by following their instructions. We realized that there is a need to set additional parameters as environment variables and memory configuration parameters for successful installation.

The parameter settings are specific to cluster resources and are not easily available on a single website. Also, once Hadoop was installed, we could not run BDA applications on it.

In this paper, we share our experiences and challenges faced in Hadoop cluster setup along with their solutions. We have enumerated errors encountered during Hadoop installation and running a MapReduce job. This paper provides details of various memory configuration parameters, their settings for successful MapReduce job execution and the way we have calculated various values for our cluster.

The solutions discussed here for Hadoop installation have been successfully tested in our Hadoop environment and can be referred to create a multi-machine Hadoop cluster in a University lab environment. Also, the settings required for executing a MapReduce job have also been successfully tested.

Rest of our paper is organized as follows: Sect. 2 introduces Hadoop basics, HDFS, Map Reduce Framework and YARN. Section 3 presents Installation of a Hadoop cluster and various challenges faced during this process. Section 4 explains the implementation details to run a MapReduce job on Hadoop cluster. Concluding remarks are discussed in the last section.

2 Hadoop Basics

Apache Hadoop is a software library framework used for distributed storage and distributed processing of voluminous collection of data on a cluster of commodity computing machines [15]. It can be created from commodity hardware machines. Apache Hadoop presents a scalable, flexible and reliable distributed computing framework for big data. It supports scaling from a single machine to thousands of commodity machines where each machine provides its individual storage and computation to the cluster. For fault tolerance, Hadoop depends on its library to identify and manage failures at the application layer instead of depending on the hardware. Therefore, Hadoop delivers a highly-available (HA) service on top of the computer clusters, though each node is susceptible to failure. Hadoop stack offers services and tools for data storage, data access, data processing, data security and other data management operations. Few reasons for Hadoop popularity are its capability to store, process and analyze enormously large volumes of structured/unstructured and semi-structured data in a fast and reliable manner, at a low-cost. The holistic perspective of Hadoop framework provides importance to its four core components - (a) *Hadoop Common, (b) Hadoop Distributed File Systems (HDFS), (c) Hadoop MapReduce,* and (d) *Hadoop YARN. Common* provides Java utilities, libraries, operating system level abstractions and Java files/scripts required for running Hadoop [14]. The other three components are discussed in the following subsections.

2.1 Hadoop Distributed File System (HDFS)

HDFS is a Java-based distributed file system used by Apache Hadoop that provides high performance data access over the Hadoop cluster and can store data up to 200 PB [13]. In HDFS, a single large file is divided into parts and can be stored on multiple machines across the cluster. It has been designed using master/slave architecture [33]. A HDFS cluster contains one *NameNode*, one *SecondaryNameNode* and many *DataNodes*. The *NameNode* acts as a master server that stores the HDFS file system namespace and its metadata. It also stores mapping of the files to blocks along with their physical location. For the clients, it administers access to the files. Secondary *NameNode* is a special dedicated node in HDFS cluster whose main task is to regularly update the metadata on *NameNode*. It checkpoints *NameNode* file system namespace, but is not a replacement of primary *NameNode*.

The *DataNodes* control and manage storage available on the nodes where they run. DataNodes can store and retrieve data blocks when directed by *NameNode*. The *DataNodes* send heartbeat messages and Block Reports to *NameNode* at regular intervals, to inform that they are live and functioning correctly. Block report is a detailed record of all blocks contained in a *DataNode*. Fault tolerance in HDFS is achieved by block replication, with three being the default replication factor [16]. The *NameNode* is responsible for replication of blocks in multiple *DataNodes*. The replication factor and block size are configurable parameters and can be set as per application requirement. The presence of a single *NameNode* in a cluster simplifies overall architecture of the Hadoop ecosystem [28].

2.2 Hadoop MapReduce

Hadoop MapReduce is a simple programming model for developing BDA applications that are capable of processing extremely large datasets in parallel, on Hadoop clusters, in a fault-tolerant and reliable manner. The key benefit of MapReduce is its capability to easily scale-up processing of data over multiple cluster nodes [17]. Once an application has been written using the MapReduce programming model, scaling of application to hundreds or thousands of cluster machines is merely a configuration setting [26].

MapReduce signifies two distinct and separate functions called mapper and reducer [25]. Mapper captures input data and transforms it into another data set, where individual input data elements are split up into tuples (key/value pairs). Reducer receives mapper's output as its input and combines the tuples into a smaller set of tuples. Reduce job is always executed after completion of the map task. The input and output dataset of mapper and reducer functions are stored in HDFS [16]. HDFS inherently takes care of scheduling and monitoring and automatic re-execution of unsuccessful tasks [19] if required.

2.3 Yet Another Resource Negotiator (YARN)

Apache YARN is a cluster and resource management abstraction layer of Apache Hadoop. It supports different data processing engines, i.e. batch, stream, interactive, and graph processing to process data that is stored in HDFS [27]. It is also responsible for job scheduling. YARN is also considered as the data operating system for Hadoop. YARN widens the scope of Hadoop to other growing technologies, so that they can reap benefits of HDFS [20]. In YARN, the basic unit of processing capacity is known as a container. A container encapsulates the available resources, like, CPU and memory [21]. It is a locale where actual work occurs. It is a logical bundle of resources, like, memory, CPU and disk that is bound to a particular node.

YARN takes into consideration all computing resources available on every node of the Hadoop cluster. Depending on availability of these resources, it considers resource requirements from various applications submitted to the cluster. It provides processing capability to applications by assigning containers. For example, each MapReduce task of a submitted job runs in a container. An application (job) may require one or more containers for its execution. A set of physical resources including CPU core and RAM are assigned to each container. A single Hadoop node in a cluster is capable of running several containers, in parallel.

YARN contains a master daemon called as *Global ResourceManager* (runs on master node), slave daemon called *NodeManager* (run on slave nodes) and an *Application Master* (AM). *ResourceManager* (RM) manages assignments of CPU and memory across all nodes. It mediates available system resources among competing applications. RM has two main elements: *ResourceScheduler* and *ApplicationManager*, as shown in Fig. 1. Scheduler takes care of assigning resources to different programs running in the Hadoop cluster. *ApplicationManager* accepts and initiates new jobs, negotiates first container required for executing *ApplicationMaster* [22]. *NodeManager* monitors containers for their resource usage and reports it to the *ResourceManager*. It also traces the health of the cluster node on which it is running. *ApplicationMaster* negotiates resources from *ResourceManager* and co-ordinates with one or more *NodeManager* for task execution and monitoring. It manages the application lifecycle. There is one *ApplicationMaster* for one application.

Workflow of Client Request for a MapReduce Job: When a client application is submitted to YARN framework, then based on application type, *ApplicationMaster* is decided. *ResourceManager* negotiates with *NodeManager* to obtain a container for executing *Application Master* instance. Once an ApplicationMaster instance is initiated successfully, it gets registered with *ResourceManager*. *ApplicationMaster* talks with *ResourceManager* for its resource requirements on a specific node, and then receives actual resources from *NodeManager*. Application codes running on containers report their status to *ApplicationMaster* periodically. During job execution, all nodes of the cluster (*ResourceManager* and *NodeManager*) store and fetch data from HDFS as shown in Fig. 1. After job completion, *ApplicationMaster* de-registers itself with *ResourceManager* and the used containers are released.

3 Hadoop Cluster Setup

Hadoop cluster can be set up using low cost, affordable and easy to obtain commodity hardware. We installed Hadoop on commodity machines having Ubuntu operating system. If a Linux-like operating system is not available, then there is a need to install a virtual box and an instance of CentOS/Linux /Ubuntu/Fedora operating system for Hadoop to be installed over it. To install Hadoop on a single machine, minimum system requirements are - (i) 4 GB RAM (ii) core i3 processor (iii) 50 GB hard disk space, with a network of 1Mbps speed. However, higher the disk space and RAM

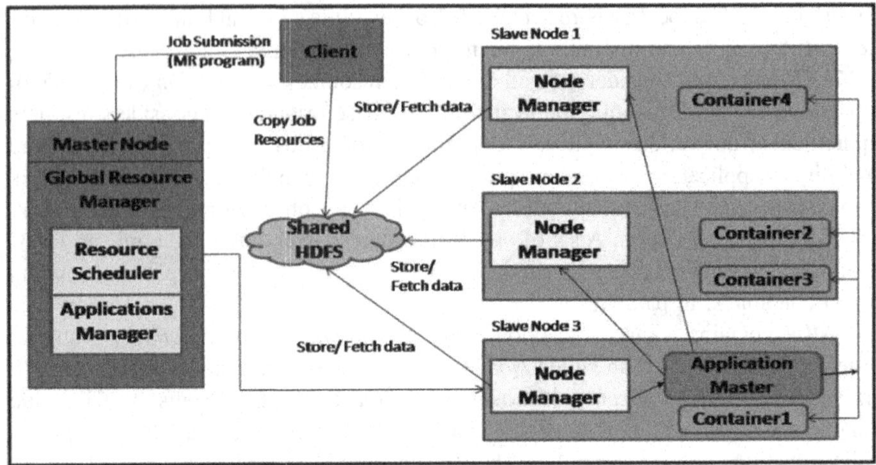

Fig. 1. Container management in executing a MapReduce job

capacity, faster will be the computational speed of the cluster. So, recommended RAM for cluster nodes is 8 GB. Systems with lower configuration than the minimum suggested requirements may take more time to process and fail to perform too.

Here, we discuss the hardware and software requirement for setting a three node Hadoop cluster.

3.1 Setting a 3-node Hadoop Cluster

For setting a three node Hadoop cluster, we identified three machines having Ubuntu 20.04 LTS operating system connected using Local Area Network. The hardware configuration details of the three machines are shown in Table 1.

Table 1. Hardware configurations of machines chosen for Hadoop Cluster

Machine	Processor type	OS type	RAM	Disk (in GB)	Node type
1	Intel Core i7- 3770 CPU @ 3.40 GHZ x 8	64-bit	8	1000	Master
2	AMD A6-5350M APU with Radeon HD Graphics	64-bit	8	300	Slave 1
3	AMD A6-5350M APU with Radeon HD Graphics	64-bit	8	300	Slave 2

3.2 Challenges in Installing Apache Hadoop 3.x

For installation of Hadoop, we referred several articles [8–11]. We tried to install Hadoop using the steps described in these articles, but found that the details were not sufficient for successful installation of Hadoop. Then, we found an article [12], which was more detailed. We followed the installation steps from this article.

For setting a three node Hadoop cluster, the first step is to install single node Hadoop setup on all the three machines. However, we could not install Hadoop successfully due to several problems. To fix the problems, we referred to other sites. Here, we provide details of the challenges faced by us during installation and the proposed solutions.

Challenge 1: During installation, a separate Hadoop user is required to be created. This isolates the Hadoop file system from Linux file system and deals with all Hadoop related activities. We created a Hadoop user named *hduser* to access HDFS and MapReduce. The *hduser* should be given *superuser* privileges otherwise installation steps will fail. It is a critical step and was missing in the [12]. To provide *superuser* permission to *hduser*, we did the following-

The *sudoers* file is used by Linux/Unix administrators to allocate system rights to its users. We added *hduse*r entry in /etc/sudoers/ file as follows-

hduser ALL=(ALL:ALL) ALL

This command gives superuser permissions to *hduser*.

Challenge 2: The steps of installation have to be executed in two different user modes - *hduser* and *normal user*. But, the distinction between these two modes is not clearly mentioned in the installation process. We categorized the installation steps to be executed in different user modes as presented in the Table 2 below.

Table 2. List of commands to be executed in different user modes

Normal user	Hadoop *hduser*
Installing Oracle Java 8	Configuring SSH
Creating Hadoop user for accessing HDFS and MapReduce	Downloading latest Apache Hadoop source from Apache mirrors
Installing SSH	Updating Hadoop configuration files • User profile file - .bashrc • Configuration files i. hadoop-env.sh ii. mapred-site.xml iii. core-site.xml iv. yarn-site.xml v. hdfs-site.xml
Disabling IPv6	Format NameNode
	Start all Hadoop daemons (dfs/yarn)
	Track/Monitor/Verify

Challenge 3: The prerequisite steps, and installation steps till Update Hadoop Configuration Files are appropriately mentioned in [12]. However, when we executed the following command to initialize HDFS -

hduser@deepali:/usr/local/hadoop/etc/hadoop $ hdfs namenode –format

we encountered an error message, *"No such file or directory".*

To fix this error we established that the environment variable ($PATH) was not set for Hadoop. This setting was not mentioned in [12]. We set $PATH by giving the following command:

hduser@deepali:/usr/local/hadoop/etc/hadoop$set $PATH=/usr/local/hadoop/bin

This setting tells the system to check the mentioned path for all HDFS and Hadoop commands. But, $PATH variable is set only for the current session. In order to persist these changes for subsequent login sessions, we edited ~ /.profile file in *superuser* mode as shown in Fig. 2.

```
hduser@deepali:/usr/local/hadoop/etc/hadoop$)gedit
~/.profile
      # if running bash
      if [ -n "$BASH_VERSION" ]; then
          # include .bashrc if it exists
          if [ -f "$HOME/.bashrc" ]; then
          . "$HOME/.bashrc"
          fi
      fi
      # set PATH so it includes user's private bin
      if it exists
      if [ -d "$HOME/bin" ] ; then
          PATH="$HOME/bin:$PATH"
      fi
      if [ -d "/usr/local/hadoop/bin" ] ; then
          PATH="/usr/local/hadoop/bin:$PATH"
      fi
      if [ -d "/usr/local/hadoop/sbin" ] ; then
          PATH="/usr/local/hadoop/sbin:$PATH"
      fi
```

Fig. 2. Settings in ~ /.profile file in *superuser* mode

After successful installation of Hadoop on the three single nodes, next step is to configured in a multi-node cluster setup [13]. In our cluster setup, one machine was configured as *MasterNode* that runs NameNode, *SecondaryNameNode* and *ResourceManager* as Java processes and the other two machines were *SlaveNodes* that run Java processes for *NodeManager* and *DataNode*. Figure 3 and Fig. 4 show the DataNode and Resource manager interface after successful installation of Hadoop.

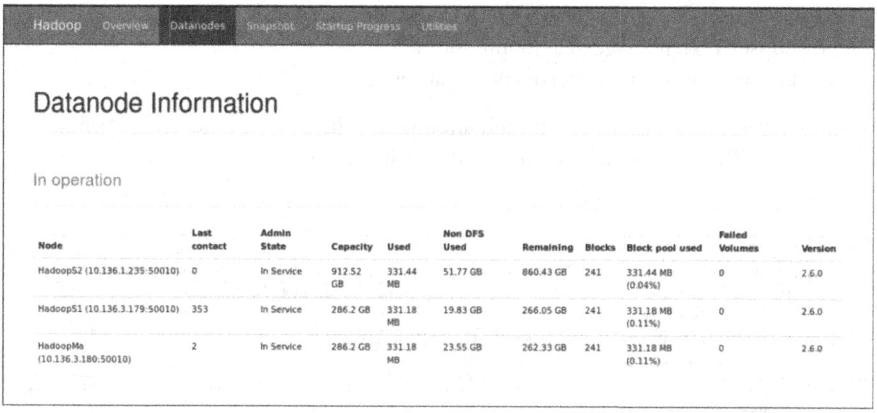

Datanode Information

In operation

Node	Last contact	Admin State	Capacity	Used	Non DFS Used	Remaining	Blocks	Block pool used	Failed Volumes	Version
HadoopS2 (10.136.1.235:50010)	0	In Service	912.52 GB	331.44 MB	51.77 GB	860.43 GB	241	331.44 MB (0.04%)	0	2.6.0
HadoopS1 (10.136.3.179:50010)	353	In Service	286.2 GB	331.18 MB	19.83 GB	266.05 GB	241	331.18 MB (0.11%)	0	2.6.0
HadoopMa (10.136.3.180:50010)	2	In Service	286.2 GB	331.18 MB	23.55 GB	262.33 GB	241	331.18 MB (0.11%)	0	2.6.0

Fig. 3. DataNode Interface showing 3 nodes in operation in multimode Hadoop

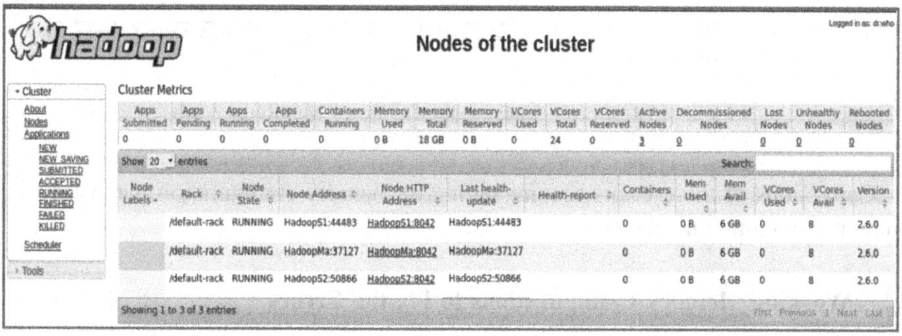

Nodes of the cluster

Cluster Metrics

Apps Submitted	Apps Pending	Apps Running	Apps Completed	Containers Running	Memory Used	Memory Total	Memory Reserved	VCores Used	VCores Total	VCores Reserved	Active Nodes	Decommissioned Nodes	Lost Nodes	Unhealthy Nodes	Rebooted Nodes
0	0	0	0	0	0 B	18 GB	0 B	0	24	0	3	0	0	0	0

Node Labels	Rack	Node State	Node Address	Node HTTP Address	Last health-update	Health-report	Containers	Mem Used	Mem Avail	VCores Used	VCores Avail	Version
	/default-rack	RUNNING	HadoopS1:44483	HadoopS1:8042	HadoopS1:44483		0	0 B	6 GB	0	8	2.6.0
	/default-rack	RUNNING	HadoopMa:37127	HadoopMa:8042	HadoopMa:37127		0	0 B	6 GB	0	8	2.6.0
	/default-rack	RUNNING	HadoopS2:50866	HadoopS2:8042	HadoopS2:50866		0	0 B	6 GB	0	8	2.6.0

Showing 1 to 3 of 3 entries

Fig. 4. Resource Manager Interface showing aggregate cluster metrics

4 Running a MapReduce Job on Hadoop Cluster

Having installed a multi-node Hadoop cluster, our next task was to run a MR Job on it. For this we downloaded Hadoop-core-1.2.1.jar file and kept it in the same folder where the Java MapReduce program was stored. Hadoop-core-1.2.1.jar file is required to compile and execute MR programs. We compiled the MapReduce java program having mapper and reducer functions. We created an input directory in HDFS and moved the input data file for MR job into this directory. When this job was run from one of our cluster nodes, it failed. After repeated unsuccessful trials, we analyzed the log files maintained by Hadoop. The following subsections describe the errors encountered and their proposed solution.

4.1 Errors Outline

The following log files were analyzed to know the error messages logged by Hadoop.

- Hadoop-hduser-DataNode-HadoopMaster.log
- Hadoop-hduser-NameNode-HadoopMaster.log

- Hadoop-hduser-SecondaryNameNode-HadoopMaster.log
- Yarn-hduser-nodemanager-Hadoopmaster.log
- Yarn-hduser-resourcemanager-Hadoopmaster.log

After careful and exhaustive examination of log files, we found errors behind the failure of MapReduce job which are listed below in Fig. 5:

Error1	Container is running beyond memory limits Container [pid=XXX, containerID=container_XXX] is running beyond physical memory limits. Killing container
Error2	Java Heap space Out Of Memory, INFO mapred.JobClient: Task Id : attempt_XXX, Status : FAILED on node node1, Error: Java heap space
Error3	Container killed by the ApplicationMaster, Container killed on request. Exit code is 143 Container exited with a non-zero exit code 143
Error4	Mapper killed with an error, Current usage: XXX of physical memory used; XXX of virtual memory used. Killing container. (displays container id)
Error5	Mapper process runs out of heap memory throwing a java out of memory exceptions, java.lang.RuntimeException: java.lang.OutOfMemoryError
Error6	Exception from container-launch, INFO mapreduce.Job : Job job_XXX failed with state FAILED due to: Application application_XXX failed 2 times due to AM
Error7	Container for appattempt_XXX exited with exit Code: 1 due to: Exception from container-launch. Container exited with a non-zero exit code 1.

Fig. 5. List of errors causing the failure of MapReduce job

Corrections of these errors require setting of memory configuration parameters in Hadoop configuration files [20].

4.2 Working Memory Configurations to Fix the Errors

This section describes memory configuration parameters settings that are required to fix errors mentioned in the above section for successfully running a MapReduce job. Configuration of these parameters is done in *yarn-site.xml* and *mapred-site.xml* file [23, 24]. These files are editable by *hduser* only. The configuration parameters and their settings are shown in Fig. 6. A brief description of these parameters is as follows:

1. ***yarn.nodemanager.resource.memory-mb*** **-** This configuration parameter, contained in *yarn-site.xml,* sets the amount of resource memory (MB) that can be assigned to containers in the NodeManager. It is calculated as follows-
   Resource Memory (MB) = Total Physical Memory of a node – Reserved Memory where reserved memory is the RAM required by system in addition to other Hadoop processes. If the cluster node's physical memory is 8 GB, recommended reserved memory is 2 GB. Each machine in our Hadoop cluster has 8 GB RAM. We assigned available resource memory for YARN as 6144 MB (multiple of block size- 512 MB) on each node.
2. ***yarn.scheduler.minimum-allocation-mb*** **-** This configuration parameter, contained in *yarn-site.xml,* is used to set minimum memory (MB) to be allocated to each container on its creation at ResourceManager. It is the lowest size of container specified in MB. Its value depends on the amount of available RAM. Its recommended value is 512 MB for nodes having 4–8 GB physical memory.

3. ***yarn.nodemanager.vmem-pmem-ratio*** - This configuration parameter, contained in *yarn-site.xml,* is used to set the ratio of virtual memory (vmem) to physical memory (pmem) for running a Map/Reduce task. NodeManager monitors memory usage (physical and virtual) of the yarn container. If this virtual memory goes beyond "yarn.nodemanager.vmem-pmem-ratio" times the "mapreduce.reduce.memory.mb' or "mapreduce.map.memory.mb', then the container automatically gets killed by the Node Manager. The value 2.1shown in Table 4 indicates that vmem is set to twice the size of pmem.
4. ***yarn.scheduler.maximum-allocation-mb*** - This configuration parameter, contained in *yarn-site.xml,* is required to set maximum memory allocation (MB) for every container requested by the ResourceManager. Fundamentally, it means ResourceManager can assign memory to each container in increments of "yarn. scheduler.minimum-allocation-mb" and this value should not surpass "yarn. scheduler.maximum-allocation-mb". It is calculated as: Number of containers times RAM allocated to each container
5. ***mapreduce.map.memory.mb*** - The configuration parameter, contained in *mapred-site.xml,* is used to set the upper memory limit which Hadoop permits to allocate to a Mapper process in MBs. This parameter signifies maximum memory each Map task can take during a MapReduce job execution. Since each Map task will execute in a different container, hence this memory setting must be set to at least equal or more than minimum container allocation in YARN. Its default value is 512 MB. If this limit is surpassed, Mapper will be killed by Hadoop the with an error message indicating that the container is running beyond physical memory limits. Its value should be equal or more than RAM per container.
6. ***mapreduce.reduce.memory.mb*** - This configuration parameter, contained in *mapred-site.xml,* is used to set the upper memory limit which Hadoop allocates to a reducer process in MBs. It signifies how much maximum memory each Reducer task can take during a MapReduce job execution. This memory setting must be either greater than or equal to minimum container allocation of the YARN. Generally the Reducer's memory is set higher than the mapper's memory. It may be because the number of reducer task is less than the number of mapper task, and reducers aggregate records from 'n' number of mappers. Its value should be twice the value of RAM per container.
7. ***mapreduce.map.java.opts*** - This configuration parameter, contained in *mapred-site.xml,* is used to set JVM heap size for mapper job. JVMs are run for every container executing Map as well as for Reduce tasks. This value must be set to a value less than Map and Reduce memory set in mapred-site.xml file, so that this value is within the limits of memory allocated to the container by YARN. Each Mapper and Reducer is a java process and we need some reserve memory to store the java code as well. Hence, Map/Reducer memory should be greater than JVM heap size. Its value can be calculated 0.8 times RAM per container
8. ***mapreduce.reduce.java.opts-*** This configuration parameter, contained in *mapred-site.xml,* is used to set JVM heap size for reducer task and its value can be calculated as 0.8 * 2 times RAM per container.

Parameter Name	Parameter Setting Configuration
mapreduce.map.memory.mb	<name>yarn.nodemanager.resource.memory-mb </name> <value>6144</value>
yarn.scheduler.minimum-allocation-mb	<name>yarn.scheduler.minumum-allocation-mb</name> <value>512</value>
yarn.nodemanager.vmem-pmem-ratio	<name>yarn.nodemanager.vmem-pmem-ratio </name> <value>2.1</value>
yarn.scheduler.maximum-allocation-mb	<name>yarn.scheduler. maximum-allocation-mb</name> <value>6144</value>
mapreduce.map.memory.mb	<name>mapreduce.map. memory.mb</name> <value>1024</value>
mapreduce.reduce.memory.mb	<name>mapreduce.reduce.memory.mb</name> <value>2048</value>
mapreduce.map.java.opts	<name>mapreduce. map.java.opts</name> <value>-Xmx512m</value>
mapreduce.reduce.java.opts	<name>mapreduce. reduce.java.opts</name> <value>-Xmx1024m</value>

Fig. 6. Memory configuration parameters and their settings

After having set Hadoop memory configuration parameters, we executed MapReduce programs successfully. Figure 7 and Fig. 8 show the command line interface and resource manager interface after completion of MapReduce job.

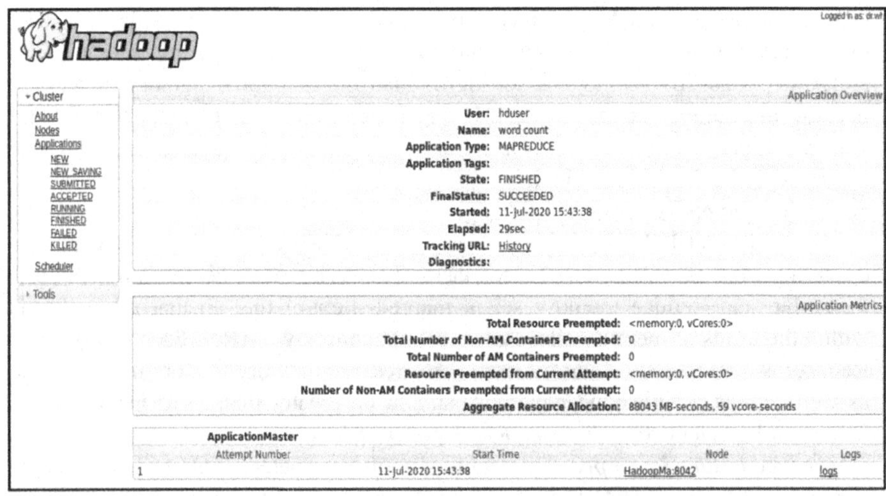

Fig. 7. Interface showing successful completion of MapReduce job

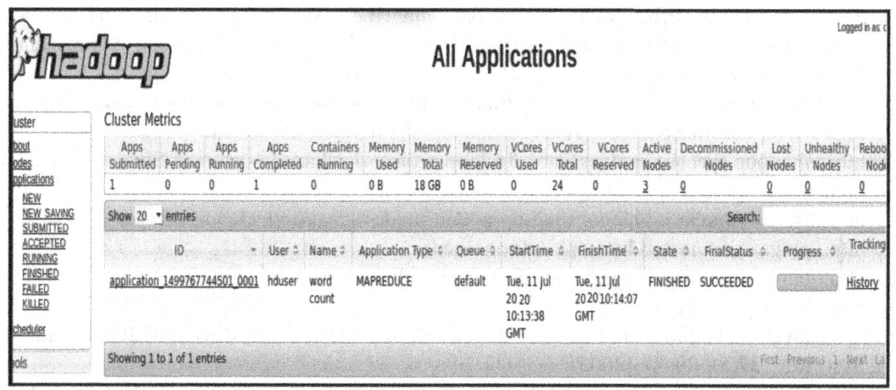

Fig. 8. Resource Manager Interface showing successful completion of MapReduce job

5 Conclusion

With the growing demand of big data professionals in industry, it becomes necessary that university students should get an opportunity to learn BDA tools and techniques as part of their course curriculum. In order to meet this objective, first, we provide details to set a multi-node Hadoop cluster in a University environment using commodity hardware machines. The paper describes various Hadoop environment variable settings required to successfully install a Hadoop cluster. Second, we outline errors encountered in execution of a MapReduce program when configuration parameters are not set as per cluster resources. Third, we delineate working parameter settings in Hadoop xml files, required to run a MapReduce job in a lab environment. The experiences and leanings presented here will help the academic community in setting up Hadoop and using it for analytic purposes.

References

1. Bi, Z., Cochran, D.: Big data analytics with applications. J. Manage. Anal. **1**(4), 249–265 (2014)
2. Picciano, A.G.: The evolution of big data and learning analytics in American higher education. J. Asynchron. Learn. Netw. **16**(3), 9–20 (2012)
3. White, T.: Hadoop: The Definitive Guide. O'Reilly Media, Inc. (2012)
4. Verma, C., Pandey, R., Katiyar, D.: Evaluating of file systems, applications and MapReduce logs to support functional analysis. In: Proceedings of the International Conference on Communication and Computing Systems, ICCCS 2016, Gurgaon, India, 9–11 September 2016, p. 11. CRC Press (February 2017)
5. Dean, J., Ghemawat, S.: MapReduce: simplified data processing on large clusters. Commun. ACM **51**(1), 107–113 (2008)
6. Siemens, G., Long, P.: Penetrating the fog: analytics in learning and education. EDUCAUSE Rev. **46**(5), 30 (2011)

7. Ngo, L.B., Duffy, E.B., Apon, A.W.: Teaching HDFS/MapReduce systems concepts to undergraduates. In: 2014 IEEE International Parallel & Distributed Processing Symposium Workshops (IPDPSW), pp. 1114–1121. IEEE (May 2014)
8. http://www.michael-noll.com/tutorials/running-hadoop-on-ubuntu-linux-multi-node-cluster/
9. https://www.tutorialspoint.com/hadoop/hadoop_multi_node_cluster.htm
10. https://hadoop.apache.org/docs/stable/hadoop-project-dist/hadoop-common/SingleCluster.html
11. https://www.edureka.co/blog/setting-up-a-multi-node-cluster-in-hadoop-2.X
12. http://pingax.com/install-hadoop2-6-0-on-ubuntu
13. http://pingax.com/install-apache-hadoop-ubuntu-cluster-setup
14. http://hadoop.apache.org/
15. Ghemawat, S., Gobioff, H., Leung, S.-T.: The Google file system. ACM SIGOPS Operating Syst. Rev. **37**(5), 29–43 (2003)
16. Shvachko, K., Kuang, H., Radia, S., Chansler, R.: The hadoop distributed file system. In: 2010 IEEE 26th symposium on Mass Storage Systems and Technologies (MSST), pp. 1–10. IEEE (May 2010)
17. Dean, J., Ghemawat, S.: MapReduce: a flexible data processing tool. Commun. ACM **53**(1), 72–77 (2010)
18. Verma, A., Cherkasova, L., Campbell, R.H.: Resource provisioning framework for mapreduce jobs with performance goals. In: Kon, F., Kermarrec, A.-M. (eds.) Middleware 2011, pp. 165–186. Springer, Heidelberg (2011). https://doi.org/10.1007/978-3-642-25821-3_9
19. Singh, D., Reddy, C.K.: A survey on platforms for big data analytics. J. Big Data **2**(1), 1–20 (2014). https://doi.org/10.1186/s40537-014-0008-6
20. Vavilapalli, V.K., et al.: Apache Hadoop YARN: yet another resource negotiator. In: Proceedings of the 4th Annual Symposium on Cloud Computing, p. 5. ACM (October 2013)
21. https://hortonworks.com/blog/apache-hadoop-yarn-concepts-and-applications/
22. https://hadoop.apache.org/docs/current/hadoop-yarn/hadoop-yarn-site/YARN.html
23. Bakshi, R.: How to plan and configure YARN and MapReduce 2 in HDP 2.0 (September 2013). https://hortonworks.com/blog/how-to-plan-and-configure-yarn-in-hdp-2-0/
24. https://www.ibm.com/support/knowledgecenter/en/SSZJPZ_11.5.0/com.ibm.swg.im.iis.ishadoop.doc/topics/configuring_hadoop.html
25. Khan, I., Naqvi, S.K., Alam, M., Rizvi, S.N.A.: An efficient framework for real-time tweet classification. Int. J. Inf. Technol. **9**(2), 215–221 (2017). https://doi.org/10.1007/s41870-017-0015-x
26. Glushkova, D., Jovanovic, P., Abelló, A.: Mapreduce performance model for Hadoop 2.x. Inf. Syst. **79**, 32–43 (2019)
27. Monu, M., Pal, S.: A review on storage and large-scale processing of data-sets using MapReduce, YARN, SPARK, AVRO, MongoDB (April 4, 2019) (2019)
28. Ahad, M.A., Biswas, R.: Handling small size files in Hadoop: challenges, opportunities, and review. In: Nayak, J., Abraham, A., Krishna, B.M., Chandra Sekhar, G.T., Das, A.K. (eds.) Soft Computing in Data Analytics. AISC, vol. 758, pp. 653–663. Springer, Singapore (2019). https://doi.org/10.1007/978-981-13-0514-6_62
29. Gupta, M., Singla, N.: Evolution of cloud in big data with Hadoop on Docker platform. In: Web Services: Concepts, Methodologies, Tools, and Applications, pp. 1601–1622. IGI Global (2019)
30. Thind, J.S., Simon, R.: Implementation of Big Data in cloud computing with optimized Apache Hadoop. In: 2019 3rd International conference on Electronics, Communication and Aerospace Technology (ICECA), pp. 997–1001. IEEE (June 2019)

31. Trujillo, G., Kim, C., Jones, S., Garcia, R., Murray, J.: Virtualizing Hadoop: How to Install, Deploy, and Optimize Hadoop in a Virtualized Architecture. VMware Press (2015)
32. Gummaraju, J., et al.: U.S. Patent No. 10,193,963. U.S. Patent and Trademark Office, Washington, DC (2019)
33. Bharti, U., Bajaj, D., Goel, A., Gupta, S.C.: Identifying requirements for Big Data analytics and mapping to Hadoop tools. Int. J. Recent Technol. Eng. **8**(3), 4384–4392 (2019)
34. https://docs.aws.amazon.com/emr/latest/ManagementGuide/emr-what-is-emr.html. Accessed 20 Nov 2020

Plagiarism Detection of Online Submissions Using High Level Fuzzy Petri Nets in Pandemic Times

Pooja Jain[1,3](✉), Vaibhav Agasti[1,3], and Tapan Kumar[2,3]

[1] Department of Computer Science and Engineering, Nagpur, India
[2] Department of Electronics and Communication Engineering, Nagpur, India
[3] Indian Institute of Information Technology, Nagpur, India

Abstract. Source code plagiarism is a growing problem due to the emergence of the internet, open source community etc. In current pandemic times, institutes are adopting online classes and online assignment submissions. While submitting online, many times, programmers present someone else's work as their own. The detection of such plagiarism is crucial because plagiarism is essentially a form of theft. The plagiarizer benefits from the work that he/she did not create. This paper proposes an algorithm to detect plagiarism in source codes by comparing the Abstract Syntax Trees (AST) of the respective source codes. The comparison is done by first properly encoding the obtained ASTs into strings and then comparing the strings by using a Global Sequence Alignment technique. A fuzzy decision maker then makes the final decision based on the output of the sequence alignment algorithm.

Keywords: Plagiarism detection · Fuzzy petri nets · Abstract syntax trees · Global sequence alignment technique

1 Introduction

Software development is a crucial responsibility of software engineers and of students pursuing computer science/information technology major. Various software are designed in different languages and using different techniques [1]. Therefore, the project leaders assign various tasks to the engineers and similarly, teachers assign coding projects/assignments to the students. Many times, due to the emergence of the open-source community, programmers copy someone else's code and present them as their own work. This act of presenting someone else's work as your own is termed as plagiarism. In other words, intentionally claiming works done by others as one's own product [2]. In covid-19 during lockdown, most of the institutes are adopting online mode of educations. They have started online classes along with online submission of projects and assignments for engineering students. Hence, plagiarism detection becomes all the more important.

This plagiarism often goes undetected, as it is very inefficient and time-consuming for project managers and teachers to manually detect it. An automated plagiarism detection mechanism is therefore needed to compare the two source codes.

R. S. Tomar et al. (Eds.): CNC 2020, CCIS 1502, pp. 72–86, 2021.
https://doi.org/10.1007/978-981-16-8896-6_6

This paper discusses a fuzzy logic based approach to detect similarity between two given source codes. First, an Abstract Syntax Tree (AST) of both the source codes is constructed. The AST is then encoded into strings. Once the encoding is done, Sequence Alignment is used to extract the similarity features of the two strings. Finally, the similarity features are given as an input to a fuzzy-decision machine that gives the decision on whether the code is plagiarized or not.

2 Literature Survey

1. Text based approach:
   In this particular approach [3], the source code is considered as pure text. The two programs are therefore compared as if they are sequences of lines. The two programs are compared to find the matching lines of strings. If a threshold number of lines are the same, it is concluded that plagiarism exists.
   The drawbacks of text based approach are:
   a. They do not detect renaming of identifiers.
   b. They are ineffective in detecting plagiarism if a statement/ comment is added/deleted.
   c. They are ineffective if line breaks or extra white spaces are added.
2. Token based approach
   In this method [4], the source code is parsed and written as a sequence of tokens. A token is defined as a word appearing in the source code. The obtained sequence of tokens is processed to find the duplicate subsequences. The technique ensures robustness against formatting and spacing.
   Kamiya, Kusumoto et al. [5] described a tool based on this principle. It is called the CCFinder. Lexical rules were used to convert each word in the source code into a token which would remove the effect of changes made to functions names and variables. Other similar tools are CP-miner, described by Li, Lu et al. [6] and JPlag described by Prechelt, Malpohl et al. [7]. Schleimer, Wilkerson et al. [8] described a document fingerprinting approach which is used to detect plagiarism based on the token based approach.
   While the token based approach generally gives better results than text-based approach, it is found to be less effective if unnecessary variables or functions are declared in the source code.
3. Program Dependency Graph based approach
   This approach [9] contains the data flow and control flow information of a program. The PDG carries semantic information of the source code. In this approach, a set of PDGs are calculated for the two source codes. Once the PDGs are available, an isomorphic subgraph matching algorithm is used to find the similar subgraphs.
   The advantage of PDG-based detection algorithm as per Bellon, Koschke et al. [10] is that it can help in the detection of non-contiguous code clones. The other detection techniques mentioned in the paper are less effective in detecting them. A non-contiguous code clone is defined as having elements that are non-consecutively located on the source code.
   The PDG-based detection algorithm has a disadvantage that it cannot detect contiguous code clones as effectively as the other approaches. Also, Krinke [11] stated

is their paper that the PDG-based detection cannot be applied to practical software systems as it is time consuming.

4. Metrics based approach

   The metrics based approach [12] gathers different metrics for code fragments and makes a comparison of the metrics vectors. Various techniques use different metrics for plagiarism detection. For instance, a combination of metrics called fingerprinting functions are calculated for one or more syntactic units such as statements, classes, methods, etc. Then these fingerprinting functions are compared with each another to find the clones.

   The computational cost of this approach is very high, sometimes even polynomial.

5. AST based Approach

   Zhao et al. [13] described the structure of AST and a way to compare them. Since the AST is a complex structure, the method proposed calculating the hash value of the ASTs and then comparing them. The paper also proposed a variant to minimize the number of false positive detections. The papers [20-32] deal with the intelligent information retrieval using different machine learning approaches.

6. High Level Fuzzy Petri Nets

   Dr. Carl Petri proposed the petri net theory [14]. The High Level Fuzzy Petri Net is a more general representation model that can integrate several modelling formalisms into a single complicated system. The authors [28] gave a multi agent perspective for intelligent systems (Table 1).

Table 1. Comparison of petri nets used in papers

Paper	Conclusion
[15]	The model preserves agreement as well as the possibility of protecting services against misbehavior of malevolent services
[16]	The study characterizes the relationship between the performance of FCM clustering and the distribution of the "true" cluster sizes
[17]	An easy human fall detection algorithm was developed on the basis of enormous use of smart phones containing multiple sensors
[18]	A model was developed to solve the reasoning problems
[19]	An algorithm whose objective is to train the HLFPN structure to perform functions like pattern recognition, data clustering, pattern classification, optimization etc. was developed
[20]	The proposed hierarchical structure of HLFPN make the process of managing the complex systems easy with the help of decomposition and also facilitates reusability
[21]	The proposed model and corresponding application to predict stock prices was developed
[22]	The proposed HLFPN model integrates qualitative and quantitative tools for decision-making

3 Proposed Method

The concepts and tools used for the algorithm are described below:

Abstract Syntax Trees (AST):
Abstract syntax tree (AST), is the represents the source code in the form of the abstract syntactic structure. The constructs are denoted by the nodes of the tree.

Jones [23] mentions that AST captures the essential structure of the input data in a tree form, in addition to removing the unnecessary syntactic details.

Welty [24] proposed a method to represent code level knowledge using an ontology which is based on AST.

Sequence Alignment:
It is a way to calculate the relationship between the strings by adding spaces or by shifting the position of alphabets. Vladimir [25] presents the algorithm in a concise manner. Sequence alignment is widely used in the field of bioinformatics.

The algorithm that is used in this paper is Needleman-Wunsch algorithm. The algorithm basically divides a large problem into many smaller problems. Now in order to find the optical solution to the larger problem, it used the combination of the solutions to the smaller problems.

Fuzzy Petri Nets:
Petri nets are a mathematical and graphical modeling tool, which is asynchronous, concurrent, parallel, distributed, parallel, stochastic and nondeterministic. Murata [26] showed that fuzzy petri nets can be used to analyze and model various systems. This paper adopts Mamdani's fuzzy implication rule type [27] to make a decision on the plagiarized code.

An Abstract Syntax Tree can be constructed by performing lexical analysis on the source code followed by the syntax analysis. The sequence of tokens obtained from lexical analysis is fed to the syntax analyzer to produce the AST (Fig. 1).

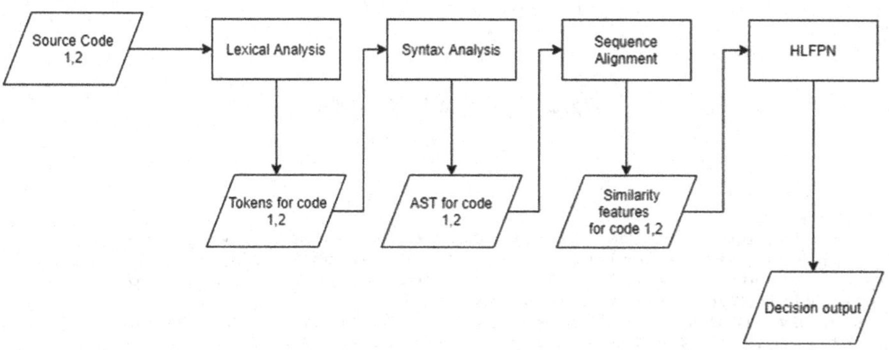

Fig. 1. Flowchart depiction of procedure for plagiarism detection

4 Procedure for Plagiarism Detection

1. Given n source codes, an Abstract Syntax Tree for the respective programs is constructed.
2. Once an AST for a program is constructed, it is then encoded in string format for future evaluation purposes.

3. The encoded strings are then processed to extract similarity features from them using Global Sequence Alignment.
4. Once the similarity features of given source codes are available, they are given as an input to a fuzzy decision maker which makes the decision on whether plagiarism exists between any two of the input similarity feature sets.

The experiment was done on source code written in Java programming language, but it can be easily extended to any language as far as it's syntax is known.

Creation of AST

Given a source code in Java, we perform lexical analysis followed by syntax analysis to obtain an abstract syntax tree of the source code. Lexical analysis is done to capture all the identifiers used in the code and syntax analysis checks the syntax of the code by parsing it and creating the AST.

Encoding the AST in String Format

Once the AST is created, it is encoded in an appropriate string format. The XML format was used for this experiment. Figure 2 indicates a simple program written in Java language. The result after encoding the AST of the respective program are shown in Fig. 3.

```
public class add
{
    public static void main(String[] args)
    {
        int a=3,b=5;
        int c=a+b;
    }
}
```

Fig. 2. A simple Java program

```
<CompilationUnit><TypeDeclaration><Modifier>public</Modifier>
<SimpleName>add</SimpleName><MethodDeclaration><Modifier>
public</Modifier><Modifier>static</Modifier><PrimitiveType>void
</PrimitiveType><SimpleName>main</SimpleName>
<SingleVariableDeclaration><ArrayType><SimpleType><SimpleName>
String</SimpleName></SimpleType><Dimension>[]</Dimension>
</ArrayType><SimpleName>args</SimpleName>
</SingleVariableDeclaration><Block><VariableDeclarationStatement>
<PrimitiveType>int</PrimitiveType><VariableDeclarationFragment>
<SimpleName>a</SimpleName><NumberLiteral>3</NumberLiteral>
</VariableDeclarationFragment><VariableDeclarationFragment>
<SimpleName>b</SimpleName><NumberLiteral>5</NumberLiteral>
</VariableDeclarationFragment></VariableDeclarationStatement>
<VariableDeclarationStatement><PrimitiveType>int</PrimitiveType>
<VariableDeclarationFragment><SimpleName>c</SimpleName>
<InfixExpression><SimpleName>a</SimpleName><SimpleName>b</SimpleName>
</InfixExpression></VariableDeclarationFragment>
</VariableDeclarationStatement></Block></MethodDeclaration>
</TypeDeclaration></CompilationUnit>
```

Fig. 3. Example of encoded abstract syntax tree

Using Sequence Alignment to Extract Similarity Features

Once the ASTs of two given source files are encoded in string format, sequence alignment is used to extract similarity features between the two strings. The three similarity features of interest here are:

1. Match ratio: This similarity feature is captured in the parameter m_r, which is the ratio of number of matching characters in the two strings to the size of a string.
2. Mismatch ratio: This similarity feature is captured in the parameter mm_r, which is the ratio of number of mismatching characters in the two strings to the size of a string.
3. Gap ratio: This similarity feature is captured in the parameter g_r, which is the ratio of number of gaps to the size of a string.

The three similarity features are given as an input to a fuzzy decision maker which evaluates them to tell whether the two programs represented by these two sets of features are plagiarised, that is, are a copy of each other.

Given the two similar codes (Fig. 4 and Fig. 5) for calculating n-thfibonaccinumber, the three features are were found as follows:

1. $m_r = 90.78$
2. $mm_r = 1.76$
3. $g_r = 7.46$

This output is given to the fuzzy decision maker.

```
class fibonacciA {
        static int fib(int n)
        {
                /* Declare an array to store Fibonacci numbers. */
                int f[] = new int[n + 1];
                int i;

                /* 0th and 1st number of the series are 0 and 1*/
                f[0] = 0;

                if (n > 0) {
                        f[1] = 1;

                        for (i = 2; i <= n; i++) {
                        /* Add the previous 2 numbers in the series
                        and store it */
                        f[i] = f[i - 1] + f[i - 2];
                        }
                }

                return f[n];
        }

        public static void main(String args[])
        {
                int n = 9;
                System.out.println(fib(n));
        }
}
```

Fig. 4. Java program-I to calculate n-th fibonacci number

```
class fibonacciB {
        static int fibonacci(int n)
        {
                int dp[] = new int[n + 1];
                int i;
                dp[0] = 0;

                if (n > 0) {
                        dp[1] = 1;

                        for (i = 2; i <= n; i++)
                        {
                                dp[i] = dp[i - 1] + dp[i - 2];
                        }
                }

                return dp[n];
        }

        public static void main(String args[])
        {
                int n = 9;
                int nthNumber=fibonacci(n);
                System.out.println(nthNumber);
        }
}
```

Fig. 5. Java program-II to calculate n-th fibonacci number

5 Fuzzy Decision Maker

The High Level Fuzzy Petri Net is used to make decisions based on the three input parameters (match ratio, mismatch ratio and gap ratio) whether the given source code are plagiarised. Three fuzzy sets, HIGH, MEDIUM and LOW are used for this purpose. The membership functions of the three sets is given below:

6 Membership Function

For decision making, three features are used, which are:

the ratio of total number of mismatches to the length of the sequence (mmr),
the ratio of total number of matches to the length of the sequence (mr),
and the ratio of total number of gaps to the length of the sequence (mg).

With the three input features, the membership functions of Low, Middle, and High [28] are defined as:

$$\mu H(x) = 1, \ when\ x \geq 90$$

$$\mu H(x) = \frac{1}{20}(x - 70)\ when\ 70 < x < 90$$

$$\mu H(x) = 0\ when\ x \leq 70$$

$$\mu M(x) = 0, \ when\ x \geq 80$$

$$\mu M(x) = \frac{-1}{30}(x - 80)\ when\ 50 \leq x < 80$$

$$\mu M(x) = \frac{1}{30}(x - 20)\ when\ 20 < x < 50$$

$$\mu M(x) = 0, \; when \; x \leq 20$$

$$\mu L(x) = 0, \; when \; x \geq 30$$

$$\mu L(x) = \frac{-1}{20}(x - 30) \; when \; 10 < x < 30$$

$$\mu L(x) = 1, \; when \; x \leq 10$$

The plagiarism output (P) will belong to either STRONG, INTERMEDIATE or WEAK fuzzy set.

The following rule base is used for decision making:

IF m_r is HIGH, THEN P is STRONG
IF m_r is MEDIUM, THEN P is INTERMEDIATE
IF m_r is LOW, THEN P is WEAK

IF mm_r is HIGH, THEN P is WEAK
IF mm_r is MEDIUM, THEN P is INTERMEDIATE
IF mm_r is LOW, THEN P is STRONG

IF g_r is HIGH, THEN P is WEAK
IF g_r is MEDIUM, THEN P is INTERMEDIATE
IF g_r is LOW, THEN P is STRONG

Based on the rule based, the decision is made. The membership of input features are as calculated and they are evaluated by the fuzzy decision maker to make the decision.

In the two source codes given in figure (figureNum), the fuzzy decision maker outputs PLAGIARISED as the decision.

7 Results

The following scenarios of a standard program were worked upon using the proposed algorithm. One example of these scenarios is given below.

The base program used for the examples is given in Fig. 6. Variants of this program were created according to the scenarios and the proposed algorithm was executed.

```
class BaseProgram{
        static int fib(int n) {
                int f[] = new int[n + 1];
                int i;
                f[0] = 0;
                if (n > 0) {
                        f[1] = 1;
                        for (i = 2; i <= n; i++)
                                f[i] = f[i - 1] + f[i - 2];
                }
                return f[n];
        }
        public static void main(String args[]) {
                int n = 9;
                System.out.println(fib(n));
        }
}
```

Fig. 6. Base program

1. Renaming the identifiers (Fig. 7)

```
class IdentifierRenamed{
        static int fibonacci(int num) {
                int dp[] = new int[num + 1];
                int index;
                dp[0] = 0;
                if (num > 0) {
                        dp[1] = 1;
                        for (index = 2; index <= num; index++)
                                dp[index] = dp[index - 1] + dp[index - 2];
                }
                return dp[num];
        }
        public static void main(String args[]) {
                int num = 9;
                System.out.println(fibonacci(num));
        }
}
```

Fig. 7. Identifier renamed

Parameters:
  m_r: 97.45
  mm_r: 0.4
  m_g: 2.15
Output:
  PLAGIARISED

2. Reordering the code blocks (Fig. 8):

```
class CodeBlocksReordered{
        public static void main(String args[]) {
                int n = 9;
                System.out.println(fib(n));
        }
        static int fib(int n) {
                int f[] = new int[n + 1];
                int i;
                f[0] = 0;
                if (n > 0) {
                        f[1] = 1;
                        for (i = 2; i <= n; i++)
                                f[i] = f[i - 1] + f[i - 2];
                }
                return f[n];
        }
}
```

Fig. 8. Reordering the code blocks

Parameters:
  m_r: 57.74
  mm_r: 0.0
  m_g: 42.26
Output:
  PLAGIARISED

3. Reordering statements within the same block (Fig. 9)

```
class StatementsReordered{
        static int fib(int n) {
                int f[] = new int[n + 1];
                f[0] = 0;
                int i = 2;
                if (n > 0) {
                        f[1] = 1;
                        for (; i <= n; i++)
                                f[i] = f[i - 1] + f[i - 2];
                }
                return f[n];
        }
        public static void main(String args[]) {
                System.out.println(fib(9));
        }
}
```

Fig. 9. Statements reordering

Parameters:
  m_r: 82.19
  mm_r: 3.56
  m_g: 14.25

Output:
PLAGIARISED

4. Changing the white spaces/formatting (Fig. 10)

```
class WhiteSpacesChanged{
        static int fib(int n) {
                int f[] = new int[n + 1]; int i;
                f[0] = 0;

                if (n > 0) {
                        f[1] = 1;
                        for (i = 2; i <= n; i++)
                        {
                                f[i] = f[i - 1] + f[i - 2];
                        }
                }

                return f[n];
        }
        public static void main(String args[]) {
                int n = 9; System.out.println(fib(n));
        }
}
```

Fig. 10. White space formatting

Parameters:
m_r: 99.02
mm_r: 0.22
m_g: 0.76
Output:
PLAGIARISED

5. Adding/changing comments (Fig. 11)

```
class ModifyingComments{
        static int fib(int n) {                         //function definition
                int f[] = new int[n + 1];               //create an integer array
                int i;
                f[0] = 0;
                if (n > 0) {
                        f[1] = 1;
                        for (i = 2; i <= n; i++)                //calcluate f[i]
                                f[i] = f[i - 1] + f[i - 2];
                }
                return f[n];
        }
        public static void main(String args[]) {
                int n = 9;                              //setting the value of n to 9
                System.out.println(fib(n));             //printing the value
        }
}
```

Fig. 11. Comment modification

Parameters:
m_r: 100

mm_r: 0
m_g: 0
Output:
PLAGIARISED

Changing the order of operations and operands (Fig. 12)

```
class OperandReordering{
        static int fib(int n) {
                int f[] = new int[n + 1];
                int i;
                f[0] = 0;
                if (n > 0) {
                        f[1] = 1;
                        for (i = 2; i <= n; i++)
                                f[i] = f[i - 2] + f[i - 1];
                }
                return f[n];
        }
        public static void main(String args[]) {
                int n = 9;
                System.out.println(fib(n));
        }
}
```

Fig. 12. Changing order of operands

Parameters:
m_r: 91.44
mm_r: 1.64
m_g: 6.92
Output:
PLAGIARISED

Adding redundant statements (Fig. 13)

```
class RedundantStatements{
        static int fib(int n) {
                int f[] = new int[n + 1];
                int i;
                f[0] = 0;
                int x=0,y=1;
                if (n > 0) {
                        f[1] = 1;
                        for (i = 2; i <= n; i++)
                                f[i] = f[i - 1] + f[i - 2];
                }
                return f[n];
        }
        public static void main(String args[]) {
                int n = 9;
                int x=0,y=1;
                int z=x+y;
                System.out.println(fib(n));
        }
}
```

Fig. 13. Adding redundant statements

Parameters:
m_r: 76.93
mm_r: 0.15
m_g: 22.92
Output:
PLAGIARISED

6. Changing the data type of the variable (Fig. 14)

```
class DatatypesChanged{
        static long fib(int n) {
                long f[] = new long [n + 1];
                int i;
                f[0] = 0;
                if (n > 0) {
                        f[1] = 1;
                        for (i = 2; i <= n; i++)
                                f[i] = f[i - 1] + f[i - 2];
                }
                return f[n];
        }
        public static void main(String args[]) {
                int n = 9;
                System.out.println(fib(n));
        }
}
```

Fig. 14. Data type changed from int to long

Parameters:
m_r: 99.27
mm_r: 0.41
m_g: 0.32
Output:
PLAGIARISED

8 Conclusion

The paper discussed an Abstract Syntax Tree based approach to detect plagiarism between two programs. In covid-19 during lockdown, most of the institutes are adopting online mode of educations. They have started online classes along with online submission of projects and assignments for engineering students. Hence, plagiarism detection becomes all the more important.

A fuzzy decision maker was used to make a decision based on the input parameters which represented the similarity features identified by the Sequence Alignment algorithm- Needleman Wunsh. The algorithm described was thus effective in following scenarios:

- When identifiers are renamed
- When code blocks are reordered.
- When statements within a code block are reordered.
- When white spaces and formatting is/are changed.
- When comments are changed/added,
- When the order of operands and operation is changed within an expression.
- When redundant statements are added.
- When the data type of the variables is changed.

References

1. Humphrey: A Discipline for Software Engineering. Addison-Wesley Longman Publishing Co., Inc
2. Lim, E.Q.Y., Nather, A.: What Is Plagiarism? Planning Your Research and How to Write It, pp. 283–293 (2015). https://doi.org/10.1142/9789814651059_0016
3. Zhao, J., Kunfeng, X., Yilun, F., Baojiang, C.: An AST-based code plagiarism detection algorithm. In: 10th International Conference on Broadband and Wireless Computing, Communication and Applications (BWCCA) (2015)
4. Hamid, A.B., Stan, J.: Efficient token based clone detection with flexible tokenization. In: Proceedings of the 6th Joint Meeting of The European Software Engineering Conference and The ACM SIGSOFT Symposium on The Foundations of Software Engineering (2007)
5. Kamiya, T., Kusumoto, S., Inoue, K.: CCFinder: a multilinguistic token-based code clone detection system for large scale source code. IEEE Trans. Softw. Eng. **28**(7), 654–670 (2002)
6. Li, Z., Lu, S., Myagmar, S., Zhou, Y.: CP-Miner: a tool for finding copy-paste and related bugs in operating system code. In: Proceedings of the 6th Conference on Symposium on Operation Systems Design and Implementation, pp. 289–302 (2004)
7. Prechelt, L., Malpohl, G., Phillipsen, M.: Finding plagiarisms among a set of programs with JPlag. J. Univ. Comput. Sci. **8**(11), 1016–1038 (2002)
8. Schleimer, S., Wilkerson, D.S., Aiken, A.: Winnowing: local algorithms for document fingerprinting. In: SIGMOD ACM, pp. 76–85 (2003)
9. Ferrante, J., Ottenstein, K., Warren, J.D.: The program dependence graph and its use in optimization. ACM Trans. Program. Lang. Syst. **9**(3), 319–331 (1987)
10. Bellon, S., Koschke, R., Antoniol, G., Krinke, J., Merlo, E.: Comparison and evaluation of clone detection tools. IEEE Trans. Softw. Eng. **31**(10), 804–818 (2007)
11. Krinke, J.: Identifying similar code with program dependence graphs. In: Proceeding of the 8th Working Conference on Reverse Engineering, pp. 301–309 (2001)
12. Mayrand, J., Leblanc, C., Merlo, E.: Experiment on the automatic detection of function clones in a software system using metrics. In: 1996 Proceedings of International Conference on Software Maintenance (1996)
13. Zhao, J., Xia, K., Fu, Y., Cui, B.: An AST-based code plagiarism detection algorithm. In: 10th International Conference on Broadband and Wireless Computing, Communication and Applications (BWCCA)
14. Carl, P.: KommunikationmitAutomaten, dissertation (1962)
15. Bartoletti, M., Tiziana, C., Michele, P.G.: Lending Petri nets. Sci. Comput. Program. **112**(1), 75–101 (2015)

16. Zhou, K., Yang, S.: Exploring the uniform effect of FCM clustering: a data distribution perspective. Knowl. Based Syst. **96**, 76–83 (2016)
17. Shen, V.R.L., Lai, H.Y., Lai, A.F.: The implementation of a smartphone-based fall detection system using a high-level fuzzy Petri net. Appl. Soft Comput. **26**(1), 390–400 (2015)
18. Shen, V.R.L.: Knowledge representation using high-level fuzzy Petri nets. IEEE Trans. Syst. Man. Cybernet. Part A Syst. Humans **36**(6), 2120–2127 (2006)
19. Shen, V.R.L.: Reinforcement learning for high-level fuzzy Petri nets. IEEE Trans. Syst. Man Cybernet. Part B Cybernet. **33**(2), 351–362 (2003)
20. Liu, K., Lee, J., Chiang, W.: High-level fuzzy Petri nets as a basis for managing symbolic and numerical information. Int. J. Artif. Intell. Tools **9**(4), 569–588 (2000)
21. Victor. R.L., Shen, R.-K.S., Cheng-Ying, Y., Wei-Chen, L., Tzer-Shyong, C.: A stock market prediction system based on high level fuzzy Petri nets. Int. J. Uncertainty Fuzziness Knowl. Based Syst. **26**(5), 771−808 (2018). https://doi.org/10.1142/S0218488518500356
22. Liu, K.: A high-level fuzzy Petri nets model for integrating quantitative and qualitative decision making. Int. J. Uncertainty Fuzziness Knowl. Based Syst. **15**(3), 253–284 (2007)
23. Jones, J.: Abstract Syntax Tree Implementation Idioms. University of Alabama, Alabama (2016)
24. Welty, C.A.: Augmenting abstract syntax trees for program understanding. In: Proceedings 12th IEEE International Conference Automated Software Engineering. IEEE, Incline Village, NV (1997)
25. Vladimir: The Needleman-Wunsch algorithm for sequence alignment. In: 7th Melbourne Bioinformatics Course
26. Murata, T.: Petri nets: Properties, analysis and applications. Proc. IEEE **77**(4), 541–580 (1989)
27. Mamdani, E.H.: Application of fuzzy logic to approximate reasoning using linguistic systems. IEEE Trans. Comput. **26**(12), 1182–1191 (1977)
28. Jain, P., Dahiya, D.: Architecture of a library management system using gaia extended for multi agent systems. In: International Conference on Information Intelligence, Systems, Technology and Management, pp. 340–349. Springer, Berlin, Heidelberg (2011)
29. Bai, Y., Wang, D.: Fundamentals of fuzzy logic control — fuzzy sets, fuzzy rules and defuzzifications. In: Bai, Y., Zhuang, H., Wang, D. (eds.) Advanced Fuzzy Logic Technologies in Industrial Applications. Advances in Industrial Control. Springer, London (2006)
30. Jain, P., Dahiya, D.: An intelligent multi agent framework for e-commerce using case based reasoning and argumentation for negotiation. In: International Conference on Information Systems, Technology and Management, pp. 164–175. Springer, Berlin, Heidelberg (2012)

Design of Methodology and a Comparative Analysis of Trigram Technique in Similarity of Textual Data

Ranjeet Kumar[1(✉)] and Sumant Kumar Tiwari[2]

[1] Meerut Institute of Engineering and Technology, Meerut, UP, India
ranjeetkumar@gmail.com

[2] ICFAI Business School (IBS), ICFAI Foundation for Higher Education, Hyderabad, India
sumant@ibsindia.org

Abstract. In this knowledge era information sharing and its searching is upgrading day by day by new innovative technology to do this. The major challenge in the academia and scientific community about the similarity of content and method producing for publication or for research purposes. In the academic and scientific organizations it is matter of fact that the scientific and research publications must be plagiarism free. In the submitted documents for the publication from the academia and research organization can be written with the use of free available text on the internet or from the free copyrighted documents having in the local corpus. In this paper, the comparative study has been performed to analyze the textual similarity between two or more documents. The methodology of continuous trigram and its applications for the finding the matching textual content of the similar text from the local corpus as well as from the internet. In the present paper, the comparative analysis of different techniques and their working applications of the similarity finding and retrieval process have been performed.

Keywords: Textual similarity · Text retrieval · Text matching · Textual plagiarism · Tri-gram technique · N-gram technique

1 Introduction

In recent age of internet the content is easily accessible to the users to use for their own practice whether it is textual content or any other type of content used for different context. In this scenario, more cases of similarity and duplicacy of content are coming are in the knowledge. The academia and scientific community are working on many challenges to overcome this issue by developing methodology to find out the different cases related to similarity of content. There is a need of some new applications or methodology by which the plagiarism can be found in the textual matters. The efforts have been made in many ways and did comparative study of very initial and some recent techniques to solve the issue. In the academic or research scenario textual similarity is major issue whether it is partial or fully copied, it comes under the plagiarism or copyrights violation of the actual author. For fair use text, figure, graph,

R. S. Tomar et al. (Eds.): CNC 2020, CCIS 1502, pp. 87–99, 2021.
https://doi.org/10.1007/978-981-16-8896-6_7

source code or contents may be used under the 'Fair use' practice and it should be valuated accordingly. To mitigate the issue related to the textual plagiarism different approach and methodology has been discussed in the literature and some technique has been targeted to develop some applications for finding the content similarity. Many applications and methodology prosed by recent developers to automate the system for the similarity finding in the document. In the process to automatic the system for finding similarity, many factors or components which have to be considered. There are some issue of reference cited in the article for the increasing the citation number in the research documents. These different issues related to plagiarism cases and it should be deal separately because it is completed process and it depends upon the structure of documents. In general in some general purposes it might be considered for some extent. In the same line the content used from self-publication is justified or not? In this context, in the paper published (Kumar and Tripathi 2017) has analyzed the cases and their working methodology. In this current paper, some modification in the previous used technique of a trigram methodology with on the consideration of some suitable text count new output has been generated from the automated plagiarism detection system for the textual contents.

Similarity finding and searching the pattern to avoid exact copying from different resources available to produce own material, the term is 'plagiarism' is the working interest since long time. Denning (1995) has suggested a concept of libraries and created for academic works. The main purpose of his suggestion was to avoid such copied material in publications whether it is academic or scientific publications in the different forms. In the other context of self-plagiarism, Samuelson suggested that 30% shared similarity is acceptable for self- plagiarism (Samuelson 1994). But in the academic context it is not clearly mentioned in the literature however, the researcher are still finding the way to avoid this context from the academic publication. In the process of developing a methodology to avoid exact similarity the assumption made by the developer to choose word by word similarity in context of text. If it is considered the 40% of similarity and then we have to define the 40%. The exact solution to define the percentage count is still not clear. It is assumption of developer and they are counting the word or taking overall material percentage which contain figure, table, flow charts, diagram etc. If in the methodology all the content material is counted then the similarity percentage will not be justified, then how we can proceed to define the exact textual plagiarism and its percentage count. Hence it is required to do a comprehensive examination of what constitutes self-plagiarism. In this context academic and scientific concern should be made to take a consideration to educate about related issues to avoid it. To quantify the issues of similarity finding, the basic two approaches has been discussed by the researchers i) the local (local repository or direct) and ii) global (in large set of data available on internet globally or indirect) approach. In their research (Ahlgren *et al.* 2003; van Eck and Waltman 2009) they suggested the findings related to similarity issues in the two documents. If we consider the first approach of local repository, it is based on direct matching between two documents in the repository. In another method of global approach, it is based on local document with another documents which is available on internet or indirect sources (Colliander and Ahlgren 2011), in this co-occurrences (eventually normalized) has to measure for the similarity between their profiles or between two objects.

In this context many researchers have been proposed different methodology to detect similarity in the documents the Lancaster and Culwin 2005, have suggested the method of classifying the metrics which was used for similarity findings in the documents. In the suggested method the introduced metrics in two simple ways. First based on number of documents considered in the calculation of metrics the method is classified accordingly and in second case it depends upon the computational complexity of design methodology for the similarity finding. In their research such as (Brin et al. 1995) introduced the fingerprints methods which was defined by statistical measures of consecutive of N characters in the documents which he proposed as n-gram in the text. In another research finding by (Stein and Zu Eissen 2006; Schleimer et al. 2003), where introduced as hashed value of n-grams as fingerprints. Some researchers such as (Aslam and Frost 2003), and language model measure (Zhai and Lafferty 2001) introduced probabilistic approach and language model to measure the sentences in the documents The present paper, the work is based on trigram method and it has been proposed some extra measures according to the required output and application requirement. The model is designed based on trigram method of searching the text in the document but it is not taking only three consecutive character, the selection of characters based on similarity finding. It is designed to display the output with two columnar display with sources of the copied material to avoid any discrepancies. The system will generate the complete report regarding the plagiarism detection of the documents.

2 Related Research

In the previous decade many techniques and methodologies have been used for the automated plagiarism detection. The major development came in this plagiarism detection system are based on local repository or for college assignment or some of them are for web data. But as internet resources increased day by day and there was a need of automated system to check all the available sources the web based application introduced and the natural language processing technique used for plagiarism detection in text documents and many other forms like within the text and multiple text documents. In this context of multiple text the researcher (Brin 1995; Shivakumar and Garcia-Molina 1996; Lyon et al. 2001; Broder 1998) introduced multiple text searching of common length n, where n can be defined or may be chosen as per requirement or method application. In the method defined, n may be made fixed then the substrings are said to be *n*-grams. In this n-gram technique the substring can be restricted on any number of strings depending upon the algorithm used. According to the application and requirement of the substring the value of *n* may be chosen for finding the similarity of text from the documents. The value of *n* cannot be chosen a very small like 1 or 2 nor big since in the document not all text or other material are usually fully copied verbatim from the source document.

In the article published by (Clough P.D. 2003) mentioned different techniques whether it is copy detection, parts of information retrieval, comparison with documents, authorship attribution these all applied to the plagiarism detection issues. For example, string matching and overlap of LCS, the proportion of shared content words, particularly those occurring only once, CopyCatch (Woolls and Coulthard 1998), the overlap of consecutive word sequences or word n-grams e.g. Ferret (Lyon et al. 2001), SCAM (Shivakumar and Garcia-Molina 1996), COPS (Brin et al. 1995), Koala (Heintz 1996), and compressed versions of the texts (Medori et al. 2002) Methods have also been developed to visualize the similarity between texts including VAST [12], Dotplot (Church and Helfman 1993), Bandit8 and Duploc (Ducasse et al. 1999). In another methodology of the text matching of the submitted document statistical method used in detecting plagiarism is "Latent Semantic Analysis" (LSA). By using the LSA the word similarity and the extraction of the word sense or meaning and then compare it for the similarity check in the body of the text. Other context of the plagiarism is paraphrased documents and this can be handled by different approaches or methodologies such as semantic similarity which can be used to grade the content in the documents and these semantics can be identified ad used for plagiarism detection. There are different approaches such as cosine similarity method can be used to find out semantic relevance among passages in minimal computational cost.

Many researchers have been suggested better approach to find out the similarity in the documents in their research Adams and Meltzer proposed (Adams and Meltzer 1993) query term based solution which is based on trigrams and inverted files approach for exact matches in the sentences. In many ways and researcher community N-gram approach fond suitable in many forms of plagiarism detection and claimed by researcher (Cavnar 1994) the tri-gram base approach is more suitable that word count method and got 100% recall with high precision in the test experiments performed by them. He recommended the method of trigram for retrieval of words fragments and TREC-2's has also found trigram an affective metric with promising results. The usability of the method of N-gram increases rapidly, since N-grams are (Canvar W.B. 1995; Cohen 1995) language-independent, it can be used for different collections of document in different languages. It is found suitable with word based systems for effective retrieval of compound nouns in the Korean documents (Lee and Ahn 1996). Also in another research published by The method of N-grams can be used (Cavnar and Trenkle 1994; Damashek 1995] which describes the suitability of N-gram in multilingual documents and its distinguisher factor between documents to gauge topical similarity between documents in the same language. Another research published by (Kumar and Tripathi 2013, 2014, 2015) N-gram based analysis performed for methodologies used in similarity search in text documents. There are another sort of different used in the area of text retrieval are mentioned in the research based on N-grams (Canvar W.B. 1995; Huffman 1996; Robertson and Willett 1992) and found robust in finding of spelling errors in the languages or differences and garbling of text. Application of N-gram are different types and researchers still finding many other ways to explore the method such as I-Match (Chowdhury et al. 2002) an intelligent system based on fingerprints and it filters out terms based on inverse document frequency in the document. For the implementation, first applying pre-processing approach to remove frequent and rarest terms from the documents. In this approach system are generating report about near to exact copy and it is based on ranking and weight assigning method for importance terms in the document.

Many others development earlier published by researchers based on feature vectors. Such in 1976 Ottenstein proposed such a system. Another similar system based on feature vector later reported. Another approach based on Rabin-Karp Algorithm with Windowing algorithm introduced by (Schleimer et al. 2003) called MOSS (Measure of Software Similarity) for the plagiarism detection. However it wasn't of much useful for detecting content plagiarism as it will fail to detect the semantics associated with the document.

In this paper, the system has designed based on both local repository based and internet based sources also. The comparative study based on software's currently available has been performed and analyzed that only word or fingerprints set of data categories detected in search. Also the majority of software's currently available and in use are detecting program source texts in number of word format. The present proposed system is based on sentences and paragraphs chunks and its performance is prominent.

3 Implementation of Methodology

Plagiarism is the most shouted problems in the academic and publications area and it became a major challenge to keep the research articles free from plagiarism. There are number of efforts going and researchers are working in this regards. The number of applications has been developed and day by day it is growing advanced. In the literature we have mentioned some of the developed applications and product which has some significant use in the shouted problem.

In this paper the approach designed to detect near copied and exact copied material in the document. It is not based only on word count and fingerprints of the document. It is search based on longest sequence or terms which copied from any source and then it will generate the results. For that purpose we defined a continuous trigram technique to match the textual data with each documents with another and find the longest sequence and then calculate the similarity measure for plagiarism. The propose system worked on local repository as well as on internet. The system detects the longest sequence of the sentences and if it is continued with extent of word to line and beyond of the sentences then it count the similarity of the text and show in the results section of the output. In the Fig. 1 given below the system working model is described which is proposed in this present paper. It shows the complete working process of the proposed methodology.

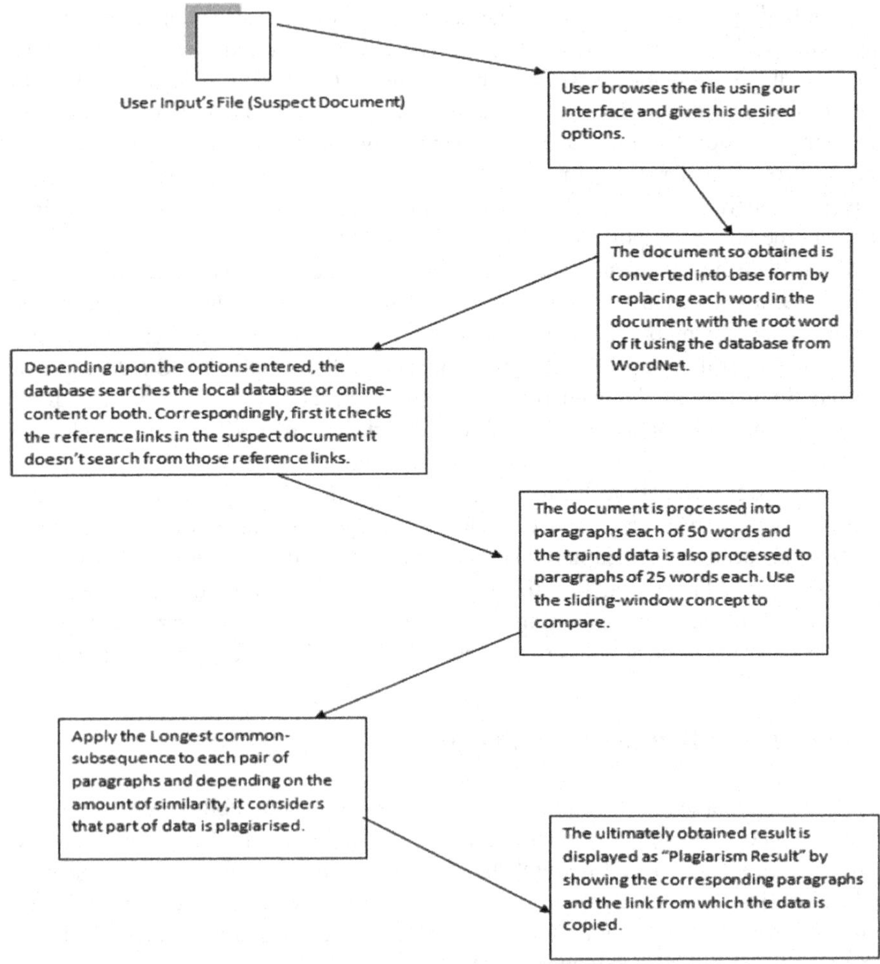

Fig. 1. Process diagram of the methodology and designed system

3.1 Methodology Design

The methodology designed in the present paper is based on two main modules. In this, i) for local repository document and ii) for resources copied from Internet and other online resources used for copying the material. In the both of the proposed module there is option of specific search, that means in the local database we have given a option to the user to search the plagiarism with specific files only and generate the plagiarism results. In the same line in the internet based search we have given option to the user to opt some free websites like Wikipedia or Encyclopedia web sites for free from searching and plagiarism criteria for some extents. In the initial steps for the plagiarism checkup user can follow these criteria and options for the better and optimum result generation for a particular input query file. The system will perform the initial steps of stemming and finding the root word of the each and every word in the query input document with the help of wordnet. The steps for the ditto or exact copying type of cases in plagiarism detection initially converted all the sentences and word into its root words after stemming.

The designed system is taking input from users as query document in pdf or word file format and after processing which included pre-processing of the query document and then checking the similarity search. The system is designed based on local repository and for internet sources based search, so system is providing the user to choose any of the two for plagiarism check whether the input query files will check on the local database or in the internet. After processing the system will generate the results in the two columnar display format.

3.2 Extractions of Links and Downloading the Similar Contents

After pre-processing of the submitted document for the plagiarism check, the system will search based on choice submitted by the user like local repository or internet sources, it will search the similar content in the available documents and then system will extract the similar documents. Now, we generate query of trigram like 1–10, 11–20, and so on and then the process of finding the similar content in these entire content in the internet with the help of search engines. In this process we get the links of the similar contents and we download the respective contents from the results obtained in the searching process.

In the searching process for neglecting the some free open source web sites, we have created a list of some websites addresses and when the link extraction process starts and encounters such addresses we skip the links.

3.3 Finding Textual Similarity

This module will generate the similarity report based on downloaded documents. For generating this report all the suspected documents will be divided into several paragraphs with words value assigned. These approach will be applied on both type of sources whether it is local repository or internet sources. Now the searching module is applied to compare the query documents with the downloaded documents for the textual similarity.

After the above process, comparing the query document with suspected docuemnts and finding the corresponding paragraphs using the Longest Common Subsequence Algorithm to get the common data of the two paragraphs. This is done at the cost of para-phrasing concept which involves searching and comparing the given line by considering all the possible positions of words.

4 Techniques and Methods Related to Concepts

We are analysing the algorithms which can be categorized based on the problem solving techniques. These algorithms are designed to handle the different problems and textual retrieval.

The techniques and methodology is divided into four major categories, String-based, Corpus-based, Knowledge-based, and Hybrid text similarities;

4.1 String Based Similarity

One of the oldest text similarity finding technique is based on String-based and it used currently in many applications due to its simple measurement approach. It is based on string sequences and character composition. It can be categorised into two major categories of similarity functions i.e. character-based similarity functions, and token-based similarity functions.

The Character-based Similarity also called sequence-based or edit distance (ED) measurement. In this approach similarity calculated based on edited distance between two strings, (Wang et al. 2011) (including insertion, deletion and substitution) between them.

Another application of string based approach is term-based similarity also known as token-based. In this application each string models as a set of tokens. For calculating the similarity we are taking tokens such as words. Based on query tokens corresponds with sets of tokens we can find out the string similarity measurement (Yu et al. 2016). If the similarity is found, the string pair is flagged as being similar or duplicate. The main drawback of this application on character-based is when we are applying it on larger string, it will take time and very complex in nature.

4.2 Corpus Based Search

In this similarity methods semantic approach is used for comparing the text. Initially we have to create one large corpora for similarity search with the query text and based on similarity of the query text with the corpora determines the similarity between two concepts. In the corpora of text known data or text we are storing which is going to match with the query text and if similarity identified, the similar text storing in the separate bin for determining the similarity index. The corpus we can use in any language related the searching the similarity of the query text (Kulkarni et al. 2016). The ultimate target of the application is to find out the query text with the text in the corpus.

4.3 Knowledge-Base Similarity

In the research of R. Mihalcea, discussed about the technique based on information which is used from semantic textual networks and based on similarity with query text and semantic similarity measures, identify the degree of words similarity is called a knowledge-based similarity measures (Mihalcea et al. 2006). In this concept of Knowledge-based similarity we also can measure of semantic relatedness along with semantic similarity. Based on knowledge base it introduced by (Budanitsky and Hirst 2006) it specifies two interchangeable concepts while relatedness associates concepts semantically. In this semantic methodology it interconnects with facts, rules defined conclusion on specific domains and the it is designed a knowledge representation in general it includes rules network semantics, logical propositions and conclusions.

5 Comparative Analysis with Different Methodologies

The present paper describes practical test cases based on daily work experiences and as per requirement the concept of trigram for three consecutive words has been modified for near to exact copied and exact copied material. The main idea of 3 words has been modified in different level of words categories for better improvements of the results. Some of the major techniques and their working has been analysed and it is presented below.

5.1 Fingerprinting Technique

In this method of "fingerprints", it contrast to the above mentioned approach, the invention is limited primarily to the repository of e-contents compiled by the user. It is limited for the same type of work assignments of the students and the essays. When large set of data on the internet and access the similarity with web applications, the results of the plagiarism detection affected.

5.2 Set of Word Metrics Technique

A) In this approach the use of set of words as a metrics, known as simple metrics.
   - It is used to detect inter-corporal type of similarity finding using paired metrics within a corpus.
   - In this method an approach of direct comparison of all possible pairs of sub normal values scaled to be between 0 and 100, although 0.0 to 1.0 could equally be used.
   - In the above metrics search most likely highest ranked and similarity index terms has chosen to be the most worthy in terms of similarity investigation.

B) Similarity Calculations
   - In this it compares the found metrics based on dividing submission down into their simple component parts.
   - Based on sentences claims and word claims generated from a subsection it compare for similarity in text.

Example-

Three word fragments-

Man is running on the ground

____ Man is running ____is running on _____running on the _____on the ground_____ and so on …

Note* *The above methodology is primarily directed to finding the plagiarism on the word level inclusion of stop words and stemming. Since, it finally does string matching. Again the window size selected is of only 3 words. This report basically based on the word count matches. Since, no direct evidence of plagiarism is seen by a common man. Through our experiments, we have arrived at the appropriate modified* *technique of the trigram with size 6–8 words, which gives best direct evidence on the amount of content copied, the content and where from it is copied.*

5.3 Ferret Systems Principles

In this Ferret based system a short strings is considered for the similarity search (three word in a string). In the processing of method selected set of text are converted into characteristics trigrams and these compared in pairs for similarity finding. After finding the similarity results using resemblance metric will be generated. On the basis of this resemblance metric level it can be decided the documents comes under plagiarism or not.

Note* *In the technique offerret system, the text document is compared by the string matching algorithm. There is document or words limitation in the technique for searching or uploading the document into the process for plagiarism check up. Another issue of limited number of words and files processing has been found in the technique which makes it very limited in use and tedious for bigger data applications.*

6 Results and Discussions

In the present paper, the addressed methodology has been implemented with the user friendly frontend development which is providing the options to search the input query text for the similarity finding. In the above discussion the local repository search, web search and specific search has been discussed, the input query text for the similarity search we have been given options for different search options to the user for their better search results.

In the current situation of the academic scenario, for the protection of copyrighted digital data is tedious and challenging task and also to maintain the originality in the research and academic literature. The number of applications developed in this regards to keep the originality in this research and academic data. The major techniques and methods used in the development of text similarity has been discussed in the Sects. 4 and 5 of the present paper. There are different set of applications for different areas of target document which has to be check the textual similarity. Some of them are only for students assignments and essays written in the classrooms. Some applications developed for limited number of words and files and some were developed which has wide scope and used differently like trigram, variable words count, etc.

Due to access of online resources and increasing the use of internet if it is taking into consideration a review of results on the basis of discussion made in this paper it reveals that in the decade of 90's and thereafter easy copying of their contents allured many authors to opt for plagiarism resulting into increasing % of cases of the plagiarism.

7 Conclusion

The recent research and developments in this area of textual similarity search in the research and academic documents through free available data on internet and in a local corpus is making new advancement day by day with new methodological approach and techniques. In the present paper, the modification based on requirement of finding longest word counts has been performed and it is based on the longest sequence of the similarity matches and then count the plagiarism portions in a chunk of data with paraphrasing applications. The results of the developed systems have been tested and it is satisfactory. In this approach maximum longest similar text finding is the target to find out the text chunks copied from any source. The more emphasis given to the time taken in the process of the input data for the plagiarism check-up. For the accuracy of the similarity checkup not only check similarity based on 3 words but it counts the longest words chunk and then decide to have plagiarism or not and then show in the results section. The present paper also address different techniques and methods for most used application in the textual similarity search and discussed about the working methodology of each techniques and methodology for the comparative analysis of discussed methods for the better results for similarity search in the text documents.

References

Lancaster, T., Culwin, F.: Classifications of plagiarism detection engines. Innovation Teach. Learn. Inf. Comput. Sci. **4**(2), 1–16 (2005)

Brin, S., Davis, J., Garcia Molina, H.: Copy detection mechanisms for digital documents. In: Proceedings of the 1995 ACM SIGMOD International Conference on Management of Data, San Jose, CA, pp. 398–409 (1995)

Stein, B., Zu Eissen, S.M.: Near similarity search and plagiarism analysis. In: Proceeding of 29th Annual Conference of the German Classification Society, pp. 430–437 (2006)

Ranjeet, K., Tripathi, R.C.: Text mining and similarity search using extended tri-gram algorithm in the reference based local repository dataset. Elsevier Procedia Comput. Sci. **65**, 911–919 (2015)

Ranjeet, K., Tripathi, R.C.: A trigram word selection methodology to detect textual similarity with comparative analysis of similar techniques. In: IEEE Fourth International Conference on Communication Systems and Network Technologies, pp. 383–387 (2014)

Schleimer, S., Wilkerson, D.S., Aiken, A. Winnowing: local algorithm for document fingerprinting. In: Proceedings of the ACM SIGMOD International Conference on Management of Data, pp. 76–85 (2003)

Ranjeet, K., Tripathi, R.C.: An analysis of automated detection techniques of textual similarity in research documents. Int. J. Adv. Sci. Technol. **56**, 99–110 (2013)

Samuelson, P.: Self plagiarism or fair use. Commun. ACM **37**(8), 21–25 (1994)

Denning, P.J.: Plagiarism on web, editorial. Commun. ACM **38**(12), 29 (1995)

Ahlgren, P., Jarneving, B., Rousseau, R.: Requirements for a co-citation similarity measure, with special reference to Pearson's correlation coefficient. J. Am. Soc. Inform. Sci. Technol. **54**(6), 550–560 (2003)

van Eck, N.J., Waltman, L.: How to normalize co-occurrence data? An analysis of some wellknown similarity measures. J. Am. Soc. Inf. Sci. Technol. **60**(8), 1635–1651 (2009)

Kumar, R., Tripathi, R.C.: An analysis of the impact of introducing the plagiarism detection system in an institute of higher education. J. Inf. Knowl. Manage. **16**(02), 1750011 (2017)

Colliander, C., Ahlgren, P.: Experimental comparison of first and second-order similarities in a scientometric context. Scientometric **90**, 675–685 (2011)

Aslam, J.A., Frost, M.: An information-theoretic measure for document similarity. In: Proceedings of the 26th International ACM/SIGIR Conference on Research and Development in Information Retrieval, pp. 449–450 (2003)

Zhai, C., Lafferty, J.: A study of smoothing methods for language models applied to ad-hoc information retrieval. In: Proceedings of the 24th Annual International ACM/SIGIR Conference on Research and Development in Information Retrieval, New Orleans, Louisiana, United States, pp. 334–342 (2001)

Shivakumar, N., Garcia-Molina, H.: Building a scalable and accurate copy detection mechanism. In: Proceedings of 1st ACM Conference on Digital Libraries, DL 96 (1996)

Lyon, C., Malcolm, J., Dickerson, B.: Detecting short passages of similar text in large document collections. In: Proceedings of the 2001 Conference on Empirical Methods in Natural Language Processing, pp. 118–125 (2001)

Broder, A.Z.: On the Resemblance and Containment of Documents, Compression and Complexity of Sequences. IEEE Computer Society, Washington, DC (1998)

Clough, P.D.: Measuring Text Reuse, Ph.D. thesis, University of Sheffield CopyCatch Product (2003). https://www.copycatchgold.com/

Wise, M.: YAP3 improved detection of similarities in computer programs and other texts. Presented at SIGCSE 96, pp. 130–134 (1996)

Prechelt, L., Malpohl, G., Philippsen, M.: JPlag Finding plagiarisms among a set of programs, Faculty of Informatics, University of Karlsruhe, Technical Report 2000-1 (2000)

Woolls, D., Coulthard, M.: Tools for the trade. Forensic Linguist. **5**(1), 33–57 (1998)

Heintze, N.: Scalable document fingerprinting. In: Proceedings of the Second USENIX Workshop on Electronic Commerce (1996)

Medori, J., Atwell, E., Gent, P., Souter, C.: Customising a copying-identi.er for biomedical science student reports: comparing simple and smart analyses. In: O'Neill, M., Sutcliffe, R.F. E., Ryan, C., Eaton, M., Griffith, N.J.L. (eds.) AICS 2002. LNCS (LNAI), vol. 2464, pp. 228–233. Springer, Heidelberg (2002). https://doi.org/10.1007/3-540-45750-X_31

Church, K.W., Helfman, J.I.: Dotplot a program for exploring self-similarity in millions of lines of text and code. J. Comput. Graph. Stat. **2**(2), 153–174 (1993)

Ducasse, S., Rieger, M., Demeyer, S.: A language independent approach for detecting duplicated code. In: Proceedings of the International Conference on Software Maintenance ICSM 99, pp. 109–118. IEEE (1999)

Adams, E.S., Meltzer, A.C.: Trigrams as index elements in full text retrieval observations and experimental results. In: ACM Computer Science Conference, February (1993)

Cavnar, W.B.: N-gram-Based Text Filtering for TREC-2. In: The Second Text Retrieval Conference (TREC-2), February (1994)

Cohen, J.D.: Highlights: language- and domain-independent automatic indexing terms for abstracting. J. Am. Soc. Inf. Sci. **46**(3), 162–174 (1995)

Lee, J.H., Ahn, J.S.: Using n-grams for Korean text retrieval. In: 19th Annual International ACM SIGIR Conference on Research and Development in Information Retrieval (1996)

Cavnar, W.B., Trenkle, J.M.: N-gram-based text categorization. In: Symposium on Document Analysis and Information Retrieval, April (1994)

Damashek, M.: Gauging similarity with n-grams: language-independent categorization of text. Science **267**(5199), 843–848 (1995)

Huffman, S.: Acquaintance: Language-Independent Document Categorization by N-grams. In: The Fourth Text Retrieval Conference (TREC-4), October (1996)

Robertson, A.M., Willett, P.: Searching for historical word-forms in a database of 17th-century english text using spelling-correction methods. In: 15th Annual International ACM SIGIR Conference on Research and Development in Information Retrieval (1992)

Chowdhury, A., Frieder, O., Grossman, D., McCabe, M.: Collection statistics for fast duplicate document detection. ACM Trans. Inf. Syst. **20**(2), 171–191 (2002)

Ottenstein, K.J.: An algorithmic approach to the detection and prevention of plagiarism. SIGCSE Bull. **8**(4), 30–41 (1976)

Wang, J., Li, G., Fe, J.: Fast-join: an efficient method for fuzzy token matching based string similarity join. In: 2011 IEEE 27th International Conference on Data Engineering, pp. 458–469 (2011)

Yu, M., Li, G., Deng, D., Feng, J.: String similarity search and join: a survey. Front. Comp. Sci. **10**(3), 399–417 (2016). https://doi.org/10.1007/s11704-015-5900-5

Kulkarni, A., More, C., Kulkarni, M., Bhandekar, V.: Text analytic tools for semantic similarity. Imp. J. Interdiscip. Res. **2**(5), 2454–1362 (2016)

Mihalcea, R., Corley, C., Strapparava, C., et al.: Corpus-based and knowledge-based measures of text semantic similarity. In: AAAI, vol. 6, pp. 775–780 (2006)

Budanitsky, A., Hirst, G.: Evaluating wordnet-based measures of lexical semantic relatedness. Comput. Linguist. **32**(1), 13–47 (2006)

Cavnar, W.B.: N-gram-Based Text Filtering for TREC-2. In: The Second Text Retrieval Conference (TREC-2), February (1995)

A Framework to Identify Color Blindness Charts Using Image Processing and CNN

Kritika Dhawale[1], Ankit Singh Vohra[2], Pooja Jain[2], and Tapan Kumar[1(✉)]

[1] Department of ECE, Indian Institute of Information Technology, Nagpur, India
[2] Department of CSE, Indian Institute of Information Technology, Nagpur, India

Abstract. Color vision deficit (sometimes known as colour blindness) is a term used to describe a set of diseases that impact colour perception. People take many color blindness tests while consulting an Eye Specialist to check if they are suffering from this deficiency. This test is conducted by showing different types of color blindness charts to the patient and then asking him/her to read those charts. In this paper, we make the machine learn the color blindness charts and identify the pattern present in it, using Image processing and Deep learning. Charts may contain a single digit or double-digit number or any unrecognized pattern. For this, we collected color blindness charts from the internet, preprocessed and augmented them for training purposes using CNN. Deep Learning is a method in which a computer software learns statistical patterns in data so that it can recognise or help us distinguish between the patterns in the charts. The model learns about the various attributes based on the photos and represents the data mathematically, organising it in space:

Keywords: Convolution neural networks (CNN) · Color blindness · K-means color clustering · Morphology · Skeletonizing

1 Introduction

Color blindness (colour vision deficit, or CVD) affects one in every 12 males (8%) and one in every 200 women worldwide. To put the numbers in context, there are about 300 million colorblind people who struggle every day, with 99% of them suffering from red-green colorblindness. Computer vision is the scientific study of methods that computers and other systems use to do a certain activity successfully and autonomously without the need for clear and precise human instructions. Because such an algorithm allows computers to learn and make predictions on their own, computers can learn and make predictions. In general, training data is created to make predictions rather than being explicitly programmed to accomplish the task using machine learning algorithms based on sample data. The methods have been utilised in a wide range of applications, including stock prediction, recommendation systems, email filtering, object categorization, and computer vision, such as autonomous driving, when developing an algorithm with precise instructions to execute the task is impossible.

We built a model for the person who wants to take a color blindness test without actually visiting an Eye Specialist at his own place. The charts that the patient will

R. S. Tomar et al. (Eds.): CNC 2020, CCIS 1502, pp. 100–109, 2021.
https://doi.org/10.1007/978-981-16-8896-6_8

recognize shall be then verified by our pre-trained model and give the correct results. The pre-trained model is built by preprocessing the charts, augmenting them and then passing onto a Convolutional Neural Network for training purpose. The classified pattern can be a single digit from 1-9 or any noisy, unrecognized pattern. CNN is one of the best techniques to achieve this kind of task. As an improvement and future work, better data preprocessing can be done to extract the features and the patterns should be more clear and visible so that CNN will yield better accuracy. Different models, other than Neural Networks, like a Random Forest may also be tried out (Figs. 1 and 2).

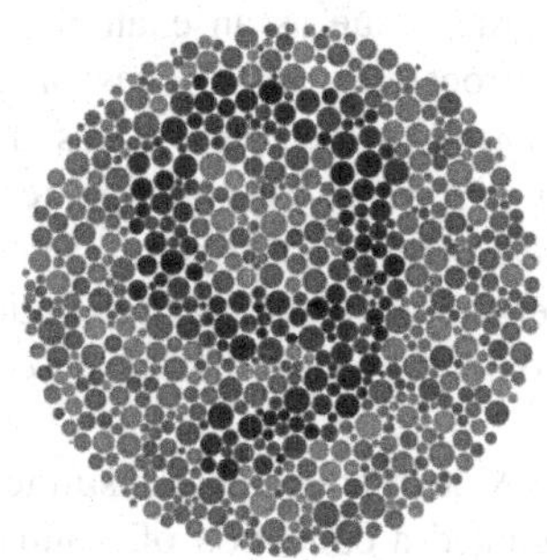

Fig. 1. Chart with a single digit-9

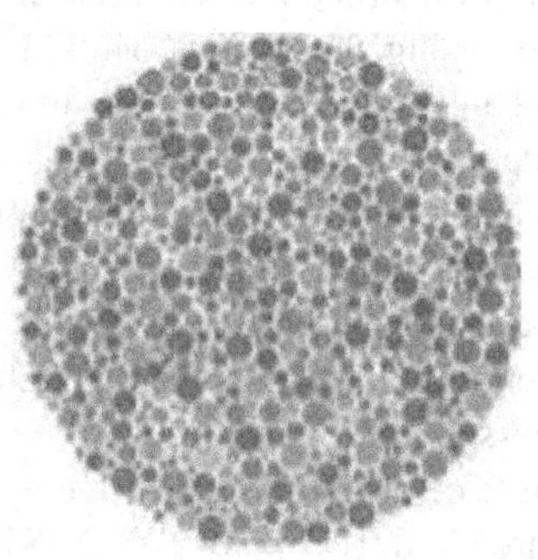

Fig. 2. Chart with an unrecognized pattern

2 Related Work

Xiao-Xiao Niu et al. [1] gave an outcross model of incorporating the collaboration of two prevalent classifiers: Convolutional Neural Network (CNN) and Support Vector Machine (SVM), which have demonstrated outcomes in perceiving various sorts of examples. In this, CNN functions as a trainable element extractor and SVM proceeds as a recognizer. This outcross model consequently separates highlights from the crude pictures and creates the forecasts. Correlations with different examinations on a similar database demonstrate that this combination has accomplished better outcomes: an acknowledgment pace of 99.81% without dismissal, and an acknowledgment pace of 94.40% with 5.60% dismissal.

Qizhe Xie et al. [2] presented a simple self-preparing strategy that achieves 88.4% top-1 exactness on ImageNet, which is 2.0% better than the best in class model, which necessitates 3.5 billion pitifully tagged Instagram photos. It raises ImageNet-A main 1 exactness from 61.0 to 83.7% on strength test sets, lowers ImageNet-C mean debasement mistake from 45.7 to 28.3, and lowers ImageNet-P mean flip rate from 27.8 to 12.2. To achieve this, he trained an EfficientNet model on named ImageNet images and then used it as an educator to generate pseudo names for 300 million unlabeled images. At that point, he trained a bigger EfficientNet as an understudy model on the mix of named and pseudo marked pictures and repeated this procedure by returning the understudy as the instructor. During the age of the pseudo marks, the educator isn't loud with the goal that the pseudo names are as exact as could reasonably be expected.

Nonetheless, during the learning of the understudy, he infused clamor, for example, dropout, stochastic profundity and information expansion through RandAugment to the understudy with the goal that the understudy sums up superior to the educator.

Using the CIFAR10 dataset and three types of the Convolutional Neural Network, Kuntal Kumar Pal et al. [3] proved the importance of preprocessing methods for picture grouping. The results clearly reveal that for all three systems, Zero Component Analysis (ZCA) outperforms both Mean Normalization and Standardization approaches, making it the most important preprocessing strategy for image grouping using Convolutional Neural Networks.

A brief instructional briefing on information preparation is presented, along with its benefits, using the serious MNIST transcribed digits order issue as an example. He showed up and examined the impact of different preprocessing approaches on the presentation of three CNNs, LeNet, Network3, and DropConnect, as well as their gatherings. Focusing, versatile distortion, interpretation, pivot, and various mixtures of these were among the alterations broken down. Their research reveals that information preprocessing methods, such as the combination of versatile twisting and revolution, together with gatherings have a high potential to additionally improve the cutting edge exactness in MNIST grouping.

"Best of the Web" by Li Deng [4] contributed the Modified National Institute of Standards and Technology (MNIST) assets, which included a collection of manually written digit images that are widely used in optical character recognition and AI research. In general, to advance AI and example acknowledgment research, a few standard databases have emerged in which transcribed digits are preprocessed, including normalisation and standardisation, so that analysts can consider the acknowledgment aftereffects of their strategies on a standard premise. The MNIST dataset of handwritten digits, which is freely available, has become a standard for evaluating machine learning methods for a variety of uses.

Luis Perez et al. [5] investigated and contrasted various arrangements with the issue of information growth in picture grouping. They falsely compelled their entrance to information to a little subset of the ImageNet dataset, and thought about every datum expansion method thusly. One of the more effective information growth techniques is the customary changes referenced previously. They likewise explore different avenues regarding GANs to create pictures of various styles. At long last, proposed a technique to permit a neural net to learn enlargements that best improve the classifier, which we call neural expansion. They examined the triumphs and inadequacies of this technique on different datasets.

As per Denker et al. [6], he clarified the strategy for improved diminishing or skeletonizing manually written characters or other variable-line-width pictures. This technique examines a format set over the picture to be diminished. Every format has a particular game plan of dim and light pixels. At any rate one of those layouts incorporates either multiple pixels per column or multiple lines of pixels. An odd number is a decent decision. Besides, the layouts are picked so every format can unequivocally erase picture pixels without thought of the impact of such erasures on the conduct of different formats. In this manner the formats are autonomous of one another.

Khalid Saeed et al. [7], in their paper focuses on three angles firmly identified with one another: first, it introduces the best in class in the field of reducing procedures by depicting broad notions of the most significant computations and comparing them. It also proposes another declining calculation with intriguing qualities in terms of handling quality and calculation lucidity, both of which are improved using models. Finally, the paper analyses parallelization difficulties for declining calculations that are typically consecutive. The proposed calculation's main advantage is its comprehensiveness, which makes it useful and flexible for a wide range of applications. The authors [14–17] discuss usage of various machine learning models in different domains.

3 Methodology

The process flow which was followed to develop the model to detect digits from the Color Blindness Charts starts with Data Collection. 54 Color Blindness charts were collected which had some digits from 1-9 and then these charts were processed to make it understandable by the machine. The processed charts were pass to CNN and ANN for feature extraction and classification. The Fig. 3 explain the flow of the operations applied.

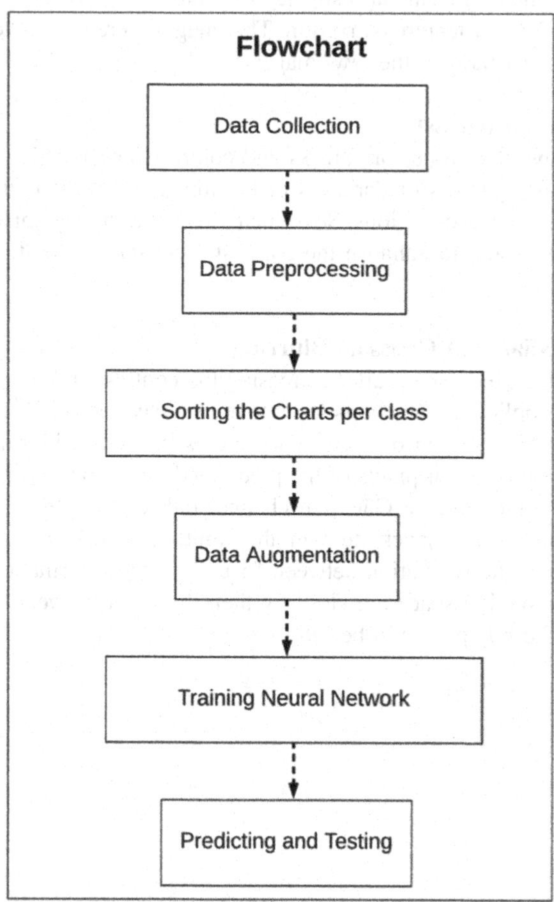

Fig. 3. Flow of the methods applied

3.1 Data Exploration

We collected various charts from the internet as there was not a specified dataset to achieve our task. Overall there were 54 color blindness charts. But as this number was very less, we augmented those 54 images after pre-processing them.

3.2 Data Pre-processing

To identify the digits from the Color Blindness charts, it is important to first preprocess the images and make them clear and black and white so that the machine can be trained on it using neural networks. So after going through a lot of research work we need to apply the following image processing methodologies in sequence to ensure that the images are processed.

3.2.1 Resize Image

The color blindness charts which were available were of size 492 * 492, so it was important to bring them to a standard smaller size like 225 * 225 or 250 * 250 which can be passed to CNN for feature extraction. The images were resized to 250 * 250 by maintaining the aspect ratio of the raw images.

3.2.2 Increase the Contrast

An image must have the proper brightness and contrast for easy viewing. Brightness refers to the overall lightness or darkness of the image. Contrast is the difference in brightness between objects or regions. So to increase the brightness some value us to be added to RGB Pixels and to enhance the contrast a constant is multiplied with these pixels.

3.2.3 Apply Median and Gaussian Blurring

Since the images are pretty sharp after increasing the contrast and brightness, blurring technique is to be applied on the charts to remove excessive noise. To blur the images, Gaussian Blur and Median blur of openCV can be used. Median blur takes the middle of the considerable number of pixels of the predefined piece size and in gaussian haze the picture is convolved with a Gaussian channel rather than the case channel. The Gaussian blur changes the speck item in the limitless dimensional space into the Gaussian capacity of the separation between focuses in the information space: If two focuses in the information space are close by then the point between the vectors that speak to them in the bit space will be little.

3.2.4 Apply K-Means Color Clustering

Number K will determine how many color clusters we will use, in our case its 5. Assign each pixel value to the closest cluster. Compute and place the new centroid of each cluster. Reassign the pixel values to the new closest cluster. If there is any reassignment, again redo the steps orelse we have found the dominant colors in the image.

3.2.5 Convert to Grayscale

For any image processing, it's better to convert the image to grayscale first as, the color information doesn't help us identify important edges or other features. The reason for differentiating grayscale images from any other sort of color image is that less information needs to be provided for each pixel while reducing the complexity of the code.

3.2.6 Apply Thresholding

The digits are all clear but it is an obvious improvement. They do not look very handwritten and are too thick. Also, they are not fully white on a black background. To overcome this, we will use thresholding. We will be trying a range of threshold values until we reach a particular percent of white range. We will start at a threshold of 0 up to 255 with an increment of 10 until we are in the 0.1–0.28 range [8] (Figs. 4 and 5).

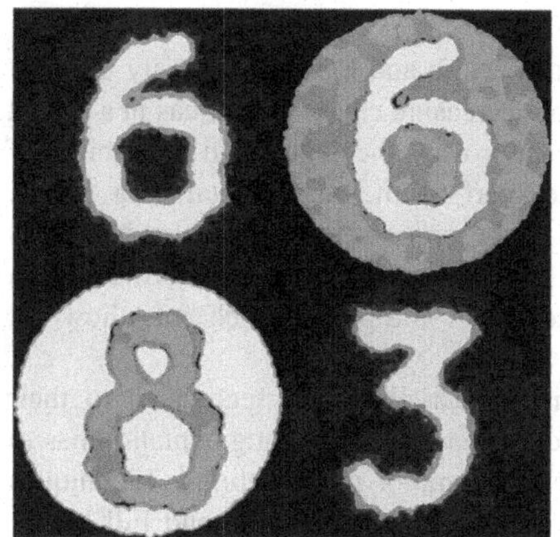

Fig. 4. Before thresholding

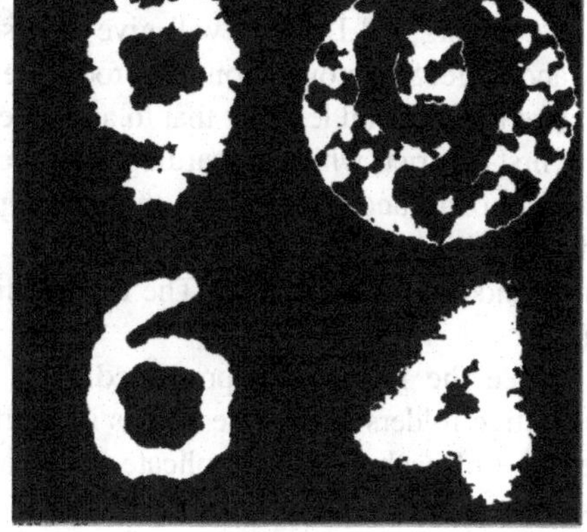

Fig. 5. After thresholding

3.2.7 Morphology Open, Close, Erosion

The purpose of morphological actions is to remove flaws from the picture's structure. The processes examine a photograph that includes an organising component, which is a small shape or layout. Morphology opening removes little elements from a picture's closer view, putting them out of sight, while closure removes small gaps in the forefront, transforming small foundation islands into frontal space. These techniques can also be used to find specific shapes in a photograph. Erosion and Dilation are two key morphological activities. Erosion adds pixels to the limits of articles in a picture, while Dilation expels pixels on object limits [9, 10] (Fig. 6).

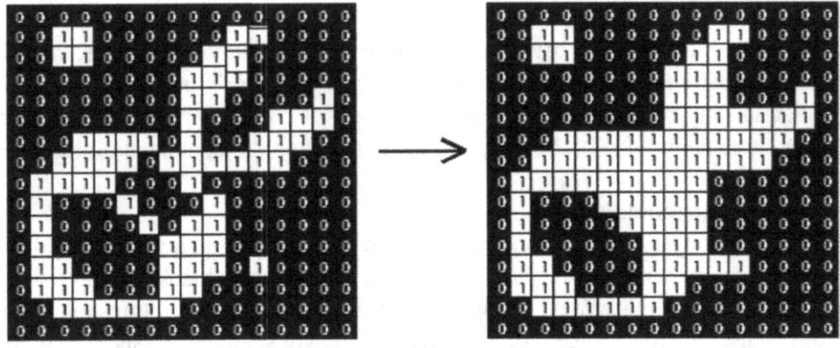

Fig. 6. Morphology [11]

3.2.8 Skeletonizing and Dilation

Skeletonizing and Dilation will give us a steady width and look increasingly uniform by and large. Skeletonization is a procedure for decreasing closer view areas in a paired picture to a skeletal leftover that to a great extent protects the degree and availability of the first district while discarding the greater part of the first frontal area pixels. Skeletonizing and Dilation are the last steps of the processing of the color blindness charts. All the charts follow the steps from 1.1 to 1.8 in order to be transformed into a more understandable format. The Intermediate output of a particular chart is shown in Fig. 7.

Once the images are processed they will be classified and segregated to their respective folders and as the data is in insufficient amount, Image augmentation has to be done of each class to replicate the images with minor modifications. Techniques used to augment the image were: ROtation, Shear, Brightness, Zoom and Fill Mode. Total 100 images were generated of each class using the augmenting techniques which are sufficient to train a CNN for feature extraction and an ANN for classification.

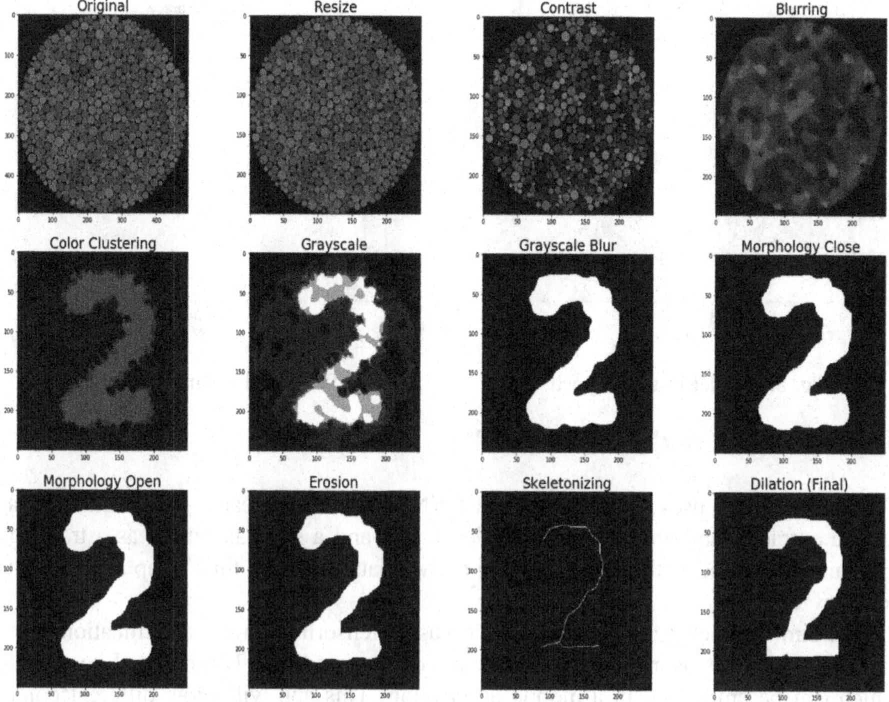

Fig. 7. Pre-processing of the charts in a grid

3.3 Algorithms and Techniques Used

CNN: Convolutional neural networks (CNN) are used for feature extraction and have become well-known as a result of the various designs available in some frameworks. The CNN's Convolution section is made up of two primary components: Convolution layers and Pooling Layers. By computing the output of neurons coupled to local layers, the convolution layers increase depth. Down-sampling is performed by pooling layers. The feature vectors are extracted from the input photos using CNN. Based on the feature vector provided by CNN, an ANN model classifies the input [12, 13].

4 Results

So, after training the Neural Network we get an accuracy of around 99% in training data as well as testing data. It was easy to obtain such high accuracy because of the processing involved in the preliminary steps. The Model Accuracy and Model Loss Graphs are plotted with respect to every epoch during the training and validation phase. More efforts were based on the processing of images rather than choosing a very complex CNN model as once the images are processed this dataset appears similar to the MNIST data and for such varied images, a small CNN was chosen which was sufficient to give high accuracy (Figs. 8 and 9).

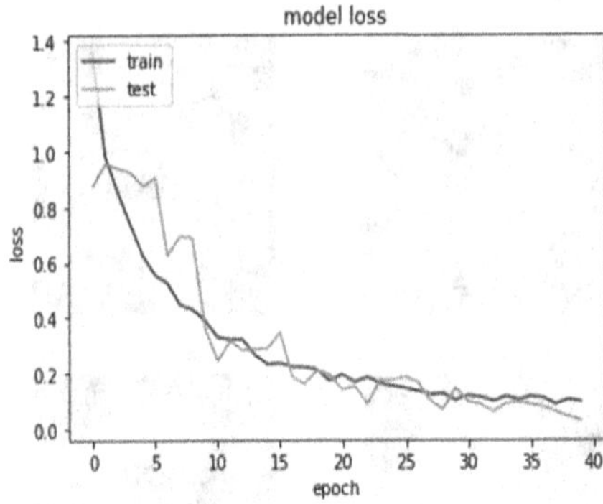

Fig. 8. Model loss per epoch

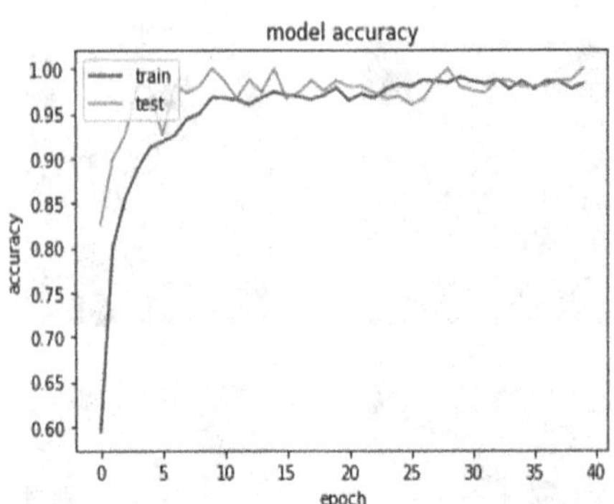

Fig. 9. Model accuracy per epoch

5 Conclusion and Future Work

The current study uses setups that use a CNN architecture created from scratch as a feature extractor and an ANN with hidden layers and a softmax output as a training mechanism to forecast the final class. On the validation set, the final setup achieves an accuracy of 0.99.

We aim to develop a mobile application using tensorflow image classification. The model trained on tensorflow and Keras can be converted to a Tensorflow Lite model which can be embedded in a mobile application. This app will show different color blindness charts and will ask the user to enter the digit which appears to them. So after showing a series of charts, the application will be able to give results about the degree of color blindness the user is affected with. So, anyone can install the app and can check whether he/she is having any difficulty in reading these charts without visiting an Eye Specialist.

References

1. Niu, X.X., Suen, C.Y.: A novel hybrid CNN–SVM classifier for recognizing handwritten digits. Pattern Recogn. **45**(4), 1318–1325 (2012)
2. Xie, Q., Hovy, E., Luong, M.T., Le, Q.V.: Self-training with Noisy Student improves ImageNet classification (2019). arXiv preprint. arXiv:1911.04252
3. Pal, K.K., Sudeep, K.S.: Preprocessing for image classification by convolutional neural networks. In: 2016 IEEE International Conference on Recent Trends in Electronics, Information and Communication Technology (RTEICT), pp. 1778–1781. IEEE, (2016)
4. Deng, L.: The MNIST database of handwritten digit images for machine learning research [best of the web]. IEEE Signal Process. Mag. **29**(6), 141–142 (2012)
5. Perez, L., Wang, J.: The effectiveness of data augmentation in image classification using deep learning (2017). arXiv preprint, arXiv:1712.04621
6. Denker, J.S., et al.: U.S. Patent No. 5,224,179. U.S. Patent and Trademark Office, Washington, DC (1993)

7. Saeed, K., Tabędzki, M., Rybnik, M., Adamski, M.: K3M: A universal algorithm for image skeletonization and a review of thinning techniques. Int. J. Appl. Math. Comput. Sci. **20**(2), 317–335 (2010)
8. Thrasher, C.W., Shustorovich, A., Thompson, S.M., Amtrup, J.W., Macciola, A.: U.S. Patent No. 10,242,285. U.S. Patent and Trademark Office, Washington, DC (2019)
9. Serra, J., Soille, P. (eds.): Mathematical Morphology and Its Applications to Image Processing, vol. 2. Springer Science & Business Media (2012)
10. Shih, F.Y.: Image Processing and Mathematical Morphology: Fundamentals and Applications. CRC Press, Boca Raton (2017)
11. http://homepages.inf.ed.ac.uk/rbf/HIPR2/close.htm. Accessed 15 Feb 2020
12. He, T., Zhang, Z., Zhang, H., Zhang, Z., Xie, J., Li, M.: Bag of tricks for image classification with convolutional neural networks. In: Proceedings of the IEEE Conference on Computer Vision and Pattern Recognition, pp. 558–567 (2019)
13. Alvear-Sandoval, R.F., Sancho-Gómez, J.L., Figueiras-Vidal, A.R.: On improving CNNs performance: the case of MNIST. Inf. Fusion **52**, 106–109 (2019)
14. Sharma, Y., Gaurav, A., Pooja, J., Tapan, K.: Vector representation of words for sentiment analysis using GloVe. In: 2017 International Conference on Intelligent Communication and Computational Techniques (ICCT), pp. 279–284. IEEE (2017)
15. Pinto, J., Pooja, J., Tapan, K.: Hadoop distributed computing clusters for fault prediction. In: 2016 International Computer Science and Engineering Conference (ICSEC), pp. 1–6. IEEE (2016)
16. Pinto, J., Pooja, J., Tapan, K.: Hadoop cluster monitoring and fault analysis in real time. In: 2016 International Conference on Recent Advances and Innovations in Engineering (ICRAIE), pp. 1–6. IEEE (2016)
17. Kumar, T., Vansha, K., Pooja, J.: Cognitive radio: a network structure perspective. In: Information and Communication Technology, pp. 229–237. Springer, Singapore (2018). https://doi.org/10.1007/978-981-10-5508-9_22

Crop Yield Quantity and Price Prediction: An Ensemble Approach

Drashi Jain, Choudhary Nikita, and Megha Kamble(✉)

Department of Computer Science and Engineering, LNCT Excellence Bhopal, Bhopal, India
meghak@lnct.ac.in

Abstract. Agriculture is critical to the Indian economy. However, agriculture in India is undergoing a structural transition that is resulting in a catastrophe. The only way to get out of this dilemma is to do everything possible to make agriculture a lucrative business and to encourage farmers to maintain crop production. As part of this endeavor, this model would use machine learning to assist farmers in making proper crop decisions. Using Random Forest machine learning methods, this model focuses on predicting the right grain price depending on climatic conditions and crop productivity based on historical data. In addition, android application has been developed.

Keywords: Random forest · Decision tree · Soil profile · Ensemble machine learning model

1 Introduction

The quantity of grains required by the population in a given year is heavily influenced by population growth and weather changes. Because of the sudden change in weather conditions, grains are occasionally damaged and hence are not sent to market, increasing market demand. It's also difficult to anticipate the weather at times. As a result, the following chapter will explain how quantity and price predictions are made (Figs. 1, 2 and 3).

(a)

(b)

Fig. 1. (a) Wheat (b) Barley

R. S. Tomar et al. (Eds.): CNC 2020, CCIS 1502, pp. 110–120, 2021.
https://doi.org/10.1007/978-981-16-8896-6_9

(a) (b)

Fig. 2. (a) Millet (b) Rice

Fig. 3. Soyabean oilseed

Working on 5 grains from 5 zones of India we have got the best result. The grains are –

- Wheat (Major producer – Utter Pradesh)
- Barley (Major producer – Rajasthan)
- Millet (Major producer – Karnataka)
- Rice (Major producer – West Bengal)
- Soyabean Oilseed (Major producer – Madhya Pradesh)

These states have different climate and varies in soil condition as well.

The data for the model comes from the machine learning technique that was used to train it. Farmers used to forecast their production based on previous year's yield results. Thus, there are various ways or algorithms [6] for this type of data analytics in crop prediction, and we can predict crop production using those algorithms. People nowadays are unaware of the importance of cultivating crops at the appropriate time and location. There is no correct remedy or technology to overcome the circumstance faced after assessing all of the concerns and problems such as weather, temperature, and various other aspects. Accurate information regarding crop production history is critical when making judgments about agricultural risk management. As a result, this chapter presents a method for predicting the grain price and yield of a crop based on climatic conditions and historical data. Before cultivating onto the field, the farmer will check the crop's production per acre.

The work's major goals are to:

a. Employ machine learning techniques to anticipate grain price and crop yield.
b. To correctly examine and interpret the data in order to make better forecasts.
c. To make machine learning models perform better.
d. Create an Android application that is simple to use.

1.1 Related Work

Majority of Asian population has influenced their culture, diets and economic condition by the most common agricultural food. For ex. More than 50% of the Indian population has rice as the primary source of nutrition. To achieve the target of large production, productive lands, human settlement, intensive cultivation process of rice, high quality fertilizer, high quality food seed, moderate artificial climate are some of the required facts. But the farmers may not have exact awareness of some of the manmade factors such as precise use of fertilizer, proper measure to prevent and cure the disease. Many diseases considered as minor, may become serious in many rice growing areas [1]. The bibliography is listing the significant contributions over the world and India [8]. With this reference list, significant achievements and importance is state in the following sections.

Smart Farming [2] is not only focused on the analysis of data acquired through various sources like historical, time series, geographical and location dependent or atomization instruments, but implementation of advanced technology, such as drone or robots to name it a real smart system. Smart systems should possess the abilities to record the data and analyze it to make decision, which is more accurate and precise as compared to human expertise. smart farming employs IoT kind of hardware, electronic interface and cloud storage to capture the data and all these things can be user friendly handled by mobile app kind of simple application to which every single person has access these days, without strong acquaintance of technical knowledge. It works in a manner that the data is organized, accessible all the time and on every aspect of field operation that can be monitored remotely from anywhere in the world.

Smart Farming [2, 3] is a budding notion in which the activity to manage the farms is carried out using up to date Information and Communication Technologies. various hardware devices and software computational techniques can be used to amplify the magnitude and quality of production, increase safety, automatic controlling of environment, field related resources, remote monitoring, hazard avoidance. At the other side, it also optimizes the human labor, soil nutritional element, it lessens dependence on human expertise and approximate measures. It also lessens the dependence on climatic condition which hamper the crop yield. Smart farming or agriculture comprises of sensors for detecting soil moisture, water, sunlight amount, humidity and temperature in weather conditions, and other supporting and ambient factors. It also comprises historical data analysis where seasonal changes affected crop yield, time series analysis, data analysis where data is contributed to the government agencies for reporting purpose. It also comprises of satellite imagery-based applications, rainfall measures, floods and disaster-based measures and such relational data is to be assessed.

Smart agriculture [4, 5] research aims to provide a decision-making support system or framework for overall agricultural management to address the issues of population growth and relative crop yield, climate change and relative crop yield, technological gain, from planting and watering of crops to remote monitoring of health and harvesting of the plants. Deep learning (DL) [5] incorporates a up to date procedure for image processing and big data analysis with huge potential. Deep learning is a recent tool these days in the agricultural domain. It has already been successfully applied to other domains. The chapter analyses the specific employed models for image data taken from the authenticate sources, the performance of iterations, the employed software app and the likelihood of real-time application to evaluate the crop disease, prototype is rice crop. deep learning offers high precision outperforming other image processing techniques.

2 Proposed Model

The easiest way to the work done in this is based on following ML models:

Bagging: Random forest, for every response y, there are n inputs. Prediction is done by binary tree, at each node, a test to input is applied, mean squared error determines the value and left or right subbranch. Eventually leaf made is prediction node. Feature values are preferred to be categorical. Leaf node is class label. Prediction score of each node is averaged.

Random forest – It's a supervised machine learning algorithm that's commonly used to solve classification and regression problems. It constructs decision trees from various samples, using the majority vote for classification and the average for regression (Fig. 4).

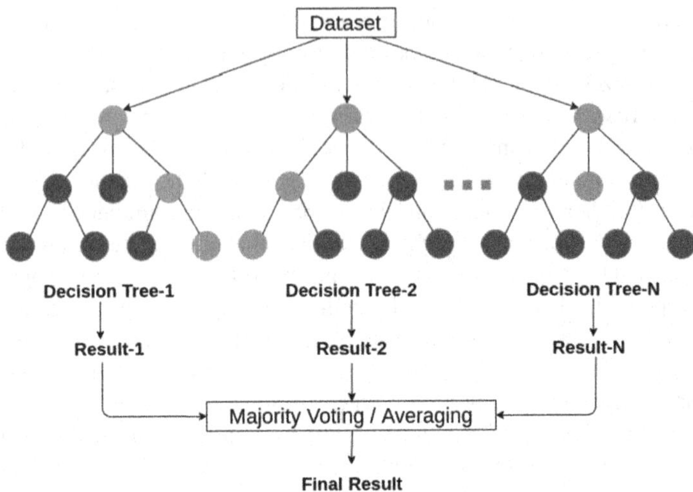

Fig. 4. Proposed architecture

One of the most essential characteristics of the random forest algorithm is that it can handle data sets with both continuous and categorical variables, as in regression and classification. for classification difficulties, it produces superior results.

Python Libraries. 1. Seaborn - Seaborn is a Python package based on matplotlib that is open-source. It's used for exploratory data analysis and data visualisation. With dataframes and the Pandas library, Seaborn is a breeze to use. The graphs that are created can also be readily altered.

2. Matplotlib - Matplotlib is a python visualisation toolkit with a low-level graph plotting library. John D. Hunter is the creator of Matplotlib. Matplotlib is free and open source software that we can utilise. For platform compatibility, Matplotlib is largely written in Python, with a few segments written in C, Objective-C, and JavaScript.

3. NumPy - NumPy is a Python library that allows you to do things with numbers. NumPy is a Python library for working with arrays. The acronym NumPy stands for "Numerical Python."

4. Pandas - Pandas is a valuable data analysis library. It has the ability to manipulate and analyse data. Pandas provide data structures that are both strong and simple to use, as well as the ability to quickly perform operations on them.

5. Sklearn - Scikit-learn is a free Python machine learning library. Support vector machines, random forests, and k-neighbors are among the algorithms included.

2.1 Analysis

To put the model into action, we chose the Indian state of Uttar Pradesh for grain wheat. To construct the system, historical data about the crop and the climate at the district level was required. This information was taken from the official website www.data.gov.in, and it includes information on the state, district, season, crop, area, and production. Temperature, precipitation, windspeed, and the crop's minimal support price were all acquired through Kaggle.

It was a matter of great concern to get the authentic data to train the machine learning model used for the same. The dataset has been collected form the two authentic government approved sites so as to get the accurate result.

Following figures are the snapshots of the datasets that have been used for this project (Fig. 5).

	month	population	temp	maxtemp	mintemp	precipitation	windspeed	msp	dayofprec	production	price
0	1-Jan-00	1056575549	17.3	22.2	7.8	0.0	5.9	610	0	76369.00	4077.33
1	1-Feb-00	1056575550	20.2	24.8	11.0	0.0	7.9	610	0	76369.00	4281.47
2	1-Mar-00	1056575551	23.8	32.0	14.0	0.0	9.0	610	0	76369.00	4201.94
3	1-Apr-00	1056575552	32.2	39.4	25.0	0.6	9.1	610	1	76369.00	4120.83
4	1-May-00	1056575553	32.0	39.1	25.1	0.0	9.5	610	0	76369.00	4357.91
...	...	...	...	...	...	...	...	...	...	...	...
249	1-Oct-20	1380004385	27.9	34.9	20.9	0.0	2.4	1975	0	107592.00	14947.04
250	1-Nov-20	1380004385	20.8	28.2	13.4	21.2	2.5	1975	2	107592.00	15651.92
251	1-Dec-20	1380004385	16.5	23.4	9.6	0.0	3.2	1975	0	107592.00	16006.59
252	1-Jan-21	1393409038	15.0	21.0	9.1	1.0	3.6	2035	1	111895.68	17395.20
253	1-Feb-21	1393409038	20.5	28.4	12.5	5.0	3.9	2035	2	111895.68	17522.70

254 rows × 11 columns

Fig. 5. Wheat grain dataset for proposed model

Dataset fields

1. Month: In our dataset we take first row as a month from 1-Jan-00 to 1-Feb-21.
2. Population: This figure comes from the World Development Indicators and represents the annual change in agricultural output compared to previous years. Growth in the population.
3. Temperature: Even if only for a short time, high temperatures have an impact on crop growth. Temperature is measured in degrees Celsius.
4. Max-temperature: The month's maximum or highest temperature.
5. Min-temp: The lowest temperature ever recorded in that month.
6. Precipitation: Precipitation is a type of liquid or solid water particle that falls from the atmosphere and lands on the Earth's surface.
7. Windspeed: is a fundamental atmospheric quantity created by air flowing from high to low pressure, usually as a result of changes in pressure.
8. MSP (Minimum Support Price): This is a guaranteed minimum price that acts as a safety net or insurance for farmers when they sell specific commodities.
9. Days of precipitation: No. of days of rainfall.

2.2 Implementation

2.2.1 Program Code

The experimental setup includes programme listings or programme commands in the text using Python and the Google Cloud environment for the provided data set and number of epochs.

1. Import Libraries

```
import seaborn as sns
import matplotlib.pyplot as plt
import numpy as np
import pandas as pd
from sklearn import linear_model
from sklearn.ensemble import RandomForestRegressor
from sklearn.ensemble import AdaBoostRegressor
```

2. importing dataset

```
from sklearn.model_selection import train_test_split
af = pd.read_csv('wheat1.csv')
```

3. Preparing data for training for production

```
p = af[['population','temp','maxtemp',
'mintemp', 'precipitation','windspeed','
msp','dayofprec']]
q = af['production']
```

4. Training the data for prodution

```
p_train, p_test, q_train, q_test = train
_test_split(p, q, test_size = 0.3, random_
state = 0)
regressor = RandomForestRegressor(n_esti
mators = 100)
regressor.fit(p_train, q_train)
boosted_tree = AdaBoostRegressor(base_es
timator=None, n_estimators=200)
boosted_tree.fit(p_train, q_train)
q_pred = boosted_tree.predict(p_test)
```

5. Evaluating the algorithm

```
accuracy = boosted_tree.score(p_test,q_test)
print(accuracy*100,'%')
```

6. Plotting graph for production

```
plt.figure(figsize=(5,5))
plt.scatter(q_test,q_pred, c='crimson')
plt.yscale('linear')
plt.xscale('linear')
p1 = max(max(q_pred), max(q_test))
p2 = min(min(q_pred), min(q_test))
plt.plot([p1, p2], [p1, p2], 'b-')
plt.xlabel('True Values', fontsize=15)
plt.ylabel('Predictions', fontsize=15)
plt.axis('equal')
plt.show()
```

2.3 Data Processing

```
p=af[['population', 'temp','maxtemp','mintemp', 'precipit
ation','windspeed','msp','dayofprec','production']]
q=af['price']
```

2.4 Price Prediction

```
p_train, p_test, q_train, q_test=train_test_split(p, q, tes
t_size=0.4, random_state=0)
regressor=RandomForestRegressor(n_estimators=100)
regressor.fit(p_train, q_train)
boosted_tree=AdaBoostRegressor(base_estimator=None, n_est
imators=200)
boosted_tree.fit(p_train, q_train)
q_pred=boosted_tree.predict(p_test)
```

3 Results and Validation

After training the data with machine learning model (Figs. 6 and 7),

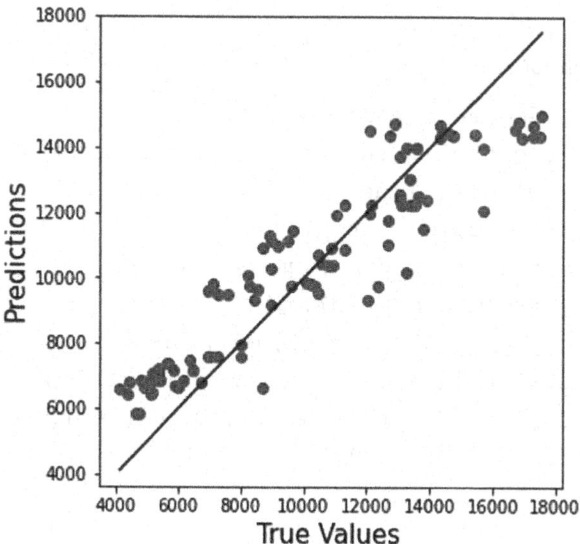

Fig. 6. Prediction v/s actual values (crop price)

- Predicted value of yield and actual value shows an accuracy of approximately 97%.
- Predicted value of price and actual value shows an accuracy of approximately 95%.

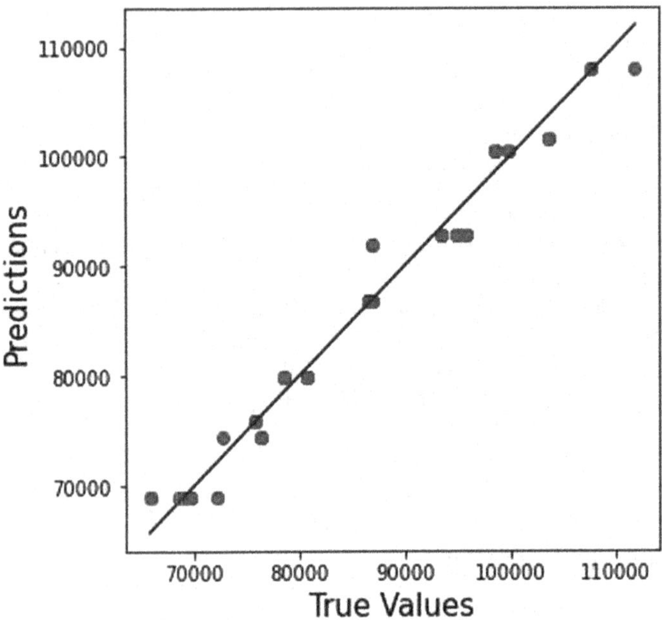

Fig. 7. Prediction v/s actual values (crop production)

Plotting graph for price

```
plt.figure(figsize=(5,5))
plt.scatter(q_test,q_pred, c='crimson')
plt.yscale('linear')
  plt.xscale('linear')
p1 = max(max(q_pred), max(q_test))
p2 = min(min(q_pred), min(q_test))
plt.plot([p1, p2], [p1, p2], 'b-')
plt.xlabel('True Values', fontsize=15)
plt.ylabel('Predictions', fontsize=15)
plt.axis('equal')
plt.show()
```

Evaluating the algorithm

```
accuracy = boosted_tree.score(p_test,q_test)
print(accuracy*100,'%')
```

4 Conclusion

Crop yield and price prediction utilising sophisticated machine learning algorithms may help crop planners make better judgments. Our programme predicts the best output in terms of quality and quantity for the farmer. Farmers also receive information regarding their intended or expected yield price. With climate change, they can acquire information on quantity and price for their grains based on their demands.

Time series prediction using neural networks is a critical tool for understanding global agricultural commodity futures pricing and, more importantly, for lowering uncertainty and risk in agricultural markets.

The government can use our approach to see if there is any form of grain black-marketing going on. Consider the following scenario: If the population and production both grow every year, and if there is a dramatic increase in the reliance on a particular grain for the same population. The government can use this to see whether there is any black-marketing going on.

Increase the number of grains consumed, as well as pulses and fruits. To achieve accurate results, advanced machine learning and deep learning are used. Increasing the dataset by evaluating the soil profile in terms of nutrients and soil quality.

References

1. Agila, N., Senthil Kumar, P.: An efficient crop identification using deep learning. Int. J. Scientific Technol. Res. **9**(01), 2805–2808 (2020)
2. Santos, L., Santos, F.N., Oliveira, P.M., Shinde, P.: Deep learning applications in agriculture: a short review. In: Silva, M.F., Lima, J.L., Reis, L.P., Sanfeliu, A., Tardioli, D. (eds.) Robot 2019: Fourth Iberian Robotics Conference: Advances in Robotics, Volume 1, pp. 139–151. Springer International Publishing, Cham (2020). https://doi.org/10.1007/978-3-030-35990-4_12
3. Yan, G., et al.: Plant disease identification based on deep learning algorithm in smart farming. Hindawi Discrete Dynamics Nature Soc. **2020**, 1−11 (2020). Article ID 2479172. https://doi.org/10.1155/2020/2479172
4. El-Helly, M., El-Beltagy, S., Rafea, A.: Image analysis-based interface for diagnostic expert systems. In: Proceedings of the Winter International Symposium on Information and Communication Technologies, pp. 1–6. Trinity College Dublin, Cancun, Mexico (2004)
5. Tellaeche, A., Burgos-Artizzu, X.P., Pajares, G., Ribeiro, A.: A vision-based method for weeds identification through the Bayesian decision theory. Patt. Recogn. **41**(2), 521–530 (2008)

6. Landge, P.S., Patil, S.A., Khot, D.S., Otari, O.D., Malavkar, U.G.: Automatic detection and classification of plant disease through image processing. Int. J. Adv. Res. Comput. Sci. Softw. Eng. **3**(7), 798–801 (2013)
7. Hakkim, V.M.A., Abhilash, J.E., Ajay, G.A.J., Mufeedha, K.: Precision farming: the future of indian agriculture. J. Appl. Biol. Biotechnol. **4**(06), 068–072 (2016)
8. Tripathi, R., et al: Precision Agriculture in India: Opportunities and Challenges (2013)

Study on Cluster-Based Pattern Recognition Using Recommendation System

Shailendra Chaurasia, Prashant Shrivastava, Megha Kamble(✉), and Bhanupriya Chouksey

Computer Science Department, LNCT Excellence Bhopal, Bhopal, India
meghak@lnct.ac.in

Abstract. The recommendations system has growing relevance to internet service and overload of information is one of the most critical incidents that users meet on the Internet. To make suggestions based on similar interests between users or items, Recommender Systems uses collective filtering. Clusters shall classify population or data points so that data points in the same category are more comparable to other data points in the same category and differ from data points in other categories. Pattern detection and matching include parameters such as average, correlation, and mutual information, etc. The PR can be used as a classification method for extracting and grouping patterns into various groups. PR is a classification method. PR is an intermediary process. In this review, we researched data mining, Clustering, Recommendation systems, Pattern Recognition, and described different types of recommendation systems as well as defined various methods of clustering & pattern recognition.

Keywords: Data mining · Clustering · Recommendation systems · Pattern recognition · Personalized or non-personalized recommendation system

1 Introduction

Data mining (DM) may also be viewed as a complicated task because techniques utilized may be very specific or data do not necessarily exist at a single location. In this extraction phase, the data stored previously are modified to continue forecasting and forecasting. It involves the convergence of different heterogeneous data sources. The main concerns are the usage of mining or user interface methods, different forms of data, and performance problems. The primary word used in data mining literature is the exploration of information. DM is often called Knowledge Discovery in Database (KDD) i.e. analysis of valuable data structures or facts. The processing of analysis data for future projection is the discovery of knowledge. To satisfy the need for analyzes of the high quantity data sets accessible, data management productivity employs several fields such as machine learning, processing of information, statistics, and visualization [1].

Clustering is helpful in various contexts for scanning, sorting, decision making, and mechanical training, including data mining, record analysis, image segmentation, and pattern recognition. Unlike all such situations in the past (for example statistical models) there is little information obtainable about data & decision-makers should create as assumptions as possible about the proof. These restrictions provide the basis for the

R. S. Tomar et al. (Eds.): CNC 2020, CCIS 1502, pp. 121–131, 2021.
https://doi.org/10.1007/978-981-16-8896-6_10

clustering approach to determine its structure preliminarily by analyzing linkages between data points. The word "clustering" is used in many research contexts to build ways to process unlabeled data. Clustering is a division of data and associated classes of objects. Active research is carried out on clustering in many areas, such as analytics, machine learning algos. Clustering is useful for various scenarios for searching, sorting, decision making, and mechanical training, including data mining, record scanning, imaging segmentation, and pattern detection. In all other situations, however, no previous knowledge (e.g. mathematical models) is available about the data, and the decision-maker should draw a few conclusions as possible about proof [2].

Recommendation Systems (RSs) should have enough quantity of data to make recommendations. There are two types of data collected: implicit and explicit data. The primary goal of data collection is to learn about users' preferences to provide appropriate recommendations. If a user rates item through a certain interface, then explicit feedback is provided. When a user purchases an item, it indicates that the user likes it; when a user returns an item, it constitutes implicit feedback. One may classify the method as CBA (Content-based Approach), CFA (Collaborative Filtering Approach), or HA (Hybrid Approach). CBRS recommends items based on both the user profile and the item description. CFA would recommend goods depending on the identities of prior raters. A hybrid approach is based on both content and collaborative filtering. RS are systems that provide recommendations depends upon user's preferences & therefore customize consumers.This method is also predicted on the 'rate' or 'preference' the consumer is given to the object. They are used in various fields such as films, books, music, foods, restaurants, etc. [3].

In this digital world, the pattern is all around. A pattern can be observable either physically or by applying algorithms mathematically. Pattern Recognition is a mechanism using machine learning algorithms to identify patterns. The recognition of patterns may be classified as a classification of data based on previously gathered information or data from and/or pattern representation. The application potential is one of the essential aspects of pattern recognition. Pattern detection is the ability to identify feature arrangements or data providing information about a specific device or data collection. In a technical context, a pattern may be repeated data sequences over time, which can be employed to predict patterns, certain image feature setups, frequent words and sentences combined in natural language processing (NLP), or unique behavioral clusters on the network which may imply an attack, among other nearly endless opportunities [4, 5].

2 Clustering

Clustering is a technique of combining items or data into clusters where objects are strongly communicated within-cluster but very distinct from objects in other clusters. In attribute values that define an entity, differences and resemblance are stated. For data conveying, categorizing, data loosening, development of models, identification of outliers, etc., clustering methods are used. Both clustering approaches have a similar style in finding clusters that represent each cluster. The similarity metric and input path cluster center help to form a cluster closest to or closest to the cluster.

Clustering may be the most significant unproven ignorance problem, so like any other such problem it has to search for framework in an unnamed data set.

2.1 Clustering Methods

2.1.1 Partitioning Method

The clusters are created in a single step in the trendy partial clustering method as an alternative to several steps. At the end of clusters, only one normal cluster is formed, although various cluster groups can be established internally K-means, k-medoids are the best widely used partitioning methods.

2.1.2 Hierarchical Method

Is a cluster exam method that is used to create a cluster picking order. After amerger or split decision is finalized, it is important to make adjustments to the importance of clean hierarchical clustering techniques to the kinds of hierarchical methods are available overall:

- Agglomerative approach
- Divisive approach.

2.1.3 Density-Based Method

The clustering algorithm based on density attempts to find clusters based on data points density in s regions. The basic clustering hint is that the location of a particular radius (Eps) requires at least a minimum of instances in any case at the cluster point (MinPts). DBSCAN (Density-based Spatial Clustering of Noise Applications) is one of the most popular frequency-oriented grouping protocols.

2.1.4 DBSCAN Method

The clustering method on basis of density based on link regions is the clustering density method used to handle device or database spatial data with noise. Its customs for the output of the cluster the high-density region and the additional region which has small density is labeled outwards of the cluster. The number of clusters in advance is not appropriate.

2.1.5 Grid-Based Method

This approach uses a space-led methodology in which a set in space is subdivided into cells that regulate the supply of the input objects. A multi-resolution grid layout is routine in the Grid-based Clustering process. It measures the object space into a certain number of cells that are used to the system a grid structure on which all cluster operations take place.

2.1.6 Model-Based Method

Model clustering methods are focused on-premise that data are produced by a combination of the underlying distribution of probabilities and optimize the fit between the data and mathematical model. Choosing a suitable applicant from the model also poses a major challenge in the face of an unknown distributor. Moreover,probability clustering is highly computational, especially when the data scale is very high [6–8].

3 Recommendation Systems

Recommendation systems apply DM methods and approaches to predict the interest of users in products and services among the large volume of items available. Customers are confronted with overloaded information. A recommendation system as illustrated in Fig. 1 is software that forecasts valuable product information using the previous user interest and expectations. The quality of search items will improve with this. And for both consumers and e-commerce websites profit.

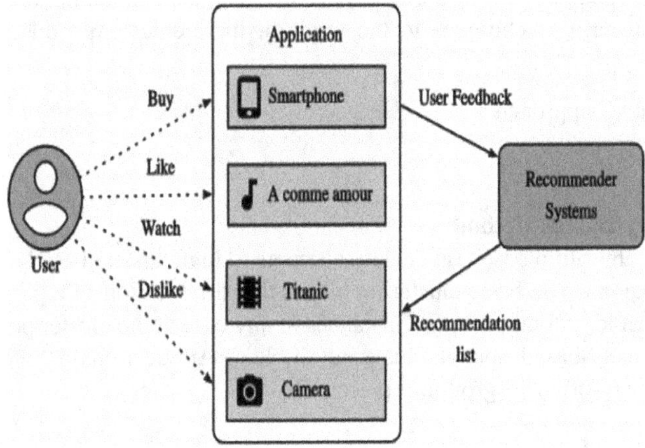

Fig. 1. Illustration of the recommendation process

3.1 Personalized Recommendation System (PRS)

PR allows digital integration of data in any format that is relevant to the user to be made available. Customized recommendations are divided into five types based on the method used in developing them as listed in Table 1:

3.1.1 Content-Based Filtering

CBFA suggests an element to consumers based on a product overview and a users' interest profile. CBFA is based on individual data and does not take into consideration the contributions of other users.

3.1.2 Collaborative Filtering

CFA user history database in the form of user ratings on objects. Collaborative filtering techniques often encounter three issues: cold start, sparsity, & scalability. A shared filtering approach is recommended to particular users when those websites are also preferred by similar users.

- User-based approach: user-based approach recommends users with similar taste interests. It matches the user according to the rating given.
- Item-based: Item-based advance is based on objects that are equally classified by the consumer.

3.1.3 Demographic Approach

A demographic recommendation is a method that relies entirely on user awareness. Sex, age, language abilities, disability, ethnic origin, mobility, employment position, homeownership, and location are all characteristics of the population. The software recommends goods based on customer demographic similarities.

3.1.4 Knowledge-Based Filtering Approach

Framework for knowledge recommendation focuses on the classification of objects of user interest. Simple facts. It is a technique for simultaneously filtering and filtering content.

3.1.5 Hybrid Approach

A hybrid method is a combination of the aforementioned approaches. In certain instances, combining cooperative filters with content-based filters may be more successful.

3.2 Non-personalized Recommendation System (NPRS)

NPRS papers focused on the product average of other consumers. Regardless of the user, each consumer gets the same reviews.

Table 1. Advantages and disadvantages of recommendation methods

Sr. No	Methods	Advantages	Disadvantages
1	Content-based filtering	1. There is no need for data from other users	1. A material analysis is needed to determine the item's properties
		2. There is no issue with a cold start	2. The goods' standards cannot be quantified
		3. May propose uncommon and fresh products	
2	Collaborative filtering	1. No knowledge of item characteristics is required for demographic suggestions	1. The accuracy of the suggestions depends on the scale of the data collection
		2. These will suggest beyond the particular user's interests	2. The methodology has difficulty with the cold beginning
3	Demographic	1. It does not depend on ratings of user items, it suggests every object to the customer	1. Demographic data processing contributes to data security issues
			2. Issue of durability and plasticity [9]

3.3 Challenges and Issues

3.3.1 Cold-Start

The recommendation to new users is difficult as its profile is almost empty & no products have yet been rated so that the program has no taste. It's called a cold start. This problem is addressed by an inquiry into certain recommended systems when creating a profile. Papers may also start cold when new and not categorized in the system beforehand. These two issues can also be addressed using hybrid methods.

3.3.2 Trust

People with short history can't have a voice that talks to people with a long history. The faith issue arises for the evaluation of a certain customer. Users could solve the problem by distributing goals.

3.3.3 Scalability

Due to increasing users and products, the framework requires more time to analyze information and make recommendations. Many of the resources are used to identify consumers and items with identical specifications.

3.3.4 Sparsity

Some customers in online stores with a huge no. of users & goods have always valued only a few things. Systems usually suggest creating user communities with their profiles via collaboration with others. These are suggested by the systems. If just a few products are evaluated by a customer, then his/her taste may be readily identified and connected to the wrong place. Lack of knowledge is the question.

3.3.5 Privacy

The most important issue was secrecy. The system needs to collect as much information as possible on the customer, including demographic details, & data on the position of a specific user to provide the most reliable and appropriate recommendation, many online shops provide effective privacy security with the use of advanced algos & programs [10].

In various applications, recommendation systems are utilized, such as news recommendations, movie recommendations, product recommendations, etc.
Recommendation systems merits are:

- The system is always up-to-date
- Recommend items as per user's preference
- Removal of redundant data

Demerits of Recommendation Systems are:

- Important data to make precise recommendations
- Changing users' preferences
- Difficulties with performance & scalability of many data
- Privacy is a problem [11].

4 Pattern Recognition (PR)

The pattern recognition and matching operation include parameters like mean, correlation, mutual knowledge, etc. Pattern recognition can be seen as a method in which patterns can be extracted and categorized from the dataset in the classification process. Pattern recognition and matching operation PR deals with the development & design of systems that identify data patterns. The aim of a PR system is therefore to examine & describe the real-world scene that is useful for the mission. Sensors are used to record natural world measurements classified by the PR process. A variety of PR meanings were given over the years. Watanabe describes an “As opposed to chaos; it’s an object that can be called loosely.” Described the PR as the area for machine detection in noisy or complex environments with meaningful regularities. PR is an overarching concept used to define a broad range of issues including recognition, description, classification, and pattern grouping [12, 13].

4.1 Pattern Recognition Models

Depending on the data analysis and classification process, pattern recognition models can be divided into different categories. Models may be used for the identification of patterns independently or dependently. The various model recognition models used are as follows:

4.1.1 Statistical Model

Every pattern is represented in terms of features by the statistic method of pattern recognition. Features are selected to allow non-overlapping space for different patterns. The probabilistic essence of both knowing that we are attempting to interpret and the way we are to convey it is understood. The features selected lead to function rooms that cluster recognizably, i.e. the correct interclass distance. It works very well. The decision limit is calculated following the study of the probability distribution of a pattern of class. This shows patterns for pre-processing operations that are appropriate for training. Features are chosen for training patterns study.

4.1.2 Structural Model

A series of complex patterns are outlined in the structural approach of pattern recognition by the number of subpatterns and grammatical rules by which these subpatterns are related. This model is about the structure and tries to identify an overall trend. The structural explanation language of structures and their structure is known as the pattern explanation language. Increased language descriptivity increases device complexity for syntax analysis.

4.1.3 Template Matching

Model Template matching of all pattern recognition models is the simplest and most primitive. Seamlessness is measured among 2 samples, curves, or pixels. Pattern recognized fits stored models whether rotating or scalar changes. This model relies on the efficiency of the processed models. The correlation function is used as a recognition feature & adapted to the training collection available. This approach is not available because amid distorted patterns it works.

4.1.4 Neural Network-Based Model

Neuron-like systems are parallel processing neural networks. An infield of classification, neural networks have an efficient result. It can change its weight and learn to use other recognition techniques. Perceptron is an early model of neurons. The arrangement is of two layers. When the output function of the perceptron is a phase, problems with classification occur when the function is linear rather than regression problems. MLP and RBF feed-in networks are the most frequently used pattern classification family in neural networks. Depending on the application criteria, different forms of neural networks are used.

4.1.5 Fuzzy Based Model

Pattern recognition plays an important role in complexity models which cannot be entirely understood by probabilistic theory: 'The intimate relationship of concept and pattern detection and classification between fuzzy sets depends very fundamentally on the fact that most schools in real-world are fluid in nature.' For fluctuating partitions of data sets, memantine techniques are used. A weighted distance similarity is also utilized to achieve a similarity level among the unknown meaning of form and type of reference.

4.1.6 Hybrid Model

The importance of fuzzy models in the identification of patterns is in the modeling of complexity which the theory of probabilism cannot understand. 'The close relationship between the concept of fuzzy sets & pattern recognition & classification is very fundamental because of the fluidity of the majority of real-world schools.' To generate fluid partitions of data sets, semantical techniques are applied. A weighted discrepancy between the form description and the reference type is also used to achieve a degree of similarity [14].

5 Literature Review

Zhang, X.-Y., et al. [2020] providea comprehensive introduction of research on solid pattern recognition in the sense to break three fundamental & implicit assumptions: closed world assumptions, separate & equivalent assumptions, & assumption of clean and broad data that forms the basis for most model models. In fact, in a complex, open, evolving world, our brains are constantly and increasingly strong in learning concepts with very few examples, under poor or noisy supervision. There are significant variations, related to these three conclusions, between human intelligence and artificial intelligence. The study will now analyze the limitations and inconveniences of current methods and recognize potential criteria for rigorous pattern recognition following substantial progress in improved accuracy [15].

Rajalakshmi, M., et al. [2019] aims to demonstrate the advantages and problems of different approaches used to establish the identification method. This paper enables researchers to develop new methods that will offer greater accuracy and lower error levels in good architecture and environments. Unconstructed handwritings like cursive, block, & tilt are key bottlenecks in this system that cause a great deal of difference in written modes, overlaps, and interconnections among characters. These systems have been developed to ensure high precision & reliability. This work summarizes numerous techniques in the written recognition method that can help researchers to identify the research gap in this field. The future scope of this work is to apply robust technology to ensure greater precision and lower error rates [16].

Aiwen Luo et al. [2019] Secure, effective, and robust walking are important for biped robots since all difficulties in real environments must be addressed. They suggest in this document utilize of a pattern-recognition scheme depends upon calculated force-sensory data from various surfaces to change the biped robot's stochastic speed. On a rigid surface, walking pattern accuracy of more than 98% is achieved to ensure pattern recognition depends upon force sensors as a valid indicator for speed change. [17].

Ahmed, M., Imtiaz, M.T., Khan, R. (2018) When the world goes global, when it comes to movies, people have plenty to choose from. In the world of films, you can choose from different genres, cultures, and languages. This poses the problem of recommending movies for automated systems users. There has been a good amount of work in this area to present. But the renovation space is always available. This article proposed a master-learning approach to suggest the development of a neural network for each cluster for users using the K-means clustering algorithm for separated related users [18].

Kaushik, S. (2018). Most recommendation systems are based on collaborative filtering technologies which are one of the most effective recommendation systems technology. The current methodology, however, suffers from the problem of performance, because it is necessary to determine the index of similarities for each user pair, to recognize their environmental conditions and scalability issues, in which millions of users and products have to make several recommendations per second. In the latest user-driven suggestions system the second biggest challenge is to measure the distances using various mathematical operations for better adjacent. This paper offers the efficient clustering algorithm of the K Means. Their experimental comparison in time, iteration, and root mean quadrangle error with current collaborative filtration techniques and k-means is present. Experimental results demonstrate the more reliable, slimmer, and precise recommendation method of clustering using effective k means [19].

Dabre, C., and Despande, A. (2017). With the recent growth of the internet as well as the growth of web services it is difficult to search for the necessary information you need as well as time-consuming. Recommendation systems in recent years have become more and more common and are being used in a variety of fields comprising movies, music, news, and books. This paper introduces a modern and effective way to group items and a recommendation framework based on weight. This paper focuses on the methods of clustering and the RFM ranking of the commodity [20].

Chen, Z., and Li, Z. (2016). The recommendation system has played a growing role in Internet services, overload of information is one of the most significant events on the Internet for users. A personalized system of recommendations is an efficient way of resolving the current issue. The difficulties of the extreme scarcity of user reviews are becoming increasingly serious with the creation of a collaborative recommendation with heterogeneous explicit feedbacks, such as 5-star rating systems. In this paper, we proposed a User Cluster (UCC) collaborative recommendation algorithm. They suggest a method to improve the accuracy of the score forecast, increasing the similarity of the successful user to achieve a more practical user similarity. Experimental findings suggest that on average, the proposed algorithm increased efficiency with the use of sparse data and the low-lying environment by 5.73% [21].

6 Conclusion

The recommendation system is nowadays broadly used. RS can be categorized into content-based collaborative filtering & hybrid approach. There are several data mining (DM) algorithms used in RS. Recommender or recommendation systems are a system that provides recommendations to users according to their tastes. Also, it is a system that can guide the user in a personalized way. It has been applied to a variety of applications. This survey paper defines several recommendation methods utilized in several systems. Clustering is helpful in various contexts for scanning, sorting, decision making, and mechanical training, including data mining, record analysis, image segmentation, and pattern recognition. Pattern recognition can be defined as data classification based on expertise or data obtained from and/or pattern representation previously acquired. pattern recognition. Finally, this survey will be very beneficial for further study.

References

1. Charmi, M.: Basics of data mining: a survey paper. Int. J. Trend Res. Dev. **4**(2), ISSN: 2394–9333. www.ijtrd.com
2. Vivek, K.: A survey on clustering algorithms for heterogeneous WSNs. Int. J. Adv. Networking Appl. **2**(4), 745–754 (2011)
3. Adomavicius, G., Tuzhilin, A.: Towards the next generation of recommender systems: a survey of the state-of-the-art and possible extensions. IEEE Transactions on Knowledge and Data Engineering, pp. 734–749 (2005)
4. https://whatis.techtarget.com/definition/pattern-recognition
5. https://www.geeksforgeeks.org/pattern-recognition-introduction/#: ~ :text=Pattern%20recognition%20is%20the%20process,patterns%20and%2For%20their%20representation
6. Kavita, N.: Data mining clustering methods: a review. Int. J. Adv. Res. Comput. Sci. Softw. Eng. **5**(4), 13−16 (2015)
7. Mann, A.K., Kaur, N.: Review paper on clustering techniques. Glob. J. Comput. Sci. Tech. (C) **13**(5 V.I), 42–47 (2013)
8. Lavanya, N.: Survey on various clustering techniques in data mining. Int. J. Sci. Res. **5**(12), 2319–7064 (2015)
9. Yagnesh, G., Patel, V., Patel, P.: A survey on various techniques of recommendation system in web mining. Int. J. Eng. Dev. Res. **3**(4) (2015). ISSN: 2321-9939
10. Mukta, K., et al.: Survey paper on recommendation system. Int. J. Comput. Sci. Inf. Technol. **3**(2), 3460–3462 (2012)
11. Susan, T., Jayalekshmi, S.: Survey on data mining techniques for recommendation systems. J. Emerg. Technol. Innovative Res. **2**(6), 1–5 (2015)

12. Paolanti, M., Frontoni, E.: Multidisciplinary pattern recognition applications: a review. Comput. Sci. Rev. **37**, 100276 (2020). https://doi.org/10.1016/j.cosrev.2020.100276
13. http://jprr.org/index.php/jprr/article/view/744
14. Seema, A., Rajeshwar, D.: Pattern recognition techniques: a review. Int. J. Comput. Sci. Telecommun. **3**(8), 25–29 (2012)
15. Zhang, X.-Y., Liu, C.-L., Suen, C.Y.: Towards robust pattern recognition: a review. Proc. IEEE **108**(6), 894–922 (2020). https://doi.org/10.1109/jproc.2020.2989782
16. Rajalakshmi, M., Saranya, P., Shanmugavadivu, P.: Pattern recognition-recognition of handwritten document using convolutional neural networks. In: 2019 IEEE International Conference on Intelligent Techniques in Control, Optimization, and Signal Processing (INCOS) (2019). https://doi.org/10.1109/incos45849.2019.8951342
17. Aiwen, L., Sandip, B., Tapas, K.M., Sunandan, D.: Dynamic pattern-recognition-based walking speed adjustment for stable biped-robot movement under changing surface conditions. In: 2019 IEEE 8th Global Conference on Consumer Electronics (GCCE) (2019)
18. Ahmed, M., Imtiaz, M.T., Khan, R.: Movie recommendation system using clustering and pattern recognition network. In: 2018 IEEE 8th Annual Computing and Communication Workshop and Conference (CCWC) (2018). https://doi.org/10.1109/ccwc.2018.8301695
19. Kaushik, S.: An enhanced recommendation system using the proposed efficient K means user-based clustering algorithm. In: 2018 International Conference on Advances in Computing, Communication Control, and Networking (ICACCCN) (2018). https://doi.org/10.1109/icacccn.2018.8748693
20. Dabre, C., Despande, A.: Recommendation system using clustering method based on item category and weight. In: 2017 International Conference on Current Trends in Computer, Electrical, Electronics, and Communication (CTCEEC) (2017). https://doi.org/10.1109/ctceec.2017.8455107
21. Chen, Z., Li, Z.: A collaborative recommendation algorithm based on user cluster classification. In: 2016 4th International Conference on Cloud Computing and Intelligence Systems (CCIS) (2016). https://doi.org/10.1109/ccis.2016.7790265

Networking and Information Security

A Novel Shoulder Surfing Resistant Password Authentication Scheme

Shailja Varshney(✉)

Department of Computer Engineering, Z.H. College of Engineering and Technology, Aligarh Muslim University, Aligarh, India
ShailjaVarahney@zhcet.ac.in

Abstract. Usability and security challenges with standard text passwords lead researchers and professionals to consider more complex authentication strategies. This paper analyzes the traditional text-based password scheme and their challenges and provides the solution over their drawbacks. This paper discusses different kinds of attacks by which authentication schemes can be compromised. The objective of this paper is to propose a new user authentication scheme to reduce the risk of identity theft. This text-based password scheme prevents shoulder surfing and is easy to use. The scheme can be used to create more secure passwords that are memorable.

Keywords: Security · Text password · Authentication · Shoulder surfing

1 Introduction

Humans mostly consider the problem in computer security systems. When humans interact with the computer system, there are three important factors: authentication, security and development of the secure systems. In this paper problem of system authentication is focused. The frequently used computer authentication method is, to submit a user name and a text password for a user. Most of the time text-based passwords suffer from shoulder surfing attacks. Here some techniques of shifting the text-based password are applied by which the password is secured from shoulder surfing attack, guessing attack, dictionary attack and other types of attacks. In this password scheme, every time a different password will be entered when a user login to the system. This password will be generated by the given formula so that no one can guess the password easily. This scheme has large password space so it is typical to recognize the password by brute force attack.

2 Background

2.1 Authentication Method

Authentication method can be split broadly into three major areas:

- Token-based authentication

R. S. Tomar et al. (Eds.): CNC 2020, CCIS 1502, pp. 135–143, 2021.
https://doi.org/10.1007/978-981-16-8896-6_11

- Biometric-based authentication
- Knowledge-based authentication

Bank cards and smart cards etc. are mostly used in the token-based authentication method. Most of the time, token-based authentication systems use knowledge-based passwords to improve the security of the system. For example, ATM cards are used with a PIN password for authentication purpose [1].

Fingerprint, iris scan, face recognition etc. are based on biometric authentication technique [2]. There are some drawbacks with this method like security systems based on this method can be costly and the identification process can be dull and it can be unreliable as well. But, this type of authentication method gives more security than other authentication methods.

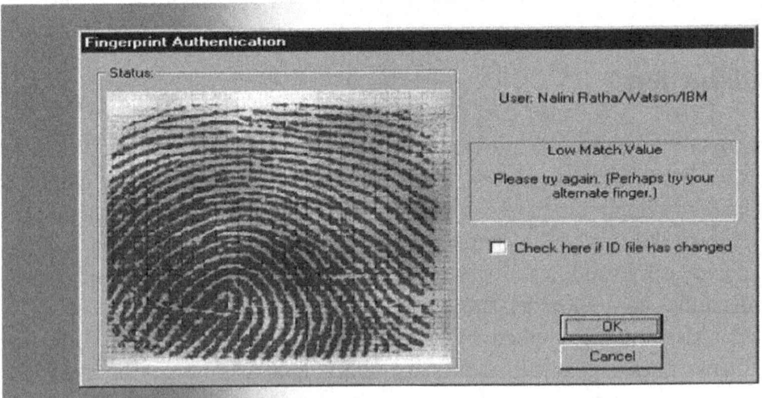

Knowledge-based authentication methods are used often. This method uses text-based passwords and picture-based passwords for authentication purpose [3, 4]. Picture-based password method is also divided into two parts: recognition- based and recall-based method. In the recognition-based method, the user gives a set of images during registration time, and the user is authenticated by recognition of the given images [5]. But in recall-based password, the user is authenticated by asking some questions that are given by the user at the registration time [6].

2.2 Possible Attack on Password

Brute Force Attack: In this type of attack, the attacker tries all possible combination of letters and numbers to break the password. Larger password space reduces the strength of this attack [7, 8].

Shoulder Surfing: In case of shoulder surfing, the text- based password has more risk because if the user uses the system in such a place where CCTV camera is available, the entered password can be captured by the CCTV camera and the attacker can break the password by zooming it [9-11].

Spyware Attack: Spyware is software which gains information about a person or organization without their knowledge, and sends information to unauthorized person or machine [12].

Dictionary Attack: In this type of attack, the attacker tries guessing passwords that are most common such as name, date of birth, etc. [7, 8].

Phishing Attack: In this type of attack, the attacker makes the fake website in which the user enters their password and the attacker steals it [13, 14].

3 Proposed Method

In this system, a user has to register before login. In this scheme, a registration page is provided which contains the user name and text-based password fields. Once the user is registered, he /she can login by entering a text password in the login page. To protect the authentication process from the attacks some crypto algorithm is applied to the given password.

User authentication system provides some functionality –

3.1 Registration

Firstly, the user has to register in this authentication process system. For the registration purpose there is a sign-up page in which user has to enter the username, password, confirm- password and then click on submit. By clicking on the submit button, all the given information is stored in the database.

3.2 Login

After successful registration, the login page is opened. In the login page, a random number is automatically generated by the system. The user enters their username and crypto password which is obtained by applying our scheme in order to login to the authentication system. This password is different every time the user wants to login.

3.2.1 Password Technique

In this system, the user can generate an alphanumeric password, length within 5 to 12 characters. At the login page, a random number generates. With the help of this random number and applied formula user can secure their password from various attacks.

Suppose a password is “khan029”, and at the login page, random number 15 is generated by the system. So by applying the formula given below:

$$((\text{random\_val} * 2) + 2)\%(\text{length} - 2)$$

“mjcp241” string is generated as a new password. Here “length” represents the length of the registered password which is 7 in this example. After applying these values in the given formula, 2 is generated it means the ASCII value of all the characters increased by 2.

3.3 Testing the System (Results)

Suppose, a user register in this Authentication system by some values such as –

Username- Ravi
Password- ravi123
Confirm password- ravi123

After clicking on the submit button, user gets registered for this system.

Now, the user goes for the login process. At the login page, a random value is displayed and by this value, user calculates how much the letters or digits must be shifted for the correct password. User get a random value “13”, so ((13 * 2) + 2) % (7 −2). With the help of this calculation, the user gets 3. So it means ASCII value of all the digits and letters must be shifted by 3, so the password after the calculation is “udyl456”. Here 7 is the length of the password that was registered.

On successful login, a welcome page is opened where a logout button appears for logout from the system.

4 Implementation

In this paper, we have developed a simple system for authentication process that has a registration page, a login page and welcome page to implement the proposed scheme.

4.1 Registration Page

Fig. 1. Registration page

In this page, the user will be registered by entering the user name and password. The password should be alphanumeric only, no special character and the length of the password should be 5 to12 (Fig. 1).

4.2 Login Page

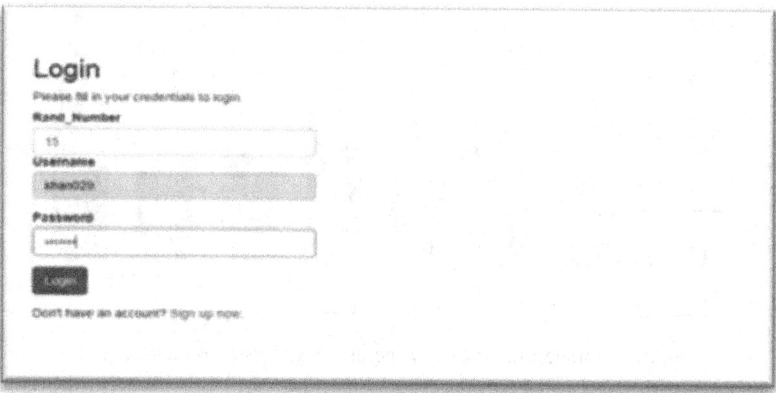

Fig. 2. Login page

Now login page will open. User is authenticated by entering the correct username and crypto password, calculated using our proposed scheme (Fig. 2).

5 User Study

In this Section, we describe the result of our scheme that is distributed into three major factors: Time taken to login and register, user-friendliness and secure from various attacks. To analyze our system we have performed user study on 30 peoples (Table 1).

5.1 Time Taken to Login and Register

Table 1. Table of users

User	Register	Login
Richa	11 s	25 s
Rakhee	17 s	24 s
Prakhar	15 s	22 s
Pallavi	19 s	26 s
Mukul	15 s	24 s
Ram	18 s	17 s
Anuja	15 s	35 s

To analyze our scheme, we have explained our scheme to these 30 peoples and asked them to register and login in this scheme. We observed the time that is taken by the user for register and login to the system.

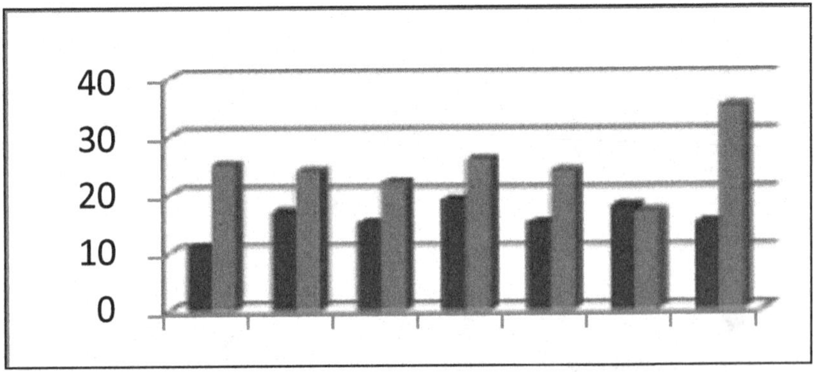

Fig. 3. Average time taken by the user for registration and login

Here average registration time is 16 s, and the average login time is 25 s. So this text password strategy is easy to use, more secure and user-friendly (Fig. 3).

5.2 User Friendliness

This scheme is user-friendly due to some reasons:

- User mostly uses text-based password scheme because he/she familiar with this scheme. Text- based password scheme has some drawbacks like shoulder surfing attack, dictionary attack and this scheme is secure from these attacks. In this scheme user can create their password from alphanumeric characters, i.e., 62 characters [A…Z, a….z, 0…9].
- User is not required to perform any complex calculation for the crypto password.

5.3 Secure from Various Attacks

To analyze our scheme, we discuss about the security of the system from some various attacks:

1) Shoulder Surfing Attack:
   It is secure from shoulder surfing attack because every time there will be a different crypto password when the user wants to login to the system. So, the attacker cannot guess the password by shoulder surfing attack. We have tested our scheme against shoulder surfing attack. Users are invited to login to the system in the presence of shoulder suffers and they are allowed to observe the login session for 5 to 8 times. They failed to guess the password.

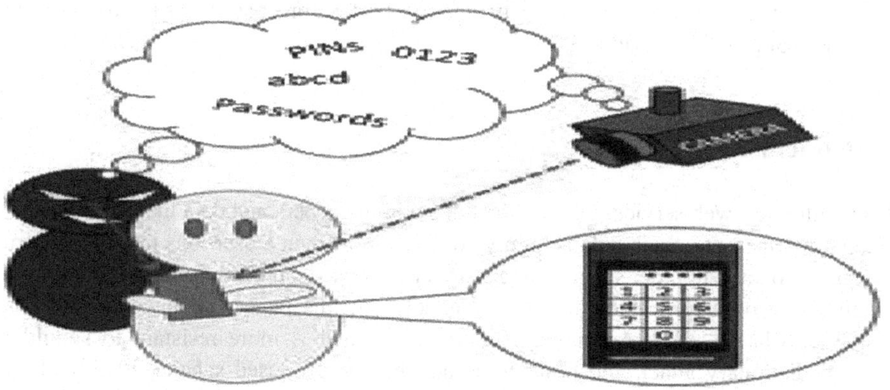

Fig. 4. Shoulder surfing attack

2) Dictionary Attack:
   The crypto password is the combination of any random numbers and charters [case sensitive] that are not present in any dictionary. So this scheme is also secure from the dictionary attack.
3) Brute-Force Attack:
   The password space of this scheme is large, i.e $2.1 * 10^{14}$. Large password space minimized the risk of brute force attack (Fig. 4).

6 Password Space

Password space is calculated to check the strength of the password against the brute-force attack. Here the password space is-

$$PS = A^N$$

Where A = all possible alphanumeric keywords. Here N is 62.

N = Length of the password

Here the minimum value of N is 5 and the maximum is 12. Here we calculate the password strength for N = 8 i.e., $2.1 * 10^{14}$.

7 Comparison with Traditional Password Scheme

Our proposed scheme provides advantages over the traditional password schemes:

- The Scheme provides large password space (10^{14}) that minimized the risk of brute-force attack.
- The crypto password is different every time when the user wants to login, so it is secure from shoulder surfing attack.
- This password scheme is easy to use, not provide any complex calculation for the password.
- This scheme provides the security against brute- force attack, shoulder surfing attack and dictionary attack.

8 Conclusion

Users often use web services and applications with their personal data like bank details, Aadhar number, etc. Such data is highly confidential. When a user logs into the system at a public place, shoulder surfing attacks are not uncommon. Traditional authentication schemes are often prone to fall to such attacks. In this paper, we have proposed a simple text-based password authentication system that is more resistant to shoulder surfing, dictionary attack and brute force attack. The proposed scheme is difficult to crack because of high password space and is easy to use as proved by the user study.

This system may be further improved by improving the password space and performing a user study on a larger scale.

References

1. Clarke, N.L., Furnell, S.M.: Authentication of users on mobile Telephones-A survey of attitudes and practices. Comput. Secur. **24**, 519–527 (2005)
2. Rajesh, K.: Continuous user authentication via unlabelled. In: IEEE International Joint Conference on Biometrics (IJCB 2017), Denver, Colorado. Syracuse University, NY, USA

3. Ziran, Z., XiyuLiu, L.Y., Zhaocheng, L.: A hybrid password authentication scheme based on shape and text. J. Comput. **5**(5) (2010)
4. Johnson Durai, A.R., Vinayan, V.: A novel crave-char based password entry system resistant to shoulder-surfing. Joseph's College of Arts and Science (Autonomous), Cuddalore, vol. 3, no. 3, pp. 273–276 (2014)
5. Xiaoyuan, S., Ying, Z., Owen, G.S.: Graphical passwords: a survey. In: 2005, 21st Annual Computer Security Applications Conference
6. Atish, N., Rajesh, B.: Analysis of knowledge based authentication system using persuasive cued click points. In: 7th International Conference on Communication, Computing and Virtualization (2016)
7. Alain Forget: A World With Many Authentication Schemes. A Thesis at Carleton University, November (2012)
8. Lashkari, A.H., Abdul Manaf, A., Masrom, M., Daud, S.M.: Security evaluation for graphical password. In: Cherifi, H., Zain, J.M., El-Qawasmeh, E. (eds.) DICTAP 2011. CCIS, vol. 166, pp. 431–444. Springer, Heidelberg (2011). https://doi.org/10.1007/978-3-642-21984-9_37
9. Sun, H.-M., Chen, S.-T., Cheng, J.-H.-Y.: A Shoulder surfing resistant graphical authentication system. IEEE Trans. Dependable Secure Comput. **15**(2), 180–193 (2018)
10. Sobradoand, L., Birget, J.-C.: Graphical passwords. Department of Computer Science, Rutgers University, An Electronic Bulletin for Undergraduate Research, vol. 4 (2002)
11. Wiedenbeck, S., Waters, J., Sobrado, L., Birget, J.C.: Design and evaluation of a shoulder-surfing resistant graphical password scheme. In: Proceeding of Advanced Visual Interface (AVI2006), pp.23−26 (2006)
12. Zainab, Z., Ayesha, K., Sarosh Umar, M., Muneeb, H.K.: One-tip secure: next-gen of text-based password. In: Information and Communication Technology for Competitive Strategies, pp. 235–243. Springer, Singapore (2019)
13. Akanksha, G., Vijaya, W.: A study of various password authentication techniques. In: International Conference on Advances in Science and Technology (ICAST) (2014)
14. Ramsha, F., Nadia, S., Sarosh Umar, M., Muneeb, H.K.: A novel text-based user authentication scheme using pseudo-dynamic password. In: Information and Communication Technology for Competitive Strategies, pp. 177–186. Springer, Singapore (2019)

MITM Attack on Modification of Diffie-Hellman Key Exchange Algorithm

Vijay Kumar Yadav[1(✉)], Rakesh Kumar Yadav[1], Brijesh Kumar Chaurasia[2], Shekhar Verma[1], and S. Venkatesan[1]

[1] Department of IT Deoghat, Indian Institute of Information Technology Allahabad, Jhalwa, Allahabad, UP, India
pcl2014002@iiita.ac.in

[2] Indian Institute of Information Technology, Lucknow, Lucknow, India

Abstract. After going through past research, it is observed that the security of data depends on five important key features such as authentication, data Integrity, mutual authentication between two parties, non-repudiation, and key exchange algorithm. Even if one of these features fail then it may breach security in real-world scenarios. The Diffie-Hellman Key Exchange (DHKE) algorithm allows securing one feature called key exchange in the cryptography field. However, this key exchange algorithm is unable to provide authentication. As a result, this key exchange scheme is prone to a hostile attack named as Man-In-The-Middle Attack (MITM). To solve this type of attack, a novel algorithm has been proposed called modification of the DHKE algorithm. In this algorithm, they claim that the MITM attack on classical DHKE can be prevented by applying the necessary functionalities like encryption and Zero-Knowledge Proof (ZKP). Although, after going through result analysis and working techniques, it is observed that the modified DHKE algorithm is still suffering from MITM attack. In this paper, the main objective is to develop an algorithm for finding out this type of security flaw in the existing modified DH algorithm which includes the concept of required authentication and encryption functions and able to perform the MITM attack on the existing modified DHKE algorithm.

Keywords: Diffie-Hellman key exchange · Zero knowledge proof · Man-in-the-middle attack · Modification of Diffie-Hellman key exchange

1 Introduction

The generation, storage and communication of data are expanding day by day at a rapid rate. So there would be a possibility of compromising the confidentiality, integrity and availability of sensitive data [12,14]. The need of the hour is to secure the data and work on its security aspects. Many researchers are doing experiments to search the perfect way to provide the security to data in an

R. S. Tomar et al. (Eds.): CNC 2020, CCIS 1502, pp. 144–155, 2021.
https://doi.org/10.1007/978-981-16-8896-6_12

efficient way so that it can't be compromised by any unauthorized third party. Hence, cryptography came up as a solution to secure the data by encrypting it. Many public key cryptosystems were proposed after the DH Seminal Paper [3]. Most of them are based on number-theory problems, for example Rivest, Shamir, Adleman (RSA) encryption scheme, ElGamal encryption [6,7,9,10]. Various crypto schemes based upon combinational problems also exists such as Wagner-Magyarik cryptosystem based on the Word Problem, out of both the number theory problems gain higher weight age than the combinational due to efficiency reasons. The modified DHKE algorithm came into existence when DH Algorithms failed to prevent the MITM attack. The DH protocol is used for securely exchanging communication secret key over an insecure channel. The major drawback of DHKE is that it fails to provide authentication between the communicating parties and as a result, this exchange scheme is vulnerable to an attack known as MITM. In the existing Modified DH protocol, the required property that is encryption and end-to-end entity authentication are implemented to resist the MITM attack. But the problem is that we can still able to perform the MITM attack on the existing algorithm. This vulnerability violates the Confidentiality, Integrity, and Availability (CIA) characteristics of sensitive information and the privacy of communicating users. It gives the permission to access the secret key by any unauthorized users. Hence, the main objective is to implement a technique to perform MITM on the existing Modified DHKE Algorithm to find the security flaw. This paper aims to improve the security of Modified DH Key Exchange Agreement by seeking out this type of security hole (MITM vulnerability) so that we can able to fix it for secure key exchange over an untrusted medium.

2 Related Work

Diffie-Hellman Key Exchange: The DHKE protocol allows two party to share secret information over insecure channel [3]. Two parties Alice and Bob choose a large prime number p and a non-zero integer g (primitive root) and make both p and g public. The key exchange algorithm proceeds as follows.

Step 1: Alice takes a private number $x \in Z_p^*$, computes $R_1 = g^x mod\ p$ and sends this R_1 to Bob. Similarly, Bob takes a private number $y \in Z$ computes $R_2 = g^y mod\ p$ and sends this R_2 to Alice.

Step 2: After Alice received the value of R_2, she computes $Key_{Alice} = R_2^x mod\ p = g^{yx} mod\ p$. Similarly Bob computes $Key_{Bob} = R_1^x mod\ p = g^{xy} mod\ p$. This makes $Key_{Alice} = Key_{bob}$ as the common key. The DHKE is based on the hardness of computational DH problem.

Elliptic Curve Diffie-Hellman Key Exchange: Alice and Bob agree on an elliptic curve $E(F_p)$ and point $P \in E(F_p)$. The key exchange steps are as under

Step 1: Alice takes a secret integer m_a, calculates $Q_a = m_a P$ and sends this Q_a to the Bob. Similarly Bob calculates $Q_b = m_b P$ and sends to this to Alice.

Step 2: Alice prepares $Key_{Alice} = m_a Q_b = m_a m_b P$, and Bob creates $Key_{Bob} = m_b Q_a = m_b m_a P$ $=Key_{Alice}$ to obtain the shared key [1].

Ring-LWE Based Diffie-Hellman Key Exchange: In ring-LWE based DH-like key exchange algorithm [4,14], two users exchange a single ring-LWE "*sample*" or public key each to arrive at approximate or "*noisy*" agreement on the ring element. In this protocol, both Alice and Bob agree on a public "big" $a \in R_q = \frac{Z_q[x]}{(x^n+1)}$, where R_q is a polynomial ring. The key exchange steps are as under

Step 1: Alice takes random *"small"* $s, e \in R_q$, computes $b = a.s + e$ and sends this b to Bob. Similarly, Bob takes, $s', e' \in R_q$ computes b' = a . s' + e' and sends this b' to Alice.

Step 2: After Alice receives the value of b', she computes the shared secret Key_{Alice} = s . b' = s.(a.s'+e') ≈ s.a.s', similarly Bob calculates Key_{Bob} = s'. b = s'.(a.s + e) ≈ s.a.s'. This makes $Key_{Alice} = Key_{Bob}$.

2.1 Security Issues with DH Key Exchange Algorithm

As mentioned above that DH protocol by itself is not able to establish the authentication feature of communicating users during the transmission of sensitive information over a channel [8]. As a result, it is prone to two attacks: a) Discrete Logarithm Computation b) MITM

Discrete Logarithm Computation Attack: If Eve (The attacker) wants to compute the shared secret key g^{xy}, then he can intercept R_1 and R_2 to get x and y respectively such as $log_g g^x = x$ and $log_g g^y = y$ (as we know that g is known to public.) Now, it will calculate the secret key as g^{xy}. As a result, the secret key is not private to authenticated parties anymore. To defend the DH protocol from the Discrete Logarithm Computation Attack, there are some recommendations:

a) The prime number p should be very large as possible (about more than 300 digits).
b) The generator g must be member of the multiplicative group $< Z_p^*, x >$.
c) The selected large random numbers should be used once that means destroyed after being used.

Man-In-The-Middle Attack: The DHKE algorithm is open to MITM attack in which the attacker sets itself to between the victims such as he or she can able to intercept whole conversation transferring from the sender to receiver and even more inject new one. As we know that generator g is known to public, the attacker itself can computes own public key as g^z and sends to Bob. When Bob responses by sending her reply, all replies are intercepted by the attacker. Here, the attacker is able to generate two keys: first one is shared between the attacker and the sender (Alice) and the other one is shared between the attacker and the receiver (Bob). For example: Active eavesdropping is a form of MITM attack. The following Table 1 explains the working flow diagram of MITM attack on Classical DHKE Algorithm.

3 Zero Knowledge Proof Protocol and Modification of DH Key Exchange Algorithm

Zero-Knowledge Proof (ZKP) protocol is a type of challenge/response authentication protocol that allows two parties to verify the legitimacy of the secret key without showing anything about secret to each-other [5]. The prover must respond to all challenges generated by the Verifier to prove its identity. This process can be within a number of rounds. In every single round, the verifier's confidence will be increased that the Prover is honest. Here, the verifier can't cheat to Prover as it doesn't have any type of knowledge about secret and also this protocol is repeated as number of time until verifier will be convinced. So verifier is unable to calculate the prover's secret. Embedding honest behavior while maintain privacy is the most valuable use of the ZKPs within the cryptography protocols [11].

Table 1. MITM attack on DHKE

Public parameter creation		
Both parties agree on a group $\mathcal{G}_q$ of prime order and security parameter 1^n with generators $g \in \mathcal{G}_q \backslash \{1\}$		
Sender	**Attacker**	**Receiver**
Selections of input parameter		
Input : Chooses a secret value $x \in \mathcal{G}_q$	*Input :* Chooses a secret value $z \in \mathcal{G}_q$	*Input :* Chooses a secret value $y \in \mathcal{G}_q$
The MITM attack		
Sender computes $R_1 = \{g^x\}$ *mod* p, and sends R_1 to receiver.		
	Attacker intercepts R_1 and keeps it secretively, then computes $R_3 = \{g^z\}$ *mod* p, and sends R_3 to both sender and receiver.	
	Attacker computes key $K_{AS} = R_1^z$ *mod* $p = g^{xz}$ *mod* p	Receiver computes $R_2 = \{g^y\}$ *mod* p and sends to the sender
After receiving the value of R_3 Sender computes $K_{AS} = R_3^x$ *mod* $p = g^{zx}$ *mod* p	Attacker intercepts R_2 and keeps it secretively, and computes key K_{AR} $= R_2^z$ *mod* $p = g^{yz}$ *mod* p	Receiver will calculate its secret key with the help of R_3 as $K_{AR} = \{R_3^y\}$ *mod* $p = g^{zy}$ *mod* p

3.1 Definition of ZKP

ZKP model can be defined as an interactive proof system that is (P, V) where P is considered as Prover and V is considered as Verifier. This system (P, V) is used for verifying a language membership statement for language over {0,1}. There are three major properties of ZKP protocol as following:

Completeness: The proof system will be complete only if statement is correct and the honest prover can able to satisfy to the honest verifier about this fact.

Soundness: The proof system will be sound if the statement is incorrect, then no insidious prover can satisfy to honest verifier about the truthfulness of the statement besides with small probability.

Zero-Knowledge: If the statement is correct, there should not be any possibility to calculate any information about statement other than the fact that the statement is true.

3.2 Modification of DH Key Exchange Algorithm

Modification of Diffie–Hellman Key Exchange Algorithm for Zero Knowledge Proof in 2012 explained ZKP based on DH key exchange protocol [6]. The proposed ZKP algorithm is implemented in two stages: the first stage explains the ZKP version-1 that is based on the basic of DH algorithm and in the second stage, an algorithm has been developed as ZKP version-2 that resists the MITM attack. In this proposed algorithm, both users (Prover and Verifier) will exchange the non-hidden data, but they won't reveal their secret information to each other for getting the unique secret key.

The existing Modified DH algorithm satisfied all required major properties of Zero-Knowledge Protocol and able to resist the known attack that is MITM attack. The description of modified DH key exchange algorithm is given in Fig. 1.

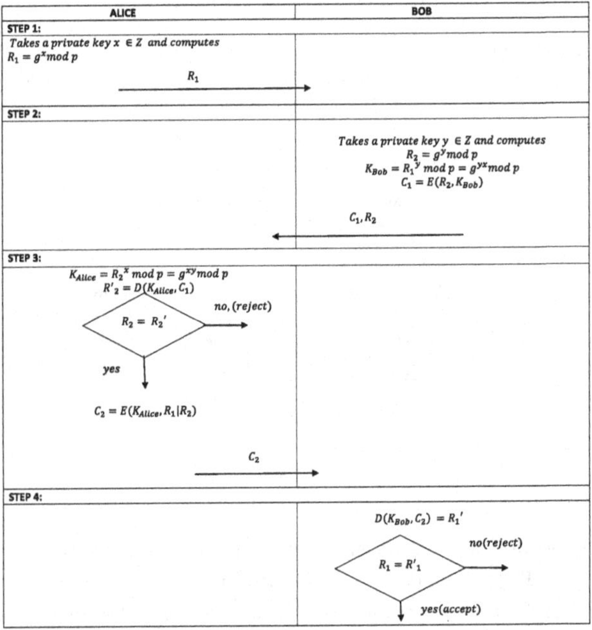

Fig. 1. Modification of DH key exchange algorithm

3.3 Comparison of Classical DH with Modified DH Algorithm

Improving the DH Secure Key Exchange in 2005 presented two modification of Classical DH Algorithm [2]. The first one is about to alter the domain of integers with $n = 2p^t$ and Z_n is cyclic. And the other one is about to change the domain to Gaussian Arithmetic $Z * [i]$. On comparing Classical DH with these two modifications, it showed that the generated symmetric key length with proposed two modifications is greater than classical DH. Even more, the proposed two modification of DH are much secure than the DH algorithm as both modification will take much time to be guessed. The following Fig. 2 represents the time comparison to compute secret key between two proposed modification of DH method and classical method:

4 Proposed Methodology

DH protocol is prone to MITM attack. The term "MITM" attack is a hostile attack that allows an attacker to relay and intercept all transferred data over open and insecure communication channel between two system [3]. For example, in an http transaction process, TCP connection establishment between client and server is main task. By applying some strategies, the attacker divides this single TCP connection into two connections, one for the client and the attacker and second for the attacker and the server. Once the connection is compromised by the attacker, the attacker will act as a proxy that can intercepts all communication over channel. This problem of MITM attack is solved in the implemented ZKP that is based on modified DH algorithm to ZKP protocol [6]. To defend against MITM attack, the end to end authentication and encryption of reply must need to implement. ZKP Version-2 resists this kind of attack by achieving major properties of ZKP protocol- Completeness, Soundness and Zero-Knowledge. But, there is still possibility of MITM attack in the proposed ZKP based on Modified DH algorithm. This kind of vulnerability makes it insecure and inefficient algorithm for communication over channel.

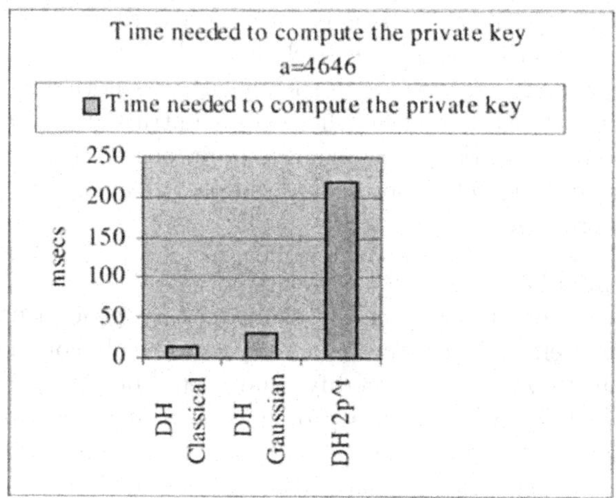

Fig. 2. Comparison analysis of classical DH and multiplicative DH [10]

4.1 Proposed Algorithm

Table 2. Symbol table of proposed algorithm

Symbol	Description
Alice	The prover that needs to prove her identity
Bob	The verifier that tests the legitimacy of prover
Eve	The attacker who will try to trick the prover
$E(K, R)$	Encryption of reply R using one's private key K
$D(K, R)$	Decryption of reply R using one's private key K
$R_1 \mid R_2$	Concatenation of both public keys R_1 and R_2

The implemented algorithm performs the MITM on the Modified DH Key exchange algorithm to expose its vulnerability (weakness) that is used for getting secure communication between two systems. In the proposed algorithm, two prime numbers p and g are selected by the trusted third party(trusted vendors) that are known to the public as said to be public numbers and can be sent in public through the internet. Where p is considered as a large prime number and g is called as primitive root of order $(p-1)$ in multiplicative group of integer modulo $< Z_p^*, x >$, called as generator. The basic notations used in the proposed algorithm is given in Table 2. The secret keys, one to be shared between sender and attacker and another one is to be shared between attacker and receiver respectively are as follows:

$$K_{Alice-Eve} = g^{xz} \mod p, \text{ and } K_{Bob-Eve} = g^{yz} \mod p$$

Once both Alice (Prover) and Bob (Verifier) are authenticated to Eve(Attacker) that leads as a result establishment of two connection-one between Alice and Eve and second one between Eve and Bob. Now the attacker can impersonate the whole communication over an open and untrusted network that uses the Modified DH algorithm for secure key exchange. The attacker acts as an active eavesdropper between Alice and Bob in such a way that both will rely that they are communicating directly to each-other over a untrusted private network. In protocol 1, it shows the working flow diagram of proposed Algorithm to perform MITM attack on existing ZKP protocol based on DH algorithm. The attacker generated two secret keys:

1) One to be shared between Alice and Eve
2) The other one to be share between Bob and Eve. After generating two different keys for both users, the attacker can relays the whole communication and intercept them to view, alter (modify) and even more inject new messages. This process will violate the privacy of the communicating users. This type of security flaw is dangerous for network based communication. Nowadays, everything is on network and data also transferred digitally over insecure channel. Hence, we should aware of this type of vulnerability like MITM attack in the network.

Protocol 1. MITM Attack on modified DHKE

Common Parameters: Both parties agree on a group $\mathcal{G}_q$ of prime order and security parameter 1^n, with generators $g \in \mathcal{G}_q \backslash \{1\}$

Inputs: Sender chooses x secret as $x \in \mathcal{G}_q$, Eve chooses z input as a secret $z \in \mathcal{G}_q$, and Receiver chooses y secret as $y \in \mathcal{G}_q$.

Outputs: Sender $K_{SR} = g^{xz}$ $modp$, Eve $K_{ES} = g^{xz}$ $modp$, $K_{ER} = g^{yz}$ $modp$, and Receiver $K_{RE} = g^{xy}$ $modp$

The Algorithm:

1. **Sender** Computes $R_1 = \{g^x\}$ $mod\ p$, and sends R_1 to receiver
2. **Attacker** Intercepts R_1 and keeps it secretively, and computes $R_3 = \{g^z\}$ $mod\ p$, sends R_3 to receiver.
3. **Receiver** Computes $R_2 = \{g^y\}$ $mod\ p$. Receiver will calculate its secret key with the help of R_3 as $K_{Bob} = \{R_3^y\}$ $mod\ p$ and encrypt either R_2 or R_3 with its secret key as $C_{Bob} = E\{K_{Bob}, R_2|R_3\}$. Now, receiver sends R_2 along with encrypted data as the pairs (R_2, C_{Bob}) to sender.
4. **Attacker** But, pairs (R_2, C_{Bob}) are intercepted by attacker and never reach to sender. Attacker computes its secret key to be shared with sender as $K_{Eve-Alice} = \{R_1^z\}$ $mod\ p$ and calculates the encrypted reply with key $K_{Eve-Alice}$ as $C_{Eve-Alice} = E\{K_{Eve-Alice}, R_3\}$. Attacker sends to sender the pairs $(R_3, C_{Eve-Alice})$ as sender will understand that data is coming from honest party.
5. **Sender** Computes its secret key as $K_{Alice} = \{R_3^x\}$ $mod\ p$ and then decrypts the received encrypted message as $R_1^{'} = D\{K_{Alice}, C_{Eve-Alice}\}$ and check that whether $R_1^{'} == R_3$, if it does not hold the condition then abort the connection otherwise attacker is verified to sender. The sender computes its encrypted data as $C_{Alice} = E\{K_{Alice}, R_1|R_3\}$ and sends to receiver.
6. **Attacker** Decrypts it with secret key $K_{Eve-Alice}$ as $R_3^{'} = D\{K_{Eve-Alice}, C_{Alice}\}$. The attacker will check that whether $R_3^{'} == R_1$, if it does not hold the condition then abort the connection otherwise sender is verified to attacker. The attacker computes its secret key to be shared with receiver as $K_{Eve-Bob} = \{R_2^z\}$ $mod\ p$ and decrypt the received encrypted message from receiver with $K_{Eve-Bob}$ as $R_3^{''} = D\{K_{Eve-Bob}, C_{Bob}\}$. and check that whether $R_3^{''} == R_2$, if it does not hold the this equality condition then abort the connection otherwise receiver is verified to attacker. The attacket encrypts either R_3 or R_2 as $C_{Eve-Bob} = E\{K_{Eve-Bob}, R_3|R_2\}$ and sends it to receiver.
7. **Receiver** Decrypts the received encrypted message with the help of its secret key K_{Bob} as $R_2^{'} = D\{K_{Bob}, C_{Eve-Bob}\}$. and check that whether $R_2^{'} == R_3$, if it does not hold the condition then abort the connection otherwise attacker is authenticated to receiver.

5 Implementation

Aim is to find out the vulnerability in existing ZKP protocol based on Modified DH Algorithm that is used for communication between two parties over an untrusted channel. As it is presented in the seminar paper that the existing modified DH agreement is able to resist the MITM attack by providing the encryption and mutual authentication. But, the problem is that there is still possibility of MITM attack in the existing modified protocol that makes it in-efficient in context of secure communication. MITM is attack in which the attacker sets itself between two users as make them believe that both users are communicating directly to each-other. All the test and implementation is performed on the Sage Math tool. The result obtained from the proposed research is mainly implemented in Python language. The python language is a programming language which is high level in nature. It is an interactive, general-purpose interpreted, object oriented. It can be easily integrated with many languages like C, C++ and Java etc. Here, first create the environment to run the Python Language. In this implemented program, we show the MITM attack on the proposed Modified DH protocol. For getting to access the services of cryptographic library and mathematical packages, we first create the environment through installing the Sage Math tool.

5.1 Sage Math Platform

"Sage Math (System for Algebra and Geometry Experimentation) is a free open-source mathematical software that has numerous mathematical features such as algebra, combinatorics, numerical mathematics, number theory, and calculus [13]. It is implemented on top of many existing open-source packages such as: Numpy, SciPy, matplotlib, Sympy, Maxima, GAP, FLINT, R and many more." Description of Hardware and Software: Desktop (PC- 2GB RAM), 80 GB Hard Drives, Ubuntu OS, and Sage Math Tool (Python Language).

5.2 MITM Attack on Existing Modified DH Agreement

The existing Modified DHKey Exchange Algorithm is able to resist the MITM attack during the communication between two or more authenticated users over an insecure channel. MITM is an attack which causes a whole communication to be impersonated by the untrusted third party resulting in loss of confidentiality, integrity, privacy and availability of common user's sensitive information. At the time of attack, the unauthenticated person is trying to make independent connections with the communicating users and impersonate all the information between them and pretending them as they are communicating directly to each-other over an insecure channel. But the fact is that the entire communication is controlled by the attacker. The attacker can able to modify, view and even inject new messages. It can be called as the vulnerability (weakness) of the Modification of DH protocol which compromises the internet security. The research work emphasizes on this kind of vulnerability and proposed algorithm is to show this weakness by performing the MITM on existing Modified DH algorithm.

6 Result Analysis

The classical DH Key algorithm doesn't provide end-to-end entity authentication itself during the communication over insecure medium. Hence, it is prone to MITM attack that allows an attacker to relay all messages and to intercept all communication without giving any type of hint of its presence to communicating parties. This type of vulnerability makes an in-efficient algorithm to existing ZKP algorithm based on DH Key Exchange Algorithm that is used for exchanging the secret key securely. Table 3 shows that how the attacker is performing the MITM attack by making the communicating parties rely that they are directly exchanging the messages to each-other over an insecure untrusted channel. As shown in Table 3, the attacker performs the same operation as both communicating parties such as it chooses the large random number and calculates its secret key for both users. Here, the attacker Eve generated two different secret keys such as one is shareable between Eve itself and Alice whether the other one is shareable between Eve and Bob. After creating the different secret keys for both users, the attacker Eve provides mutual authentication feature to both Alice and Bob for proving that he is honest user. As a result, the attacker Eve can alter or modify, view the communicating traffic between Alice and Bob and even more inject the new one. For performing MITM attack, we took 3 as a generator and 15 as a large prime number that are announced in public. The key length range, we choose, is 32 to 64 bit. We also calculated the time in seconds needed to perform the MITM attack on existing DH algorithm based on given generator, prime number and key length range.

7 Security Analysis

The existing ZKP protocol based on DH agreement is still prone to MITM attack. Hence, the existing modified algorithm is not efficient to use for exchanging the private key. For exposing the security flaw of Modified DH algorithm, here we performed the MITM attack. If the attacker can get access to sensitive information without revealing its presence, then that attacker is taking advantage of this type of security flaw (vulnerability).This technique is sometimes called as exploiting the security weakness. On comparing the classical DH key exchange protocol, existing modification of DH key exchange algorithm and the proposed algorithm in Table 3. As shown in this table, the time is computed in seconds to perform the DH algorithm, existing modified DH algorithm and proposed

Table 3. Comparison of classical DH, existing DH and proposed algorithm

Algorithm	64 bit	128 bit	256 bit	512 bit
Classical DH algorithm	0.39	0.45	0.40	0.41
Modified DH algorithm	0.39	0.40	0.42	0.44
Proposed algorithm	0.78	0.80	0.86	0.89

algorithm on basis of different key length in bit format. The Table shows the comparison of different algorithm. Here, from the above graph it has been concluded that total time to perform the classical DH and existing modified DH algorithm is less than that of proposed algorithm. Hence, there is possibility to prevent the MITM attack by assuming a threshold time. If the computation time of performing classical DH and existing algorithm will reach to its threshold time, then it will update its large prime number so that the attacker could not able to calculate the correct secret key for both sender and receiver, even if the attacker has access to all public values such as prime number and generator.

8 Conclusion and Future Work

Our motive is to improve the security or exposing the vulnerability (weakness) by seeking out security hole that is MITM attack, so that we can be fixed securely. Moreover, also prove that the existing ZKP protocol version-2 based on DH Key Exchange agreement is not secure to use for securely exchanging the secret keys over an untrusted network by providing the encryption of data and mutual authentication techniques. It is necessary to take a big step to secure key exchange algorithm because the security can only be guaranteed by maintaining efficiency of communicating traffic over an insecure network. Adding more security to the algorithm will reduce more security issues and challenges and ensure a safe and secure key exchange algorithm. Security is the field where every day new attacks are introduced. Therefore, we always need to find the solutions for these attacks. As a future scope of the proposed algorithm can suggest that we should go for the techniques to prevent such attacks. This may have some limitations but it will help securing the key exchange algorithm from attackers. As in result chapter, it has been explained that during the communication, the sender will update the large prime number value and then distribute to receiver so that the attacker could not able to listen whole communication.

References

1. Barker, E., Chen, L., Keller, S., Roginsky, A., Vassilev, A., Davis, R.: Recommendation for pair-wise key-establishment schemes using discrete logarithm cryptography. Technical report, National Institute of Standards and Technology (2017)
2. Bhattacharya, P., Debbabi, M., Otrok, H.: Improving the Diffie-Hellman secure key exchange. In: 2005 International Conference on Wireless Networks, Communications and Mobile Computing, vol. 1, pp. 193–197. IEEE (2005)
3. Diffie, W., Hellman, M.: New directions in cryptography. IEEE Trans. Inf. Theory **22**(6), 644–654 (1976)
4. Ding, J., Xie, X., Lin, X.: A simple provably secure key exchange scheme based on the learning with errors problem. IACR Cryptology EPrint Arch. **2012**, 688 (2012)
5. Feige, U., Fiat, A., Shamir, A.: Zero-knowledge proofs of identity. J. Cryptol. **1**(2), 77–94 (1988). https://doi.org/10.1007/BF02351717

6. Ibrahem, M.K.: Modification of Diffie-Hellman key exchange algorithm for zero knowledge proof. In: 2012 International Conference on Future Communication Networks, pp. 147–152. IEEE (2012)
7. Kleinjung, T., et al.: Factorization of a 768-Bit RSA modulus. In: Rabin, T. (ed.) CRYPTO 2010. LNCS, vol. 6223, pp. 333–350. Springer, Heidelberg (2010). https://doi.org/10.1007/978-3-642-14623-7_18
8. Merkle, R.C.: Secure communications over insecure channels. Commun. ACM **21**(4), 294–299 (1978)
9. Milanov, E.: The RSA algorithm. RSA Laboratories, pp. 1–11 (2009)
10. Schnorr, C.P., Jakobsson, M.: Security of signed ElGamal encryption. In: Okamoto, T. (ed.) ASIACRYPT 2000. LNCS, vol. 1976, pp. 73–89. Springer, Heidelberg (2000). https://doi.org/10.1007/3-540-44448-3_7
11. Simmons, G.J., Purdy, G.B.: Zero-knowledge proofs of identity and veracity of transaction receipts. In: Barstow, D., et al. (eds.) EUROCRYPT 1988. LNCS, vol. 330, pp. 35–49. Springer, Heidelberg (1988). https://doi.org/10.1007/3-540-45961-8_4
12. Yadav, R.K., Verma, S., Venkatesan, S., et al.: Regularization on a rapidly varying manifold. Int. J. Mach. Learn. Cybern. **11**, 1–20 (2020)
13. Yadav, V.K., Anand, A., Verma, S., Venkatesan, S.: Private computation of the Schulze voting method over the cloud. Cluster Comput. **234**, 1–15 (2019)
14. Yadav, V.K., Venkatesan, S., Verma, S.: Man in the middle attack on NTRU key exchange. In: Verma, S., Tomar, R.S., Chaurasia, B.K., Singh, V., Abawajy, J. (eds.) CNC 2018. CCIS, vol. 839, pp. 251–261. Springer, Singapore (2019). https://doi.org/10.1007/978-981-13-2372-0_22

Reinventing ICTM for Sustainability and Growth - An Interdisciplinary Approach

Sumant Kumar Tewari[1,2](✉)

[1] Operations and IT, ICFAI Business School (IBS), Hyderabad, India
sumant@ibsindia.org

[2] The ICFAI Foundation for Higher Education (IFHE), (Deemed to Be University U/S of UGC Act 1956), Hyderabad, India

Abstract. In dynamic business environment sustainability and growth of manufacturing industry is highly dependent on the integration of various disciplines of business. This research identifies three important constructs and their items or variables which belong to three different disciplines namely marketing, operations and ICT. Later hierarchical relationship among the interdisciplinary items has been established with the help of ISM technique. After this items are classified into various classes by using MICMAC analysis. This research identifies ICTM variables as a critical variable in the integration process because of their higher driving power.

Keywords: ICT · ICTM · System integration · Sustainability

1 Introduction

In the era of globalization and liberalization, business environment has become very dynamic [1]. Sustainability of conventional organizations which have not integrated their various functional areas has become very tough [2]. Business organizations are facing the intense competition on the front of cost, quality, profit margin, variation in demand, product innovation, reachability and quick response to customers' demand. Individual functional areas of business organization have limited scope to perform if they work in isolation. Literature evidence that if, various functional areas of business work together as a system then synergic effect can be observed easily [3]. This could be easily understood by an illustration that marketing department creates or identifies the demand, operations department creates goods and services to fulfill that demand and finance takes care of flow of money in the system. Information and communication technology (ICT) works as a facilitator that helps in executing various business functions effectively and efficiently. This paper tries to associates the different disciplines of business together by establishing the hierarchical relationship among their variables or items so that organizations can understand their driving and dependence role and take action accordingly. Objectives of this research have been achieved through Interpretive Structural Modeling model (ISM) and MICMAC analysis. Through extensive literature review three construct namely marketing efficiency, operational leadership and ICT and their variables or items has been identified. Later data from various academicians and practitioners has been collected through

R. S. Tomar et al. (Eds.): CNC 2020, CCIS 1502, pp. 156–166, 2021.
https://doi.org/10.1007/978-981-16-8896-6_13

questionnaire having categorical response for establishing the relationship between the items of interdisciplinary constructs. Research indicates that ICTM variables have highest driving power which reflects its importance in various activities of business and it requirement for sustainability and growth.

2 Literature Review

Sustainability and growth of any manufacturing organization depends of its performance in dynamic business environment [2]. Performance of any organization is measured on two fronts namely market positions and financial positions [4]. Market performance deals with market share, customer satisfaction, competitive position in market etc. while financial performance deals with return on investment, profit margin, revenue, etc. [5]. In business organizations marketing department is hold responsible for these activities. It is true that it is the responsibility of marketing department to create or identify the demand, sale the product or services, generate revenue and ensure customer retention. Beyond a limit marketing department cannot perform well if it works in isolation. For illustration operation department of any company is not producing quality and innovative products at affordable price to meet the customers demand then at what extent marketing people call sell it in the market could be easily understood. Operations department cannot accurately define the short term and long term demand of the product, customers' expectations from the product etc. without the help of marketing department. Literature evidence the raising need of integration over the period of time. ICT has potential to integrate the various departments of organizations effectively and efficiently [6]. ICT brings transparency in the system by providing quality information. This transparency brings trust among stakeholders that is very necessary for building an organization as a system. This research has identified three key disciplines of any business.

2.1 Marketing Efficiency

Marketing efficiency is explained by the ratio of marketing outcome and input in marketing activities. This efficiency measures have both components qualitative and quantitative which is further classified into financial and non-financial measures [4]. Financial measure is called financial performance while non-financial measure is called market performance. In this study two constructs of marketing efficiency, market performance and financial performance [7, 8] is considered.

2.2 Operational Leadership

Operational leadership indicates the better operational performance of the organization than their competitors on the front of quality, cost, product innovation, time to market, and delivery dependability [5, 9]. This research has taken these five items of operational leadership for study.

2.3 ICTM

Information and communication technology management covers adoption and usage of ICT for increasing the organizational performance. ICT is considered is facilitator which enhances the performance of any process or activity. So, alignment of ICT strategies with overall business strategy is required to harness its full capacity [5, 10]. This study has considered two items of ICTM construct level of adoption and strategic alignment.

Table 1. Research construct, items and literature reference

Construct	Items	Code	Literature reference
Marketing efficiency	Market performance	M1	[4, 5, 7, 8, 11–13]
	Financial performance	M2	
Operational leadership	Cost	O1	[5, 9, 14–17]
	Quality	O2	
	Delivery dependability	O3	
	Product innovation	O4	
	Time to market	O5	
ICTM	Strategic alignment	I1	[5, 6, 10, 18, 19]
	Level of adoption	I2	

3 Research Methodology

Through extensive literature review two constructs operational leadership and information and communication technology management and their items has been identified that are directly and/or indirectly related with the marketing efficiency construct. Various researches evidence the significant relationship between the construct marketing efficiency, operational leadership and ICTM [5]. This research identifies nine items (Table 1) related to these three interdisciplinary constructs. To predict the hierarchical relationship between these items ISM technique has been used where the judgment of group of experts is used to identify the relationship between the items. Structural self-interaction matrix (SSIM) has been used to collect the information from group of experts having academicians and practitioners from the field of marketing, finance, operations and ICT management who were involved in research and publish papers in reputed journals or provide consultancy services or working for reputed manufacturing firms in India. Creation of sampling frame was based on snowball technique, professional networking sites and websites of reputed organizations related to education and manufacturing.

3.1 Data Collection

In this study 25 manufacturing firms from different industry including FMCG, electrical & electronics, automotive and chemical and 6 academic institutes of India were identified. Later data was collected from 32 industry experts and 24 academicians with the help of questionnaire.

3.2 Interpretive Structural Modeling (ISM)

The ISM was first proposed by J. Warfield in 1973 [24] to analyze the complex socioeconomic system [23–25]. In this approach complex system is analyzed systematically and presented in graphical form which is further used for analytical interpretation [26].

Expert opinions are used to decide the relationship among the items. The steps involved in constructing an ISM [27, 28] are as follows:

Step 1: Identify the Factors
Step 2: Identify the Contextual Relationship
Step 3: Develop the structural Self-Interaction Matrix (SSIM)
Step 4: Prepare the Reachability Matrix
Step 5: Prepare the Canonical Matrix
Step 6: Develop the diagraph
Step 7: Remove the transitivity from the diagraph
Step 8: Convert the diagraph to ISM
Step 9: Model Review

3.2.1 Structural Self-interaction Matrix (SSIM)

With the inputs from the rigorous literature review, the items from different discipline are identified. Qualitative study where experts' opinion has been considered for identifying the causal relationship among the items has been used. For presenting the directional relationship between items (i (row) and j (column)) four symbols namely 'V', 'A', 'X' and 'O' have been used (Table 2) and following rules has been followed:

V: Item i determines Item j.
A: Item j determines Item i.
X: Item i determines Item j and Item j determines Item i.
O: Item i and Item j are not related.

Table 2. Structural self-interaction matrix (SSIM)

Code	I2	I1	O5	O4	O3	O2	O1	M2	M1
M1	A	A	A	A	A	A	A	X	
M2	A	A	A	A	A	A	A		
O1	A	A	A	A	A	X			
O2	A	A	A	A	A				
O3	A	A	V	O					
O4	A	A	V						
O5	A	A							
I1	V								
I2									

3.2.2 Initial Reachability Matrix (IRM)

IRM is a binary matrix which is developed by substituting the symbols of SSIM by 0 and 1. Substitution rules are mentioned in Table 3.

Table 3. Substitution rules for creating IRM from SSIM

IF the value at (i, j) position in the SSIM is	Then entry in the reachability matrix
V	Value at (i, j) = 1 and Value at (j, i) = 0
A	Value at (i, j) = 0 and Value at (j, i) = 1
X	Value at (i, j) = 1 and Value at (j, i) = 1
O	Value at (i, j) = 0 and Value at (j, i) = 0

Incorporation of transitivity in IRM provides the final reachability matrix as shown in Table 4.

Table 4. Final reachability matrix

Code	M1	M2	O1	O2	O3	O4	O5	I1	I2
M1	**1**	1	0	0	0	0	0	0	0
M2	1	**1**	0	0	0	0	0	0	0
O1	1	1	**1**	1	0	0	0	0	0
O2	1	1	1	**1**	0	0	0	0	0
O3	1	1	1	1	**1**	0	1	0	0
O4	1	1	1	1	0	**1**	1	0	0
O5	1	1	1	1	0	0	**1**	0	0
I1	1	1	1	1	1	1	1	**1**	1
I2	1	1	1	1	1	1	1	0	**1**

3.2.3 Level Partitions

Level Partition is carried out to find the level of the factors [24]. Reachability matrix is used for this purpose. Reachability set presenting the driving power of elements and antecedent set presenting the dependence power of elements are identified. After this the intersection set are developed for all the items. If the intersection and reachability set are same for the item(s) then they are leveled. Once the levels are identified for item (s) it is eliminated from the reachability and antecedent set of other items. Same process is repeated until all items are leveled (Table 5). These levels are used for placing the items level wise and building the digraph or directed graph.

Table 5. Level partitions

Iteration 1				
Factors	Reachability matrix	Antecedent set	Intersection set	Level
M1	M1,M2	M1,M2,O1,O2,O3,O4,O5,I1, I2	M1,M2	I
M2	M1,M2	M1,M2,O1,O2,O3,O4,O5,I1, I2	M1,M2	I
O1	M1,M2,O1,O2	O1,O2,O3,O4,O5,I1,I2	O1,O2	
O2	M1,M2,O1,O2	O1,O2,O3,O4,O5,I1,I2	O1,O2	
O3	M1,M2,O1,O2,O3,O5	O3,I1,I2	O3	
O4	M1,M2,O1,O2,O4,O5	O4,I1,I2	O4	
O5	M1,M2,O1,O2,O5	O3,O4,O5,I1,I2	O5	
I1	M1,M2,O1,O2,O3,O4,O5,I1, I2	I1	I1	
I2	M1,M2,O1,O2,O3,O4,O5,I2	I1,I2	I2	
Iteration 1I				
Factors	Reachability matrix	Antecedent set	Intersection set	Level
O1	O1,O2	O1,O2,O3,O4,O5,I1,I2	O1,O2	II
O2	O1,O2	O1,O2,O3,O4,O5,I1,I2	O1,O2	II
O3	O1,O2,O3,O5	O3,I1,I2	O3	
O4	O1,O2,O4,O5	O4,I1,I2	O4	
O5	O1,O2,O5	O3,O4,O5,I1,I2	O5	
I1	O1,O2,O3,O4,O5,I1,I2	I1	I1	
I2	O1,O2,O3,O4,O5,I2	I1,I2	I2	
Iteration 1II				
Factors	Reachability matrix	Antecedent set	Intersection set	Level
O3	O3,O5	O3,I1,I2	O3	
O4	O4,O5	O4,I1,I2	O4	
O5	O5	O3,O4,O5,I1,I2	O5	III
I1	O3,O4,O5,I1,I2	I1	I1	
I2	O3,O4,O5,I2	I1,I2	I2	
Iteration 1V				
Factors	Reachability matrix	Antecedent set	Intersection set	Level
O3	O3	O3,I1,I2	O3	IV
O4	O4	O4,I1,I2	O4	IV
I1	O3,O4,I1,I2	I1	I1	
I2	O3,O4,I2	I1,I2	I2	
Iteration 1V				
Factors	Reachability matrix	Antecedent set	Intersection set	Level
I1	I1,I2	I1	I1	
I2	I2	I1,I2	I2	V
Iteration 1V				
Factors	Reachability matrix	Antecedent set	Intersection set	Level
I1	I1	I1	I1	VI

3.2.4 Building the Digraph (ISM Model)

The ISM hierarchy is the graphical form of the reachability matrix where items are placed in levels and arrows are used to present the directional relationship between them. Finally ISM model is created by removing all transitivity (Fig. 1).

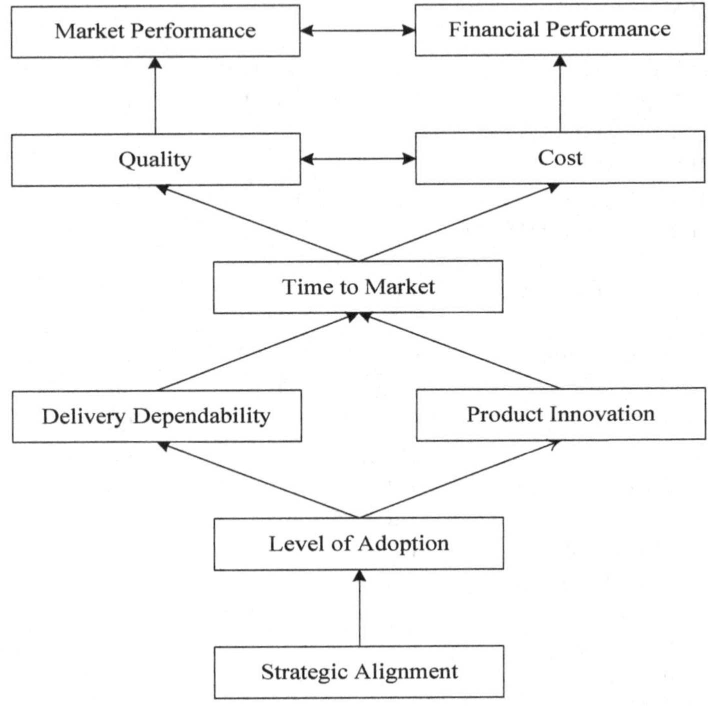

Fig. 1. ISM model of research items

Table 6. Driving and dependence power of items

Code	M1	M2	O1	O2	O3	O4	O5	I1	I2	DrP
M1	**1**	1	0	0	0	0	0	0	0	**2**
M2	1	**1**	0	0	0	0	0	0	0	**2**
O1	1	1	**1**	1	0	0	0	0	0	**4**
O2	1	1	1	**1**	0	0	0	0	0	**4**
O3	1	1	1	1	**1**	0	1	0	0	**6**
O4	1	1	1	1	0	**1**	1	0	0	**6**
O5	1	1	1	1	0	0	**1**	0	0	**5**
I1	1	1	1	1	1	1	1	**1**	1	**9**
I2	1	1	1	1	1	1	1	0	**1**	**8**
DP	**9**	**9**	**7**	**7**	**3**	**3**	**5**	**1**	**2**	

Note: DP-Dependence Power; DrP-Driving Power

3.3 MICMAC Analysis

Final reachability matrix (Table 4) is used to calculate the driving and dependence power of the items (Table 6). Sum of each row presents the driving power of respective item while sum of each column presents the dependence power of respective item.

Driving and Dependence power values of items, computed in Table 6, is used for the analysis where items are classified into various groups (Fig. 2).

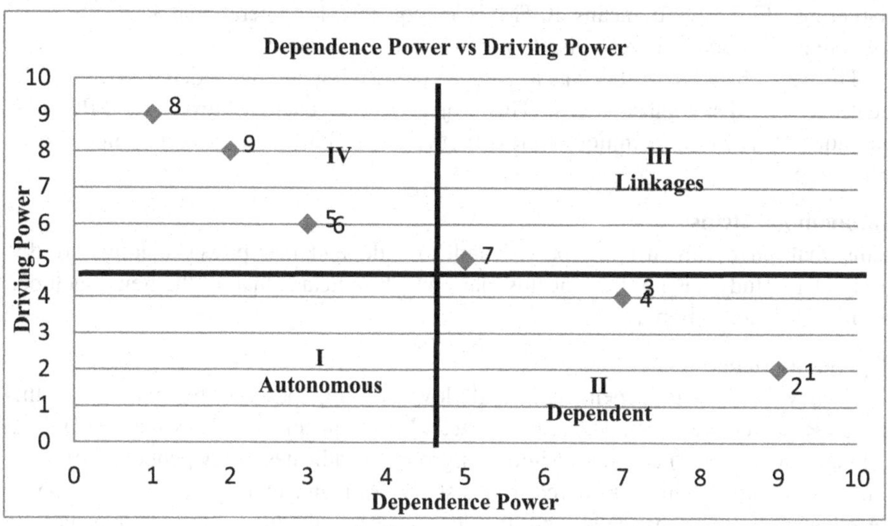

Fig. 2. MICMAC analysis of research items

4 Key Findings and Discussion

This research identifies three interdisciplinary constructs and their items with the help of extensive literature review. Through ISM technique, hierarchy level, driving power and dependence power of each item has been identified. Later items are placed according to their hierarchy and relationship between them is represented with the help of directed arrows. After removing the transitive dependency it provided diagram which graphically represents the arrangements of items and relationship between them and is called ISM model (Fig. 1).

Analysis of ISM model provide us information that items of ICTM construct, strategic alignment (I1) and level of adoption (I2) have occupied lower level (V and VI) in the model. Strategic alignment influences the level of ICT adoption in the manufacturing organizations. So if the ICT strategy is alignment with overall strategy of organization then it determines the level of ICT adoption in the organization.

Level II, III and IV has been occupied by the items of operational leadership construct. 'Delivery dependability' (O3) and 'product innovation' (O4) items have occupied place at level IV and ISM model represents the lack of relationship between them but both items are dependent on 'level of ICT adoption' and have potential to determine the ‘time to market’ (O5) which has secured place at level III. ‘Cost’ (O1) and ‘Quality’ (O2) are placed at level II. ISM model shows the interdependency between these two items. These two items are directly affected by ‘time to market’ (O5) factor. ‘Cost’ and ‘Quality’ factors are directly responsible for the ‘market performance’ (M1) and ‘financial performance’ (M2) which are the items of marketing efficiency. These items are placed at level I and are interrelated.

Observation of ISM model from the construct point of view shows the direct relation between ICTM and operational leadership and operational leadership and marketing efficiency. It means ICTM is responsible for operational leadership and operational leadership is responsible for marketing efficiency.

The next objective of this was to analyze the driving and dependence power of the identified interdisciplinary items. This objective has been achieved by MICMAC technique. MICMAC techniques classify the items into four groups which are as following:

Autonomous Items
Items that have low driving power and low dependence power belongs to this group. This study has no item for this class which indicates that all the items included in this study are important.

Dependent Items
Items having strong dependence and low driving power are placed in this group. Research items market performance (M1), financial performance (M2), cost (O1) and quality (O2) are placed into this group. It indicates the dependency of these items on the other items considered in this study. So management should careful about these factors because change in these factors occurs mainly due to changes in rest of the factors.

Linkage Items
Items that have strong driving power as well as strong dependence power are placed into this group. One item ‘time to market’ (O5) is placed into this group which indicates that it is the most sensitive item among all the items considered for this analysis. Any changes in system will affect this item.

Independent Items
Items that have high driving power and low dependence power are placed into this group. Four items ‘delivery dependency’ (O3), ‘product innovation’ (O4), ‘strategic alignment’ (I1) and ‘level of adoption’ (I2) have secured place in this group. Changes in these items will bring significant change in the system or variables.

5 Conclusion and Future Research Scope

This research is an effort to view the organizations having different discipline as a system. Moving ahead in this direction this research has identified three different constructs and associated items, related to three different disciplines namely marketing, operations and ICT. Through ISM techniques items are placed in different level and interrelationship among them has been established successfully. Later driving and dependence power of items has been calculated and used for MICMAC analysis. This research identifies ICT items has highest driving power and are responsible for achieving operational leadership as well as marketing efficiency. Items of marketing efficiency have been identified as highest dependable variable which is guided by the set of operational and ICTM activities. 'Time to market' has been identified has most sensitive variable or item which affects the entire system. In a holistic prospective research has identified as key enabler which have potential to enhance marketing efficiency by improving the market and financial performance.

Any possible bias in this research can provide scope for future research. Relationship between the items has not been assigned weight this could be done with the help of structural equation modeling (SEM). Instead of MICMAC analysis fuzzy MICMAC analysis could be used for more precise result.

References

1. Latif, Z., Mengke, Y., Danish, L.S.: The dynamics of ICT, foreign direct investment, globalization and economic growth: panel estimation robust to heterogeneity and cross-sectional dependence. Telematics Inform. **35**(2), 318–328 (2018)
2. Hong, P., Jagani, S., Kim, J., Youn, S.H.: Managing sustainability orientation: an empirical investigation of manufacturing firms. Int. J. Prod. Econ. **211**, 71–81 (2019)
3. Campos, L.M., Vazquez-Brust, D.A.: Lean and green synergies in supply chain management. Supply Chain Manag. **21**(5), 627–641 (2016)
4. Kalpan, R., Norton, D.: The balance score card-measures that derive performance. Harvard Bus. Rev. **70**, 71–79 (1993)
5. Tewari, S.K., Misra, M.: Information and communication technology: a tool for increasing marketing efficiency. Int. J. Inf. Technol. Manag. **14**(2/3), 215–231 (2015)
6. Tewari, S.K., Misra, M.: Marketing efficiency: a construct to evaluate strategic ICT adoption. Int. J. Bus. Excell. **6**(6), 735–749 (2013)
7. Ptok, A., Rupinder, P.J., Werner, J.R.: Selling, general, and administrative expense (SGA)-based metrics in marketing: conceptual and measurement challenges. J. Acad. Mark. Sci. **46** (6), 987–1011 (2018)
8. Lamberti, L., Noci, G.: Marketing strategy and marketing performance measurement system: Exploring the relationship. Eur. Manag. J. **28**(2), 139–152 (2010)
9. Santos Bento, G.D., Tontini, G.: Developing an instrument to measure lean manufacturing maturity and its relationship with operational performance. Total Qual. Manag. Bus. Excell. **29**(9–10), 977–995 (2018)
10. Nguyen, T., Sherif, J., Newby, M.: Strategies for successful CRM implementation. Inf. Manag. Comput. Secur. **15**(2), 102–115 (2007)
11. Morgan, N.A., Clark, B.H., Gooner, R.: Marketing productivity, marketing audits, and system for marketing performance assessment-Integrating multiple perspectives. J. Bus. Res. **55**, 362–375 (2002)
12. Day, G.S., Nedungadi, P.: Managerial representations of competitive advantage. J. Mark. **58** (2), 31–44 (1994)
13. Day, G.S., Fahey, L.: Valuing marketing strategies. J. Mark. **52**(July), 45–57 (1988)
14. Inman, R.A., Sale, R.S., Green, K.W., Whitten, D.: Agile manufacturing: relation to JIT, operational performance and firm performance. J. Oper. Manag. **29**(4), 343–355 (2011)

15. Vachon, S., Klassen, R.D.: Environmental management and manufacturing performance: the role of collaboration in the supply chain. Int. J. Prod. Econ. **111**(2), 299–315 (2008)
16. Lia, S., Ragu-Nathanb, B., Ragu-Nathanb, T.S., Rao, S.S.: The impact of supply chain management practices on competitive advantage and organizational performance. Int. J. Manag. Sci. **34**(2), 107–124 (2006)
17. Gunasekaran, A., Patel, C., Tirtiroglu, E.: Performance measures and metrics in a supply chain environment. Int. J. Oper. Prod. Manag. **21**(1/2), 71–87 (2001)
18. Li-Hua, R.A., Khali, T.P.: Technology management in China: a global prospective and challenging issues. J. Technol. Manag. China **1**(1), 9–26 (2006)
19. Holland, C., Naude, P.: The metamorphosis of marketing into an information handling problem. J. Bus. Ind. Mark. **19**(3), 167–177 (2004)
20. Luftman, J.N.: Competing in the Information Age Align in the San, 2nd edn. Oxford University Press, New York (2003)
21. Levy, M., Powell, P., Yetton, P.: SMEs: aligning IS and the strategic context. J. Inf. Technol. **16**(3), 133–144 (2001)
22. Bharadwaj, A.S.: A resource-based perspective on information technology capabilities and firm performance: an empirical investigation. MIS Q. **24**(1), 169–196 (2000)
23. Warfield, J.N.: A Science of Generic Design: Managing Complexity Through System Design. Lova State University Press, Lova (1994)
24. Warfield, J.N.: Towards interpretation of complex structural models. IEEE Trans. Syst. Man Cybern. **4**(5), 405–417 (1974)
25. Warfield, J.N.: Societal Systems: Planning, Policy and Complexity. Wiley, New York (1976)
26. Saxena, J.P., Sushil., Vrat, P.: Policy and Strategy Formulation: An Application of Flexible Systems Methodology. GIFT Publishing, New Delhi (2006)
27. Singh, A.N., Gupta, M.P., Ojha, A.: Identifying critical infrastructure sectors and their dependencies: an Indian scenario. Int. J. Crit. Infrastruct. Prot. **7**(2), 71–85 (2014)
28. Srivastava, A.K.: Modeling strategic performance factors for effective strategy execution. Int. J. Product. Perf. Manag. **62**(6), 554–582 (2013)
29. Tewari, S.K., Misra, M.: Driving performance of higher education industry: an Indian scenario. Int. J. Product. Perf. Manag. **70**, 2070–2091 (2020)

Quantum Key Distribution: An Ascendable Mechanism for Cryptographic Key Distribution

P. Anil(✉), Praveen Likhar(✉), and Ravi Shankar Yadav(✉)

Centre for Artificial Intelligence and Robotics (CAIR), Defence Research and Development Organisation (DRDO), Bangalore 93, India
{anilp, praveen.likhar, ravi.yadav}@cair.drdo.in

Abstract. Quantum key distribution (QKD) is a mechanism that works on quantum mechanics principles, which allows communicating users to protect their key exchange from the prying eyes of an eavesdropper. Distributing cryptographic keys among the users and guaranteeing the secrecy of these keys are major concern in cryptography. The protocols of classical key distribution are mainly depend on complexity in computation to decode the key and also on the time required to decode it. Venerable RSA algorithm based public key distribution protocol would be broken either with advancements in high computing hardware and algorithms or with the realisation of the quantum based computers with sufficient number of qubits. Whereas QKD applies the phenomena of quantum physics to ensure secure key distribution. In this paper relevant quantum mechanics principles are briefly described before explaining popular QKD protocols followed by security hacks, available commercial QKD systems & future directions.

Keywords: Cryptography · Cryptographic key distribution · Quantum cryptography · Quantum key distribution

1 Introduction

Cryptography is an art of rendering information unintelligible to any unauthorized user. Even though this field is ancient, it evolved over the centuries. The key distribution mechanism is a vital part of any cryptographic system. The most widely used classical key distribution protocol is public-key system which is based on the RSA, finite field Diffie-Hellman, and elliptic curve cryptography. However the security of these algorithms mainly depends on factorization of large integer and solution to discrete log problem. Due to this reason these algorithms are susceptible to efficient algorithm development or computational power advancement. Peter Shor proposed an algorithm for quantum based computer [1] to unriddle integer factorization and discrete log problem.

The development of QKD was motivated by the weaknesses of classical key distribution protocols. Stephen Wiesner proposed the first QKD in his paper titled "Conjugate Coding" [2]. The real breakthrough in QKD was the introduction of BB84 [3] QKD protocol by Bennett and Brassard in 1984. The QKD is an emerging

R. S. Tomar et al. (Eds.): CNC 2020, CCIS 1502, pp. 167–181, 2021.
https://doi.org/10.1007/978-981-16-8896-6_14

technology which deters intrusion or eavesdropping in a communication session by alerting the legitimate communicators about the eavesdropping by any attacker. During the last decade the QKD has been the subject of intense research efforts and led to an impressive progress and eventually the commercial QKD products are available.

Research interest in the field of QKD has been increased after it was proven that it overcomes the limitations of classical key distribution protocols. The Heisenberg uncertainty principle (HUP) and quantum entanglement are the main principles for security of QKD. As per no cloning theorem [4] derived from HUP, creating similar copy of an unknown arbitrary quantum state is impossible. As per quantum entanglement principle two particles generated from a source get entangled such that a particular characteristic is measured on one of them, the other entangled particle is observed with opposite state. Quantum teleportation is the communication process using entangled states and is the basis of Ekert's QKD protocol [5]. Quantum communication encodes information as quantum bits, or qubits, which can exist in superposition. A bit can be only 0 or 1 whereas a qubit can be 0, 1, or a superposition of both. The classical key distribution protocols unable to detect eavesdropping. Whereas QKD is proven secure against any eavesdropping attempts on a quantum communication channel. Any eavesdropping attempts change original state of quantum particle and introduce detectable anomalies.

The paper is organized in seven sections. In the second section describes fundamental QKD principles. The third section explains popular QKD protocols. The fourth section discusses practical security concerns in QKD. The fifth section covers the companies having commercial QKD products. The sixth section discusses about future directions. The seventh section concludes the paper with future perspective.

2 Fundamental QKD Principles

The QKD relies on principles of quantum mechanics. The important principles are HUP, Quantum entanglement and photon polarisation. These principles are briefly described below.

2.1 Heisenberg Uncertainty Principle (HUP)

As per the principle it is only possible to observe one of the conjugate properties with certainty. Suppose A & B are two quantum observables, then

$$\langle(\Delta A)^2\rangle\langle(\Delta B)^2\rangle \geq \frac{1}{4}\|\langle[A,B]\rangle\|^2,$$

Where, $\Delta A = A - \langle A\rangle$, $\Delta B = B - \langle B\rangle$ and $[A, B] = AB - BA$.

Therefore, $\langle(\Delta A)^2\rangle$ and $\langle(\Delta B)^2\rangle$ are variances to measure A and B uncertainty. For A and B such that $[A, B] \neq 0$, change in the A's uncertainty $\langle(\Delta A)^2\rangle$ results with opposite change in the B's uncertainty $\langle(\Delta B)^2\rangle$.

Thus, it is impossible to simultaneously measure both the conjugate properties of a quantum particle with certainty because in order to measure one of the properties inevitably disturbs the system. For example, measuring the polarisation of a photon in a direction affects all subsequent measurements. To achieve HUP QKD uses photo polarisation as conjugate attributes. Many important characteristics of QKD are derived from HUP [6].

2.2 Quantum Entanglement

The principle of quantum entanglement is the other important principle of quantum mechanics for QKD. Ekert-91(E91) protocol is a QKD protocol based on quantum entanglement. It is a correlation which exists between two quantum particles from same source in a way that a specific attribute is measured on one of them the other will be observed with opposite state. This characteristic will be held regardless of distance between the two entangled quantum particles and the particles stay entangled till isolated [7]. In 1993 Bennet et al., suggested first communication mechanism using entangled states called quantum teleportation [8].

2.3 Photon Polarisation

In QKD, a mechanism of information encoding is transmission of photons in some polarisation states. Polarisation is an electromagnetic wave characteristic that defines the oscillation direction in a plane which is perpendicular to the propagation direction. Typical polarisation state pairs used are rectilinear basis, the diagonal basis or the circular basis. All three of these bases are conjugate to each other. These polarisation state pairs are shown below in Fig. 1.

Basis	Representation	Random Bit 0	Random Bit 1
Rectilinear	+	↑	→
Diagonal	X	↗	↘
Circular	O	↺	↻

Fig. 1. Typical polarisation state pairs

3 QKD Protocols

In general, QKD protocols involve two main steps; a quantum state transmission step, to transmit and measure quantum states, and classical post processing step, to process the measured outcome to derive secret key. Based on quantum mechanics principles the QKD protocols divided in two main protocol classes; first Prepare and measure and second Entanglement based. Considering the detection schemes these can be further categories in to three classes: continuous variable, discrete variable, and distributed phase reference coding. Homodyne detection is used by the continuous variable. Whereas photon counting is used by the discrete variable and distributed-phase-reference, later on these protocols consider only those measures in which successful detection has occurred [9]. The basic idea for all Prepare and measure protocols is, Alice transmits a random secret key to Bob by encoding its bits in the polarisation states of photons and sending them to Bob.

HUP is used to guarantee the detection of the presence of Eavesdropper. Entanglement based protocols are based on photon entanglement principle. The use of entanglement in QKD protocols was first proposed by Ekert [5]. These entanglement based QKD protocols have advantage over QKD protocols based on single photon, due to inherent randomness in the quantum measurement of entangled system. Also the Entanglement based QKD systems do not require single photon source. Important QKD protocols are listed in Table 1. These protocols are grouped based on detection scheme used.

Table 1. QKD protocols

Families of protocols	Protocols
Discrete variable	BB84-BBM SARG04 B92 Six-state Ekert91 (Entanglement based) BBM92 (Entanglement based)
Continuous variable	Gaussian modulation Discrete modulation Non-Gaussian modulation
Distributed phase reference	Differential phase shift Coherent one way

3.1 Discrete-Variable Protocols

Discrete-variable protocols are the first proposed QKD protocols and still the most frequently implemented. These protocols can immediately share a perfect secret key in the absence of errors. In principal it is possible to choose any degree of freedom for discrete quantum, but polarisation is mostly preferred implementation for free-space and phase coding for fiber-based [9].

3.1.1 BB84-BBM

This protocol was proposed in 1984 by Charles Bennett and Giles Brassard [3]. This protocol is established on HUP and developed using polarised photons. This protocol uses two conjugate pairs of photon states and the states among the pair are orthogonal to one another. The BB84 protocol uses two polarization basis, rectilinear + and diagonal x, to define the states $|0\rangle$ and $|1\rangle$.

This protocol involves two phases. In the first phase, Alice randomly chooses basis, + or x, to define states, 0 or 1, and sends the photon to Bob. For each photon, Bob selects random basis for the measurement. His outcome would be either 0 or 1, unless he fails to register anything. First phase ends when the qubit transfer is complete.

In the second phase, also known as shifting phase Alice and Bob simply makes classical communication, where Bob tells Alice which photons were received, and in which basis he did the measurement; no measurement outcome is shared between Alice and Bob at this moment. Alice replies, by reviling which basis each photon was encoded in. Both accept the value corresponding to common chosen basis for measurement and reject others. Alice and Bob should now have a perfectly correlated bit string which is known as shifted key.

Alice and Bob now perform the comparison on few left over bit sequence to detect eavesdropping and to estimate the error rate. If the bits are not correlated, an error due to the presence of noise or eavesdropper must have disturbed the system. If the error rate is too high, all bits are simply discarded and the protocol has to be started over again. The resilience of BB84 protocol against eavesdropping i.e. the probability that eavesdropping escapes the detection is given by [10]

$$P_{false} = \left(1 - \frac{\lambda}{4}\right)^{n}$$

Where λ is the probability of eavesdropping a bit and n is number of bits transferred. Hence, if P_{false} is small to a sufficient degree, both Alice and Bob conclude that no eavesdropping occurred, and consequently choose derived key as their final key. Unconditional security of this protocol established by various methods [9] (Dominic Mayers [12]; Hoi-Kwong Lo and H. F. Chau [11]; Peter W. Shor and John Preskill [13]; Kraus, Gisin, and Renner, [14]).

3.1.2 SARG04

If a single photon source is used instead of attenuated laser pulse a more robost protocol can be build by utilizing the four quantum states of BB84 protocol with different way of encoding information. As a result in 2004 Scarani, Acin, Ribordy, and Gisin proposed SARG04 [15] QKD protocol. Unlike BB84 this protocol encodes the bit on basis instead of states but utilizes same BB84 four quantum states and measurement at Bob's end. In both SARG04 and BB84 the first phase are similar. In this protocol bit '0' is represented by $|0\rangle_+$ and $|1\rangle_+$ and bit '0' is represented by $|0\rangle_x$ and $|1\rangle_x$. In first phase Alice select one of the state among four and transmit to Bob. After receiving it from Alice Bob uses one of the bases for his measurement. Alice announces non-orthogonal states pair in the second phase instead of announcing bases. Alice use one of the bases for bit encoding. Bob will get correct bit if he performs measurement on the right basis. But if Bob choose the wrong basis he will not able to measure any of the states and not able to ascertain the bit. In the absence of any errors, which could be introduced as a result of eavesdropping, the sieved key size will be quarter of original key.

With the perfect implementation of single-photon SARG04 protocol achieves similar security as provided by BB84. SARG04 is more sensitive to losses as compare to BB84, and its quantum-bit-error-rate (QBER) is double of BB84. However, SARG04 is secure against PNS attacks to a greater extend as compare to BB84 [15].

3.1.3 B92

In 1992, Charles Bennett proposed B92 [16], a simplified version of BB84 which uses two nonorthogonal quantum states, instead of the four required in BB84. In rectilinear basis 0° encoded for bit 0 and 45 encoded for bit 1 on diagonal basis. Alike BB84 protocol, Alice sent randomly chosen bits to Bob via quantum channel. The bases to be used are depends upon the chosen bits. To measure the arriving photons Bob randomly chooses a basis but he will not measure anything if he chooses the wrong basis. In the Key Sifting stage Bob communicates to Alice which photons he measured, but he does not tells the measured value. All other photons which Bob does not able to measure are discarded. To verify whether the Alice's derived key is same as Bob's key privacy amplification and error correcting process continue as normal.

Man-in-middle attack on B92 is quite simple, for this an eavesdropper capture the communication, measures the captured communication and retransmit it to Bob if eavesdropper is able to measure the bit sent by Alice, and send nothing when fails. Thus, a powerful reference pulse is also used to secure B92 against intercept-resend attack alongside two quantum states which encodes a bit. Tamaki et al. [17, 18] proved unconditional security for implementation based on single photon. Koashi [19] and Tamaki et al. [20] proved unconditional security for strong reference pulse implementations.

3.1.4 Six-State

This protocol was first mentioned back in 1984 by Bennett et al. as a possible extension of BB84. It was rediscovered and studied in greater detail in 1998 by Bruß [21] and by Bechmann-Pasquinucci and Gisin [22] in 1999. The working of this protocol is identical to BB84 but instead of using four states for bit encoding this protocol utilise six states. The Six-state protocol can tolerate more noise as compared to the BB84 or SARG04 protocols because in this protocol channel estimation becomes "tomographically complete," i.e. the characteristic of the channel is completely described by the measured parameters. However the major drawback of six-state protocol is reduction in the rate of key distribution by two third against half in case of BB84. The eavesdropping detection is easier with this protocol as it uses six states which results in higher error rate in case of any eavesdropping attempt. Its unconditional security was proved quite early by Hoi-Kwong Lo, in 2001 [23].

3.1.5 Ekert91 (Entanglement Based)

A new approach to QKD based on the principle on quantum entanglement was proposed by Artur Eckert, known as Ekert91 or E91 [5]. This protocol is based on the adaptation of Einstein-Podolsky-Rosen gedanken experimentation by Bohm. this protocol exploits Bell's theorem to detect eavesdropping. In this protocol a source emits pairs of entangled particles and transmits one photon to Alice and the other to Bob. To perform the measurement random basis are chosen by Alice and Bob. In the key shifting phase they inform each other over the classical channel about the bases used for their measurements. Due to the quantum entanglement property both Alice and Bob will have binary complement bit sequence corresponding to the measurements where they used the same bases. To detect eavesdropper presence Alice and Bob scrutinise the photon where they performed measurement on different bases.

3.1.6 BBM92 (Entanglement Based)

This protocol [24] is based on the principle on quantum entanglement and was proposed by Charles Bennett et al. in the year 1992. This is the entanglement version of BB84 protocol. This protocol is similar to Ekert91 protocol but uses only two analyzers as compare to three in the case of Ekert91. In this protocol if Alice and Bob perform the measurement using same analyzer state than there will be a perfect anti-correlation between their measurements. In second phase, Alice and Bob communicate over classical channel to determine measurements corresponding to pairs of entangled photons. From the selected measurements both choose the measurements for which the bases were same. After this either of them inverts the bits to obtain the same bit string.

3.2 Continuous-Variable Protocols

An alternative approach to QKD other than the Discrete-variable coding which requires photon counting techniques has been suggested. In this new approach photon counters are replaced by faster and more efficient standard telecom p-i-n photodiodes. Measurement schemes corresponding to this approach are based on homodyne detection and measured data are real amplitudes instead of discrete events and hence called continuous-variable (CV) QKD [25].

3.2.1 Gaussian Modulation Protocols

Gaussian Protocols Using Squeesed Light Source and Homodyne Measurement: The first Gaussian QKD protocol was proposed in 2001 by Cerf, Lévy and Van Assche [26]. A modulated squeesed state of light with a Gaussian distribution in one quadrature is the base behind this protocol. The homodyne detection is the mechanism used for measurement in this protocol. By randomly selecting the quadrature for homodyne measurement Bob measure the key and then applies the key shifting. This protocol can be considered as continuous-variable version of BB84 as the average state transmitted from Alice is identical irrespective of selected basis. The requirement of squeesed light source is the major limitation of this protocol.

Gaussian Protocols Using Coherent States of Light and Homodyne Measurement: To overcome the need of squeesed light source a Gaussian QKD protocol was proposed in 2002 by Grosshans and Grangier [27]. In this protocol squeesed light is replaced with coherent states of light and modulated with a Gaussian distribution in both quadratures. The homodyne detection is still the mechanism used for measurement. Unlike the first Gaussian protocol this protocol does not require key shifting because Alice simply discards the data corresponding to the quadrature that is not measured by Bob.

Gaussian Protocols Using Coherent States of Light and Heterodyne Measurement: There is loss of efficiency in the above protocol because Alice discards the half of the transmitted data. To improve the efficiency a new Gaussian QKD protocol was proposed in 2004 by Weedbrook et al. [28]. Only difference in this protocol with compare to the above mentioned protocol is that the measurement technique is heterodyne in place of homodyne. In this technique simultaneous measurements are performed for both the quadratures. The main disadvantage of this protocol is reception of two noisier quadratures as compared to single quadrature resultant due to the additional requirement of vacuum noise unit. But advantages of this protocol are an increase in the key rate and elimination of random selection for quadrature.

Gaussian Protocols Using Squeesed Light Source and Heterodyne Measurement: In 2007 García-Patrón proposed a new Gaussian QKD protocol [29] using squeesed light source and heterodyne measurement. In this protocol Alice uses squeesed light source to send the data and Bob performs heterodyne measurements. Even though it requires squeesed light source it provides highest range and rate amongst all Gaussian protocols.

3.2.2 Discrete-Modulation Protocols

In protocol design it is advantageous to keep lowest possible signals by minimising the number of monitored parameters during the measurement process. For this reason, a discrete modulation protocol [30] has been devised by Silberhorn et al., in 2002. This protocol combines a finite set of signals along with measurement schemes used in the continuous-variable protocols.

In these protocols the signals comprise of coherent state weak signals pulse alongside a phase reference strong signals pulse. Alice transmits these signals at a phase difference of 0 or Π. Bob then performs homodyne or heterodyne detection using local oscillator. If Bob performs homodyne detection he has to randomly choose one of the two relevant quadratures measurements. Among these quadratures, one is used to measure bit value and other is used to limit eavesdropping. Or Bob can perform heterodyne detection instead of homodyne detection to monitor both quadratures simultaneously. The security claim of discrete-modulation protocols is established by the fact that signal pulses which are weak in nature represent nonorthogonal states of signals.

3.2.3 Non- Gaussian Modulation Protocols

In April 2011 a new Continuous variable QKD protocol [31] based on non-Gaussian modulation was proposed by Leverrier and Grangier. According to authors the reason to use non-Gaussian modulation is that current coding methods don't permit for effective procedure for reconciliation at lower SNR ratio with Gaussian data. With the binary-input additive white Gaussian noise (BI-AWGN) channel these protocols reduce the problem for reverse reconciliation to the problem for channel coding. Compare to the protocols which employs Gaussian modulation these protocols perform the reconciliation expeditiously [31].

3.3 Distributed-Phase-Reference Protocols

New categories of protocols are conceived by some researchers which are neither discrete-variable nor continuous-variable protocols. Similar to discrete-variable protocols these protocols derive their key with the realisation of discrete variable. These protocols monitor the quantum channel by observing the phase coherence of subsequent pulses. That's why this category of protocols is known as distributed-phase reference protocols [9].

3.3.1 Differential Phase Shift

DPS-QKD protocol has been proposed by Inoue K et al., [32, 33]. In this protocol Alice sent to Bob a train of weakly coherent pulses modulating each coherent pulse randomly by $\{0, \pi\}$. In this protocol encoding of the bits are carried out using the phase difference of two adjacent phases. If phase difference between two adjacent phases is 0 then the bit is encoded as 0 otherwise 1. One-bit delay circuit is used by the Bob to detect differential phase.

3.3.2 Coherent One-Way

A Coherent One-Way (COW) [34, 35] protocol with the aim of achieving high key generation rate was proposed by G Nicolas et al. In this protocol bit 0 is encoded with μ-0 pulse sequence and bit 1 encoded with 0-μ pulse sequence, where μ is mean photon number during a definite time intervals. By measuring arrival time the two states can be optimally recognized. Alice can also send μ-μ which is also called decoy sequences to enhance the security. When a "1–0" or decoy sequences is coded, estimation of channel can be determined by inspecting coherence among non-empty consecutive pulses.

4 Security of QKD Systems

4.1 Unconditional Security of QKD Protocols

In QKD system Eve cannot obtain any information about a quantum transmission without being detected because measurement of quantum states modifies the quantum system. Therefore Eve cannot eavesdrop without disturbing the QKD system even by using infinite computational resources and time or a quantum computer. The unconditional security of QKD protocols immune the QKD system from undetected eavesdropping. But there are some assumptions for unconditional security proof of QKD protocols. These assumptions are, Eve cannot affect Alice's and Bob's creation or detection of photons or inspect their devices, random number generator use to set QKD equipment must be truly random and the Classical authentication should be unconditionally secure.

4.2 Practical Security Concerns in QKD/Side Channel Attacks on QKD

In principles QKD relies on physics and should be infinitely more difficult to crack than classical cryptography approaches. The QKD is perfectly secure in principle however loopholes may arise because of the imperfection in effectuation of QKD protocols or inadequacies in constituents of the QKD system. The QKD attacks did not target the QKD protocol but the loopholes in the implementation of the QKD system. Many attacks demonstrated on the commercially available QKD systems. Brief description of important attacks is as follows.

4.2.1 PNS Attack

In a realistic environment, currently it is impractical for equipment to reliably and efficiently produce and detect single photons because photons in large quantity are present in a signal pulse. That's why in practice QKD systems often use laser pulses attenuated to a very low level called Weak coherent pulses (WCP). WCP contain a very low photon quantity. If in this pulse two or more photons present the eavesdropper can keep one of them and send the left ones to Bob. This logic is used by Brassard et al. in devising Photon number splitting (PNS) attack [36]. To execute this attack Eve observes the pulse to count the photons and if it contains two or more photons she retain one and forward the rest. To get the key Eve measured the retained photons after knowing the declared basis by Alice. Due to very low probability of multi-photon beam emission it is very difficult to execute PNS attack practically [6].

4.2.2 Faked-State Attacks

Faked states attack [37] on a quantum cryptosystem is an intercept & resend attack. This attack is mostly unsuccessful in cases where regeneration of quantum states is attempted. But sometimes legitimate parties can fall in to trap due to their imperfect setups. The Eve can execute this attack by sending faked states by light pulses and make legitimate user believe as they are observing original quantum states. In this attack instead of reconstructing the original states Eve generates faked states which get detected by the legitimate parties without any alarm. This attack is very specific to schemes and QKD devices [37].

4.2.3 FPB-probe Attack

Fuchs–Peres–Brandt (FPB) probe attack describes the most general way in which a powerful individual attack can be performed against single-photon polarisation based BB84 QKD through a controlled NOT gate. In this attack qubit send by Alice turns to control-qubit input and the qubit received by Bob turns to the control-qubit output. Subsequently the input target-qubit is supplied by Eve to determine the output target-qubit. Minimum-error-probability projective measurement is used in FPB probe to determining output states of target qubit which are correlated with Bob's shifted value correctly received bit [38].

4.2.4 Detector Control Attack Using Tailored Bright Illumination

Through experimentation it is demonstrated that by employing a bright illumination, especially tailored for launching attack, an eavesdropper could able to control remotely the detectors of few commercial QKD devices. With this the eavesdropper is able to get the final secret key without the detection of eavesdropping [39]. This attack is executed by impelling an avalanche photodiode (APD) to function in linear manner without responding to single photon but can be operated by tailored bright illumination in a deterministic way. Gerhardt et al. demonstrated a practical execution of this attack on a QKD system [40].

4.2.5 Phase-Remapping Attack

Xu. F. et al. demonstrated an attack in which sender's dependency on time for phase modulation during preparation of a quantum state is exploited for covertly modifying distinguishable quantum states [41]. It is discoverable under most QKD protocols because it introduces a high error rate.

4.2.6 Thermal Blinding of Gated Detectors Attack

Lars Lydersen et al. [42] demonstrated an attack on Clavis2 commercial QKD system, in which the avalanche photo diodes are heated with bright illumination methods to blind the detectors. This attack is known as 'Thermal Blinding of Gated Detectors' and it exploits avalanche photo diodes in linear manner to eavesdrop QKD implementations. Once the detectors get blinded the short bright pulses can able to trigger detectors again. Detection of this attack becomes more difficult with the systems which have pauses between packets transmission. Leveraging thermal inertia the Eve is able to execute this attack before eavesdropping [42].

4.2.7 After-Gate Attack

This attack involves Eve blocking the signals from Alice and then sending bright pulses as faked states after the avalanche photodiode gate when the APD is in linear mode. Due to invariable error rate of faked stated this attack remains undetected. This allows eavesdropper to transmit detection events to the legitimate user without any errors [43].

4.2.8 Time-Shift Attack

Through this attack an attacker can get some information of secret key by exploiting variations among detector's efficiency of identifying single photon at receiving end. The time-shift attack against practical quantum key distribution systems has been demonstrated successfully by Y. Zhao et al. [44].

5 Commercial QKD Systems

ID Quantique [45] was first company who bring this new technology to the market. In 2007, it used this technology as first public application, to secure a network used for vote counting in an election in Geneva. IDQ's developed QKD based solutions like Cerberis and Clavis^2 for protect storage and point-to-point backbone networks. MagiQ Technologies [46] also developed QPN 8505 quantum cryptography system which combines traditional VPN security technology and Quantum Key Distribution. QuintessenceLabs [47] is developing high performance QKD systems with state of art research in continuous variable and bright laser quantum cryptography. SeQureNet a paris based company, Qasky [48] a china based company and Qubitekk [49] a California based company also offers commercial quantum key distribution systems. Other companies having active research in this area include HP, Mitsubishi, Toshiba, NEC, IBM and NTT.

6 Future Directions

To make this technology more popular technical development is required to increase the key bit rate which is right now few Mbps and to achieve greater distances. Further innovation on the technology side is needed to develop trusted quantum repeaters. Further research in the area of satellite QKD technology is required to overcome issues like unpredictable environmental and atmospheric conditions. To develop the trust among the users there should be a security certification process for QKD systems. It is also required to plan strategies for evaluating security of the QKD systems.

7 Conclusion

The QKD facilitates sharing of cryptographic keys, secrecy of which is assured by the quantum physics laws. QKD devices have evolved from laboratory demonstration models to commercial devices and over the time these devices are becoming more of a reality. Latest QKD devices has achieved key distribution rate of the order of Mbps. These devices have been demonstrated for a distance of hundreds of kilometer through free space and optical fiber links. However, for hundreds or thousands kilometer quantum cryptography faces some challenges. To increase the transmission distance, further research are required for the implementation of the reliable and efficient quantum repeaters and the development of the Satellite QKD. Equally to achieve higher key distribution rates faster electronics and efficient synchronisation need to be accomplished.

The major breakthrough in the history of QKD was the use of IDQ's Cerberis encryption system by Geneva government in the year of 2007 [50–52] to secure the network processing of voting results. The 'quantum Stadium project' [53] was the most successful application of QKD in which this technology was applied in the FIFA football world cup 2010 in Durban, South Africa to generate and distribute cryptographic keys to secure a data connection between the offsite Joint Operations Centre and Moses Mabhida Stadium at Durban. At University of Waterloo in June 2017 team lead by Thomas Jennewein demonstrated quantum key distribution between a moving aircraft and a ground transmitter using optical links [54]. These links were setup exploiting tracking feedback to two-axis motors directed by a substantial beacon lasers and an imaging camera on each sides. QKD signals from source were directed using a telescope from ground station and aimed to the aircraft receiver. Research team lead by Juan Yin carried out an experimentation to demonstrate key distribution through entangled photon pairs between two ground locations at a distance of 1200 kms. This experimentation employed two satellites to establish a quantum link between two ground stations [55]. Recently at Peking University and Beijing University researchers lead by Hong Guo able to achieve QKD over 49.85 km through commercial fiber networks [56]. With 202.81 km of ultralow-loss optical fiber they also experimented long distance continuous-variable QKD by applying highly-efficient reconciliation procedures and appropriately moderating excess noise.

The main issues in QKD are side channel attacks, lack of standards and process for security certification. Side channel attacks takes advantage of the imperfect implementation of the QKD protocols. Device-independent quantum key distribution (DIQKD)

[57, 58] is currently being researched by the scientific community as a strategy to deal with side channel attack on QKD. Over the last two decades extensive research and implementation work ameliorated our knowledge about security of QKD. Lot of work has been done in the area of QKD to fill the gap between theory and its implementation and to overcome the most of known weakness. To establish QKD system certification procedures and QKD standards, an Industry Specification Group was formed at the European Telecom Institute (ETSI) in Sophia-Antipolis, France [59, 60]. This evolution in the development of QKD gives a new dimension to the next generation key distribution. We conclude the paper with the hope that in the near future highly efficient, low-cost QKD systems will be eventually realised in everyday usage.

References

1. Shor, P.: Polynomial-time algorithms for prime factorization and discrete logarithms on a quantum computer (1996). e-print arXiv:quant-ph/9508027v2
2. Wiesner, S.: Conjugate coding. SIGACT News **15**, 78–88 (1983)
3. Bennett, C.H., Brassard, G.: Quantum cryptography: public key distribution and coin tossing. In: Proceedings of the IEEE International Conference on Computers, systems and Signal Processing, Bangalore, India, pp. 175–179 (1984)
4. Wooters, W., Zurek, W.: A single quantum cannot be cloned. Nature **299**, 802–803 (1982)
5. Ekert, A.K.: Quantum cryptography based on Bell's theorem. Phys. Rev. Lett. **67**(6), 661–663 (1991)
6. Gisin, N., Ribordy, G., Tittel, W., Zbinden, H.: Quantum cryptography. Rev. Mod. Phys. **74**, 145 (2001)
7. Bennett, C.H., DiVincenzo, D.P.: Quantum information and computation. Nature **404**, 247–255 (2000)
8. Bennett, C.H., Brassard, G., Crepeau, C., Jozsa, R., Peres, A., Wootters, W.: Teleporting an unknown quantum state via dual classical and Einstein-Podolsky-Rosen channels. Phys. Rev. Lett. **70**(13), 1895–1899 (1993)
9. Scarani, V., Bechmann-Pasquinucci, H., Cerf, N.J., Dušek, M., Lütkenhaus, N., Peev, M.: The security of practical quantum key distribution. Rev. Mod. Phys. **81**, 1301–1350 (2009)
10. Lomonaco, Jr., S.J.: A Quick Glance at Quantum Cryptography (1998). arXiv:quant-ph/9811056v1
11. Lo, H., Chau, H.: Unconditional security of quantum key distribution over arbitrarily long distances. Science **283**, 2050–2056 (1999)
12. Mayers, D.: Unconditionally secure quantum bit commitment is impossible. Phys. Rev. Lett. **78**, 3414–3417 (1997)
13. Shor, P., Preskill, J.: Simple proof of security of the BB84 quantum key distribution protocol. Phys. Rev. Lett. **85**, 441–444 (2000)
14. Kraus, B., Gisin, N., Renner, R.: Lower and upper bounds on the secret key rate for QKD protocols using one—way classical communication. Phys. Rev. Lett. **95**, 080501 (2005)
15. Scarani, V., Acin, A., Ribordy, G., Gisin, N.: Quantum cryptography protocols robust against photon number splitting attacks for weak laser pulse implementations. Phys. Rev. Lett. **92**, 057901 (2004)
16. Bennett, C.H.: Quantum cryptography using any two nonorthogonal states. Phys. Rev. Lett. **68**(21), 3121–3124 (1992)
17. Tamaki, K., Koashi, M., Imoto, N.: Phys. Rev. Lett. **90**, 167904 (2003)

18. Tamaki, K., Lütkenhaus, N.: Phys. Rev. A **69**, 032316 (2004)
19. Koashi, M.: Unconditional security of coherent-state quantum key distribution with a strong phase-reference pulse. Phys. Rev. Lett. **93**, 120501 (2004)
20. Tamaki, K., Lo, H.-K.: Unconditionally secure key distillation from multiphotons. Phys. Rev. A **73**, 010302 (2006)
21. Bruß, D.: Optimal Eavesdropping in Quantum Cryptography with Six States (1998). e-print arXiv:quant-ph/9805019v2
22. Bechmann-Pasquinucci, H., Gisin, N.: Incoherent and coherent eavesdropping in the six-state protocol of quantum cryptography. Phys. Rev. A **59**, 4238–4248 (1999)
23. Lo, H.-K.: Quantum Inf. Comput. **1**, 81 (2001)
24. Bennett, C., Gilles Brassard, N., Mermin, D.: Quantum cryptography without Bell's theorem. Phys. Rev. Lett. **68**(5), 557–559 (1992)
25. Ralph, T.C.: Continuous variable quantum cryptography. Phys. Rev. A **61**(1), 010303 (1999)
26. Cerf, N.J., Lévy, M., Van Assche, G.: Quantum distribution of gaussian keys using squeezed states. Phys. Rev. A **63**, 052311 (2001)
27. Grosshans, F., Grangier, P.: Continuous variable quantum cryptography using coherent states. Phys. Rev. Letter **88**, 057902 (2002)
28. Weedbrook, C., Lance, A.M., Bowen, W.P., Symul, T., Ralph, T.C., Lam, P.K.: Quantum cryptography without switching. Phys. Rev. Lett. **93**, 17054 (2004)
29. García-Patrón R.R.: Quantum Information with Optical Continuous Variables : from Bell Tests to Key Distributions. Ph.D. thesis, Université Libre de Bruxelles (2007)
30. Silberhorn, C., Ralph, T.C., Lütkenhaus, N., Leuchs, G.: Continuous Variable Quantum Cryptography - beating the 3 dB loss limit (2002). e-print arXiv:quant-ph/0204064v3
31. Leverrier, A., Grangier, P.: Continuous-variable quantum key distribution protocols with a non-Gaussian modulation. Phys. Rev. A **83**, 042312 (2011)
32. Inoue, K., Waks, E., Yamamoto, Y.: Differential-phase-shift quantum key distribution. Phys. Rev. Lett. **89**, 037902 (2002)
33. Inoue, K., Waks, E., Yamamoto, Y.: Differential-phase-shift quantum key distribution using coherent light. Phys. Rev. A. **68**, 022317 (2003)
34. Gisin, N., Ribordy, G., Zbinden, H., Stucki, D., Brunner, N., Scarani, V.: Towards practical and fast Quantum Cryptography (2004). e-print arXiv:quant-ph/0411022
35. Stucki, D., Brunner, N., Gisin, N., Scarani, V., Zbinden, H.: Fast and simple one-way quantum key distribution. Appl. Phys. Lett. **87**, 19418 (2005)
36. Brassard, G., Lutkenhaus, N., Mor, T., Sanders, B.C.: Limitations on practical quantum cryptography. Phys. Rev. Lett. **85**(6), 1330–1333 (2000)
37. Makarov, V., Hjelme, D.R.: Faked states attack on quantum cryptosystems. J. Mod. Opt. **52** (5), 691–705 (2005)
38. Shapiro, J.H.: Performance analysis for brandt's conclusive entangling probe. Quant. Inform. Process. 5, 11–24 (2006). eprint: arXiv:quant-ph/0510009v1
39. Lydersen, L., Wiechers, C., Wittmann, C., Elser, D., Skaar, J., Makarov, V.: Hacking commercial quantum cryptography systems by tailored bright illumination. Nat. Photonics **4**, 686 (2010)
40. Gerhardt, I., Liu, Q., Lamas-Linares, A., Skaar, J., Kurtsiefer, C., Makarov, V.: Perfect eavesdropping on a quantum cryptography system (2010). eprint arXiv:quant-ph/1011.0105
41. Xu, F., Qi, B., Lo, H.-K.: Experimental demonstration of phase-remapping attack in a practical quantum key distribution system. New J. Phys. **12**, 113026 (2010)
42. Lydersen, L., Wiechers, C., Wittmann, C., Elser, D., Skaar, J., Makarov, V.: Thermal blinding of gated detectors in quantum cryptography. Opt. Express **18**, 27938 (2010)

43. Wiechers, C., et al.: After-gate attack on a quantum cryptosystem. New J. Phy. **13**, 013043 (2011)
44. Zhao, Y., Fung, C.-H.F., Qi, B., Chen, C., Lo, H.-K.: Quantum hacking: Experimental demonstration of time-shift attack against practical quantum-key-distribution systems (2011). e-print arXiv:quant-ph/0704.3253v3
45. http://www.idquantique.com
46. http://www.magiqtech.com/MagiQ/Home.html
47. http://www.quintessencelabs.com/quantum-cryptography.php
48. http://www.qasky.com/EN/default.asp
49. http://qubitekk.com
50. Jordans, F.: Swiss Call New Vote Encryption System Unbreakable. http://technewsworld.com/
51. https://www.idquantique.com/idq-celebrates-10-year-anniversary-of-the-worlds-first-real-life-quantum-cryptography-installation/
52. Centre for Quantum Technology (CQT). a Research Group in the School of Physics at the University of KwaZulu-Natal, ANNUAL REPORT (2010)
53. http://fifa.com/worldcup/news/durban-high-tech-stadium-1217593
54. Pugh, C.J., et al.: Airborne demonstration of a quantum key distribution receiver payload. Quant. Sci. Technol. **2**, 024009 (2017)
55. Yin, J., et al.: Satellite-based entanglement distribution over 1200 kilometres. Science **356**, 1140–1144 (2017). https://doi.org/10.1126/science.aan3211
56. Zhang, Y.-C., et al.: Continuous-variable QKD over 50 km commercial fiber. Quant. Sci. Technol. **4**, 035006 (2019)
57. Pironio, S., et al.: Device-independent quantum key distribution secure against adversaries with no long-term quantum memory. Phys. Rev. X **3**, 031007 (2013). https://doi.org/10.1103/PhysRevX.3.031007
58. Zapatero, V., Curty, M.: Long-distance device-independent quantum key distribution. Sci. Rep. **9**, 17749 (2019). https://doi.org/10.1038/s41598-019-53803-0
59. https://www.etsi.org/technologies/quantum-key-distribution
60. Thomas, L., Gaby, L.: Standardization of quantum key distribution and the ETSI standardization initiative ISG-QKD. New J. Phys. **11**, 055051 (2009)

Video Summary Based on Visual and Mid-level Semantic Features

Rajnish K. Ranjan[1], Yachana Bhawsar[1(✉)], and Amrita Aman[2(✉)]

[1] Department of Computer Science and Engineering, Goverment Women's Polytechnic, Bhopa 462016, India
[2] Technocrats Institute of Technology, Bhopal 462022, India

Abstract. The continuous creation of digital media mainly video has caused a tremendous growth of digital content. To make accessible of such a large volume of videos, a number of techniques have been proposed. To summarize video of the different domain, researchers have targeted visual information contained in frames. But visual features only are not enough to create a semantic summary. In this work, we proposed a methodology for generating semantic based static summary of original videos. This method considers visual features like color, shape, textures etc.; and optical flow motion as middle level semantic feature. Along with these features, flipped scale invariant feature transform (F-SIFT) has been applied because of its invariance to scale, rotation or lighting changes in images. In the real world, it is common to observe flip like transformation in images, it is because of symmetric view of images, opposite capture viewpoint or it may be by artificial flipping. Another benefit of proposed application is that, along with semantic video summary user may have different length of summary according to their interest. Technically length of the summary is varying just by changing threshold in a different iteration of the key-frames extraction process. Proposed technique has been tested on different datasets, mainly videos available on YACVID dataset and UCF_Sports dataset. Interestingness about the proposed technique is that, users have the choice to select short length, medium length or longer length video_summary.

Keywords: Key-frame · Video summary · Semantic features · SIFT · Texture

1 Introduction

This will not surprise if we say this is the advance technical era as the huge demand of multimedia application is rapidly increasing day by day. It is not easy to store and manage the tremendous volume of data. Today there are many recent smart developments of computing technology and network infrastructure so storing and manging of data is possible. Various fields like entertainment or astronomy involved multimedia. These fields require high quality multimedia, which needs huge amount of memory and time (longer in length). This idea is not good in present scenario. Managing huge amount of data should be effective and efficient for the success of these multimedia applications. Efficiency should be measured in terms of time, memory or transfer from one network to another network. These challenges are the major part of the efficiency.

R. S. Tomar et al. (Eds.): CNC 2020, CCIS 1502, pp. 182–197, 2021.
https://doi.org/10.1007/978-981-16-8896-6_15

To overcome the same problems many researchers have worked. A lot of great research has been done in the field of video summarization and still this field requires some smart work for describing semantic meaning of the original content. The main motive of our work is to get a meaningful summary of videos especially in sports domain. There is no need to devote whole time for watching full videos to understand the complete scenario; instead a person can get most informative content or highlights only from original videos using proposed application. A video summary is mainly time and memory management process. It can also be used in emergency cases like surveillance or medical videos effectively. Our earlier work for video summary [1] tackles few problems like semantic meaning preserved in generated summary. This work is more interesting for users as they have multiple choices for different length videos summary and it is possible just by filtering or collecting key frames on different threshold.

A video is a collection of two dimensional images which are displayed at the fixed rate. In image processing term, 2-D images are called frames. Those frames which have prior and subsequent frame knowledge are called key frames. These key frames are arranged in temporal order to form video summary. Therefore key frames play an important role to generate summary of any video. Basically, frames are the smallest unit of video and collection of frames merge together and develop a shot, collection of shots come together to develop a scene and a number of scenes come together to develop a video. Video summary can be achieved by two ways: (1) Video is created by many scenes, and a scene is created by many shots then a shot is created by frames as described in Fig. 1. A shot boundary is described by Yeo et al. [2], are the camera action which take place in between start and end operations. A shot is also defined as collection of many successive frames. (2) In the second way of video summary, key frames are identified and these frames are extracted from the original videos directly. Summery of the video produced by associating all key frames [3] in temporal order. Video summery that is produced may be either dynamic or static.

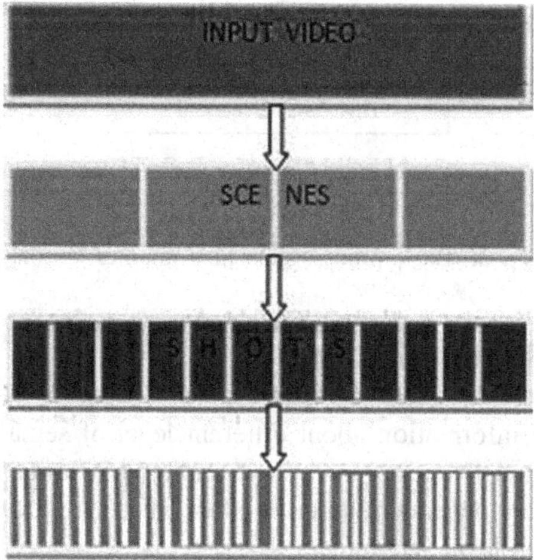

Fig. 1. Video fragmentation: video -> scenes -> shots -> frames.

Summarization is described as the process of data reduction as well as length reduction. Video summary deletes the similar contents in video and forms an abstract representation of the original content. Generally video summarization categories in two ways: first is static video summarization [4, 5] and second is dynamic video summarization [6].

2 Related Work

2.1 Computer Vision Process [7]

Computer vision is a high level image processing technique that enables computer or software to process and explore images to produce symbolic information which is useful for decision making. It is basically connected with the theory behind artificial systems to extract information from images. The images can be in the form of videos, camera images, medical images etc. The computer vision methods are application specific. Some systems tend to solve an independent problem while some systems may be employed to solve a sub problem of the original application. The type of methods designed to solve a particular problem depends on whether the functionality of problem is predefined or if it needs changes during solving itself. However, some functions are primarily designed for certain application only. Figure 2 shows the basic functions which we can find in all computer vision system.

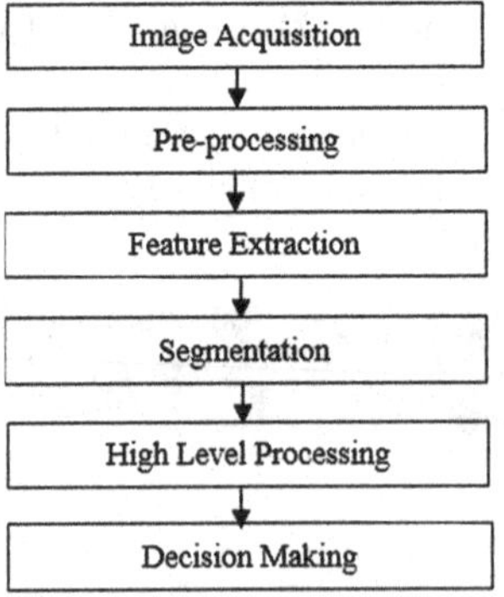

Fig. 2. Basic process flow in Computer Vision.

3 Video Semantic Information

This section gives the information about different level of semantic in sports mainly soccer. According to understanding hierarchy, semantic information can be categories in three levels and all are dependent on each other. These are low-level semantic, mid-level semantic and high-level semantic.

3.1 Low Level Semantics

Low level semantic generally considers low level visual features like dominant color, shape, texture etc. The dominant color is one of the most important features in soccer and cricket matches. It is because of camera focus mostly on the ground which is naturally green dominant color and other is crowd gathered in the stadium which is definitely not a dominant green. Thus it is easy to differentiate these two categories by the help of color histogram. But dress color code of player is negligible because of ground color and crowd in the background. In Fig. 3, dominant color region can be seen. Thus low level semantic gets struck in that type of cases. So there is a need of higher semantic understanding level which takes low level semantic feature as an input. Textures are other important low level visual features which play important role in all type of videos. As we know, texture feature is insensitive to rotation, lighting and other condition. Title textures provide important information in sport, it is shown in Fig. 4.

Fig. 3. Original image and dominant color region [8].

Fig. 4. Types of texture occurred in soccer video frames [8].

3.2 Mid Level Semantics

At the first stage of semantic space, relevant low level visual features are required to represent mid level semantic structure. And mid level semantic building block serves as rudimentary semantic for high level semantic structure. In this level of semantic one can get the play type, completion, camera view, motion, audience and some other related information. For soccer video, different coarse view of mid-level semantic exists, which is shown in Fig. 5. These are global view in which focus on cheering audience, ground and player is considered; medium view in which focus is on player's act and ground but it don't consider audience; close-up view consider close range on

Fig. 5. Different coarse view in soccer video (global, medium, close-up and audience respectively from left to right) [8].

large scale of a player, football, goal net, etc. and audience response after an event occur during play is also consider to be mid-level semantic features.

3.3 High Level Semantics

The high level semantics are quite specific i.e. turnover, touchdown, other user specified events, etc. and immediately useful for viewers. Advice to the player by coach, any action taken by referee as in Fig. 6, and some other high level action comes under high level semantics. These features are difficult to find correctly without using a lower level of semantic feature i.e. low level and middle level semantic. Thus we can say, middle level feature information is needed to represent high level semantic. In Fig. 7, we have two inference problems. First is a low level visual feature to middle level semantics and second is from mid level semantic to high level semantic.

Fig. 6. Referee detection [9].

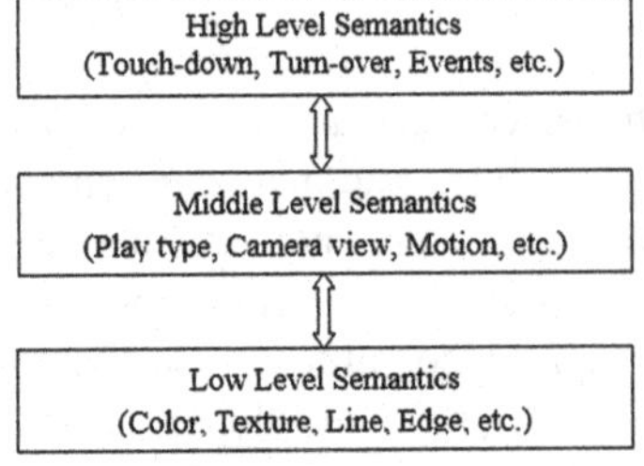

Fig. 7. Semantic space in soccer videos.

4 Feature Extraction

Feature extraction is the most important part of image processing system and accuracy of the application depends on feature selection. Thus better the feature selection better is the accuracy. Basically, feature extraction means getting visual information from images. Feature vectors contains these visual information in the feature database.

Actually, this is the main part of Image Retrieval System where feature value of images gives the image information. In Context Based Image Retrieval, feature selection from extracted features is the most important task. In it most relevant image is produced by the good feature selection procedure. Features which could be extracted are colors, textures, edges, motions, optical flow etc. There may be various representation of each feature and each feature have different representation aspects.

4.1 Color Based Features

Color feature is one the most important visual features used in image and vision processing. It is a global feature and narrates the nature of the surface of an image region correlate with the scene. Usually, color features are based on the pixel features and all pixel of the region have its own participation. As colors are not sensitive to size of image or change in direction. The color feature does not capture local object features in the image. To represent a color feature, a color histogram is the most common way to use. Apart from color histogram color.

based features include color correlograms, color moments, a mixture of Gaussian models, etc. color histogram and color moment are a simple and efficient descriptor. Extraction of color based feature depends on color spaces like RGB, HVS, HSV, YUV, YCbCr, etc. But RGB and HSV are most common color space and selection of color space method depends on applications.

4.2 Texture Based Features

For analysis of many images, texture characteristics play very important role. Image can be like natural images, medical images, sports images or remote sensing images. The meaning of texture little varies domain to domain; hence there is no specific definition of texture. According to Bagri and Johri [10] texture is a superficial phenomenon of human visual systems of natural objects. According to Li et al. [11] textures are object surface owned intrinsic visual features that are independent of color or intensity and reflect a homogeneous phenomenon in images. Basically, texture exists almost everywhere in nature and texture structure is a repeated pattern in entire image and it can be recognised by everyone. It contains crucial knowledge about the coordination of object surfaces as well as their correlations with surrounding environment. There are six texture features corresponding to human visual perception and they are coarseness, contrast, directionality, line-likeness, regularity, and roughness. Tamura is used to identify them. Analysis of textures can be done either by quantitatively or qualitatively. According to Tamura [12] six quantitative analysis of texture has been proposed which are explained below.

1) *Coarseness:* It relates the distance in grey-levels of spatial variations i.e. related to the size of primitive elements which form texture. Coarseness has a direct rel×ationship to fundamental texture features and scale, repetition rate of primitive elements. An image can have repeated texture pattern of different scales. The main goal of this method is to grab a large size as best whenever coarse texture is present and grab a small size when a micro or fine texture is present. If $A_k(x, y)$ is the average at point (x, y) over neighbourhood which has size $2^k \times 2^k$. Basically size of each point is power of two like 1 × 1, 2 × 2,.... and f(i, j) is the grey level at (x,y).

$$A_k(x, y) = \sum_i \sum_j f(i, j)/2^{2k}$$

Range of i and j varies from $(x - 2^{k-1})$ to $(x + 2^{k-1} - 1)$ and $(y - 2^{k-1})$ to $(y + 2^{k-1} - 1)$ respectively. Now by the help of Ak we will have equation to calculate difference at each point of overlapping and non-overlapping pair of neighbourhood.

$$E_{k,h} = \left|A_k\left(x + 2^{k-1},\ y\right) - A_k\left(x - 2^{k-1},\ y\right)\right|$$

Where $E_{k,h}$ is difference in horizontal direction between overlapping and non-overlapping pair.

2) *Contrast:* It measures the distribution of gray levels, which varies in an image. Also, checks to what limit it's.

distribution are biased to black or white. Generally, contrast can vary in an image by stretching or shrinking it's grey scale level. For given a picture f(x, y), we can change its contrast (only possible to change quality but not a structure of the image) by multiplying with positive constant factor c i.e. c*f(x, y). According to Tamura, contrast is approximated into four factors. The simplest analogy for Factor i) is the chain of grey-levels. Next, it can be doubtless seen that the diversification σ^2 or standard abnormality σ approximately the mean of the grey-levels probability dissolution is in a superior way preferable as contrast. As it is readily known, σ or σ^2 can measure the dispersion in the distribution. In this sense, Factor ii) reflect some extent. However, the resultant worth is undesirable for a selection in which a base hit peak is highly biased to black or white. We desire a contrast of polarization. Factor iii) says, the higher contrast in the picture have sharp edges and the last factor of Tamura defines, the repeating pattern (differs only in scale) is the reason for different contrast value in images. The kurtosis α_4 is readily known for this final cause and can be defined as

$$\alpha_4 = \mu_4/\sigma^4$$

where μ_4 is the fourth moment corresponding to mean and σ^2 is variance. Consequently, we became associated.

with σ and σ^4 for the second-step measure of study as follows:

$$\text{Contrast} = \sigma/\alpha_4^n$$

Here 'n' is positive number. In Tamura experiment it varied from 8, 4, 2, 1,1/2,1/4 and 1/8. According to Tamura's experiment n = 1/4 gives the best value of contrast.

3) *Directionality:* Directionality is a global property to the region of an image which is measure by the frequency distribution of local edges against their directional angles. It is as important feature as coarseness and contrast of the image which tells how much uniform the region is. Texture feature proposed by Tamura does not find much difference between orientations and patterns, thus it is not easy to differentiate orientation or pattern of images. But by the help of directionality, it is possible to measure the total degree of directionality in images. Hence it is satisfactory to say, directionality is one of the most important feature given by Tamura.

$$Directionality = 1 - r * n_p * \sum_p \sum_\phi (\phi - \phi_p)^2 * H_d \phi$$

In above equation 'r' represents normalizing factor which is related to quantizing levels of 'ϕ' (quantized direction code), `n_p' is total number of peaks, 'ϕ' is position of peak and 'ϕ_p' represent the pth peak position of H_d where 'H_d' represents the desired histogram.

4) *Line-Likeness:* According to Tamura, line-likeness is an element of texture that is made up or composed of lines. For this purpose for a given edge, the direction and the neighbouring edge's direction are equal or nearly equal then we consider such a group of edge points to the line. Basically, line likeness is concerned mainly with the shape of texture elements.

5) *Regularity:* Regular pattern and similarity occurred in images are measured by regularity. In Tamura terms, it.

is also called property for variations of a placement rule. Generally, in natural textures regularity is absent. But a fine texture considers being regular. It seems easy to describe the regularity in mathematical form of the repetitive pattern of objects. In reality, it is easy to synthesize a pattern in the term of mathematical expression. But it doesn't seem likely to be easy to describe regularity of natural textures pattern. Some mathematical technique exists which tell about regularity those have highly regular pattern textures. However, it is difficult to describe natural textures mathematically. On another side, measuring irregularity is also difficult without any information like shape and size of textures. Tamura assumption is if any feature of texture varies through the image, it means the image is irregular. Hence it's better to take a partition of an image called sub-image and calculate the variation of texture in each sub-image. Four independent features have been introduced above and sum of these four feature measure as a regularity.

$$Regularity = 1 - r * (F_{cor} + F_{dir} + F_{con} + F_{lin})$$

Where 'r' is normalizing factor.

6) *Roughness:* There is no standard way to describe tactile sense of roughness. Tamura says additive affect of coarseness and contrast produce roughness.

$$Roughness = F_{cor} + F_{con}$$

4.3 Motion Feature

Optical flow is the pattern for getting apparent motion feature of an object moving in consecutive frames. It is two dimensional (2D) vector fields and vectors are displacement vector of pixel moving from one position (in the first image) to other position (in the second image). Say two consecutive frame I_1 and I_2 in which a pixel in the first frame is $I_1(x, y, t)$ at time t and same pixel in frame I_2 after time dt is $I_2(x + dx, y + dy, t + dt)$ i.e. pixel displaced by (dx, dy) position in frame I_2 at time dt. Since both pixels are same and there is no change in intensity, so we can say-

$$I_2(x + dx, y + dy, t + dt) = I_1(x, y, t)$$

After applying Taylor series approximation, it would be-

$$f_x u + f_y v + f_t = 0$$

where,

$$f_x = df/dx$$

$$f_y = df/dy$$

$$u = dx/dt$$

$$v = dy/dt$$

Here f_x and f_y are image gradient (along position) and similarly f_t is gradient along time. There are two unknown variable (u, v) but there is a single equation. Hence there is no direct way to solve for (u, v). So there exists several methods to solve it, Lucas-Kanade [13] method is one of them.

5 Proposed Methodology

The proposed methodology produces static video summaries by extracting key frames based on visual features and midlevel semantic feature. Texture and color features are used as visual features; however using visual features do not guarantee effective summary of the video. In order to make meaning full or effective video summary, proposed method includes mid-level semantic features like motion feature and a local key-point descriptor called SIFT features. Basically, color and motion features are used to extract the characteristics of a video as these two features are dominant features in image and vision process domain.

5.1 Basic Flow and Algorithm Flow Chart

Development of any video summary starts from acquiring a video and dividing it into smaller unit which is called frame. The key frame selection process is the most important

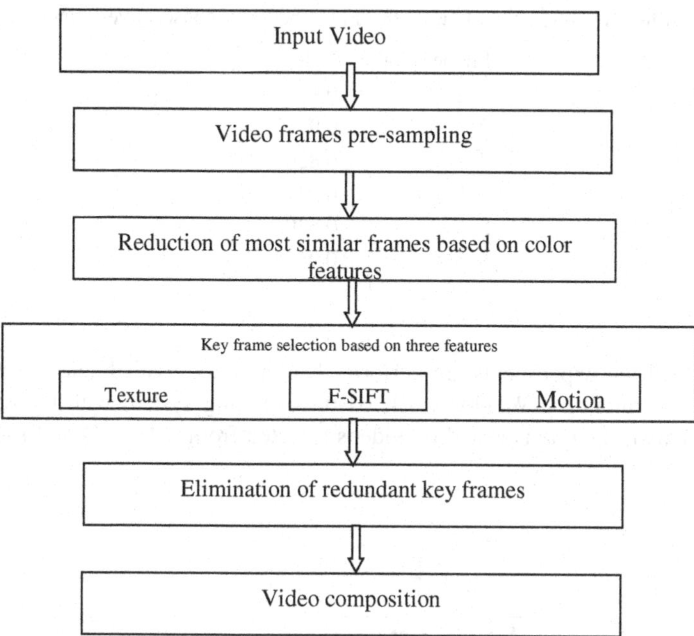

Fig. 8. Basic flow diagram of video summarization.

task of video summarization process and another important thing to be kept in mind is the duration of video summary. A summary should be of the desired length as given in input by the user. The basic block diagram of video summarization process can be depicted as in Fig. 8. It is shown in the flow diagram that taking a video as an input and extracts all the frames and save all frames. Further step is all about key frames extraction but to be good performance most similar frames can be eliminated in the beginning.

In our methodology, most similar frames are eliminated on the basis of color histogram. In first, BGR color space is converted into HSV color space then histogram comparison is applied for consecutive frames till the last frame and according to threshold most similar frame are deleted. On remaining frames, three features have been applied to get key frames. These steps can be seen in basic block diagram i.e. in Fig. 9. Now there is a chance that common frame can be selected as key frame by two or more feature extraction technique. Hence before the composition of summary, it is better to remove redundant key frames. In Fig. 9, the flow chart of applied algorithm can be seen.

6 Results and Discussion

In this section, we have put details of video summary result for different dataset along with a comparison with other existing techniques. To check the performance of proposed technique, a number of experiments with different datasets have been performed. Results of the technique show the merits and demerits to compare it to existing

Table 1. Difference of similarity Index between consecutive frames.

Frame number	Value of S_i
1–2	0.9546
2–3	0.9423
3–4	0.8268
4–5	0.9372
5–6	0.5205
6–7	0.9633

techniques. All the experiments are performed on a system with Intel(R) 2.4 GHz, 4 GB RAM and running a Windows 8.1, 64-bit operating system with the x64-based processor. This technique is tested on videos selected from YACVID and Benchmark

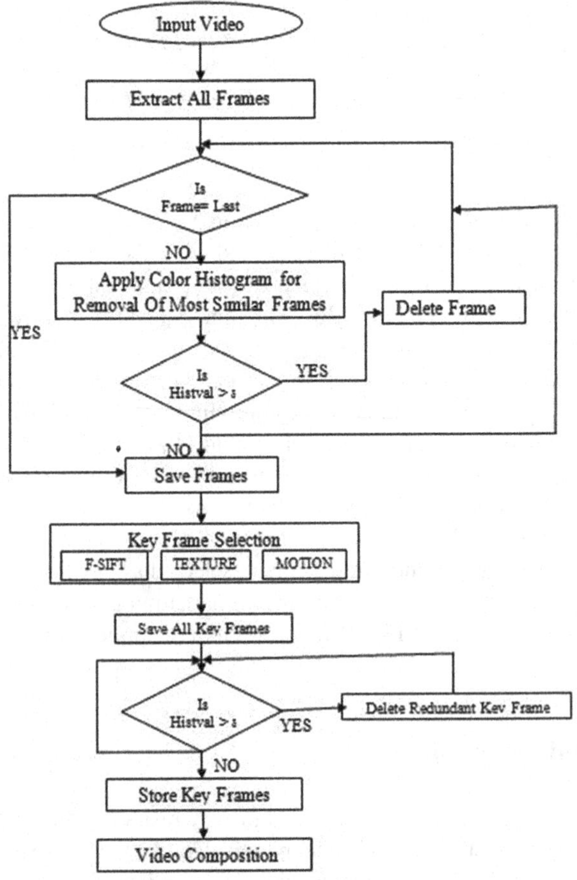

Fig. 9. Flow chart for proposed algorithm.

Table 2. Result obtained from different dataset.

date set	Video	Duration	#Frame	#KF1	#KF2
Yacvid	V85.avi	52 s	1575	129	15
Yacvid	V71.avi	4.35 min	6378	298	52
Yacvid	V86.avi	8.44 min	12974	982	123
Bench mark	Footbal.mp4	3.13 min	4569	322	36
Bench mark	Cricket.mp4	4.07 min	6173	314	48

Fig. 10. Images of soccer video- (a) Selected key frames and (b) its corresponding interest point.

data set which is a repository of digitized videos for retrieval and other research processes. And small video clip is taken from UCF_Sports (University of Central Florida) also tested.

As a number of videos have been tested on this application, few are listed in Table 2 along with some important details like duration of the video, a total number of frames and key frames (for different values of δ) generated by proposed techniques. Frame removal in this technique is based on how one frame is differing from another frame, it can be clearly understood from Table 1. It is shown that, if small changes are in frames then similarity index value S_i is close to 1 and if large change in two frames then the value of S_i is near zero.

Fig. 11. Soccer frames in gray format and its corresponding texture image.

Interest points in the frame have been identified by SIFT feature, it can be shown in Fig. 10. During execution phase of this application, all the selected key frames have been identified from all frames available for a video according to color feature. These selected key frames ensure fewer redundancies. After getting all selected key frames other features have been applied to get more informative frames, these features are flip sift which finds key object and Tamura's feature applied to get present textures in frames which can be shown in Fig. 11 and then optical motion feature applied to get all neighbour pixel have similar motion which can be shown in Fig. 12.

Fig. 12. Two consecutive frames and their pixel displacement.

According to these features, final key frames have been identified to get semantic video summary. Summarize result of soccer video (Dataset is taken from https://trecvid.nist.gov/trecvid.data.html) is displayed in Fig. 13 and Fig. 14.

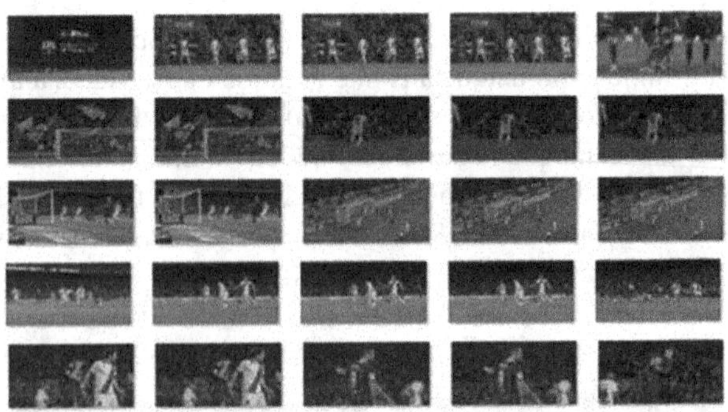

Fig. 13. Sets of soccer Video's frames.

Fig. 14. Summary result of soccer video in the form of key frames.

7 Evaluation

DATASETS: Three different data sets have been tested in proposed technique. We have taken different length of videos available in dataset. For very small video clip we have taken UCFSPORTS (https://crcv.ucf.edu/data/UCF_Sports_Action.php) data sets, for medium length (generally one to 10 min) we have taken YACVID (https://sites.google.com/site/vsummsite/download) data sets and for longer videos we have tested many videos available on YOUTUBE. Till now there is no standard frame work has been made to evaluate video summaries. According to Avila et al. [4] evaluation technique consider; summary is generated by users manually and then automatic generated summaries are evaluated based on user's summary. The Same approach is used in proposed technique. To know the effectiveness of proposed technique among other existing video summary techniques, Comparison of User Summary" (CUS) methodology has been used which is given by Avila et al. [4]. In this mechanism, comparison of automatically generated video summary is done by summary generated by users manually. After watching complete show of video user select key frames accordingly and each key frames of automatic summary is compared with user's given key frames.

There are two metrics to check the quality of produced summary, Accuracy Rate which is written as (CUS_A) and Error Rate which is written as (CUS_E). These two metrics are defined as-

$$CUS_A = n_{mAS}/n_{US}$$

$$CUS_E = n_{m'AS}/n_{US}$$

Table 3. Comparison of results with different techniques.

Technique	Dataset used	CUS_A	CUS_E
Proposed approach	Yacvid	0.917	0.42
Proposed approach	UCF sports	0.92	0.20
Proposed approach	Benchmark (YouTube)	0.78	0.46
Rajnish et al. [1]	Yacvid	0.908	0.52
VSUMM [4]	Yacvid	0.85	0.35
Local descriptor [14]	Open-video	0.88	0.35
STIMO [15]	Generic video	0.72	0.58

For UCFSPORTS data set, we have five sets of summary generated manually. Result obtained by the technique is evaluated based on manually generated summary. Accuracy is coming approx 0.92 whereas error rate is 0.20. Here n_{mAS} is a number of matching key frames of automatic summary from user key frames, $n_{m'AS}$ is a number of non-matching key frames of automatic summary from user generated key frames and n_{US} represents number of key frames from user summary. The range of CUS_A is from 0 to 1, its value will be zero if there is no key frame match with key frames generated by user summary and it will be 1 for all key frames of automated summary matches with user generated key frames. The value of CUS_E lies between 0 and n_{AS}/n_{US}. If all key frames of automated summary matches with all key frames of user summary then error rate value would be 0.

And maximum error rate would be n_{AS}/n_{US} i.e. no any key frames of automated summary matches with key frames of user summary. For good quality summary value of CUS_A would be 1 and CUS_E would be 0. Performance result with existing paper has been tabulated in Table 3.

8 Conclusion

Research in automatic video summarization improved multimedia in varieties of way in recent past. But still, research is going on in this field to get effective and efficient summary understandably and computationally. In this paper, the automatic technique to generate semantic video summary has been proposed, which has facilities to change the length of summary according to user preferences. As it is discussed in earlier sections, the summaries are a collection of key frames extracted from videos. It is difficult to capture an important event in videos by multiple visual features like color, shape and texture. Hence apart from visual features, motion feature and key-point detector and descriptor feature have been applied in proposed approach to get event holding and meaningful summaries. Proposed technique has been tested on evaluation criteria given by Avila et al. [4] by finding the probability of matching and non-matching criterion to obtained key frames to user's key frames. The proposed technique is found to be more efficient with high accuracy rate (CUS_A) in compare to existing techniques. The future scope of this technique lies in incorporating audio features to make summary more entertaining and understandable with less computation cost.

References

1. Ranjan, R.K., Agrawal, A.: Video summary based on f-sift, tamura textural and middle level semantic feature. Procedia Comput. Sci. **89**, 870–876 (2016)
2. Yeo, C.H., Zhu, Y.W., Sun, Q.B., Chang, S.F.: A Framework for subwindow shot detection. In: Proceedings of International Multimedia Modelling Conference, pp. 84–91 (2005)
3. Liu, H., Hao, H.: Key frame extraction based on improved hierarchical clustering algorithm. In: IEEE Conference on Fuzzy Systems and Knowledge Discovery(FSKD), pp. 793–797 (2014)
4. Fontes, S.E., de Avila, A., Lopes, P.B., da Luz, A., de Albuquerque, A.A.: VSUMM: a mechanism designed to produce static video summaries and a novel evaluation method. Pattern Recogn. Lett. **32**(1), 56–68 (2011)
5. Sandhu, S.K., Agrawal, A.: Summarizing videos by key frame extraction using SSIM and other visual features. In: Sixth International Conference on Computer and Communication Technology(ICCCT), pp. 209–213 (2015)
6. Lie, W.N., Hsu, K.C.: Video summarization based on semantic feature analysis and user preference. In: IEEE International Conference Sensor Network, Ubiquitous Trustworthy Compuer, pp. 486–491 (2008)

7. Moeslund, T.B., Granum, E.: A survey of computer vision based human motion capture. Comput. Vis. Image Underst. **81**(3), 231–268 (2001)
8. Qian, X.: Semantic based sport video browsing. In: Semantics in Action–Applications and Scenario, pp. 139–162 (2012)
9. Huang, C.-L., Shih, H.-C., Chao, C.-Y.: Semantic analysis of soccer video using dynamic Bayesian network. IEEE Trans. Multimedia **8**(4), 749–760 (2006)
10. Bagri, N., Johri, P.K.: A comparative study on feature extraction using texture and shape for CBIR. Int. J. Adv. Sci. Technol. **80**, 41–52 (2015)
11. Hu, W., Xie, N., Li, L., Zeng, X., Maybank, S.: A survey on visual content-based video indexing and retrieval. IEEE Trans. Syst. Man Cybern. **41**, 797–819 (2011)
12. Tamura, H., Mori, S., Yamawaki, T.: Textural features corresponding to visual perception. IEEE Trans. Syst. Man Cybern. **8**(6), 460–473 (1978)
13. Baker, S., Matthews, I.: Lucas-kanade 20 years on: a unifying framework. Int. J. Comput. Vision **56**(3), 221–255 (2004)
14. Cahunia, J.Y., Chavez, G.C.: A new method for static video summarization using local descriptors and video temporal segmentation. In: XXVI Conference on Graphics, Pattern and Image 2013, pp. 226–233 (2013)
15. Marco, F., Filippo, G., Manuela, M., Marco, P.: STIMO: still and moving video storyboard for web scenario. Multimedia Tools Appl. **46**, 47–69 (2010)

Waveletbased Selective Image Encryption Scheme Using Tinkerbell Chaotic Map

Ashish Kumar[1(✉)] and N. S. Raghava[2]

[1] Department of Information Technology, Delhi Technological University, Delhi, India
ashishkumar@dtu.ac.in

[2] Department of Electronics and Communication Engineering, Delhi Technological University, Delhi, India
nsraghava@dce.ac.in

Abstract. In this era of information technology, the exchange of information is taking place globally. In order to facilitate it, special attention is being given to network policies as well as security. The digital images contain a significant amount of information; therefore, an encryption module should be fast and processed in minimum time without facing any complexity in a shared network environment. This paper presents a novel symmetric image encryption algorithm in the wavelet transform domain based upon the properties of the Tinkerbell chaotic system along with Arnold's cat map to support confusion and diffusion. Two-Dimensional Discrete wavelet transform (2D-DWT) is used to decompose an image into its wavelet transform domain. The shuffling module is applied to the least significant coefficients using Arnold's cat map, whereas the encryption module deals with the most significant part of the image using Tinkerbell chaotic map based on the stream cipher. All the suitable parameters measure the algorithm's overall performance, and it is evident through results that it can be used for satellite and medical images to provide confidentiality.

Keywords: Discrete wavelet transform · Arnold's cat map · Tinkerbell chaotic map · Stream cipher · Selective encryption

1 Introduction

Security is a continuous process via which information is secured from several active and passive attacks. Several security mechanisms areused to ensure integrity, authentication, and confidentiality of the information [1, 2]. Cryptography is one of the primitive ways to secure information across unreliable communication networks. Cryptography schemes are of two types: (1) symmetric-key cryptography (2) asymmetric key cryptography. Since digital images communicate very frequently, thus users' privacy must be protected on untrusted communication channels. In the traditional cryptography system, it is difficult to secure large size of multimedia from intruders or attackers, and calculation of mathematical equations (built-in Encryption technique) increases overhead. Traditional algorithms are ideal for the small amount of information, but images are having an excessive amount of information and bulky in

R. S. Tomar et al. (Eds.): CNC 2020, CCIS 1502, pp. 198–208, 2021.
https://doi.org/10.1007/978-981-16-8896-6_16

size. When traditional algorithms are applied to images such as satellite images and medical images, it takesmore time to encrypt the image and increases the computational cost [4]. In the last few decades, chaotic systems have been used in the cryptography system due to the characteristics such as sensitivity, ergodicity, non-linear, unpredictability, and random-look nature, deterministic andeasy to reconstruct after filling in multimedia data [5]. Traditional cryptography schemes such as AES DES and RSA are popular algorithms designed for text data, but they are not suitable for images. Recently,chaos-based algorithms are designed for images on the principle of Shannon's theory of confusion and diffusion using pseudo-random numbers and follow the concept of traditional cryptography schemes.

A lightweight encryption scheme is achieved by a selective image encryption technique, where only a significant part of the original image is encrypted. Detection of significant part in the spatial domain as well as in frequency domain is calculated by various image processing techniques and wavelet functions, respectively [6]. When a significant part of an image is encrypted instead of full image, it reduces the computational cost and time complexity. There are more shortcomings of a conventional full image encryption scheme apart from the computational cost. It is discussed below:

(1) Pseudo-random numbers are generated as per the size of an image. Therefore, the number of iterations is increased to produce the key sequence as compared to the selective image encryption scheme.

(2) Encryption and decryption speedsare increased due to the bulky size of data or images [7].

Younis et al. proposed a scheme where 6.25–25% of the plaintext data isencrypted to decrease theencryption and decryption time [8]. Taneja et al. proposed a method to secure large size of data using Frenslet transform, where only signed bits of coefficientsare used for encryption [9]. In paper [10], selective image encryption scheme was implemented based on permutation and encryption module using 2D DWT. In [11], the Authors proposed three schemes using the same image encryption algorithm applied at different steps of JPEG compression; also, they have maintained the range of coefficients after encryption.Selective image encryption algorithms are designed on the basis of selective pixels or coefficients of the images [13, 14]. Xiang proposed a selective image encryption system, and an encryption algorithm selectively encrypts 50% of the whole image. They have used skew chaotic tent map to produce keystream to encrypt the significant component of an image [15]. Prajwalasimha proposed pseudo-Hadamard transform (PHT)-based image encryption scheme based on confusion and diffusion using S-box [16]. In [17], An object detection algorithm is applied to detect objects within the image using the Harr – cascade classification technique to increase the computation speed of encryption. The detected object is encrypted with the help of residue number system. In the year 2020, confusion and diffusion-based selective image encryption algorithm using dual hyperchaos map and DNA was proposed to secure medical images. DNA encoding and decoding rules are embedded in the selected pixel to implement the algorithm using chaotic sequences [18].

In this paper, the given input grayscale image is disintegrated into four sub-bands (LL, LH, HL, HH) by applying 2D DWT. These sub-bands contain the approximations and details coefficients of the image. LH, HL, and HH belong to multiresolution representation (MRR); these sub-bands preserve higher frequency information such as texture and edges of an image.***LL*** belongs to multiresolution approximation (MAR), which represents the lower frequency information.Lower frequency part or approximation coefficients of the image preserve characteristics of the image while higher frequency contains the details of the image. LL band is the approximation of the entire image, i.e., high significant information is allocated to the LL band. Therefore,a chaotic system deals only with the LL band [14, 19]. Many researchers have shown their interest in the spatial domain cryptosystem instead of frequency domain due to loss of information. Efficient retrieval of images with minimal loss of information at the receiver end is one of the objectives of the proposed algorithm.

2 Primarily Background

Digital images are being used as a source of information in digital imaging applications, such as surveillance, telecardiology, satellite communication. Therefore, to protect such information from the attackers or intruders on the untrusted network is the necessity of an ideal communication system. Chaotic maps are widely used for symmetric key encryption schemes to protect bulky information. In the proposed algorithm, we have used Tinkerbell chaotic map along with wavelet transform to accomplish the aim of the proposed algorithm.

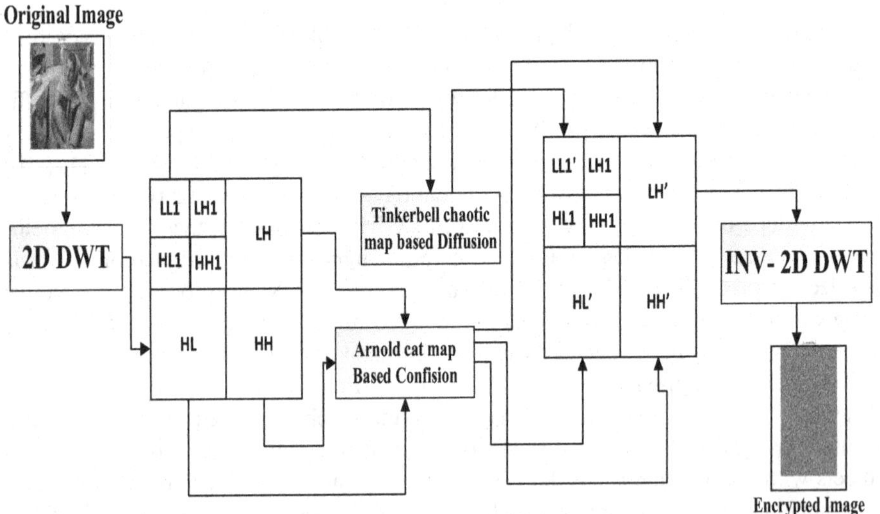

Fig. 1. Schematic diagram of the proposed architecture

2.1 Tinkerbell Chaotic Map

Tinkerbell chaotic map, a discrete-time dynamic system,is defined as two dimensional chaotic [20] map. It is assumedthat the Tinkerbell map (1) derives its name from the famous Cinderella story. The Tinkerbell map exhibits vibrant dynamics, including chaotic behavior and a range of periodic states. It is mostly used to produce chaotic sequences which are deterministic in nature and preserves pseudo randomness property.

$$\begin{aligned} x_{n+1} &= x_n^2 - y_n^2 + ax^n + by^n \\ y_{n+1} &= 2x^n y^n + cx^n + dy^n \end{aligned} \tag{1}$$

The chaotic behavior of the system depends upon the variables a, b, c, d.n defines the discrete number of iterations that areused to produce the sequence. x_0 and y_0 together work as a key for the proposed cryptosystem, the initial seed of the iterationis used to generate a pseudo-random number sequence.

2.2 Discrete Wavelet Transform

The wavelet-based transforms are broadly used in image processing techniques for compression and watermarking schemes because the time-frequency representation of a signal is possible by wavelet transforms.JPEG-2000coding standard is one of the perfect applications of DCT Transform. Wavelets are functions that derive from a single function called the mother wavelet.

In 2D DWT, low pass and high pass filters are applied toinput function or an image [21] in the horizontal direction and vertical directions and then it is downsampled by a factor of 2 to obtain approximation coefficients matrix and detail coefficients matrices; 1D DWT is applied to the image in both the directions to construct 2D DWT. The detail subbands include horizontal (HL), vertical (LH), and diagonal (HH) sub-bands of the image.The resultant values of the low pass filter represent the most significant coefficients or a low-resolution version of the original image,which is called the approximation coefficient (LL). For the subsequent level of decomposition, the approximation coefficients matrix of the previous level is decomposed into its sub-band coefficients.One level-DWT [22] and inverse discrete wavelet transform are defined by the following Eqs. (2) and (3):

$$D(a, b) = \sum_a \sum_b \mathrm{S}(a)\phi_{ab}(n) \tag{2}$$

$$S = \sum_a \sum_b \mathrm{D}(a, b)\phi_{ab}(n) \tag{3}$$

$D(a, b)$ describes the coefficient of DWT. Shift parameters and scale transform are denoted by a and b, respectively. $\phi_{ab}(n)$ represents the base time wavelet of the function. A bottom-up approach is used to reconstruct the original signal S by applying Inverse-DWT.

2.3 Arnold Cat Map

Russian mathematician Vladimir I. Arnolddevelopeda systembased upon chaos theory to shuffle an image known as Arnold cat map. It is a two-dimensional invertible chaotic map, which is used as a scrambling algorithm in cryptography schemes, also known as cat face transform [23]. Any square size image of size N*N is used as an input to produce a shuffled image and a scrambled imageis obtained by applying Eq. (4) as shown below:

$$\begin{bmatrix} x' \\ y' \end{bmatrix} = \begin{bmatrix} a & b \\ c & d \end{bmatrix} \begin{bmatrix} x \\ y \end{bmatrix} mod(N) \tag{4}$$

Here, dimension of an image is denoted by N × N, and coordinates of the pixels within an original image is denoted by x, y, and x', y', are new positioned coordinatesof an original image [24]. Reconstruction of the original image from a scrambled image is done by using Eq. (5).

$$\begin{bmatrix} x \\ y \end{bmatrix} = \begin{bmatrix} a & b \\ c & d \end{bmatrix}^{-1} \begin{bmatrix} x' \\ y' \end{bmatrix} mod(N) \tag{5}$$

3 Proposed Algorithm

In this paper, we have proposed and implemented an algorithmbased on the selective image encryption scheme. The proposed algorithm consists of the DWT, Arnold cat map and the chaotic map.In order to obtain the Frequency component, 2D-DWT up to two levels is applied to input grayscale image $I_{(x,y)}$. $LL1$ sub-band becomes an input for the encryption module and bands (LH, HL, HH) are shuffled as per Sect. 3.2. Modified bands are combined and passed to IDWT to generate the encrypted image and the decryption module is performed in the reverse order of the encryption module to obtain the decrypted image.

3.1 DWT Based Coefficients Generation

DWT is recursively applied to the image to obtain frequency coefficients, and for each call, the LL band behaves as input for the DWT. In this paper, 2D DWT is applied up to two-level. Since 2D DWT works upon the square matrix, therefore, an input image $I_{(x,y)}$ has been taken in the size of $2^m \times 2^m$.

Step (1): Implement Eq. (2) upon the input image $I_{(x,y)}$ to produce sub-band coefficient matrices LL, LH, HL, HH at level onewith the size of $2^{m/2} \times 2^{m/2}$.

Step (2): In the next level of decomposition, 2D DWT (2) is applied to LL, and the produced coefficient matrices of LL, are LL_1, LH_1, HL_1, HH_1 with the size $2^{m/4} \times 2^{m/4}$.

Step (3): Generated coefficients are used further for the confusion and diffusion process of the cryptosystem. LH, HL, HH coefficient matrices are used as input for Sect. 3.2 to shuffled the location of coefficients.

Step (4): It is observed that coefficient values are float values by applying 2D DWT. LL_1 coefficients matrix values are decomposed into two parts: (a) Integer value segment $Int(LL_1)$ (b) Fractional value $Fra(LL_1)$, and encryption is performed upon the $Int(LL_1)$ of the float numbers and later encrypted integer matrix $Enc_{int}(LL_1)$ is combined with Fractional value matrix $Fra(LL_1)$.

3.2 Shuffling Module

Arnold's cat map is performed on LH, HL, HH bands separately using Eq. (4). Arnold's cat map achieves the shuffling of coefficient locations. In this paper, twenty-five number of iterations are performed upon the coefficient matrix LH, HL, HH, and $N = 2^{m/2}$.

$$\text{Input}: \begin{bmatrix} a & b \\ c & d \end{bmatrix} = \begin{bmatrix} 1 & 1 \\ 1 & 2 \end{bmatrix}.$$
$$HL' = S(HL)_{25}; HH' = S(HH)_{25}; LH' = S(LH)_{25}$$

where $S()$ is, Arnold cat map function and subscript denotes the number of iterations.

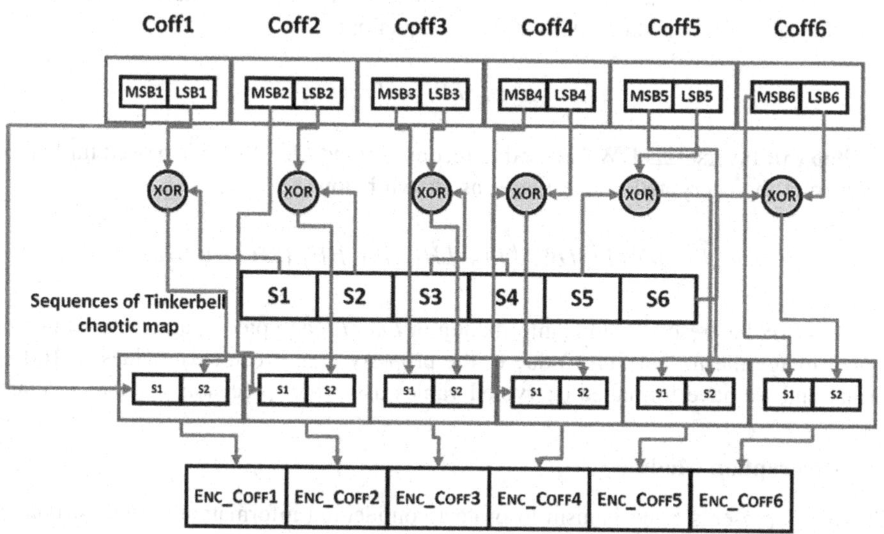

Fig. 2. Encryption module of the proposed algorithm

3.3 Encryption Module

Step (1): Tinkerbell chaotic map works as a keystream generator to produce sequences X and Y for the cryptosystem. It depends uponinitial seeds X_0 and Y_0, parameters a, b, c, d and n iterations. The size of a sequence depends upon iterations, which is defined by the size of LL_1. Thus, $2^{m/4} \times 2^{m/4}$ sequences are necessary, which are produced by applying Eq. (1).

Step (2): Experimental analysis of coefficients bands concludes that the values of the coefficients in $Int(LL_1)$ need minimum of 16 bits to preserve the entire information. Two Dimensional Tinkerbell chaotic map generates sequences and stores them as a single array by applying element multiplication between X and Y matrix. These sequences are normalized and decimal values are then converted into 10 bits [0 1024] using Eq. (6).

$$S = mod\left(|\mathrm{X} \cdot \times \mathrm{Y}| \times 10^6, 1024\right) \tag{6}$$

Step (3): Now, reshape the sequence S as per the size of $Int(LL_1)$ and keystream of sequence S is XORed with the LSB bits of $Int(LL_1)$ in a bitwise fashion until all the coefficients of $Int(LL_1)$ are XORed with sequence S. Figure 2 illustrates the encryption procedure of the proposed algorithm. matrix $Enc_{int}(LL_1)$ save all the encrypted coefficient values into it after XOR operation.

Step (4): Later, $Enc_{int}(LL_1)$ are combined with their own decimal values of $Fra(LL_1)$ of the LL_1 band as per the below equation:

$$LL_1^{'} = Enc_{int}(LL_1) + Fra(LL_1)$$

Step (5): Inverse-2D DWT is used to reconstruct the LL'. Which is passed further to reconstruct the encrypted image Enc_I as shown below:

$$Enc\_I = IDWT\left(IDWT\left(LL_1^{'}, LH_1, HL_1, HH_1\right)LH', HL'HH'\right)$$

Step (6): To preserve all the information in Enc_I, encrypted image is saved in the tagged image file format (TIFF) due to the property, i.e., it can save values in 16-bit format and we have formatted decrypted values using half-precision standard format.

3.4 Decryption Module

This paper presents a mechanism to protect confidential information within an image over the public networks. Thus, the reconstruction of a decrypted image from an encrypted image is equally important as the encryption process. Since chaotic maps are very sensitive to initial conditions, therefore using the same key pair of seeds generates the same key that is usedto decrypt an encrypted image at the receiver's end. Since the chaotic system behavior is deterministic, so reconstruction of an image using the same key pair atthe decryption end gives the decrypted image.

Step (1): Encrypted image *Enc_I* is received at the receiver end, then applying the 2D-DWT with two levels gives the coefficients of the encrypted image as per Sect. 3.1.

Step (2): Arnold map generates the original location of coefficients of HH, HL, and LH band after performing the same number of iterations.

Step (3): Now, LL_1 band is extracted from the encrypted image, and the same procedure is applied in reverse order of the encryption module.Thus, a decrypted image is generated with a minimum loss of information.

4 Experimental Results

The MATLAB R2015a software has been used to implement the proposed algorithm, the test input images,Barbara and Baboonof size 256 × 256, as shown in Fig. 3(a) and (c), respectively. The initial parameters for the Tinkerbell map are chosen as $a = 0.9, b = -0.6013, c = 2.0, d = 0.50$ to make the system chaotic. The secret symmetric key for encryption is $X_0 = 0.1231$ and $Y_0 = 0.009231$.

4.1 Cipher Image Illustration

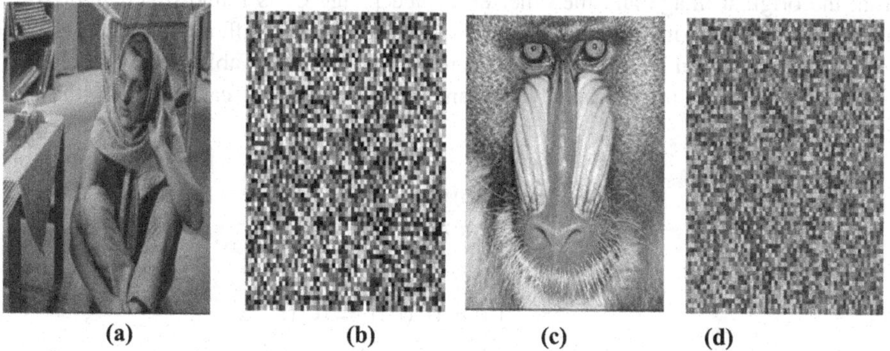

Fig. 3. Cipher image results of the Proposed algorithm (a) Original image of Lena (b) Encrypted image of Lena (c) Original image of Baboon (d) Encrypted image of Baboon

4.2 Histogram Analysis

Histogram analysis demonstrates the pictorial representation of the frequency count of all the available pixelintensity values within an image. Histogram analysis has been performed on the input images and encrypted images, and visual representation of histogram shown in Fig. 4(a), b, c and d. The x-axis defines the intensity values and the y-axis defines the count of intensity values.Uniform distribution of pixel intensity in histogram representation in Fig. 4(b) and Fig. 4(d) shows that all the pixels within an image have a similar count, and images are well encrypted.

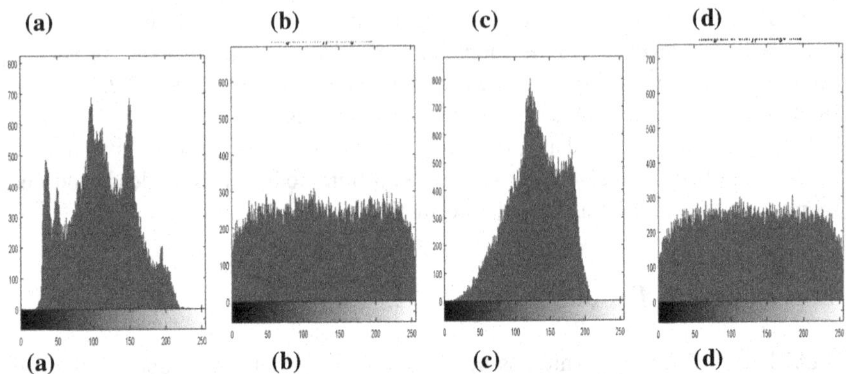

Fig. 4. Histogram Analysis (a) Original image of Lena (b) Encrypted image of Lena (c) Original image of Baboon (d) Encrypted image of Baboon

4.3 NPCR and UACI Analysis

The number of changing pixel rate (NPCR) and unified average changed intensity (UACI) tests are performed on two encrypted images. Encrypted C image originates from the original image and the other encrypted image C' is found by changing one pixel in the original imageto determine the strength against differential attack. Theoretical ideal scores of NPCR and UACI are ≅ 1 and ≅ 0.33.Table 1 shows obtained values for the input images and NPCR and UACI values are calculated by the following equations.

$$NPCR = \frac{\sum_{(i,j)} D(i,j)}{m \times n} \times 100\% \tag{7}$$

$$where\, D(i,j) \begin{cases} 1 \; if \; (C(i,j) \neq C'(i,) \\ 0 \; if \; (C(i,j) = C'(i,) \end{cases}$$

$$UACI = \frac{1}{m \times n} \left(\sum_{i,j} \frac{|C(i,j) - C'(i,j)|}{255} \right) \times 100\% \tag{8}$$

Table 1. NPCR and UACI scores of the test input images

Position	Images	Original value	Modified value	NPCR	UACI
(174,50)	Lena	70	71	0.96	0.334
(174,47)	Baboon	172	171	0.97	0.339

5 Conclusion

Chaos system is very sensitive to the initial condition means a slight change in the initial key gives a different result, and that is why intruders cannot break the cipher image.Image Reconstruction of an image at the receiver's end with a negligible difference has been achieved through the proposed algorithm with the help of TIFF image format. Only 6.3% ofcoefficients are encrypted to enhance the speed of the encryption also initial parameters increase the key size. The proposed algorithm is useful, and it hasreal-time applications to encrypt a large size of data in order to fulfill all the aspects of security. Various tests are also performed to evaluate the efficiency of the proposed algorithm, and the results of tests show that the proposed algorithm has an ample amount of substantial-quality to protect the information in a reliable manner and can resist all types of brute force attacks. Future work can also be done on different color models as well as different wavelet transforms.

References

1. Shivakumar, S.K., Sethi, S.: DXP SecurityBuilding Digital Experience Platforms, pp. 183–200. Apress, Berkeley (2019)
2. Kizza, J.M.: Computer Network Security Fundamentals. Guide to Computer Network Security, pp. 41–57. Springer, Cham (2017)
3. Gao, C., et al.: M-SSE: an effective searchable symmetric encryption with enhancedsecurity for mobile devices. IEEE Access **6,** 38860–38869 (2018)
4. Puthal, D., et al.: A dynamic prime number based efficient security mechanism for big sensing data streams. J. Comput. Syst. Sci. **83**(1), 22–42 (2017)
5. Jallouli, O.: Chaos-based security under real-time and energy constraints for the Internet of Things. Diss. (2017)
6. Som, S., et al.: A selective biplane image encryption scheme using chaotic maps. Multimed. Tools Appl. **78**(8), 10373–10400 (2019)
7. Kumar, M., Saxena, A., SatvikVuppala, S.: A survey on chaos based ImageEncryption techniques. In: Multimedia Security Using Chaotic Maps: Principles and Methodologies, pp. 1–26. Springer, Cham (2020)
8. Younis, H.A., Abdalla, T.Y., Abdalla, A.Y.: Vector quantization techniques for partial encryption ofwavelet-based compressed digital images. Iraqi J. Electr. Electron. Eng. **5**(1), 74–89 (2009)
9. Taneja, N., Raman, B., Gupta, I.: Selective image encryption in fractional wavelet domain. AUE Int. J. Electron Commun. **65**, 338–344 (2011)
10. Tresor, L., Sumbwanyambe, M.: A selective image encryption scheme based on 2D DWT, henon map and 4D Qi hyper-chaos. IEEE Access **7**, 103463–103472 (2019)
11. He, K., et al.: Robust and secure image encryption schemes during jpeg compressionprocess. Electron. Imaging **11**, 1–7 (2016)
12. Krikor, L., Bab, S., Ari, T., Shaaban, Z.: Image encryption using DCT and stream cipher. Europ. J. Sci. Res. **32**, 47–57 (2009)
13. Liu, X., Eskicioglu, A.M.: Selective encryption of multimedia content in distribution networks: Challenges and new directions. In: IASTED Communications, Internet & Information Technology CIIT, (USA), pp. 527–533 (2003)

14. Hazarika, N., Borah, S., Saikia, M.: A wavelet based partial image encryption using chaotic logistic map. In: 2014 IEEE International Conference on Advanced Communications, Control and Computing Technologies. IEEE (2014)
15. Xiang, T., Wong, K., Liao, X.: Selective image encryption using a spatiotemporal chaotic system. Chaos: An Interdisciplinary Journal of Nonlinear Science **17**(2), 0231151–02311513 (2007)
16. Prajwalasimha, S.N.: Pseudo-Hadamard Transformation-Based Image Encryption Scheme. Integrated Intelligent Computing, Communication and Security, pp. 575–583. Springer, Singapore. (2019)
17. Kelur, S., Ranjan Kumar, H.S., Raju, K.: Selective area encryption using machine learning technique. In: 2019 Innovations in Power and Advanced Computing Technologies (i-PACT), vol. 1. IEEE, pp. 1–7 (2019)
18. Akkasaligar, P.T., Biradar, S.: Selective medical image encryption using DNA cryptography. Inf. Secur. J. A Global Perspect., 1–11 (2020)
19. Lahmiri, S.: A wavelet-wavelet based processing approach for microcalcifications detection in mammograms. J. Adv. Inf. Technol. **3**(3), 162–167 (2012)
20. Ouannas, A., et al.: The fractional form of the Tinkerbell map is chaotic. Appl. Sci. **8**(12), 2640 (2018)
21. Ahmad, Afandi, AzlanMuharam, and Abbes Amira., GPU-based implementation of CABAC for 3-Dimensional Medical Image Compression. J. Telecommun. Electron. Comput. Eng. (JTEC) **9**(3–8), 45–50 (2017)
22. Kumar Ashish, and N. S. Raghava., Chaos-based steganography technique to secure information and integrity preservation of smart grid readings using wavelet. Int. J. Comput. Appl., 1–7 (2019)
23. Agilandeeswari, L., Ganesan, K.: RST invariant robust video watermarking algorithm using quaternion curvelet transform. Multimed. Tools Appl. **77**(19), 25431–25474 (2018)
24. Elkamchouchi, H., Salama, W.M., Abouelseoud, Y.: ArMTFr: a new permutation-based image encryption scheme. Int. J. Electron. Secur. Digital Forens. **11**(1), 1–28 (2019)

Computing Techniques for Efficient Networks Design

Spatial Information Preservation in Graph Convolutional Neural Network

Rakesh Kumar Yadav[1](✉), Abhishek[1], Prashant Shukla[1], Nazish Tabassum[1], Ranjeet Singh Tomar[2], and Shekhar Verma[1]

[1] Indian Institute of Information Technology Allahabad, Prayagraj, India
{pcl2014003,rsi2016006,rsi2016502,icm2014504,sverma}@iiita.ac.in
[2] ITM University, Gwalior, India
ranjeetsingh@itmuniversity.ac.in

Abstract. Convolutional Neural Networks (ConvNets or CNNs) are that class of Neural Networks that have confirm very effective in areas such as classification and image recognition. Graph convolution neural network is that area of work that deals with the generalization of well-established neural models like convnets on structured datasets as there are numerous important problems that can be framed as learning from graph data. This paper focused to overcome one of the major weaknesses GCNN poses i.e. GCNN are Translational Invariant means these neural models are unable to identify the position of one object with respect to another. For example, the model will predict a car if it sees a bunch of random car parts like wheels, steering, headlights, and so on because all the key features are there. So, the main problem is to identify that the car parts are not in the correct position relative to another. We performed the experiments on two benchmark datasets, MNIST and smallNORB, and the accuracies obtained with our proposed models are comparably high. Thus the technique is able to preserve the spatial relationship among objects in the given structured dataset is the main motivation behind this paper.

Keywords: Convolutional Neural Network · Graph convolution neural network · Translational invariant

1 Introduction

The representation of graphs [8] can be defined as vertices and edges such as $G = (V, E)$, V = vertices, E = edges. In Graph Convolutional Neural Network [2], graphs are undirected but weighted but in our case the graphs are undirected and unweighted. The information about connections among different vertices or say different nodes are stored in a matrix called as Adjacent matrix where every cell in adjacent matrix is defined as A_{ij}. If $A_{ij} \neq 0$ i.e. if A_{ij} has some value it means there is an edge connecting node i to node j and the edge has weight = value (A_{ij}).

R. S. Tomar et al. (Eds.): CNC 2020, CCIS 1502, pp. 211–222, 2021.
https://doi.org/10.1007/978-981-16-8896-6_17

1.1 Convolution Neural Network

Convolution Layer. Input layer [1] passed an array of 2 Dimensions and this array is chunk wise convoluted with filters which is defined by user and passes all through the input at least once. Formula for convolution can be defined mathematically as,

$$h(a) = f \star g = \int_{-\infty}^{+\infty} f(a - v)\partial v \tag{1}$$

When filter is convoluted with the array or say input, they result a map called an Activation map. So, basically these inputs have to convoluted with filters because this technique is used to find out features of input, in our case it is an image. This filter learned the features of given images as the filter swoop over each pixel and convolute. Initially, weights are assigned some random value and learned through backpropagation. Steps involved in back propagation technique:

- Weights need to be passed to next layer
- Dealing with loss function
- Updating weight by sending back to previous layer

Relationship between weights and errors are shown as above Fig. (1). As the weights are keep on updating, the dot keep on arriving downwards and the slowly error gets scale down.

Pooling Layer. This layer is the soul of a Neural Network. Data which we generally dealt such as images, videos and audios often have large parameters between the convolutional layer [10]. Thus to reduce them and to avoid overfitting to our model, pooling layer plays an important role. This layer generally runs with $2 * 2$ filter or more, depends on user to improve big time complexity but using this filter did not preserve the spatial relationship among images. Here in Fig. (2) an input of $4 * 4$ matrix has been trimmed or more technically downsampled to $2 * 2$ matrix output while in (iv) an input of $4 * 4$ matrix has downsampled to $3 * 3$ matrix by taking stride to 1 as depicted in above figure.

Fully Connected Layer. This is the last and fully connected layer of the convnets. All the techniques and computation to achieve best output is obtained in this layer.

1.2 Graph Convolutional Neural Network

There are few weaknesses in GCNN and thus it is the high time to think about the advancement or improvements in the current model and propose some new solutions.

GCNN weaknesses:

1. Computational cost is high.
2. Time complexity is high if model is pretty deep, training process will take much greater time. Thus need of good GPU (for complex tasks).
3. For good result, need huge amount of training data.
4. They lost spatial information of the position and orientation, thus can't encode spatial relationship into their predictions.

Thus, to overcome one of the weaknesses i.e. preservation of spatial relationship among different features like edges, then shape and after that objects or simply say, different parts of images, group of neurons often called as capsules are introduced instead of single neuron. So, what happen when GCNN uses the pooling layer. Pooling layer actually lost the internal information about the angle, pose, orientations of the components to diminish the complexities as much as possible. They route all the valuable knowledge to some neurons which might not be related to particular information. A GCNN classifies an image/audio/video by just checking if certain chunks of components is available in image/audio/video or not. And if all the chunks or components are present, then it predicts the image accordingly.

1.3 CAPSule NETwork

In a capsule network [9,11,12], higher level neurons received all the low level details, after which these higher level neurons perform some convolutions [5] methods to check whether that particular features are present there or not. Now, suppose a model which classifies two images, say human and table. Thus, if a lower neuron identified a thumb, it then obviously makes some sense to propagate this valuable knowledge to a higher level neuron that deals with identifying an arm or hand and not to that neuron that identifies table. If a higher level neurons gets all the correct details that contains angle, pose, orientation, degree of certainty and positions from lower level neurons of presence of thumb, index fingers, middle finger, ring finger, pinky finger in correct orders as well as palm and wrist, then Hand neuron can identifies it as arm. Use of group of neurons or simply say capsules, that if lower level layer identifies [13] certain pattern then these neurons output a high dimensional vector that contains all the valuable details and knowledge about the probability of the orientation, degree and its pose. After getting this vector these values fed to higher level capsules.

The launching of capsule network by professor Hinton [9] opened the ability to take full advantage of spatial relationship and importance of preserving such valuable information. The basic and simple architecture of capsnet is explained following:

1. The Input: The input to the capsnet is an 3-Dimensional image feed to Neural network same as in CNN.
2. PrimaryCaps: This primary capsule is very similar to convolution layer with only difference in the convolution of numbers of output stack from previous convolutions.

As in very first layer simple edges and curves are detected, now it's turn for finding more complex shapes from the edges found earlier. To reduce the size of input rapidly, choose larger stride while convolution.
Now there are large stack of output, so cut the stack up into different blocks or decks. We can call these blocks/deck capsule layer.
Each capsule layer has X capsules, where X defined by user. Each capsule is actually an array of n values and this array is called Vector or commonly known as pose matrix.
The old model with single pixel, it can say whether or not it found a curve/edge or not. It is more like boolean but with the capsule pixel model can store n values per location. This give more room to store more details than just whether or not we found a shape in that spot. So details we would want to store can be pose, rotation, colour, and many more. It is totally depends on user to make it model more specific towards these parameters by increasing the value of n in capsule vectors.
While during training of traditional CNN, the model cares about the correct prediction of input, but with the capsule network, there is something called "Reconstruction". So, the technique is to take the vectors of information stored already and tries to recreate the original input image. With the closeness of reconstructed output matches the original image, the model has been graded and improvised accordingly.

3. Squashing: After storing all the information in capsules, we perform one more non linearity function (previously it was ReLU) on our model. The function scales the values of vector to change length of vector so that the vectors length changes between 0 to 1 to show the actual probability.
4. Routing by Agreement: This is the essence of capsnet. In traditional convnet, pooling (mostly max pooling) is used by reducing the size of input by only passing highly activated pixel of that region to the next layer. However, here in capsnet we don't want to loose the spatial information among objects, thus in capsnet a different technique known as Routing by Agreement has been used. With this technique, model will only pass the valuable and useful information and rejects the data which is irrelevant with respect to higher level capsules. This gives the much smarter selection rather than just pass the highest, lowest or averaging the values like in max, min, or average pooling method. With traditional convnet, spatial relationship is not preserved:
In capsule network, with the help of Routing by Agreement, the feature wont agree with each other:
The above figure shows that all the parts of face are ready to be part of high Face capsule but the Palm capsule is not the part of Face capsule but of Hand capsule. Thus palm is assigned as 0 for Face capsule.
5. DigitCaps: This is the final layer of our model. This layer has number of outputs which needs to be predicted and each predicted outputs associated with the n dimensional vectors. The length of each ones vector defines the confidence of the output being found. Longer the length better will be prediction. The vector having longer vector will be the final prediction of model.

2 Material and Method

Given an image and information of each and every entities of this particular images are stored accordingly, treating the image as graph. We aim to solve this problem by using the ideas and algorithms which was proposed earlier and improve our model. The capsule network, which is also modification of CNN, shows better results for this problem. Taking the basic model of spatial preservation using capsnet, we build our own different architectures which is differ from previous work.

1. First one is using attention module [6] as on basic capsnet
2. Intermixing the different GCNN layers and capsnet accordingly.
3. Use of Low, medium and high features of GCNN with Capsnet.

2.1 CapsNet Architecture

Lets see each architecture one by one but before that it should be mentioned that each architectures implemented two routings algorithm: dynamic routing and em routing.

1. Dynamic routing:
   - Image: array of raw image
   - Relu conv1: input will be array of image
   - Primary caps layer: input is the output by relu conv1 with suitable kernel size and stride
   - Apply squash function as defined in Eq. (2)
   - Digit caps layer
     - $\mu_{j|i}$ (prediction vector) = W (transformation) $\star$ u_i (output of child neuron).
     - dynamic routing layer
       v_j = dynamic-routing $\mu_{j|i}$
       V_{ij} = normal (v_j)
       v_j is activity vector
       V_{ij} 's length is probability if child caps belongs to parent caps lies 0–1

Algorithm for Dynamic Routing:
dynamic-routing ($\mu_{j|i}$, r, l)

(a) $b_{ij} \rightarrow 0, i = layerL, j = L + 1$
(b) for itr iterations do: (itr = 3)
   - $c_i \rightarrow softmax(b_i), i = L$
   - $s_j \rightarrow \sum_i c_{ij}\mu_{j|i}, cij$
   - $v_j \rightarrow squash(s_j)$
   - $b_{ij} \rightarrow b_{ij} + v_j\mu_{j|i}$

(c) return v_j

Squash formula used

$$v_j = \frac{||s_i||^2}{1 + ||s_i||^2} \star \frac{s_i}{||s_i||} \tag{2}$$

Reconstruction loss

$$Loss = ||image - reconstructedimage|| \tag{3}$$

Feed v_j which was calculated in step (3) using above algorithm of Dynamic Routing through 3 fully connected layers with sigmoid activation function to regenerate original image. With addition to reconstruction loss, margin loss also calculated in dynamic routing.

Margin loss

$$Total_L = T_c \max(0; m_j^+ - ||v_c||)^2 + \lambda(1 - T_c) \max(0, ||v_c|| - m^-)^2 \tag{4}$$

2. EM-routing
   - Image: array of raw image
   - RELU-conv1: This layer is basic convolution layer using a suitable filter with stride 2 which outputs 32 feature maps using the ReLU as activation function.
   - Primary-caps: Apply convolution filter to convert each of the 32 feature maps into 32 primary capsules. Each and ever capsules contain a 4×4 pose matrix and an activation value. We group $4 \times 4 + 1$ neurons to generate 1 capsule.
   - CONV-caps1: calculating vote by v = pose matrix * transformation matrix μ = em-routing (activation, votes) The 16 μ from the model is shaped to form the 4×4 pose matrix of the parent capsule.
   - CONV-caps2: The input of CONV-caps2 is from output of CONV-caps1. The output capsules of ConvCaps2 are connected to the Class Capsules and it outputs one capsule per class.
   - Class-caps: This class output a vector whose length determines final activation of parent capsule. Pose-out is final pose matrix of parent.

Algorithm for Expectation Maximization Routing
EM-routing (a, V)

(a) $R_{ij} = 1\ |L + 1|$, all capsules, $i = L$ and $j = L + 1$, where L = Layers of model
(b) For itr iterations do
   - j = L+1, M-step (a, V, R, j)
   - i = L, E-step (μ, σ, a, V, i)
(c) return(a,M)

Procedure of M step:

(a) M step (activation a, assignment probability r, votes v, parent caps j)
(b) for all i belongs to layer L:

$$R_{ij} \leftarrow R_{ij} * a_i$$

(c) For all h[th] component

$$\mu_j^h \leftarrow \frac{(\sum_i R_{ij} V_{ij}^h)}{(\sum_i R_{ij})}$$

(d) For h:

$$(\sigma_j^h)^2 = \frac{(\sum_i R_{ij} (V_{ij}^h - \mu_j^h)^2)}{(\sum_i R_{ij})}$$

(e) $cost^h \leftarrow (\beta_v \log(\sigma_j h)) \sum_i R_{ij}$
(f) $\sigma_j \leftarrow sigmoid(\lambda(\beta_\alpha - \sum_h cost^h))$

λ is a parameter increased by 1 after each routing iteration and $\beta_\alpha, \beta_{n\mu}$ updated accordingly. Now, a_j is transferred to E step.

Procedure E step

(a) E step (μ, α, activation a_j, vote, child caps)
(b) As explained r for all j belongs to layer $L + 1$

(c) For all j belongs to $L + 1$

$$R_{ij} \leftarrow \frac{\alpha_j p_i}{\sum_{\mu \epsilon L+1} \alpha_\mu p_\mu}$$

In E-step, update the assignment probability R_{ij} which is calculated on the basis of new μ, α and a_j.

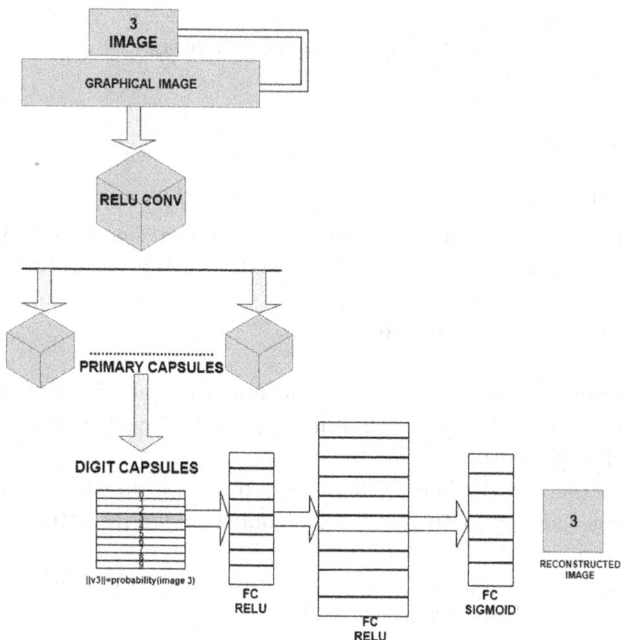

Fig. 1. Capsule network

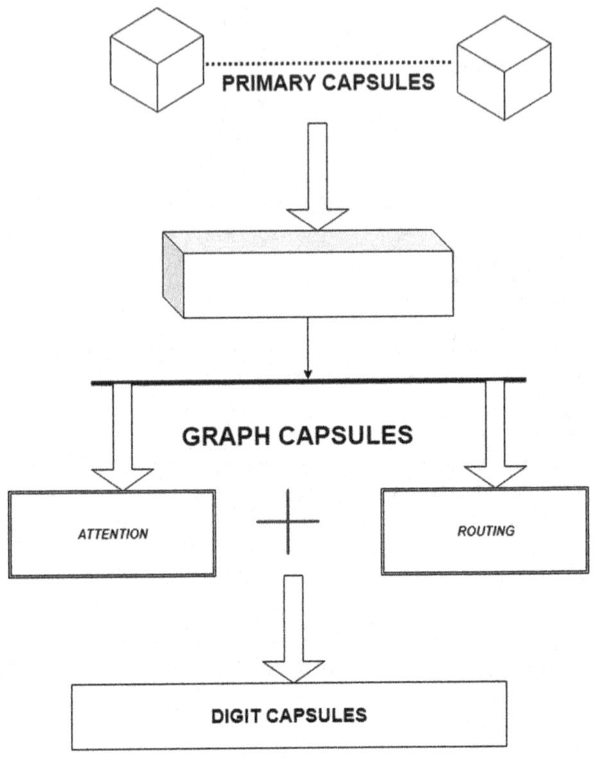

Fig. 2. Capsule attention network

3 Architecture

1. Capsnet with Attention Module
   This model introduces new capsule layer named as Graph Capsule as described in paper [7]. Thus, Graph Capsule = Attention + Routing.

   Algorithm for Attention Module
   Attention (primary caps)
   (a) a = mean(P), where P belongs to output from each primary caps.
   (b) Send the calculated 'a' to 2 fully connected layers attention1 = fully connected layer(a)
   (c) b = maximum(P), where P belongs to output from each primary caps.
   (d) Send the calculated 'b' to 2 fully connected layers attention2 = fully connected layer(b)
   (e) Now, apply node based normalization. Here we used sigmoid function scale = sigmoid(attention1,attention2)
   (f) Multiply this scale value with actual inputs.
       channel attention = scale * inputs
   (g) return channel attention

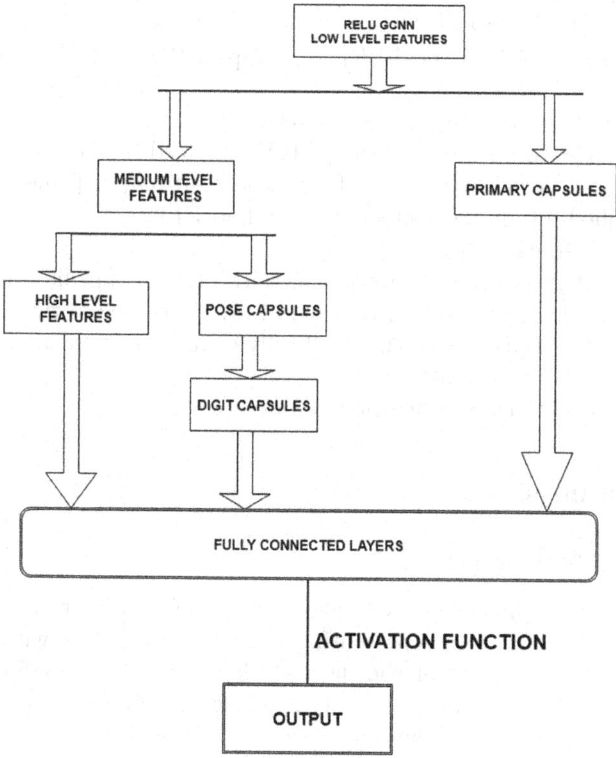

Fig. 3. Infusing layers network

2. Infuse the GCNN layers and Capsnet layers
   (a) Apply basic RELU gcnn layer
   (b) The output from this layer used as low feature and then feed into first layer of capsnet i.e. to primary layer.
   (c) The output from RELU-gcnn is then, feed to find medium level feature.
   (d) The output of medium level feature feed to next layer of capsnet which is used to find required votes and pose matrix.
   (e) The output from medium feature level is feed into high level feature layer of gcnn i.e. the final fully connected layer.
   (f) The output of second layer capsnet feed into final capsule class layer.
   (g) Now final layer of GCNN and final capsule class layer are connected to fully connected layer
   (h) Output of this final layer needs to pass by an activation function which is a softmax function.
3. Low, Medium and High features of GCNN with Capsule Network
   This model use the Low level feature of network and feed it to Capsule Network for spatial relationship preservation. Similarly, train and test the model for Medium level and High level feature respectively.

The algorithm is as follows:

(a) Find Low Level Feature (LLF) of an input. We applied 3 layers to find LLF.
(b) Feed this LLF to regular capsule Network.
(c) Now, find Medium Level Feature (MLF) and feed this to capsule Network.
(d) Finally, last layer of GCNN i.e. High Level Feature (HLF) needs to obtain. We applied 9 fully connected layers to find HLF.
(e) Feed HLF to capsnet.
(f) the output from each of capsule Network i.e. LLFcapsule, MLF-capsule, HLF-capsule are connected to a final fully connected layer.
(g) The result obtained from this final fully connected layer needs to be pass from an activation function.
Here Softmax/sigmoid function can be use.

4 Experiments

4.1 Training and Testing

Before training, the image dataset have been preprocessed, treating pixels of an image as nodes of graph, representing it as graphical data with nodes and edges. Further, the training of the data set has been done for 50 epoch and learning rate for it is exponential decay learning rate of value $1e{-}3$. The loss function is minimized using Adam optimizer [4], which shown to be better than the stochastic gradient decent.

1. MNIST: MNIST's Training dataset [6] is 55000 which is a handwritten dataset from (0–9) and tested on 10,000 datasets. Images are reshaped to $(28 \times 28 \times 1)$ dimensions, 1 indicates that images to be train are not coloured.
2. smallNORB: smalNORB's Training dataset [7] is 46800 which shows toys from various angles and in different lighting and tested on 46800 datasets.

Finally, Images are cropped to $(32 \times 32 \times 1)$ dimensions.

4.2 Metrices Used for Evaluation

Coming to the results as we have mentioned in the previous section that we have evaluated the results using two routing algorithms: dynamic routing and em routing on dataset MNIST and SmallNORB.

1. For Dynamic Routing: Total loss = Reconstruction Loss + Margin Loss
The architecture, on MNIST achieves $0:429\%$ test error rate while on small-NORB $0:434\%$ test error rate.
2. For EM Routing [3]: Spread loss is used here to minimize the error which is defined as: Total loss is:
$L = \sum_{i \neq t} \max(0; m - (\alpha_t - \alpha_i))^2$

A_t = activation of target class
A_i = activation for class i
M is initially is 0.2 but increases by 0.1 after each epoch during training. M stops reaching maximum of 0.9. The architecture, on MNIST achieves 0.068% test error rate while on smallNORB 0.0491% test error rate

5 Result

Coming to results, the Reconstructed image shows that our model preserve the Spatial information among different parts of nodes. Thus, to preserve much informations and details we must minimize Reconstruction Loss as much as possible. For MNIST data set:

The code is implemented in PYTHON and Tensorflow is used for all heavy mathematical operations as defined by equations.

Accuracy

Table 1. Results and Comparison

Accuracy (%)	CAPSnet	Model1	Model2	Model3
MNIST	99.62	99.56	84.78	84.10
smallNORB	82.1731	83.43	87.14	88.54

The time complexity is:
Epoch $*$ number_of_training_dataset $* (L1 * L2 + L2 * L3 + L3 * ...)$.
MNIST – $50 * 55000 * (L1 * L2 + L2 * L3 + L3 * ...)$ where, L1 Relu conv1 = $20 * 20 * 256$, L2 Primary caps = $6 * 6 * 8 * 32$, L3 class-caps = $10 * (4 * 4)$.

smallNORB – $50 * 46800(L1 * L2 + L2 * L3 + L3 * ...)$ where, L1 Relu conv1: $14 * 14 * 32$, L2 Primary caps: $(14 * 14 * 32)(4 * 4 + 1)$, L3 Conv-caps1: $6 * 6 * 32(4 * 4 + 1)$, L4 Conv-caps2: $4 * 4 * 32(4 * 4 + 1)$, L5 class-caps:$10 * (4 * 4 + 1)$

6 Discussion and Summary

The idea of the paper as we have mentioned many times in the above section is to spatial preservation of graphical dataset. We tried to implement such by taking various research papers of previous work as our base paper. The idea for implementing two routing algorithms: Dynamic and EM [3] for calculation of votes and prediction vector for parent-child capsules is quite satisfactory and the accuracy for testing 10,000 MNIST and 46800 data points of smallNORB for both the algorithms are quite same. But for smallNORB the accuracy is lower than MNIST. Implementing different types of models for smallNORB there is a gradual increase of accuracy but there are much rooms to improve accuracy and decrease error rate. The time taken to train our model by EM routing algorithm is much more than the time taken to train the model by Dynamic routing algorithms. Though The attention module implemented in our model does not increase the significant accuracy compared with capsnet but it does reduce the time take for training of such big data.

7 Future Scope

The paper can be extended to use more complex datasets like MNIST100 and cifar100 with different elevations and azimuths and light effect. Since we use only one channel (gray) image this work can be extended to colour image. Instead of attention module, different image processing modules can be implemented with Capsnet.

References

1. Albawi, S., Mohammed, T.A., Al-Zawi, S.: Understanding of a convolutional neural network. In: 2017 International Conference on Engineering and Technology (ICET), pp. 1–6. IEEE (2017)
2. Henaff, M., Bruna, J., LeCun, Y.: Deep convolutional networks on graph-structured data. arXiv preprint arXiv:1506.05163 (2015)
3. Hinton, G.E., Sabour, S., Frosst, N.: Matrix capsules with EM routing. In: International Conference on Learning Representations (2018)
4. Kingma, D.P., Ba, J.: Adam: a method for stochastic optimization. arXiv preprint arXiv:1412.6980 (2014)
5. Kulkarni, T.D., Whitney, W., Kohli, P., Tenenbaum, J.B.: Deep convolutional inverse graphics network. arXiv preprint arXiv:1503.03167 (2015)
6. LeCun, Y., Bottou, L., Bengio, Y., Haffner, P.: Gradient-based learning applied to document recognition. Proc. IEEE **86**(11), 2278–2324 (1998)
7. LeCun, Y., Huang, F.J., Bottou, L.: Learning methods for generic object recognition with invariance to pose and lighting. In: Proceedings of the 2004 IEEE Computer Society Conference on Computer Vision and Pattern Recognition, vol. 2, p. II-104 (2004)
8. Mathieu, M., Henaff, M., LeCun, Y.: Fast training of convolutional networks through FFTs. In: 2nd International Conference on Learning Representations, ICLR 2014 (2014)
9. Sabour, S., Frosst, N., Hinton, G.E.: Dynamic routing between capsules. arXiv preprint arXiv:1710.09829 (2017)
10. Simonyan, K., Zisserman, A.: Very deep convolutional networks for large-scale image recognition. arXiv preprint arXiv:1409.1556 (2014)
11. Xiang, C., Zhang, L., Tang, Y., Zou, W., Xu, C.: MS-CapsNet: a novel multi-scale capsule network. IEEE Sig. Process. Lett. **25**(12), 1850–1854 (2018)
12. Xinyi, Z., Chen, L.: Capsule graph neural network. In: International Conference on Learning Representations (2018)
13. Yang, M., Liu, Y., You, Z.: The Euclidean embedding learning based on convolutional neural network for stereo matching. Neurocomputing **267**, 195–200 (2017)

Graph Convolutional Neural Network Using Wavelet Transform

Rakesh Kumar Yadav[1(✉)], Abhishek[1], Prashant Shukla[1], Neelanjana Jaiswal[1], Brijesh Kumar Chaurasia[2], and Shekhar Verma[1]

[1] Indian Institute of Information Technology Allahabad, Prayagraj, India
{pcl2014003,rsi2016006,rsi2016502,ism2014005,sverma}@iiita.ac.in
[2] Indian Institute of Information Technology, Lucknow, India
brijesh@iiitl.ac.in

Abstract. Convolutional Neural Networks have brought great advancement in the field of deep learning. Graphs can be used to represent information in a natural way in many important areas of interest. CNN on graphs can be formulated either using a spatial or spectral approach. In this work, we propose a framework for designing a convolutional neural network on graphs where convolution is performed in the spectral domain. We are interested in defining the filters for convolutional layers using the wavelet transform. Wavelet transform has attracted much attention in recent years for the purpose of signal processing. The property that makes it desirable is that it can provide the time and frequency resolution of signals. The experiments have been conducted on the benchmark dataset, Cora, and the accuracies obtained with our proposed models are comparably high.

Keywords: Convolutional Neural Network · Graph convolution neural network · Wavelet transform

1 Introduction

The introduction of convolutional neural network [2,7,9] model has brought great advancement in the field of machine learning. Owing to the success of the CNN, research has been going on to generalize the CNN model to work with graphs. In a lot of diverse applications, data have the potential to be represented as graphs that can help in achieving better results. Graphs can be directed or undirected, static or dynamic etc. CNNs are able to extract the local stationary structures shared among nodes using the convolutional filters [1,7,8] which aids in decreasing the number of parameters required to train in the network. Convolutional filters can be designed in spatial as well as spectral domains. The work of [4,11,12]defines filters in spatial domain. The papers [2,4,7] define filters in spectral domain using the Fourier transform. In this work we aim at designing filters in spectral domain using wavelet transform [3,5]. Wavelet transform has the advantage over Fourier transform in the sense that it gives time as well as frequency resolution whereas Fourier transform only provides frequency resolution of the signal.

R. S. Tomar et al. (Eds.): CNC 2020, CCIS 1502, pp. 223–236, 2021.
https://doi.org/10.1007/978-981-16-8896-6_18

1.1 Convolution Neural Network

Convolution Layer. Convolutional layer is the core layer in CNN. It performs convolution on the input as well as the hidden layers and the results are passed onto the subsequent layers. Mathematically the convolution operation is defined as in Eq. 1.

$$\langle f, g \rangle = \int_{-\infty}^{+\infty} f(t-\tau)g(t-\tau)\partial\tau \tag{1}$$

As we know convolution operation requires two entities, one of which is the input and the other one is the filters which are specifically designed for this layer and determine the quality of the operation. These filters help in the extraction and learning of features. They also have parameters also known as kernel that are learned to adjust these filters during back propagation.

Pooling Layer. Pooling layer is used for reducing the dimensionality of the output maps at various layers so as to reduce the computational cost. This layer acts independently on each feature map. It is added after all or some of the convolutional layers. One thing to note here is that only the spatial dimensions are reduced. Pooling operation has no effect on the depth of the output.

Fully Connected Layer. These layers are generally added in the end after convolutional layers. This layer acts identical to the layers in regular neural network. Each neuron receives input from all the units in the previous hidden layer. Essentially it aggregates all the information from the previous convolutional layers.

1.2 Graph Convolutional Neural Network

In real life situations the data points are related. There is interconnection between them which plays a crucial role in determination of the problem. Graphs provide a useful way to represent this information. Most of the real world data exist in form of graphs. But the neural networks do not take into account the graphical interrelation of the data. Then this creates the need of Graph Convolutional Neural Networks. GCN is the CNN that take into account the graphs along with data to solve the problem at hand

Consider a graph $G(V, E)$. Every vertex has F number of features then Graph Convolutional Network takes:

- An input matrix (X) of features of dimensions NxF where N is the total count of nodes and F is the count of features per vertex.
- An adjacency matrix (A) of dimensions NxN that contains the representation of the graph.

The generalised Eq. 2 for each of layer can be given as:

$$Y(k+1) = f(Y(k), A) \tag{2}$$

with $Y(0) = X$ and $Y(K) = Z$ for graph-level outputs, where K is the count of layers.

The models then differ in how $f(.)$ is chosen. The layer-wise forward propagation rule for the simplest GCN model can be given as:

$$f(Y^K, A) = \sigma(AY^{(K)}W^{(k)})$$

Where $\sigma()$ is an activation function and $W^{(K)}$ is the weight matrix at layer k.

1.3 Spectral Graph Theory

We have our input as a graph $G(V, E)$, where E denotes the set of edges and V denotes the set of nodes. There are two matrices associated with the input. Let N be the count of vertices and F be the count of features then these matrices can be defined as:

1. Adjacency Matrix: An adjacency matrix denoted by A is of size $N \times N$ and can be defined as:

$$A = \begin{cases} w_{mn} & \text{if node m and n are connected by an edge} \\ 0 & \text{otherwise} \end{cases} \tag{3}$$

2. Feature Matrix – A feature matrix of size $N \times F$ can be defined as:

$$X = \begin{cases} x_{ij} & \text{value of j}^{\text{th}} \text{ feature for i}^{\text{th}} \text{ node} \end{cases} \tag{4}$$

3. Degree Matrix: A degree matrix denoted by D of the size $N \times N$ is a diagonal matrix which can be given as:

$$F = \begin{cases} x_{ij} & \text{value of j}^{\text{th}} \text{ feature for i}^{\text{th}} \text{ node} \end{cases} \tag{5}$$

4. Degree Matrix – A degree matrix denoted by D of the size $N \times N$ is a diagonal matrix which can be given as:

$$D = \begin{cases} d_{mn} & \text{if m = n} \\ 0 & \text{otherwise} \end{cases} \tag{6}$$

where d_{mn} is the degree of the vertex m.

Graph Laplacian – To perform signal processing on graphs we need to find the Laplacian of the graph. The eigen values and the eigen vectors of the Laplacian are then used in the calculation of Graph Fourier and Graph Wavelet Transform. Laplacian is defined by the Eq. 7,

$$L = D - A \tag{7}$$

This is the non-normalized form of the Laplacian. The normalized form of L has been defined in Eq. 8,

$$L = I - D^{-1/2}LD^{-1/2} \tag{8}$$

- L is a symmetric matrix since both D and A are also symmetric.
- It is real and positive semi-definite.
- It has non-negative eigen values and the corresponding eigenvectors which satisfy:

$$LU = \sigma U$$

- We can also say that the eigenvalue decomposition of L is given by:

$$L = U\lambda U^t$$

- The eigen values play the role of frequency.Low frequency components are represented by the smaller eigen values and vice-versa.

Fourier Transform – Fourier transform is an operation that is used for the purpose of signal processing by extracting out the frequencies present in the signal. It decomposes a signal into sine and cosine constituents. It is utilized in a wide variety of applications, like image filtering, image reconstruction and image analysis. Fourier transform converts a signal given in spatial domain to the frequency (spectral) domain as in Eq. 9.

$$\hat{f(w)} = \int_{-\infty}^{+\infty} f(t)e^{-jwt}dt \tag{9}$$

The inverse Fourier transform can be defined as:

$$f(t) = \int_{-\infty}^{+\infty} f(w)e^{-jwt}dt \tag{10}$$

Graph Fourier Transform – The signal analysis over graphs is useful in many areas of applications. Graph fourier transform is one such tool. The eigenvectors calculated from the laplacian of the graph are analogous to fourier basis. The graph fourier transform of a function f defined over the vertices of a graph G at an eigen value λ_l, is given by:

$$\hat{f(l)} = \sum_{n=1}^{N} x_l \star f(n)$$

The inverse graph Fourier transform can be given as:

$$f(n) = \sum_{n=1}^{N} x_l \star f(l)$$

where x_l is the eigen vector.

Wavelet Analysis – Wavelet transform is a rather new concept. Due to some specific properties the wavelet transform is popularly used for the purpose of signal processing. When we think of signal processing the most common term that comes to mind is Fourier expansion and Fourier transform. Fourier expansion is the representation of a function using infinite sine and cosine functions. The only downside to the Fourier transform is that it has no time resolution.

It only tells what frequencies exist in the signal but what it fails to tell is the time at which those frequencies occur and for what duration. Wavelet transform overcomes this shortcoming as it can perform both time and frequency resolution.

Wavelet
A wavelet is a short-term wave whose amplitude starts at zero, rises and then diminishes back to zero. Wavelets have become popular now-a-days for many signal processing applications. Wavelets are utilized in the representation of other functions. In wavelet algorithms data is processed at different scales which makes it different from Fourier transform. Wavelets are mathematical functions that analyze a signal by extracting the frequency components and then matching them according to scale. Wavelets are used for localizing a signal in both frequency and time that gives it edge over Fourier transform that analyzes a signal in terms of frequency and amplitude but not time.

A set of wavelets are needed for the complete analysis of data. A wavelet prototype function known as mother wavelet is used for the creation of the family of wavelets by applying translation and scaling operations. Consider a mother wavelet, then the daughter wavelets are given by the Eq. 11,

$$\Psi_{s,a}(x) = \frac{1}{s}\Psi(\frac{s-a}{x}) \tag{11}$$

Where a is the translation factor and s is the scaling factor.

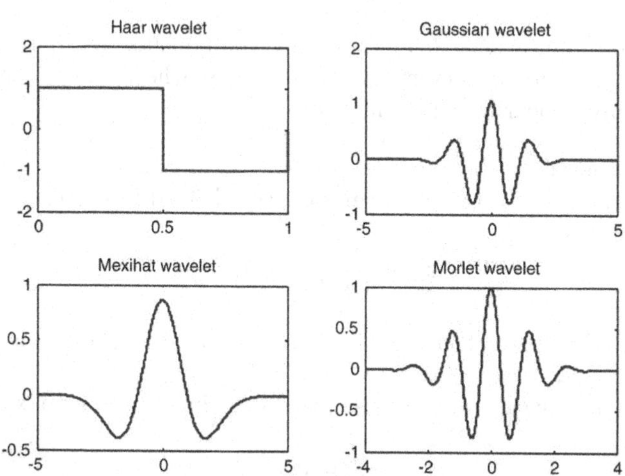

Fig. 1. Example of wavelets

Scaling in Wavelet Analysis. Scales are used to get different views of the signal. Scaling is used for the purpose of either compressing or dilating a signal. Dilation is performed using larger scales and compression using smaller scales. The meaning of scale used here is similar to that used in geographical maps.

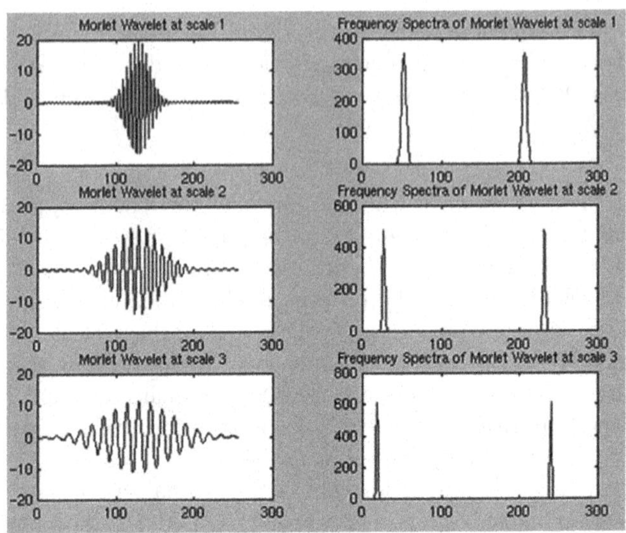

Fig. 2. Scaling of morlet wavelet

- Small scales are used to focus on the details such as spikes or discontinuity.
- Large scales are used to get an overview of the signal or the global information.
- High frequencies are represented by low scales and low frequencies by high scales.
- In real life applications, high frequency components which correspond to global information are present for the most part whereas low frequency components only appear for short durations.

Wavelet Transform

The continuous wavelet transform can be given defined in Eq. 12

$$CWT(x) = \frac{1}{\sqrt{s}} \int x(t)\Psi(\frac{s-a}{x})da \tag{12}$$

Where s is the scaling factor, a is the translation factor, and Ψ is the mother wavelet.

Therefore the wavelet transform is given by the inner product of x and wavelet coefficients Ψ:

$$\hat{x} = \Psi x$$

The signal is reconstructed using the inverse wavelet transform is given by the Eq. 13:

$$x = \Psi^{-1}\hat{x} \tag{13}$$

Benefits of Wavelet Transform

- Wavelet transform provides localization in time as well as frequency domain.
- Wavelets have the advantage of separating fine characteristics in a signal. Small wavelets can be utilized for isolating fine characteristics, whereas large wavelets can be utilized for identifying coarse characteristics.
- It is suited for signals with high-frequencies for short durations and low-frequency components for long duration.
- It can be used for compressing or de-noising a signal without causing much degradation.

2 Materials and Methods

For the input we have a graph in the form of adjacency matrix and a feature matrix describing each node. We also have the target classes for nodes. The aim of this paper is to build a GCN to solve the node classification problem. The architecture of CNN is basically divided into two parts

1. Feature Extraction
2. Node Classification

Feature Extraction part is done by the convolutional layers involved. Filters are used for extracting the features. The input feature matrix is convoluted with the set of filters. Each filter after convolution obtains a feature map and the number of filters used talks about the dimension of the feature maps i.e. the number of filters is the equal to the number of feature maps obtained.

Node classification task is done by activation function such as sigmoid, softmax or a set of Fully Connected Layers followed by the activation function. The fully connected layers help in aggregating the information extracted by the convolutional layers. Now we will discuss about each operation separately.

2.1 Convolution Layer

The steps involved in the convolution layer can be described using the flow chart given below:

2.2 Calculation of Laplacian

To design filters in the spectral domain we need to find the spectrum of the graph. The spectrum of a graph is given by its Laplacian. Graph Laplacian is calculated as follows:

$$L = D^{(-1/2)} L D^{(-1/2)} = I - D^{(-1/2)} L D^{(-1/2)}$$

where, D is the degree matrix and I is the identity matrix.

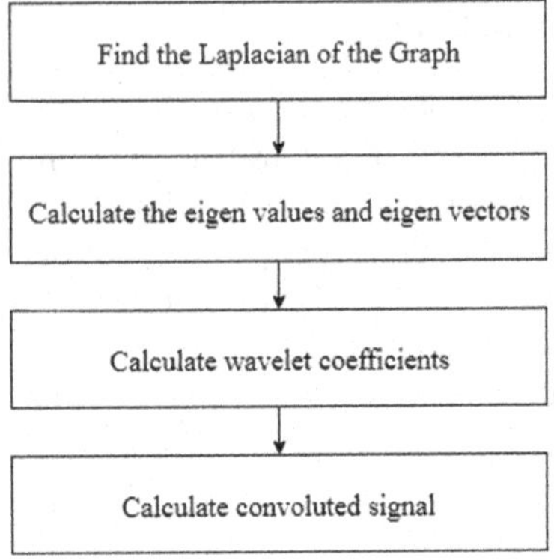

Fig. 3. Convolutional layer flowchart

This is known as the normalized form of Laplacian. The eigen vectors and eigen values are calculated from the eigen decomposition of L.

$$L = \chi^* \lambda \chi$$

where χ denote the matrix of eigen vectors, χ^* is the transpose of χ, and λ denotes the eigen values

The eigen values play the role of frequency. The eigen value components of neighbour vertices are closer.

2.3 Calculation of Wavelet Coefficients

In this work, we are defining the convolution operation using wavelet analysis. The Eq. 14 for defining the wavelet coefficients is derived from the graph fourier transform as explained in [6]. Wavelet coefficients are calculated using Eq. 14:

$$\psi = \chi_l^* g(\lambda_l) \chi_l \tag{14}$$

where χ_l are the eigenvectors, g is the kernel(wavelet) function calculated at an eigenvalue.

2.4 Graph Convolution Operation

Convolution Layer is the core layer in CNN. As already mentioned above we are defining the convolution operation in the spectral domain. The spectrum of the graph is represented using the Laplacian calculated above. The convolution operation is responsible for extracting the features which eventually helps in differentiating nodes. Now we will design filters using the wavelet coefficients calculated in the previous step. Filters defined using wavelet transform are like band pass filters.

This convolution operation is defined on the basis of convolution operation defined in [5] by replacing Fourier transform with Wavelet transform. This operation can be described using the Eq. 15,

$$Q = \psi^{-1} h \psi X \tag{15}$$

$$Y = \sigma(QW + b) \tag{16}$$

where ψ is the matrix containing wavelet coefficients, ψ^{-1} inverse is the matrix containing inverse wavelet coefficients, X is the input, feature matrix being the input for the first layer, h is the diagonal filter matrix, σ is an activation function, and b is the bias.

There are several choices for activation function such as tanh, sigmoid, ReLu. ReLu activation function is applied on the result of the Eq. 16.

3 Fully Connected Layer

In this model we have used one fully connected layer as the last layer before the prediction of the outputs. Fully connected layer operates on the feature map obtained from the last convolutional layer. The number of filters used in th fully connected layer is equal to the number of target classes present in the dataset. The operation of the FC layer is defined as follows:

$$Z = WY + B$$

where W is the weight matrix, Y is the output of the previous layer and B is the bias.

3.1 Predicting the Output Class

The output class is predicted by applying softmax on the output of the last layer. Softmax function calculates the probability of an input belonging to a class for all target classes. At the last layer we will have the scores for each of the classes. As explained above, at the end of the FC layer we have 7 scores for each of the 2708 examples. Softmax calculates the probabilities by using these scores. The class with the maximum probability is the final result. Given the scores, the probability that x belongs to a class j is computed as follows:

$$P(y = c|x) \frac{e^{x} w_c}{\sum_{k=1}^{K} e^{x} w_k} \tag{17}$$

3.2 Loss Function

The aim of the neural network model is to minimize the loss function during the backward pass in order to update weights and biases. Cross-entropy function is used as the loss function. The loss function over one node is given by the Eq. 18,

$$Loss = \sum_{c=1}^{C} q_{o,c} \log(p_{o,c}) \tag{18}$$

where, C is the number of classes q is a binary predictor $(0, 1)$ whether the output class was correct or not $p_{o,c}$ is the probability that the output is of class c This loss function is summed over all the nodes.

4 Architectures

There are 3 models proposed in this paper. These models differ in the choice of wavelet function and in the number of filters. Each of them consists of three layers.

4.1 Model 1

The wavelet function used in this model uses the itersine construction [10]. The function g calculated in Eq. 19 that uses the itersine wavelet

$$g(x) = \sin(0.5\pi \cos(\pi x)^2) \tag{19}$$

The model proposed consists of a total of 3 layers. The first two layers are Graph Convolutional layers and the last one is the fully connected layer. The mapping from one layer to another on the Cora dataset is explained below.

- First Convolutional Layer – The input for the first convolutional layer are 1208 examples, each with 1433 features. The number of filter used is 256. The output feature map for this layer is of the dimension 1208×256.
  $[1208, 1433]$ is mapped to $[1208, 256]$.
- Second Convolutional Layer – The input for this layer is the output from the previous layer. 32 filters are used for this layer. The output feature map of this layer of the dimension 1208×32.
  $[1208, 256]$ is mapped to $[1208, 32]$.
- Fully Connected Layer – The output of the second convolutional layer is the input for this layer.The number of filters used is same as the count of classes, in this case 7.
  $[1208, 32]$ is mapped to $[1208, 7]$.

4.2 Model 2

The choice of wavelet for this model is heat kernel. The Eq. 20 of heat kernel is given by,

$$g(x) = e^{-sx} \tag{20}$$

The number and type of layers is same for all the three models. However they differ in the number of filters used. The mapping from one layer to another is explained as follows:

- First Convolutional Layer – The count of filters used for this layer is 128. The output feature map of this layer of the dimension 1208×128.
  $[1208, 1433]$ is mapped to $[1208, 128]$..

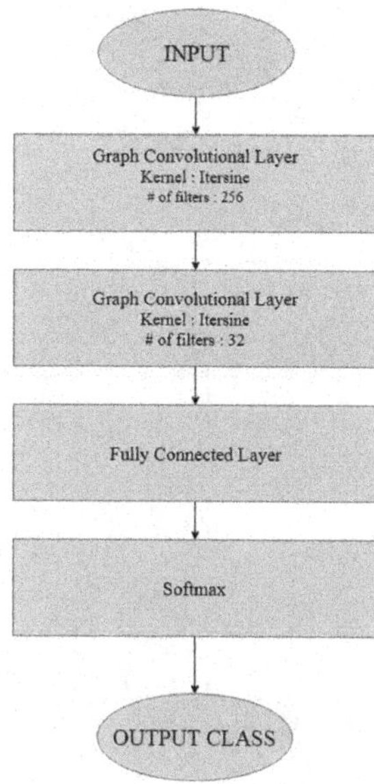

Fig. 4. Model 1

- Second Convolutional Layer – The count of filters used in this layer is 32. The output feature map for this layer of the dimension 1208 × 32.
  [1208, 128] is mapped to [1208, 32].
- Fully Connected Layer – The input for this layer is the output of the second convolutional layer. The count of filters used in this layer is same as the number of target classes, in this case 7.
  [1208, 32] is mapped to [1208, 7].

4.3 Model 3

The choice of wavelet for this model is Mexican Hat kernel. Heat kernel is given by Eq. 21,

$$g(x) = x * e^{-x} \tag{21}$$

This is the second order derivative of Gaussian. The mapping from one layer to another is explained as follows:

- First Convolutional Layer – The count of filters used in this layer is 128. The output feature map of this layer is of the dimension 1208 × 128.
  [1208, 1433] is mapped to [1208, 128].
- Second Convolutional Layer – The count of filters used in this layer is 32. The output feature map of this layer of the dimension 1208 × 32.
  [1208, 128] is mapped to [1208, 32].

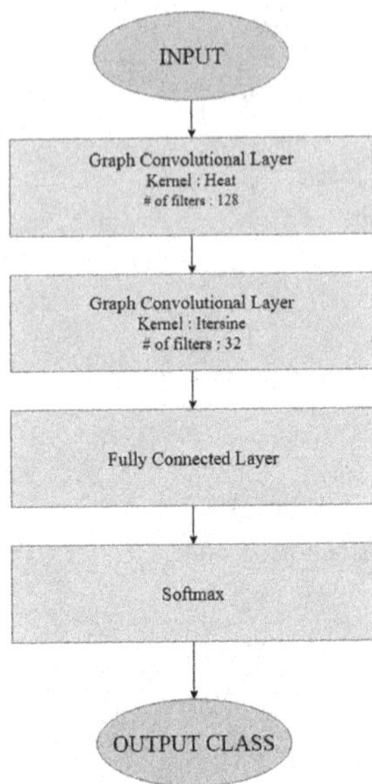

Fig. 5. Model 2

- Fully Connected Layer – The output of the second convolutional layer is the input for this layer. The number of filters used in this layer is same as the number of classes, i.e. 7.
  $[1208, 32]$ is mapped to $[1208, 7]$.

5 Experiments

Dataset – Cora dataset has been used. It is a collection of 2708 publications. Each vertex is represented according to the presence or absence of 1433 words. An entry of '0' for the absence and '1' for the presence of that word. A total of 5429 edges are present. The edges are stored in the form of adjacency matrix. The publications are categorized into one of the following seven classes:

- Neural Networks
- Case Based
- Probabilistic Methods
- Reinforcement Learning
- Genetic Algorithms
- Rule Learning
- Theory

For the purpose of testing a total of 1000 input examples are used. These are selected randomly.

5.1 Metrics Used for Evaluation

The metric that has been used for the purpose of testing is the mean accuracy.

$$\text{Mean Accuracy} = \frac{\sum_{n=1}^{N} Y}{N} * 100 \tag{22}$$

where, $Y = 1/0$ if the output is correct/incorrect and N is the number of examples used for testing.

5.2 Result

The training and testing set statistics are as follows:

- Training – 1208
- Validation – 500
- Testing – 1000

The maximum count of epochs for the purpose of training is 300. The loss function is minimized using the Adam Optimizer, which has shown to be better than the stochastic gradient decent. The loss function minimizes the actual and the predicted output. The value of learning rate parameter is set to 0.01. The metric used is the mean accuracy over testing data set. The code is implemented in PYTHON and Tensorflow is used for all heavy mathematical operations as defined by equations.

Table 1. Accuracy

S. No	Model	Accuracy (%)
1	GCN	81.2
2	Spectral CNN	73.3
3	Model 1	78.2
4	Model 2	81.9
5	Model 3	69.2

The time complexity is: epoch * number_of_training_dataset * $(L1 * L2 + L2 * L3 + L3 * ...)$

6 Discussion and Summary

The idea of this paper as we have mentioned many times in the above section is to bring out a model that helps in getting better results. We tried to implement such taking a base paper of the previous work don see from the results, some wavelets perform better than the others. Wavelet coefficients calculated from the heat kernel gave the best results. Itersine wavelet also gave good results. Mexican Hat Wavelet do not prove to be very useful in getting good results. However, Model1 and Model2 perform better than the spectral cnn method. The addition of the fully connected layer helped in speeding up the training process. The number of epoch required is significantly reduced.

7 Future Scope

Coming to the future Scope of the paper we can modify the model by defining kernel using other kind of wavelets. Lanczos approximation of the signal can also be tried. Also sharing weights among the layers can be incorporated to test how that is producing the results.

References

1. Atwood, J., Towsley, D.: Diffusion-convolutional neural networks. In: Advances in Neural Information Processing Systems, pp. 1993–2001 (2016)
2. Bruna, J., Zaremba, W., Szlam, A., LeCun, Y.: Spectral networks and locally connected networks on graphs. arXiv preprint arXiv:1312.6203 (2013)
3. Defferrard, M., Bresson, X., Vandergheynst, P.: Convolutional neural networks on graphs with fast localized spectral filtering. In: Advances in Neural Information Processing Systems, vol. 29, pp. 3844–3852 (2016)
4. Derr, T., Ma, Y., Tang, J.: Signed graph convolutional networks. In: 2018 IEEE International Conference on Data Mining (ICDM), pp. 929–934. IEEE (2018)
5. Duvenaud, D., et al.: Convolutional networks on graphs for learning molecular fingerprints. arXiv preprint arXiv:1509.09292 (2015)
6. Hammond, D.K., Vandergheynst, P., Gribonval, R.: Wavelets on graphs via spectral graph theory. Appl. Comput. Harmon. Anal. **30**(2), 129–150 (2011)
7. Henaff, M., Bruna, J., LeCun, Y.: Deep convolutional networks on graph-structured data. arXiv preprint arXiv:1506.05163 (2015)
8. Kipf, T.N., Welling, M.: Semi-supervised classification with graph convolutional networks. arXiv preprint arXiv:1609.02907 (2016)
9. Niepert, M., Garcia-Duran, A.: Towards a spectrum of graph convolutional networks. In: 2018 IEEE Data Science Workshop (DSW), pp. 244–248. IEEE (2018)
10. Perraudin, N., et al.: Gspbox: a toolbox for signal processing on graphs. arXiv preprint arXiv:1408.5781 (2014)
11. Rippel, O., Snoek, J., Adams, R.P.: Spectral representations for convolutional neural networks. arXiv preprint arXiv:1506.03767 (2015)
12. Such, F.P., et al.: Robust spatial filtering with graph convolutional neural networks. IEEE J. Sel. Top. Sig. Process. **11**(6), 884–896 (2017)

Link Prediction Computational Models: A Comparative Study

Yachana Bhawsar and Rajnish K. Ranjan(✉)

Department of Computer Science and Engineering, Govt Women's Polytechnic, Bhopal 462016, India

Abstract. The continuous creation of digital media mainly video has caused a tremendous growth of digital content. Social networks are the way to represent the relationship between entities. Analysis of a social network involves predicting links between actors or finding relationships, finding important nodes or actors, detecting communities of similar actors, etc. The data in social networks, which involves nodes, relations or contents, are huge and dynamic. There is a need of some data mining techniques to analyse such data and perform analysis. Social network analysis from a data mining perspective is also called link mining or link analysis. Earlier social networks are used only for interacting and sharing information, but it has a concept of research work. Now-a-days there are various social networking sites and it's the choice of the user to select any one of them. The competition to attract many users or actors is always there. Users want more friends or relations suggested by social networks. And users are switching to adopt the one where he/she finds more relations. To this end link prediction became the core and heart of social network analysis. There is lots of work done in social network analysis towards link prediction, but some issues and challenges are there. In this work these issues and challenges are trying to solve out. Uncertainty of social network data is the main issue, and the fuzzy soft set is applied for it. Interval-valued fuzzy soft is another variation of fuzzy soft set, applied to deal with uncertain data. Markov model is used for user's behavior prediction in the web, the same concept adopted here to find relations. Genetic algorithm-based approach considers the social graph structure into account to predict relation. Scalability is another issue; all the proposed techniques are scalable techniques of link prediction for social network analysis.

Although the proposed work is for social network data only, but it can be applied for some other applications like molecular biology, telecommunication and criminal investigation where link prediction is necessary. Adopting appropriate link prediction techniques, social networks can enhance their performance and link many people. The network, which links many people will become more popular and win the competition. Experiments are done and proposed work is compared with existing technique. It is observed that the proposed work is better than the previous approaches.

Keyword: Fuzzy soft set · Link prediction · Data mining · Interval-valued fuzzy soft set · Markov model · Genetic algorithm

R. S. Tomar et al. (Eds.): CNC 2020, CCIS 1502, pp. 237–249, 2021.
https://doi.org/10.1007/978-981-16-8896-6_19

1 Introduction

Social networks are a way to connect people and came into the scene from 1990's. Since then many social networks are created. The purpose of creating a social network was different from each other. The most popular online social network is Facebook in this age. It was initially started for a particular university, but now it is open for all users to interact and share personal or professional information.

The huge amount of raw data is generated daily by individuals on social networks. Social networks can be visualized as a graph structure, in which nodes or vertices are people or other entities and the edges are the interaction between these objects or entities [1]. Studying social network is a challenging task because of its dynamic nature. Different properties of these networks come under recent research. Social network analysis (SNA) is the analysis of large, heterogeneous, multi-relational social networks.

2 Social Network Analysis

Now-a-days Social networks are the backbone of information. Lots of challenges and issues are identified by applying data mining in social network analysis. The data generated on social networks is huge and dynamic. There is a need to find out computational models for social network analysis, which includes filtering, classifying, prediction and categorizing the data [2]. There are two ways for analysis of social networks.

3 Structure Analysis and Linkage-Based

According to Agrawal [3] to find out relevant node, community or links, analysis of the linkage is necessary. The structure of any social network contains links and nodes as a basic element.

3.1 Static Analysis and Dynamic Analysis

Static analysis is easier as compared to the dynamic analysis. Some social network like bibliographic network changes gradually and can be analyzed on batch modes, but Facebook like social network changes frequently and dynamic analysis is required.

4 Data Mining

Now-a-days mountains of data are available from various fields, and this is because of some techniques, making data in computer and digital form. To handle large-scale data a multidisciplinary approach known as data mining is available. A process that can discover new, intuitive and attractive pattern and models is data mining. It is known as KDD (knowledge discovery in databases) [4]. Data mining is the key part of the KDD.

There may be many patterns in large databases. The main data mining tasks are summarized, association, clustering, classification and trend analysis [5].

Summarization: Abstract and generalized information of data is provided by summarizing.

Association: It deals with finding a relationship or connections between objects.

Clustering: It finds out clusters or groups for objects whose classes are unknown.

Classification: It determines the class of an object based on its attributes.

Trend analysis: Discovers interesting patterns in the evolution history of the object.

5 Data Mining Approaches Used in Social Network Analysis

The uniqueness of social network data calls for novel data mining techniques. Social network data is distributed, dynamic, noisy and vast. Data mining approaches involve analysing frequently changing social network and such large data. Social network analysis based on graph theory: graph theory is the heart of the social network. The SNA approaches based on graph theory includes tasks of community detection, recommender systems and semantic webs.

Social network analysis based on opinion: there are various data mining tasks based on opinion. It involves SNA approaches for opinion mining, opinion extraction, opinion summarization and opinion formation. Social network analysis based on sentiment: social network analysis involves tasks related to sentiments. Sentiment analysis and review or ratings are the main tasks.Social network analysis based on classification: classification is an important approach in social network analysis. Classification may be unsupervised, supervised or semi-supervised depending upon the data and application.

6 Social Network Analysis Tasks

Social network analysis involves various tasks and techniques [6]. Some of them are as follows:

Influence Propagation: The task of analysis of the propagation of information, influence, innovations, infections, practices and customs through networks. Application of influence propagation is in viral marketing, outbreak detection, key blog posts finding, finding leaders or trendsetters and information feed ranking.

Community or Group Detection: Community detection involves the identification of groups of vertices. These identified vertices are more densely connected to each other as compared to the nodes of the rest of the network.

Expert Finding: If web based social network mining is explored then expert finding becomes the most important task. Identification of a person with relevant expertise or experience is the aim of the expert finding.

Expert finding is one of the most important subjects for mining from (web-based) social networks [7]. The aim of the expert finding is to identify persons with relevant expertise or experience.

Recommender System: Recommender System is a computer system that makes suggestions. Friends or people are suggested by Facebook. Movies are suggested by Netflix. Products are suggested by Amazon. Videos are suggested by YouTube.

Link Prediction: Link prediction problems deal with finding a relationship between two nodes or users of any social network.

Behavior and Mood Analysis: Users have different behavior such as sharing, posting, linking, commenting and befriending. Analysis of these behaviors is an open research area.

Opinion Mining: Mining opinion data that reside in online discussions is a way to track opinions of people on specific subjects.

7 Link Prediction in Social Networks

There are various research areas of social network analysis in which link prediction is explored by my researchers. The problem of predicting the future or existing links among nodes in a social network is termed as link prediction [8]. In link prediction problem, the focus is on the relation rather than the objects. Data mining focuses on objects and relations, link prediction focuses on relations only.

The applications of link prediction are molecular biology, criminal investigation, recommender systems and bibliographic domain. It is a binary classification problem. In most of the research papers link prediction is done using different topological features of the social network. Various classification algorithms classify future links.

The Link existence problem is the main research issue. Link existence is to predict a new link between two nodes in a social network will exist in the future or not. The Link existence problem can be extended to the other two tasks. Link weight is of concern with the different weights associated with each link and link cardinality is to

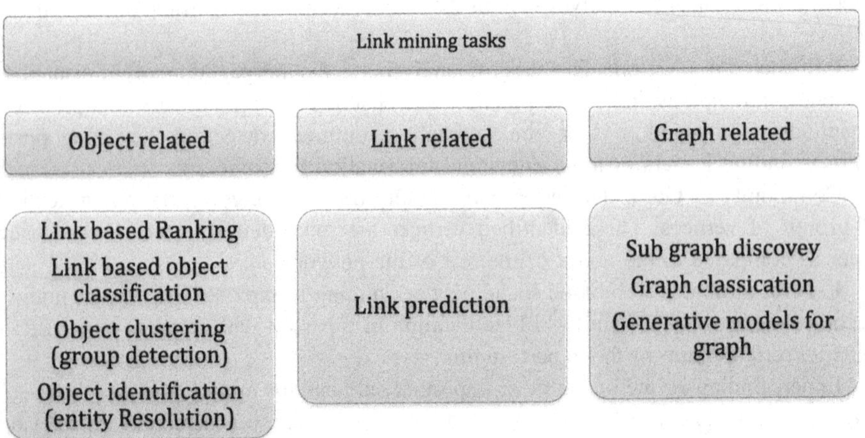

Fig. 1. Link mining tasks

deal with a number of link existences between the same pair of nodes in a social network. Link type predicts different roles of the relationship between two nodes.

The task of link prediction comes under link mining as classified by Getoor et al. [9]. According to them there are three categories of link mining tasks.

Link prediction approaches are classified as similarity-based and learning based approaches as shown in Fig. 1. Similarity of non-connected node pairs in a social network is computed. Similarity is based on measures for analysing the proximity of nodes. A score is assigned to every potential node pair (x; y). Higher score reflects that the probability of linking x and y in the future is high and vice versa. A list with scores is ranked list and it is in increasing or decreasing order which is obtained and accordingly links are predicted. Link prediction problem is treated as binary classification task in learning based approach.

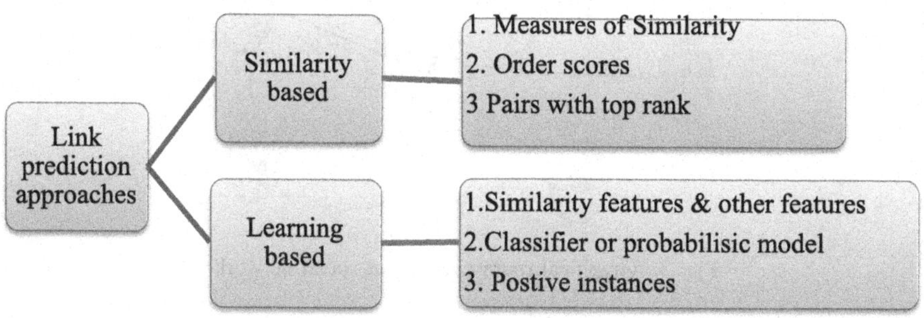

Fig. 2. Generic framework of link prediction model [10]

This problem can be solved by using typical machine learning models and probabilistic models. Nodes are described as features. There are some non-connected pair of nodes, these nodes corresponds to an instance with some class label. The pair of nodes labelled as positive or negative depending upon the result. The features associated with each node have two parts. Some features are based on similarity-based approaches and some features depend on domain knowledge about social network or attribute information.

8 Methodology

Link prediction falls under data mining technique. Here different real-world networks are analyzed which contains the variety of entity and relation. An emerging challenge for link prediction is mining under highly linked networks for understanding the knowledge behind the relationships. As multi-relational feature violates the traditional assumption of independent, so a distribution of data instances among features play the important role and it need the different approach which filters unwanted features instances. Therefore, new approaches are needed that can exploit the dependencies across the attribute and link structure.

The social network can be visualized as a graph G, in which the vertex V corresponds to a person in the network and an edge E represents some form of association between two persons. New interactions add new links in the existing network. So, link prediction in dynamic social networks is challenging task. Figure 3 illustrate link prediction. In the given figure each vertex is treated as user in the social network and each edge is treated as friendship between two users. New link that is predicted by any methodology is represented by red edge between the user as shown in Fig. 4. In the given figure new link is between user P and user Q is predicted.

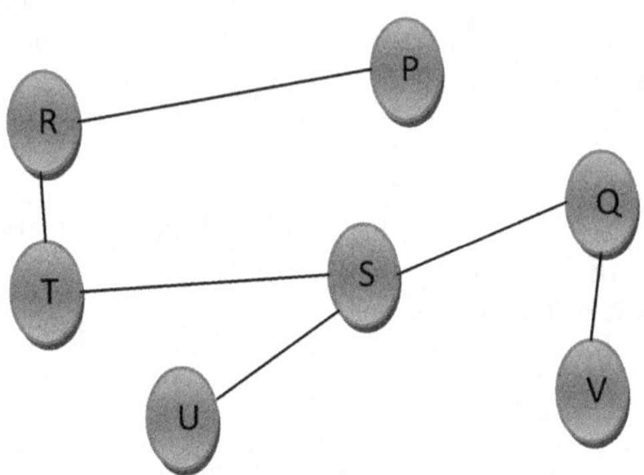

Fig. 3. Graphical representation of social network

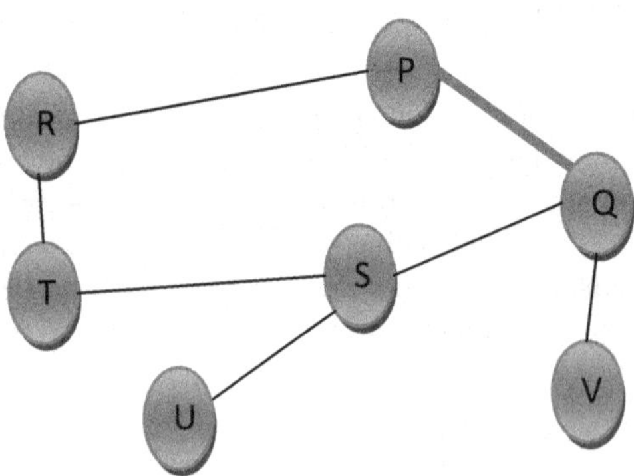

Fig. 4. Graphical representation of social network with new links

The main aim of this research work is to propose approaches of link prediction for social network environment. Following are the main objectives of the research:

9 To Develop an Approach for Link Prediction Based on Fuzzy Soft Set

Data in a social network (e.g. links, events, features) is uncertain. With uncertain data, each link in a network is associated with the probability that indicate the possibility that the link exists in the network. Fuzzy Set Theory (FST) deals with to what extent an object belongs to a particular set.

10 To Develop an Approach for Link Prediction Based on IVFSS

There has been a rapid growth of interest in developing approaches that are capable of dealing with imprecision and uncertainty. To this end, an interval-valued fuzzy soft set (IVFSS) that combines soft set theory with interval-valued fuzzy set theory has been proposed to handle imprecision and uncertainty in applications such as decision-making problems. In many fuzzy decision-making applications, the related membership functions are extremely individual, and thus, it is more reasonable to give an interval-valued data to describe a degree of membership. It is a special case of a soft set. As compared with fuzzy set, interval-valued fuzzy set has no problem of setting the membership function, which makes it very convenient and easy to apply in practice.

11 To Develop an Approach for Link Prediction Based on Markov Model

Markov model is basically used for user's behavior prediction on the web. The same concept can be used for predicting the relation on the social network. There are different orders of Markov model based on a number of previous pages considered for future prediction. The transition probability matrix should be calculated for each order. It is observed that combining all orders of the Markov model improves the result of the prediction.

12 To Develop an Approach for Link Prediction Based on Genetic Algorithm

A standard genetic algorithm evolves a constant-size population of elements (called chromosomes) by using the genetic operator of reproduction, crossover, and mutation. Each chromosome represents a candidate solution to a given problem and it is associated with a fitness value that reflects how good it is, with respect to the other solutions in the population. Network topology can be combined with genetic algorithms and by doing this we can get better results. GA based approach has chromosomes in terms of feature values between two links.

13 Result Analysis

The proposed and existing methods are implemented in Matlab tool. Results of the proposed methods are discussed in previous chapters. In this chapter a comparison of existing and proposed methods is discussed. Common neighbor, Jaccard's and Sorenson index are implemented and tested on the same dataset. In this chapter these existing algorithms are discussed and explained. Values of evaluation parameters and accuracy are calculated and compared for different number of node pairs. It is observed that the proposed approaches give more accurate results. Proposed approaches are scalable as accuracy is increase with the increase in number of node pairs.

13.1 Existing Methods

Existing link prediction measures common neighbor, Sorenson index and Jaccard's coefficients are implemented for different number of node pairs. The definition of these measures is as follows:

Common Neighbors (CN): The CN matric is the simplest model for link prediction. CN metric is widely used in problems related to link prediction [11]. For example, if there are two nodes x and y, then the CN are defined as the number of nodes that both x and y have a direct interaction with. the higher value tells about a strong probable link between x and y. Following formula were derived for this measure:

$$\boldsymbol{CN}(\boldsymbol{x},\boldsymbol{y}) = |\Gamma(\mathrm{x}) \cap \Gamma(\mathrm{y})|, \tag{1}$$

Where r(x) denotes the neighbors of node x.

CN reflects the relative similarities between node pairs because it is not normalized. Therefore, some neighbor-based metrics consider how to normalize the CN metric reasonably.

Jaccard Coefficient (JC): Size of common neighbours are normalized by Jaccard Coefficient. A higher proportion of common neighbors relative to the total number of neighbors they have given higher values for pairs of nodes. The formula for this measure is defined as:

$$\boldsymbol{JC}(\boldsymbol{x},\boldsymbol{y}) = \frac{|\Gamma(\boldsymbol{x}) \cap \Gamma(\boldsymbol{y})|}{|\Gamma(\boldsymbol{x}) \cup \Gamma(\boldsymbol{y})|} \tag{2}$$

Sorensen Index (SI): It is based on lower degrees of nodes and points out that they have higher link likelihood. The formula for this measure is as follows:

$$\boldsymbol{SI}(\boldsymbol{x},\boldsymbol{y}) = \frac{|\Gamma(\boldsymbol{x}) \cap \Gamma(\boldsymbol{y})|}{|\Gamma(\boldsymbol{x}) + \Gamma(\boldsymbol{y})|} \tag{3}$$

13.2 Comparison of Proposed Models

Existing methods Common Neighbor, Jaccard coefficient, Sorenson index are implemented for the same data set for which proposed work is implemented. The output screen of existing methods for different number of node pair is shown in following Figs. 5 , 6, 7 and 8:

Comparison of the proposed approaches and existing approaches are shown in this section. For comparison, average value of precision, recall and f-measures are calculated. Accuracy is also compared for different node pairs. Existing link prediction methods are also implemented for the same number of node pairs. These existing methods are common neighbours, Jaccard's coefficient, and Sorenson index.

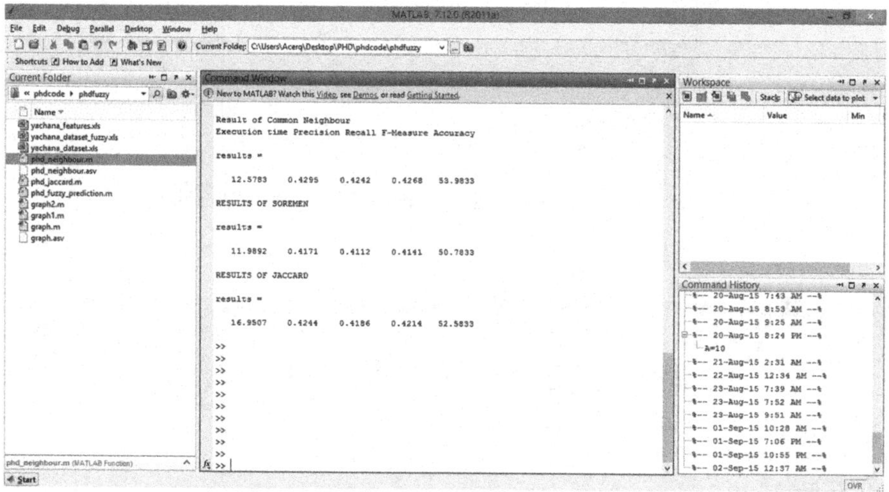

Fig. 5. Output screen of existing methods for 6k node pairs

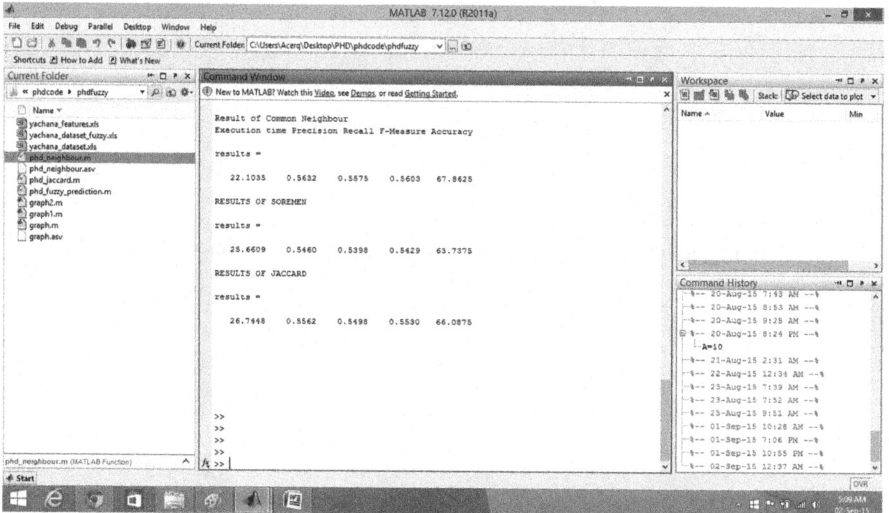

Fig. 6. Output screen of existing methods for 8k node pairs

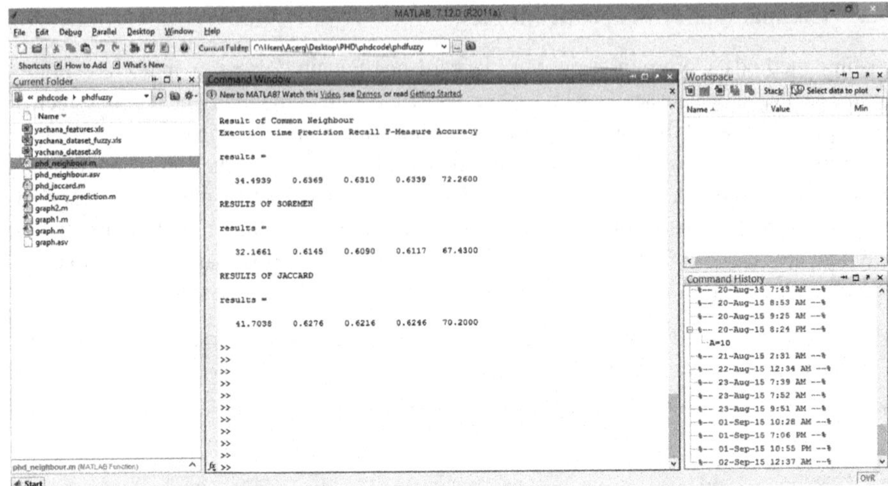

Fig. 7. Output screen of existing methods for 10k node pairs

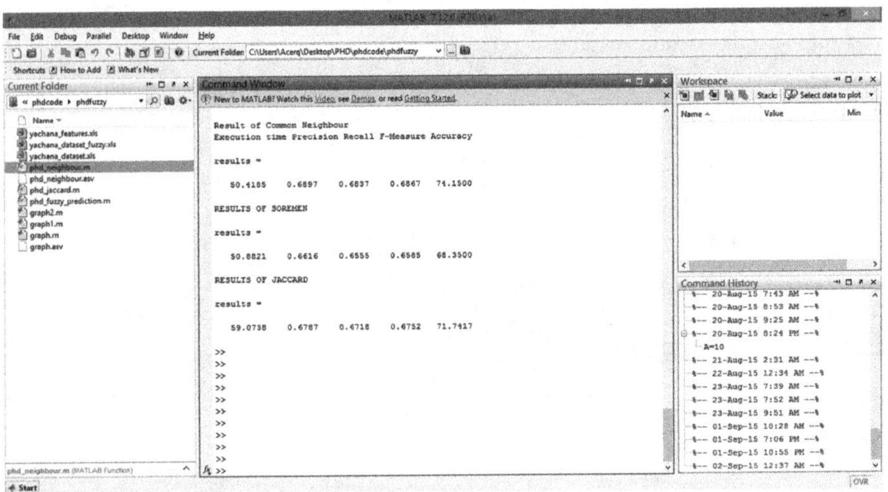

Fig. 8. Output screen of existing methods for 12k node pairs

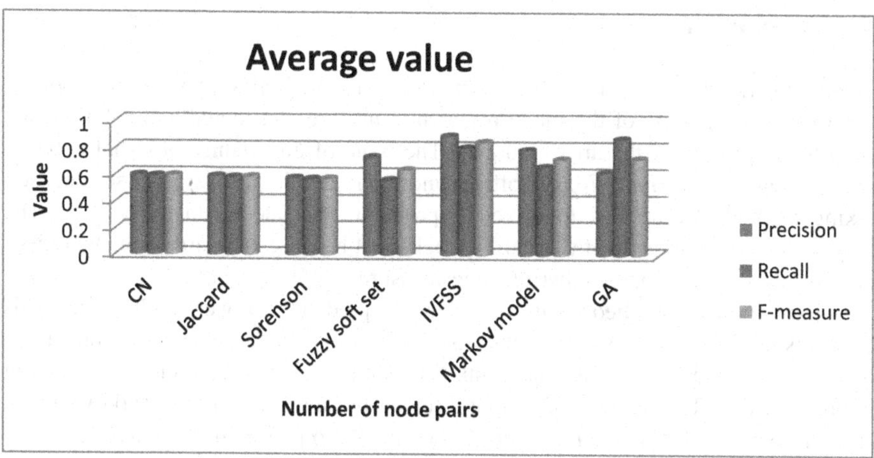

Fig. 9. Average values of evaluation parameters

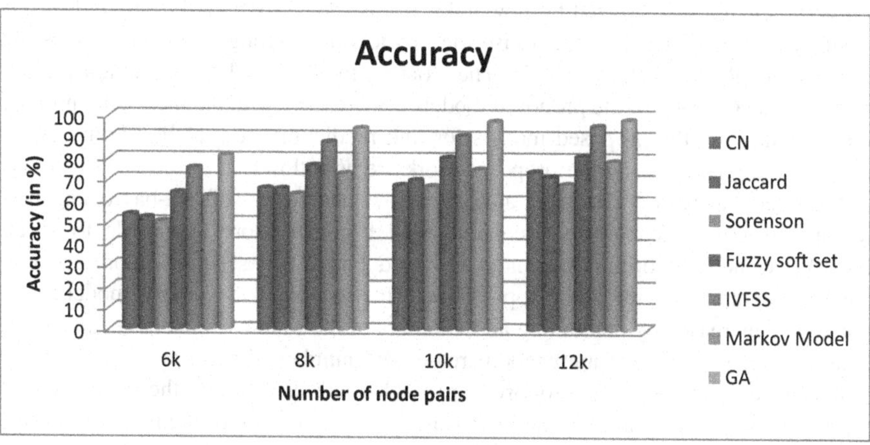

Fig. 10. Comparison of accuracy

From above Fig. 9 it is observed that average values of evaluation parameters of all proposed methods are high as compared to the existing approaches. It is analysed that Interval-valued fuzzy soft set gives better values of precision, recall and f-measures as compared to fuzzy soft set. Figure 10 show the accuracy of proposed approaches is higher than the existing models. The proposed Interval-valued fuzzy soft set gives more accurate results in comparison to another proposed fuzzy soft set model. Although Genetic algorithm-based approach gives most accurate results.

14 Conclusion

Social network analysis is a broad area in which link prediction playing an important role. In this work some of the many research issues are considered and solutions are found to adopt state-of-the art techniques. The issue of uncertainty in social network data is taken into account. Fuzzy soft set and interval-valued fuzzy soft set decision making methods are applied to solve the problem associated with uncertainty. The fuzzy soft set is combined with Jaccard's Coefficient because jacquard coefficient gives better result as compared to other existing measures.

Markov model is applied for user's behaviour prediction in web applications. This concept is used for social network analysis in this work. The user's next action can be predicted by taking previous actions. Link between two users is predicted by watching previous actions. The number of actions decided by the order of the Markov model. The work here is taken up to 4th order Markov model to predict future links. The issue of efficiency and less model building time is handled by this model.

Network structure plays important role in analysis and link prediction. The genetic algorithm-based model is used to take network structure for link prediction. The value of fitness function is optimized for new links. If this value crosses a threshold, then it is considered as predicted link otherwise the prediction is wrong. Another issue is the scalability of the prediction models. The existing models for link prediction are not scalable. The accuracy of the proposed models is increasing with the increasing number of node pairs. All the proposed models for link prediction are scalable. Some of the points that are analysed by the proposed work are as follows:

Proposed Fuzzy soft set based and interval-valued fuzzy soft set-based link prediction approaches deals with uncertainty and becomes more applicable to social networks. Genetic algorithm and interval-valued Fuzzy soft set gives more accurate results as compared with other approaches. The accuracy of Markov model-based approach is increased by combining all the orders of the Markov model. Accuracy and value of other evaluation parameters increase with number of node pairs.

It can be concluded that proposed approaches are scalable as the accuracy and values of evaluation parameters are increasing with the increase of the number of node pairs. Proposed models are suitable for large scale undirected online social networks like Facebook etc. The proposed Fuzzy soft set-based model handles uncertainty exists in social network data. Further, uncertain data can be handled more accurately by Interval-valued fuzzy soft set. The proposed Markov model is less time consuming in model building and is appropriate for fast prediction but compromises with accuracy. Genetic algorithm-based model is useful for optimization and gives better results.

References

1. Kleinberg, J., Liben-nowell, D.: The link prediction problem for social networks. In: LinkKDD (2004)
2. Yu, L., Loscalzo, S.: Social Network Analysis: Tasks and Tools. In: Social Computing, Behavioral Modeling, and Prediction. In: Salerno, J.J., Michael, J., Liu, Y.H. (ed.) pp. 151–159. Springer, Heidelberg (2008)

3. Aggarwal, C.: An introduction to social network data analytics. In: Social Network Data Analystic, charuc aggarwal, Ed., ch. 1, pp. 1-15 (2011)
4. Kamber, M., Han, I.: Data Mining Concepts and Techniques. Morgar Kaufmann (2000)
5. Han, J., Yu, P.S., Chen, M.S.: Data Mining: An Overview from a Database Prespective. IEEE Trans. Knowl. Data Eng. **8**, 866–883 (1996)
6. Wasserman, K.F.S.: Social Network Analysis: Methods and Applications. Cambridge University Press, Cambridge (1994)
7. Pavlov, R.I.: Finding Experts by Link Prediction in Coauthorship Networks. In: 2nd Interational ISWC ASWC Workshop on Finding Experts on the Web with Semantics, pp. 42–55 (2007)
8. Satuluri, V., Wang, C. : Local probabilistic model s for link prediction. In: ICDM (2007)
9. Diehl, C.P., Getoor, L.: Link Mining: A Survey. SIGKDD explorations, vol. 7, no. 2, pp. 3–12 (2005)
10. Wen, X.B., Rong, W.Y., Yu, Z.X., Peng, W.: Link Prediction in Social Networks: the State-of-the-art. Science China Information Science, vol. 58, no. 38 (2015)
11. Hamner, B., Yang, B., Cukierski, W.: Graph-based features for supervised link prediction. In: International Joint Conference on Neural Network (IJCNN '11), August 2011, pp. 1237–1244. Springer multimedia tools and applications 2010, vol. 46, pp. 47–69 (2010)

Deep Learning Approach to Load Forecasting: A Survey

Segun A. Akinola[1(✉)], Prabhat Thakur[1], Mayank S. Sharma[2(✉)], Krishna Kumar[2], and Ghanshyam Singh[1]

[1] Centre for Smart Information and Communication Systems, Department of Electrical and Electronics Engineering, University of Johannesburg, Auckland Park Kingsway Campus, Johannesburg 2006, South Africa
{akinolaa, prabhatt, ghanshyams}@uj.ac.za

[2] Department Electronics and Communication, ITM University Gwalior, Gwalior, India

Abstract. The power sector has been widely invested-in for many years. There is a need in finding lasting solutions that can ameliorate the ever-dynamic challenges attached to it which makes the researcher looking for techniques in artificial intelligence solving the complication in the power sector. Since when Artificial intelligence came to existence a lot of problems have been solved through the use of its application such as an artificial neural network (ANN), Neural Network (NN), Deep Neural Network (DNN), Machine learning (ML) and deep learning (DL). Deep learning has become a very good solving tool which makes research focus more on it to tackle a lot of problems such as forecasting tasks, modeling the non-linearity in data of many fields, computer vision, natural language processing, speech recognition, and signal processing. This updated review paper focuses on the application of deep learning (DL) that applied to solar load forecasting; the common algorithm used was shown in the literature reviews. The main reason for this review is to show the latest updated techniques using DL for forecasting that will help the researcher to select the best methods in DL for forecasting accurately. After the review it shows that deep learning performs better for forecasting showing good accuracy, finding the hidden layer.

Keywords: Deep learning · Support vector regression · Deep belief network · Root mean square error · Machine learning · Artificial neural network

1 Introduction

Machine learning had contributed immensely to the research world with different applications solving a lot of problems and bring room for new ideas in the techniques, it has been so exciting that researchers are now focusing on the area in other to get more challenges solved with bringing out more ways to solve issues. Machine learning has contributed immensely to the development of the Artificial intelligence world [1–3]. Machine learning has a technique called deep learning (DL)that focuses on the hidden layer of the network and the main aim is to make or let a system (computer)

R. S. Tomar et al. (Eds.): CNC 2020, CCIS 1502, pp. 250–262, 2021.
https://doi.org/10.1007/978-981-16-8896-6_20

understand and even think like the human brain by getting or mimicking the human brain. Artificial Intelligence (AL) which is subdivided into seven like natural language processing, expert system, cognitive modeling, robotics, machine learning, heuristics problem solving and knowledge presentation [4] the machine learning is wide. Research areas such as Bayesian network clustering, deep learning, and decision tree are all machine learning approaches. The investigation has revived by many industries on Al to be automated like picture with audio detection, research scientific assistant with respect in decision making at various critical fields. In knowing more about the machine it is said to particular learning that extracts pattern in the raw data in making a decision, the Machine learning algorithm can be divided into two learning which is supervised and unsupervised learning. The unsupervised learning algorithm is data set that has many features that learn the important properties in the structure while the supervise learning has features associated with the label [5] and it has two data set which is training and testing dataset in the learning algorithm which helps models learning from the raw data meanwhile the testing data validate the model output. On a general view, machine learning is used for solar forecasting prediction and load forecasting on many publications with different applications to it.DL is an active research area that has a lot of applications in renewable energy forecasting. Most of the applications which are generally in power forecast. Application of the DL learning algorithm which is globally published in solar power forecasting makes other techniques like the Numerical weather prediction (NWP), ANN and other methods. The aim of this research is to introduce DL algorithms like the Deep belief network (DBN), Artificial empathy (AE), and Long short-term memory (LSTM) to load and solar power forecasting. DL has more architecture than other traditional neural network dues to multiple hidden layer computation and also deep learning can be used in the building complex of the sophisticated network which applied to many fields like finance, power system, education, manufacturing, health, etc. Deep learning involves a complex computational technique that has more hidden layers that represent data differently abstracting with features in the input model moreover it can be used as an unsupervised learning algorithm in a different task. Deep learning predicts more accurately in solar forecasting prediction in getting the hidden layer, also load forecasting using deep learning has got better results as shown in the literature reviews. This paper shows the reviews of deep learning algorithm techniques on solar and load forecasting with the reviews of many previous publications.

This paper is organized as following forecasting, deep learning method Fig. 1. LSTM, Table 1. Review of deep learning on solar load forecasting, Table 2. RSME comparison, conclusion, and Fig. 2 solar prediction methods.

2 Forecasting

Forecasting is defined as the prediction of future using the previous data set, different models can be used in forecasting like ANN, DL etc., more details on forecasting methods has been done by researchers and more improved methods are coming, some are shown in this review.

2.1 Naïve Method

In looking for the cost-effective and easy method to use we look at the naïve method, this is a particular method that gets the last data to get the next prediction because it can estimate the previous periods of forecasting without restabilizing or adjusting the casual factors. It is mainly used for comparison with other sophisticated techniques [6, 7].

2.2 Linear Model

Using linear functions, the linear model predict data future which has so many methods like mean average (MA) with autoregressive (AR) though, with the hybrid-like ARMA which is the combination of both AR with MA model and another hybrid is ARIMA, the ARMA is used to predict stationary with the univariates like time series though with the AR model normally the value is assumed to be linear in future combination with past experience with the random error in a constant [8]. Meanwhile, the MA forecast by taking the nearest data number in the previous data on an average. The ARIMA can predict nonstationary with another method and it is also used for comparison [9].

2.3 Nonlinear Model

In a case where times series show linear structure the linear model will be used through many time series is nonlinear in structure, there is a limitation in linear models like ANN, Support Vector Machine (SVM)with RF. The ANN works like a human brain in architecture, with the quadratic function and polynomial complex represented. Generally, ANN is made up of layers which is the input, hidden and the output layer with connection to the node by each layer which is called the weight and can be calculated with the backpropagation technique, the SVM is in the class of supervised learning that implement approximation, time series, and classification in forecasting issues with separation between groups with borders. The SVM determines the boundary and generates multiple inputs in producing nonlinear solutions [9] while the Random forest involves the decision tree that predicts multiple on random variables [10] it can fast in solving.

3 Deep Learning

Machine learning method with multiple layers with deep artificial neural network architecture is deep learning (DL), deep learning is a network that has multiple hidden layers with the first deep learning structure by Ivakhnenko with Lapa in the year 1965 [11]. In recent time it has been a very good area which researcher is focusing at and the reason is that no power processor in training the deep architecture, recently with the power and generation increases processor which make the data generated in digitalization providing the needed infrastructure in deep learning and with this development it makes a lot of fields now use deep learning in predicting and forecasting like (a) Engineering and Computer Science (b) Health (c) Finance (d) Manufacturing and

(e) Education. One of the basic functions of deep learning is to understand methods with the aim of improving the results, optimizing the time in computing processing.

3.1 Methods of Deep Learning

3.1.1 Autoencoder (AE)

Autoencoder which is one of the feeds forward NN and is used in copying input neurons passing through the hidden layer in stacked Autoencoder [5]. The function is the main part of autoencoder $h = f(x)$ with a construction decoder $x = h(h)$, with output $x = g(f(x))$.

Mathematically, Auto-encoder is:

$$x = g(Wx + b) \tag{1}$$

The input is x, weighs is W, bias is b, the activation function is g that rectify linear function.

3.1.2 Recurrent Neural Network (RNN)

The recurrent neural network has the ability to store previously calculated inform ation in the internal memory, on like feed-forward neural network which gas no internal memory to process random input, a lot of application have been used with RNN which make it easier because of the previous parameters are significant to get the future parameters like language translation.RNN become more clear when it unfolded into a full network that the input in the hidden neuron will take input from a neuron at where it stops previously [12, 13].

3.1.3 Long Short-Term Memory (LSTM)

Long short term memory design provides loner memory to compensate for the failure of RNN model that fail on vanishing gradient descent, LSTM has internal self-loops that can be used to store information which has five elements in computational graph generally like input gate, forget gate, output gate, output state cell which is showed in Fig. 1 below. The function of the gates is reading, writing with erasing all perform in cell memory state [14]. Mathematically LSTM model is represented as follow.

Input gate is forget gate is *xo* is, update signal is *Ct* is the value *t* at time with *ht* serve as output in LSTM cell thou sigmoid function will be on and off while modifying the decision of the input gate to be on and off state and when the value in the input gate is small or nearly zero it will not change the cell memory *Ct*.

3.1.4 Deep Boltzmann Machine (DBM)

RBM architecture is like DBM neural network but has more hidden parameters with layers in RBM meanwhile DBM is not like DBN and the reason is that DBM architecture has an indirect connection among all layers like visible with multiple hidden layers (1).

3.1.5 Deep Belief Network (DBN)

In forecasting deep belief network has a two-step algorithm which is stated below:

a) DBN perform features learning reducing dimensionality input data
b) Additional layer suck as a linear layer added to forecasting

Explaining further layers in DBN has an (RBM) Boltzmann Machine restricted and it a two stochastic artificial neural network that learned to distribute above data input set which the layers organized such as funnel that helps in learning features around data. In training DBN regression we have to use two steps which are in the first step training DBN unsupervised way in contrastive divergence the topology that is abstract data in reducing set features and the second is appending ANN in training the step with one layer connecting neurons with pre-trainedtopology. The new layers will be trained with the desired target in getting the best prediction which is even possible to train the whole DBN once again.

3.1.6 Convolution Neural Network (CNN)

In convolution Neural network work in mimicking as human neuron feed-forward neural network. it a deep learning techniques that deals with the audio processing with visual, natural language processing and video recognition etc. and it is used in process of grid data topology input is *X*, kernel filter is *W* with *s* as output that is features map that can be said as continuous t time Generally CNN has three layers which build the architecture network and the first is several parallel convolution layers, another layer is detector state that rectified linear activation with lastly is stage of pooling function layer [5].

3.2 Review on Solar Load Forecasting

For every electric grid is have a robust and efficient power supply both from the renewable energy that makes smooth operation management and balance the demand with the aim of minimizing the costing and for every smart grid it really on a percentage of renewable energy integration load forecasting dynamic pricing with managing the demand for effectiveness. Table 1 shows deep learning models, types of learning, Architecture and the categories. Solar load forecasting which is very necessary when planning the operation of the power system, the power management has a vital role to play in developed or developing nations because power generation influence so many aspects of the nation-building and the economy. The good management of power in an economic boost the economical solar forecasting which plays a key role because of the cost-effectiveness need to be managed properly and predict future in other for the nation to prepare ahead, load forecasting has a major role in the power sector so as to do proper management for what to expect ahead., this paper focuses majorly on solar and load forecasting with deep learning applications which can be either short-term forecasting, mid-term forecasting, and long-term forecasting. Solar load forecast will influence with the weather condition as factor and time [15] both midterm and long-term forecasting are the function of the historical data for power with weather, the demand like the appliance and demographic data while the short term forecasting deal with the literature for the time interval with couples of hours in week as consideration. short-term load forecasting used but in a lot of applications like economy dispatch, real-time control, scheduling energy transfer. The midterm load forecasting can be used in planning the interval from a month to as much as five-year intervals for proper planning on a future power plant that will show a dynamic power system with time interval meanwhile the long-term load forecasting will have the intervals of 5 to as high as 20 years. Generally, long-term load forecasting is used to know what is needed for the generation power plant size so that the future requirement with the costing to be evaluated [13]. In this paper, the general review of both load and solar forecasting will be described on how deep learning applied in solving many problems on solar and load forecasting.

Autoencoder Deep learning algorithm used short-term load forecasting in the price of electricity [16] it is proposed by the author in the study by using (stacked denoising) which is a process of removing noise from signal for a short-term forecast with designing two-approach model in online forecasting with a day ahead and Stacked denoising autoencoder is effective which what it shows in a day ahead [17] after all the result compared with some methods like SVM, multivariate adaptive regression splinesMARS with least absolute shrinkage selected operator call Lasso [17].

In this study, Autoencoder with long short-term memory was used to forecast energy power plant in this research Autoencoder and long short-term memory were combine to forecast after which the result was compared to the ANN, LSTM with DBN [18] same method applied to 21 solar power plant because the proposed method show decrease average of RMSE to the training and testing thou in many reviews or research RMSE and MAE were normally used to estimate the performance of any proposed method and the aim to compare with other methods. In the determination of the Error, Root mean squared error and Mean Absolute Error is normally using to get the forecasting accuracy [18].

Deep leaning performance equations for RMSE and MAE are given as follows.

$$RMSE(y,x) = \sqrt{\frac{1}{N}\sum_{n=1}^{n}(y-x)^2} \tag{2}$$

$$MAE(y,x) = \frac{1}{N}\sum_{n=1}^{n}(y-x) \tag{3}$$

Input time series is X time series while predicted output time series y with a numbers N sample time series. Auto encoder and long short-term memory work greatly in the performance of the method using RMSE at 0.0713 with DB and RMSE 0.0724.

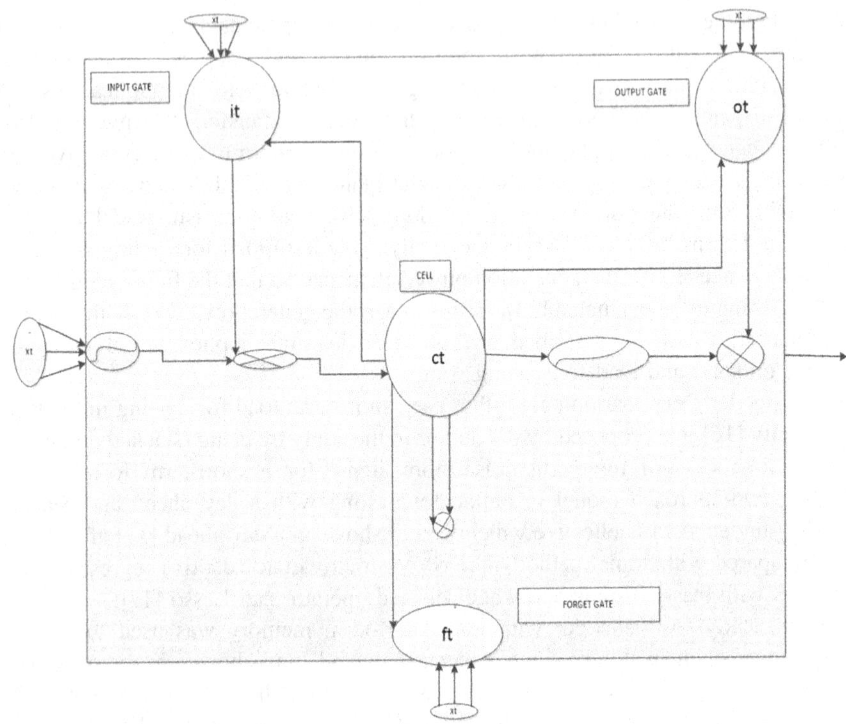

Fig. 1. LSTM cell with graph architecture

Recently research shows a household load forecasting using an uncommon approach polling Deep Recurrent Neural Network [19]. The study showed by the author which refers to that joining more layers in a neural network has a good tendency of improving forecasting performance The researcher used pool input for a group of customers in increasing data diversity with the volume data were collected from 920 smart meter customers in the Republic of Ireland. The researcher used GPU in hardware to be able in accelerating computational time with the parallelizing model and the result compared with the literature like SVR, DRNN, and ARIMA and the approach really shows a lot of improvement in the results RMSE in comparing to SVR with 13.1%, DRNN with 6.5%and ARIMA with 19.5%.

Generally, deep learning has technique is used for short-term load forecast which is the LSTM. This technique has two particular approaches building energy like LSTM based sequence and Standard LSTM [14] which is implemented to consume data of a residential load which train even tested in an hour plus a minute resolution the study shows that standard LSTM perform very well in an hour resolution but it fails in a minute resolution and in the second approach the data set performs very well when compared the results.

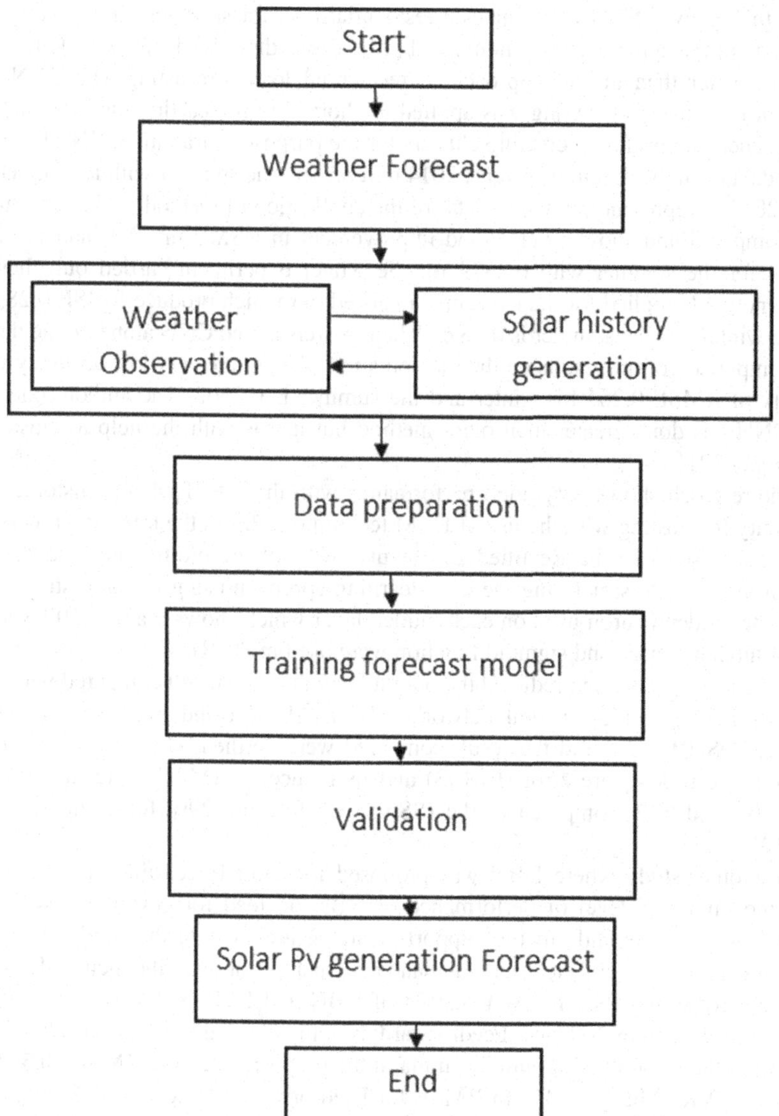

Fig. 2. Solar prediction method

In this study, LSTM investigates a residential load for short-term forecasting with the usage of the appliance in an individual [20]. The author clearly show that algorithm perform better than the art approach in residential load forecasting The CNN conjunction to K mean clustering was applied to short-term forecasting the large data set used K-mean algorithm in creating clusters for the purpose of training CNN The author select data from the month of August 2014 to represent the summer with December that same 2014 to represent the winter data for the application of method [21] after which it was compared and show a very good improvement in RSME in CNN and K means 0.2194 for the summer with 0.2379 for the winter experiment carried out, then the neural network applied for the experiment carried out which produce RMSE 0.28jkl39 for the winter and the summer is 0.2379. The researcher used CNN alone on the data so that comparison of the results on the method and CNN get the very low accuracy when we talk of RMSE 0.264 for winter and the summer is 0.2502. The author concluded that CNN has done greater than other method but it was with the help to cluster the techniques [21].

The research shows very good performance with the use of DL for customer load electricity forecasting with the use of RBM techniques [22] in the training process two cases were used like the Rectified Linear unit without the pre-training and the pre-training process. In structuring the deep learning approach using the heuristic method to get the hidden neuron used on each hidden layer which shows that in 150 layers we have 4 hidden neuron and sigmoid function were used in the RBM pre-training process while the Linear function predicted the output layer after the result compared with other methods like the sallow neural network (SNN), ARIMA and twice seasonal Holt-Winters (DSHW) [22] and the result compared were verified which show by MAPE with relative root square error (RRMS) and its reduce the (MAPE with the RMMS) with 17% and 22% compared to the (SSN) with 9% and 29% for comparing with (DSHW) [19].

In another study where DBN was proposed for short forecasting and the author want the improved level of performance of DBN on load forecasting to use a new method of ensemble and emerge support vector Regression, in this study the author used three regression and electricity demand data in application to the method [23]. The result clearly shows that the combination of DBN and SVR performs wellthanSVR, DBN with ensemble NN and Feedforward NN in the result. In the result of load demand in the Republic of South Australia in the proposed method, RMSE 30.598 and RMSE in SVR to be 44.674 with RMSE for Feedforward NN now is 38.8585 finally. Deep Boltzmann Machine (PDBM) to predict the speed of wind on wind energy the researcher gathers full data so that it is used in forecasting short-term with long-term wind speed. In predicting the speed of the wind through algorithm with one hour ahead and a day ahead which make techniques clearly show improvement in the performance by comparing with (AR) adaptive neuro, (SVM) and ANFIS for SVR [24].

Table 1. Deep learning models, types, architecture and categories.

S/N	Deep learning models	Type of learning	Architecture	Category
1	Autoencoder AE	Unsupervised	Bi-directional architecture connection with multiple hidden layers connected	Generative
2	Deep Neural Network (DNN)	Unsupervised	Multiple Hidden layers among the input with the output	Generative
3	Long Short Term Memory (LSTM)	Semi-Supervised	Connections between the output, input, forget gate with the memory cell	Generative/Discriminative
4	Deep Boltzmann Machine	Supervised	Supervised Bi-directional architecture connection with multiple hidden layers connected	Generative
5	Deep Belief Network (DBN)	Unsupervised	Partial Bi-directional architecture connection with multiple hidden layers connected	Generative
6	Convolutionary Neural Network (CNN)	Unsupervised	Multiple hidden layers connected architecture locally	Discriminative

Table 2. RSME reduction percentage comparing a method with the standards

Proposed techniques	RMSE reducing in %	The method standards
CNN and Kmeans	12. 3%	CNN
DBN with SVR	21. 2%	FNN
AE with LSTM	5.51%	MLP
PDBN	2.85%	SVR
PDRNN	19.2%	ARIMA
CNN	7.7%	NN

Table 3. Solar model prediction

Solar model prediction		
Physical models	Statistical model	Empirical model
Numerical weather prediction	Machine learning	Single parameter
Conventional methods	Time series	Temperature based
	Support vector machine	Predicting power Pv
	Neural network	Multiple parameters
	Deep learning	Sunshine house based model

Another study made for short with long-term forecasting and the short term forecasting was designed to be able for forecasting just 10 min ahead of the two hours and resulted to the 10 min ahead on MSE is 0.295 in method using in correspondence to MSE for the SVR is just 0.6340 meanwhile the long-term forecast is designed with the aim of forecasting a day ahead to the 7 days going ahead and method propose algorithm just for a day forecasting ahead and now getting result MSE 1.2926 that show improvement more than SVR which has MSE 1.3678 with this summary review the research in comparing among the methods with similar benchmark method in state of the art showing RSME percentage reducing with compared to other method.

In the reducing RMSE on the method ensemble, DBN with the SVR is excellent comparing to FNN and the method PDRN clearly shows a lot of reduction comparing with CNN with K means and ARIMA even showing the percentage of reducing in RMSE.

In this study Deep learning architecture is been used in forecasting a regenerative energy source like the use of DBN in predicting the wind speed power [25]. The use of stacked Auto-Encoder in predicting short-term wind speed [26]. Some domain suck as a special form of polynomial approximations that turn out which is very computationally expensive [27] severally has severally been used with getting successful results. Recently the probabilistic forecasting generally increases in the power forecasting field popularly with covering areas like domain statistical forecasting methods [28]. A study describes the forecasting technique with Kalman filters that are described, The physical model wasused by the author with the method scaling up for power forecasting. Looking hybrid model's area with the use of machine learning methods combining with the turbine power curves [29]. In analyzing the depth of deep learning architecture [30] has demonstrated that automatic optimization protocol can use multi approaches.

A new model was used by Cao and Lin proposed a good model in predicting solar global irradiance with the diagonal recurrent wavelet neural network (DRWNN) with a good design train algorithm, simulation to be able to show that model has the ability of getting solar irradiance that is very normally high non-linear with time changeable and which is because DRWNN join advantage in the RNN with the WNN.

4 Conclusion

This paper is an overview of solar and load forecasting perdition using deep learning techniques of the AI. Recently in the research, deep learning has shown a significant-excellent way in the estimation, predicting with forecasting on load and solar. Deep learning been the best technique with good accuracy, finding the hidden layer and work faster, the neural network is globally used in solving problems of load and solar forecasting. In this paper the focus on a review of state of art of DL on load and solar showing the outstanding performance of many of unsupervised learning such as AE algorithm to show term load forecasting which show great performance on a day ahead forecasting used for forecasting with very good results comparing to the ARIMA, SSN with DSHW. A combination of SVR and DBN shows a great performance. In Table 2 the review of state of art in DL shows the combination techniques for load and solar forecasting with excellent performance reduction in terms of RMSE thou the SVR and DBN has the highest reduction in comparison to other techniques.

References

1. Hinton, G.E., Osindero, S., Teh, Y.W.: A fast learning algorithm for deep belief nets. Neural Comput. **18**, 1527–1554 (2006)
2. Alzahrani, A., Shamsi, P., Dagli, C., Ferdowsi, M.: Solar irradiance forecasting using deep neural networks. Procedia Comput. Sci. **114**, 304–313 (2017)
3. Wei, Z., Weimin, W.: Wind speed forecasting via ensemble Kalman filter. In: 2nd International Conference on Advanced Computer Control, pp. 73–77 (2010)
4. Abdel-Hamid, O., Mohamed, A., Jiang, H.: Applying convolutional neural networks concepts to hybrid NN-HMM model for speech recognition. In: IEEE International Conference on Acoustics Speech and Signal Processing, pp. 4277–4280 (2012)
5. Goodfellow, I., Bengio, Y., Courville, A., Bengio, Y.: Deep Learning, vol. 1. MIT Press, Cambridge (2016)
6. Balkin, S.D., Ord, J.K.: Automatic neural network modeling for univariate time series. Int. J. Forecast. **16**, 509–515 (2000)
7. Stergiou, K., Christou, E.: Modelling and forecasting annual fisheries catches: comparison of regression, univariate and multivariate time series methods. Fish. Res. **25**, 105–138 (1996)
8. Adhikari, R., Agrawal, R.: An introductory study on time series modeling and forecasting. arXiv preprint arXiv:1302.6613.2013 (2013)
9. Vengertsev, D.: Deep learning architecture for univariate time series forecasting. Cs229, pp. 3–7 (2014)
10. Breiman, L.: Random forests. Mach. Learn. **45**, 5–32 (2001)
11. Ivakhnenko, A.G.E., Lapa, V.G.: Cybernetic predicting devices. CCM Information Corporation (1965)
12. LeCun, Y.: Deep learning. Nature **521**, 436 (2015)
13. Haque, M.T., Kashtiban, A.: Application of neural networks in power systems; a review. In: Proceedings of World Academy of Science, Engineering and Technology, vol. 6, pp. 1–5, June 2005. ISSN 1307-6884
14. Marin, D.L.: Building energy load forecasting using deep neural networks. In: 42nd Annual Conference of the IEEE Industrial Electronics Society, pp. 7046–7051 (2016)

15. Khatoon, S., Singh, A.K.: Effects of various factors on electric load forecasting: an overview. In: 6th IEEE Power India International Conference (PIICON), pp. 1–5 (2014)
16. Zhang, G., Patuwo, B.E., Hu, M.Y.: Forecasting with artificial neural networks: the state of the art. Int. J. Forecast. **14**, 35–62 (1998)
17. Wang, L., Zhang, Z., Chen, J.: Short-term electricity price forecasting with stacked denoising autoencoders. IEEE Trans. Power Syst. **32**, 2673–2681 (2017)
18. Gensler, A.: Deep learning for solar power forecasting—an approach using autoencoder and LSTM neural networks. In: 2016 IEEE International Conference on Systems, Man, and Cybernetics (SMC), pp. 002858–002865 (2016)
19. Shi, H., et al.: Deep learning for household load forecasting–a novel pooling deep RNN. IEEE Trans. Smart Grid **9**(5), 5271–5280 (2017)
20. Kong, W., et al.: Short-term residential load forecasting based on LSTM recurrent neural network. IEEE Trans. Smart Grid **10**, 841–851 (2019)
21. Dong, X.: Short-term load forecasting in smart grid: a combined CNN and K-means clustering approach. In: IEEE International Conference on Big Data and Smart Computing (BigComp), pp. 119–125 (2017)
22. Ryu, S.: Deep neural network based demand side short-term load forecasting. Energies **10**, 3 (2016)
23. Qiu, X.: Ensemble deep learning for regression and time series forecasting. In: 2014 IEEE Symposium on Computational Intelligence in Ensemble Learning (CIEL), pp. 1–6 (2014)
24. Zhang, C.-Y.: Predictive deep Boltzmann machine for multiperiod wind speed forecasting. IEEE Trans. Sustain. Energy **6**, 1416–1425 (2015)
25. Tao, Y.: Wind power prediction and pattern feature based on deep learning method. In: IEEE PES Asia-Pacific Power and Energy Engineering Conference, pp. 1–4 (2014)
26. Khodayar, M., Teshnehlab, M.: Robust deep neural network for wind speed prediction. In: 2015 4th Iranian Joint Congress Fuzzy and Intelligent Systems (CFIS), pp. 1–5 (2015)
27. Gensler, A., Gruber, T., Sick, B.: Blazing fast time series segmentation based on update techniques for polynomial approximations. In: IEEE 13th International Conference on Data Mining Workshops (ICDMW), pp. 1002–1011 (2013)
28. Nielsen, H.A., Madsen, H., Nielsen, T.S.: Wind power ensemble forecasting. In: Proceedings of the 2004 Global Windpower Conference and Exhibition (2004)
29. Ramirez-Rosado, I.J., Fernandez-Jimenez, L.A.: Comparison of two new short-term wind-power forecasting systems. Renewable Energy **34**, 1848–1854 (2009)
30. Sengupta, S., et al.: A review of deep learning with special emphasis on architectures, applications and recent trends. Knowl. Based Syst. **194**, 105596 (2020). ISSN 0950-7051.2020

Vehicular Technology and Applications

Optimized MAC Protocol for Lane Switching in Intersection Area

Hitender Vats(✉) and Ranjeet Singh Tomar

ITM University Gwalior, Gwalior, India
{hitender.research, ranjeetsingh}@itmuniversity.ac.in

Abstract. Enhancing Intersection's capacity via improved flow of vehicular traffic which strengthens the overall confidence of drivers is the challenge faced by vehicular control designers in ITMS utilising VANET. Equally important is designing a MAC protocol which will ensure Safety by ensuing timely delivery of Safety Messages. To tackle problem of Traffic Density enhancement we have designed a new Collision Avoidance Intersection management Algorithm (CAIA). The proposed Lane change within Intersection area increases number the vehicle crossing intersection by a factor of 1.2. We have also designed IMAC-Intersection MAC protocol customised for CAIA. Our newly designed IMAC protocol provides dedicated band in IEEE108.11 for ensuring safety of vehicle which is the paramount concern in co-operative ITMS. Since we have designed Lane change based intersection management protocol,the adaptive band allocation perfectly suits this algorithm. To increase the effective utilization of available bandwidth we have employed Physical separation of Anteena in our Simulation.

Keywords: ITMS · ITS · VANET · Cooperative driving · Multi Agent System

1 Introduction

Its a constant endeavour of city planners, scientists and engineers to make our travel experience more comfortable as far as possible. Lot of new technology are being developed and ITS-Intelligent Transportation is a right step in this direction. But much of effort has been in direction of vehicle travel on highways or on straight road including Platooning under the aegis of Cooperative Adaptive Cruise Control (CACC) mechanism. In a typical city traffic of modern world it is the Intersection Points, where flow of traffic from different direction meets, causes maximum disturbance. To solve this problem of traffic jam at intersection, till now all the researchers have divided the intersection area, both in case of Roundabout and Crossing, into small cells. To mitigate the chances of collision they make the vehicle come to halt and wait the cell to be free from any occupancy, which causes frequent stop and restarting movement of vehicle.

R. S. Tomar et al. (Eds.): CNC 2020, CCIS 1502, pp. 265–275, 2021.
https://doi.org/10.1007/978-981-16-8896-6_21

This paper tries to solve this problem from the angle of Lane rather than small cell. Also it tries to increase traffic throughput by allowing overtaking in Intersection area which is not allowed till now in normal traffic management rules. Therefore the new traffic management protocol are designed keeping safety point of view in mind while investigating the corresponding benefit of these protocol in term of efficiency and traffic queue length.

The cooperative traffic management in Intersection area require a robust and foolproof communication paradigm in VANET based ITMS. Therefore a new MAC protocol was designed and implemented on Simulator. The message set and Band allocation in IEEE 11p were subdivided to suit our designed CARA and CAIA algorithms. Since these are tailor-made MAC protocol it suits and matches perfectly with our traffic algorithm. These customised Slotted MAC protocol along with its modified version IMAC-Intersection management MAC Protocol have shown that they eliminate hidden node problem. Also due to these hybrid prioritised MAC protocols, the performance of Packet drop and prioritised safety message reception is much better.

2 Intersection Traffic Control Management System

A Crossing or any intersection can be modelled as a special case of Lane merging and Lane changing. **Umer Khan et al.** examined intelligent lane change models based on the cooperation among connected vehicles for traffic management and travel time optimization. Initial work on intersection management without Red-light was proposed by **Raravi et al**. Further mathematically modelling was done by **Uno et al.** who proposed the merge control application that was utilised for mapping cars on a lane onto different lane.

Dresner and Stone proposed an concept of autonomous intersection management (AIM) with autonomous agents which are positioned in intersection area divided in a number of cells. **J Lee and B Park** has proposed CVIC (Cooperative Vehicle Intersection Control) algorithm based on minimizing the overlaps of trajectories of conflicting vehicles at the intersection. More specifically, this system simply tries to avoid the presence of any pair of conflicting vehicles in the intersection area at the same time. **Kamal et al.** proposes a vehicle-intersection coordination scheme (VICS).

Matteo Vasirani et al. proposed A Market inspired Approach for ITMS that involves both the infrastructure and the drivers. The infrastructure agents coordinate their actions in an indirect way as competitive market participants that aim to match supply with demand. **Hesham Rakha et al.** proposed the CTR algorithm which employs individual vehicles' cumulative travel time (CTT) directly measured (under 100% market penetration rate) or estimated (under imperfect market penetrations) from environment.

Xi Zou and David Levionson focused on the use of distributed Multi Agent System which involves group cooperation of vehicle from same direction and Group competition of vehicles from different vehicles. While **Remi tachet et al.** has studied Slot-based Intersection Control which doubles the capacity. To minimise the Trip Delay due to intersection **Reza Azimi et al.** presented a Non-RSU algorithm CDAI (Collision Detection Algorithm for Intersection) using CC-IP & MP-IP.

2.1 MAC Protocol For VANET Communication

High speed of vehicle give rise to frequent slot change in message domain restricting use of cluster based scheme for MAC strategy. The predictive nature of direction of motion of vehicles add a peculiar dimension to VANET based ITS system as cars moves in on fixed direction and does not change direction all of a sudden. **MAC**-Medium Access Control Sublayer which is the basic medium access paradigm of IEEE 802.11 is carrier sense multiple access/collision avoidance or CSMA/CA.

To overcome the VANET communication problems a lot of review paper has been published which covers a whole lot of VANET and MAC protocol peculiarities in detail but **Maheshwari et al. has** presented survey of broadcast in vehicular networks. **Noh et al.** have presented an automated for situational assessment and behavioral decision in CACC. The team led by **Nguyen** presented a Hybrid TDMA/CSMA Multichannel MAC for enhanced throughput. **Wang et al.** also presented Multichannel schema for Channel Coordination. SCMAC which was Scalable and Cooperative MAC were proposed by **Cao et al**. Collision Aware MAC protocol were briefly explained by **Steinmetz et al**. Similar concept was also proposed by **Sanguesa et al.** for Hybrid Cooperative MAC.

3 Lane Change in Crossing Area Using CAIA

Intersection has been a cause of bottleneck in flow of traffic resulting in avoidable Pollution due to excessive fuel consumption and passenger discomfort inform of jerks apart from safety repercussions. The control models proposed till now creates more jerk as vehicle has to wait for occupied cell/place is to be vacated before it can proceed further. This situation arises as these models take into consideration 'distance' between vehicles- Vehicle & vehicle-roundabout.

One of the most interesting but equally challenging application of ITS is Intersection management System (ITMS). The ITMS consist of controlling traffic at intersection points with use of Inter- vehicular communication without the use of visual Traffic light presently installed out there. Intersection is nothing but an unwanted obstacle to flow of vehicle or whole of traffic. Authors have already designed CARA algorithm on similar lines for Roundabout traffic management **(Vats and Tomar).** As seen in Fig. 1, the Intersection has 4 sides (N, E, W, S) which are perpendicular to each other.

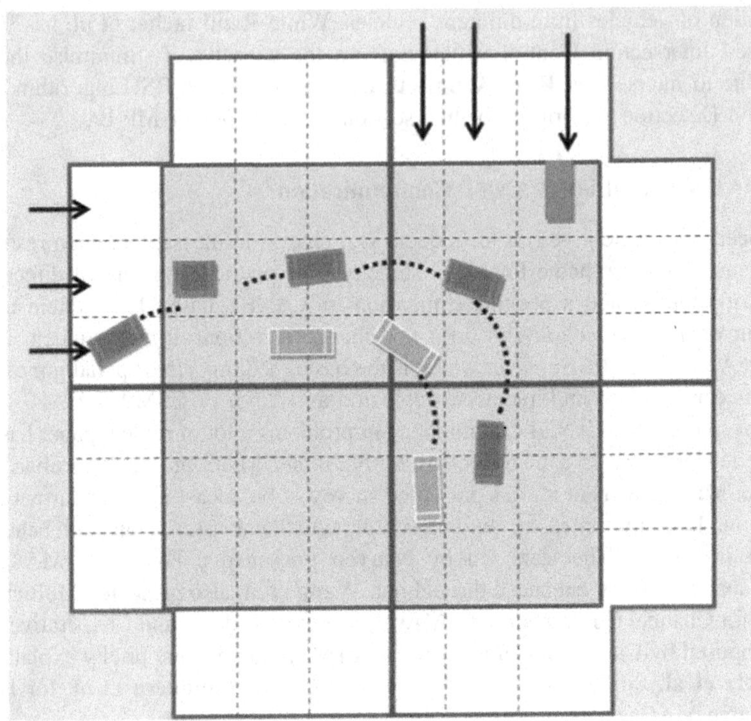

Fig. 1. Shows a lanechange in intersection area

3.1 Collision Avoidance in Intersection Algorithm (CAIA)

We have designed a new Algorithm whose basis is the fact about reusability of model invilving lane change mechanism. For analysis purpose we have modelled a 2 lane system, which will jointly constitute a 'Segment' (Fig. 2).

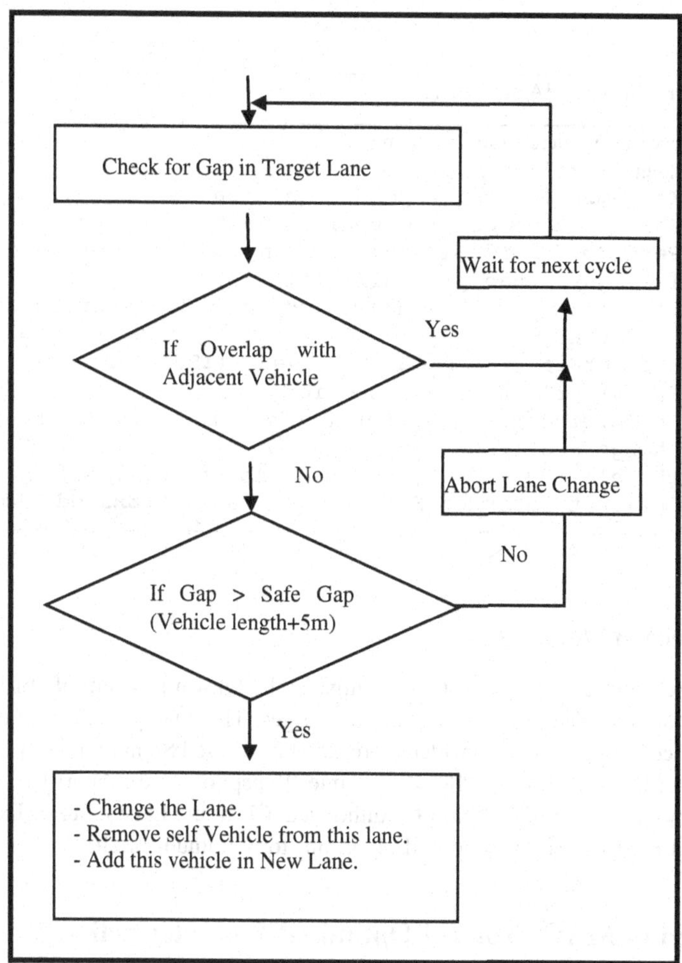

Fig. 2. Flowchart for ElectiveLC algorithm

For optional Lane change detail of other sub-algorithm like **ElectiveLC**, **ForceLC**, **I-Entry** & **I-Exit** have been worked in detail. Below depicted is the CAIA running on each car's vehicle agent.

Algorithm 1: CAIA at Vehicle

Input: Received Vehicle's movement message
Output: Transmitting Vehicle's state

```
1. Transmit Present  Speed, Position
2. Follow the preceding vehicle in Cruise Control
3. Perform LC if Required( when self-cruise velocity
   is higher than preceding Vehicle)
4. If within reach of Intersection : Transmit Intended
   Exit Lane
5. Decelerate if DECL received (ISU Performs Lane
   Entry) or Enter Intersection Segment
6. In Intersection Segment Perform Lane change if lane
   Change Received
7.  Decelerate and Join back on Abort LC Signal
8.  Exit at Intended ExitLane & Transmit Exited Signal
```

3.2 Prioritised Message List

The proposed Slotted MAC effectively mitigates the known problem of IEEE802.11p that are reliability related issues of Safety messages. The quality evaluating metric for MAC protocol which can be considered are RSSI (Received Signal Strength Indicator), PDR (Packet Delivery Ratio), PIR (Packet Inter Reception time). Abort LC, DeAccel, Compulsory LC, Present Position, LC Authorised, Clear and Lane After of Exit are the Signals that are used in our proposed algorithm for communication.

4 Design of MAC Protocol Optimised For Intersection

The communication procedure under ITMS using VANET can be classified under two phases. Vehicles having any message packet ready for transportation requests ISU. Subsequently ISU assigns the channel based upon criticality of message. The channel contention is managed by the ISU by allocation channel on Assignment band. Channel contention that is the probability of collision among request packet is managed by ISU in quite efficient manner. This proposed channel assignment is a type of Centralised MAC protocol. The flow of operation of our designed MAC protocol at the ISU is presented at Fig. 3. The complete available frequency spectrum is divided in three band namely-

- **Assignment Band (AB)-:** This band Assigns the channel on vehicle's request.
- **Road Band (RB)-:** It does the job of catering for vehicle Entering/Exiting the Intersection)
- **Turn Band (TB)-:** Used for controlling vehicle which are taking Left or right Turn.

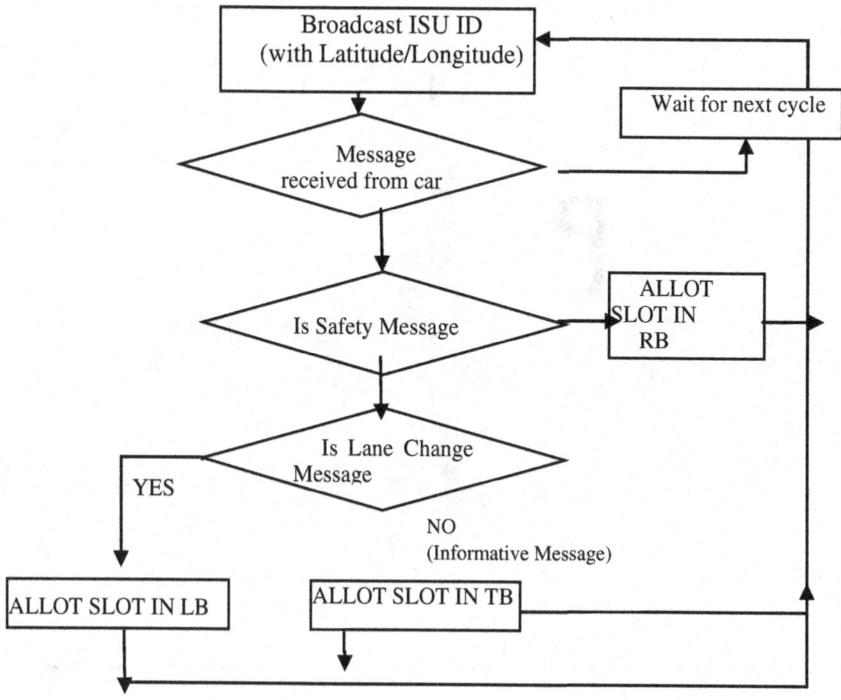

Fig. 3. Intersection MAC protocol flow chart

5 Simulation and Result

5.1 IntersectionSim

Simulation is last resort for researcher as well as Policy framework designer when ever Empirical data is not possible to obtain. Since all the vehicle present in a city cannot be converted 'Smart' at one go, which will be a very costly proposition also, all the research on VANET based ITMS system has been carried out on software based Simulators. The Simulator – "**IntersectionSim**" using OOPS based programming Language '**Python**' have been developed during VANET Project Implementation with which many responses can be obtained by our newly developed Simulator for better understanding the controller algorithms (Fig. 4).

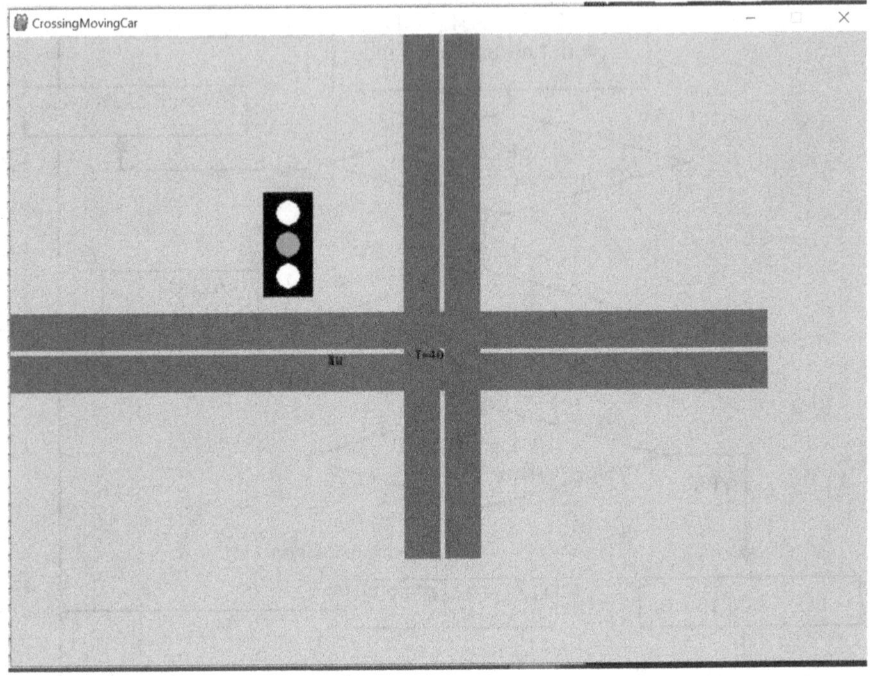

Fig. 4. Snapshots of IntersectionSim

Experimental Setup for IntersectionSim consisted of a four segments Intersection at right angle each having Two Lane with each segment of 2000 m in length.

5.2 Result Analysis

The Average Delay time was used as matric for comparison which depends upon the extra time the cars took after travelling through Intersection. The system was evaluated for various traffic density with multiple of 16 cars/min.

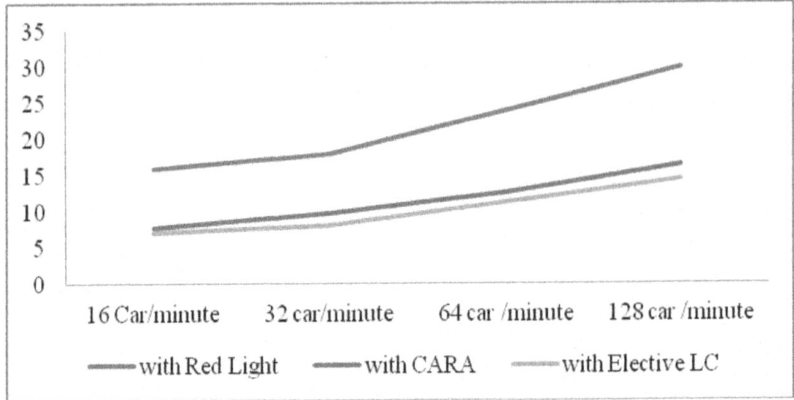

Fig. 5. Average delay time vs vehicle density chart

The Fig. 5 shows the graph of the average delay time versus the density of vehicle. It can be easily inferred from above graph that vehicles in Intersection that with CAIA algorithm the delay will be considerably reduced. The cars moving left contribute less to the delay in comparison with straight trajectories. The left as well as right turns occupies more intersection area resulting in longer wait.

The Fig. 6 shows the depiction of Packets reception ratio vs number of vehicles curve/graph. The packet reception ratio enhances with depletion in vehicle density which is in line with our hypothesis. These outcomes leads us to our conclusion that our newly designed MAC protocol will enable better as well as efficient utilisation of available frequency spectrum.

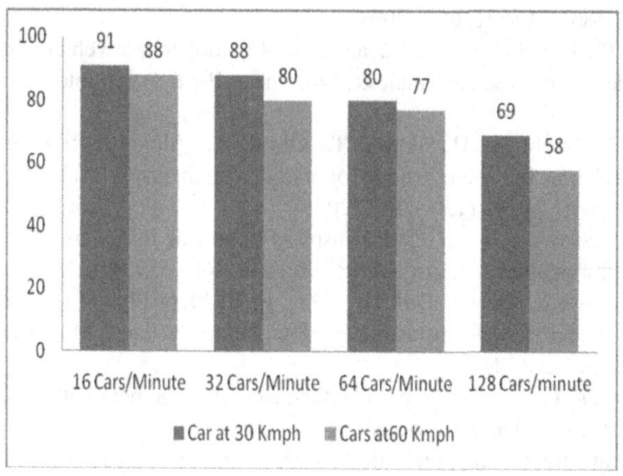

Fig. 6. Packet reception ratio vs car density

6 Conclusion

An intersection traffic management is a complicated and complex process which has got vast influence on the traffic safety involving many human lives. Right from development of means of transportation and further with automation, the number vehicle kept on increasing commemorating with passenger's comfort. This lead to arrival of a urban phenomenon of Congestion and traffic Jam on roads. To control traffic from different but conflicting direction thus avoiding accident, Red Light with Green and Red lights period were introduced keeping in mind the safety of passenger and avoiding damages to vehicles. This paper is a modest attempt to examine the possible improvisation in traffic by exploring Lane change in Intersection area of Red Light Crossing but with out compromising the safety factor and will also reduce unnecessary interference of messages. In future communication protocol for all kind of Intersection including under ITMS, can be developed.

References

1. Khan, U., Basaras, P., Schmidt-Thieme, L., Nanopoulos, A., Katsaros, D.: Analyzing cooperative lane change models for connected vehicles. In: 2014 International Conference on Connected Vehicles and Expo (ICCVE) (2014)
2. Raravi, G., Shingde, V., Ramamritham, K., Bharadia, J.: Merge algorithms for intelligent vehicles. In: Ramesh, S., Sampath, P. (eds.) Next Generation Design and Verification Methodologies for Distributed Embedded Control Systems, pp. 51–65. Springer, Dordrecht (2007). https://doi.org/10.1007/978-1-4020-6254-4_5
3. Uno, A., Sakaguchi, T., Tsugawa, S.: A merging control algorithm based on inter-vehicle communication. In: 1999 IEEE/IEEJ/JSAI International Conference on Intelligent Transportation Systems, Proceedings, pp. 783–787 (1999)
4. Dresner, K., Stone, P.: A multiagent approach to autonomous intersection management. J. Artif. Intell. Res. **31**, 591–656 (2008)
5. Lee, J., Park, B.: Development and evaluation of a cooperative vehicle intersection control algorithm under the connected vehicles environment. IEEE Trans. Intell. Transp. Syst. **13**(1), 81–90 (2012)
6. Kamal, M.A.S., Imura, J., Hayakawa, T., Ohata, A., Aihara, K.: A vehicle-intersection coordination scheme for smooth flows of traffic without using traffic lights. IEEE Trans. Intell. Transp. Syst. **16**(3), 1136–1147 (2015)
7. Vasirani, M., Ossowski, S.: A market-inspired approach for intersection management in urban road traffic networks. J. Artif. Intell. Res. **43**, 621–659 (2012)
8. Rakha, H., Zohdy, I., Du, J., Park, B., Lee, J., El-Metwally, M.: Traffic signal control enhancements under vehicle infrastructure integration systems. Mid-Atlantic Universities Transportation Center (2011)
9. Zou, X., Levinson, D.M.: Vehicle-based intersection management with intelligent agents. In: ITS America Annual Meeting Proceedings (2003)
10. Tachet, R., et al.: Revisiting street intersections using slot-based systems. PloS One **11**(3), e0149607 (2016)
11. Azimi, R., Bhatia, G., Rajkumar, R., Mudalige, P.: Intersection management using vehicular networks. In: Society for Automotive Engineers (SAE) World Congress, April 2012
12. Maheswari, R., Kumar, T.K.: Efficient way of emergency message dissemination and reliable broadcast in vehicular ad-hoc network. IJAREEI **4**, 416–421 (2015)
13. Noh, S., An, K., Han, W.: Situation assessment and behavior decision for vehicle/driver cooperative driving in highway environments. In: IEEE International Conference on Automation Science and Engineering (CASE), pp. 626–633 (2015)
14. Nguyen, V., Oo, T.Z., Chuan, P., Hong, C.S.: An efficient time slot acquisition on the hybrid TDMA/CSMA multichannel MAC in VANET. IEEE Commun. Lett. **20**(5), 970–973 (2016)
15. Wang, Q., Leng, S., Fu, H., Zhang, Y.: An IEEE 802.11p-based multichannel MAC scheme with channel coordination for vehicular ad hoc networks. IEEE Trans. Intell. Transp. Syst. **13**(2), 449–458 (2012)
16. Cao, Y., Zhang, H., Zhou, X., Yuan, D.: A scalable and cooperative MAC protocol for control channel access in VANET. IEEE Access **5**, 9682–9690 (2017)

17. Vats, H., Tomar, R.S.: Lane change in roundabout for reduced trip time. In: Verma, S., Tomar, R.S., Chaurasia, B.K., Singh, V., Abawajy, J. (eds.) CNC 2018. CCIS, vol. 839, pp. 201–212. Springer, Singapore (2019). https://doi.org/10.1007/978-981-13-2372-0_18
18. Sanguesa, J.A., Fogue, M., Garrido, P., Martinez, F.J., Cano, J.-C., Calafate, C.T.: A survey and comparative study of broadcast warning message dissemination schemes for VANETs. Mob. Inf. Syst. **2016**, 1–18 (2016)
19. Steinmetz, E., et al.: Collision-aware communication for intersection management of automated vehicles. IEEE Access **6**, 77359–77371 (2018)

Smart Vehicle-Zone: Device to Device Handoff Techniques in Vehicle Ad Hoc Networks

Sivakumar Kulanthaiyappan(✉) and Chandrasekhar Chellaih

Department of Computer Science, Periyar University, Salem, Tamilnadu, India

Abstract. Nowadays, the time-slot synchronization of rapid network devices offers an excellent strategy for 5G networks. The intelligent vehicle communications, mainly so that a massive of rapid changing devices on the different cell's with the edge, can be managed concurrently. The transport technologies with their updated information, the vehicle network has been quickly established by numerous cluster or zone connections, which link multi-tier layers, clouds, loads, etc. So, the knowledge on the device selection of related objective is missing in this scenario. It's difficult to obtain rapid information about the network and several-variety of equipment in advance. The awareness of accessibility, charge, and active handoff sessions for the proposed system will be chosen in the same way. This paper has a collaborative transfer method using D2D (Device to Device) multi-cast and D2D zones to tackle extreme resource contention caused by devices with high density and mobility. This data transfer brings vehicles, sensors, equipment, software, and roadside systems to a perfect zone link.

Keywords: Smart vehicle-zone · D2D · Handoff · Internet of Things · 5G · Internet of Vehicle

1 Introduction

The generation of networks will solve the kind of problems, difficulties, and disadvantages. It can answer any of the new challenges in which all related variables are predicted, and consumer expectations can be addressed. Apart from previous generations' standards, the technologies of 5G must not only transcend functionality as well as avoid latency, but it has to tackle upcoming new applications. This uses a very different efficiency, trustworthiness, and latency scenario. For example, it was an increased fact, technological and autonomous vehicles of the rapid changes in the area.

This work focuses a collaboration of 5G cells, and the Internet of Vehicles (IoV) for vehicle zone connectivity in the network area. Because some of these are automated, using roadmaps, in which vehicles run in the path of trivial intelligence. To make a smart vehicle zone has a necessary coverage, size, devices, range, mobility, radius, etc. with that autonomous driving in the roadmap, and first detail 5G scenario to be discussed. The 5GPP roadmap specifies latency requirements of less than 5 ms and a density of up to 100 units per square meter. It has strict territorial, constrains, and the coverage of users in areas with no shadow or other interference network coverage, such as relaying signals between vehicles. 5G connectivity would allow the mobile hotspots

R. S. Tomar et al. (Eds.): CNC 2020, CCIS 1502, pp. 276–287, 2021.
https://doi.org/10.1007/978-981-16-8896-6_22

to serve vehicles, redeploying the Internet connectivity for nearby travel users. The 5GPP proposals detail several potential scenarios in the 5G vehicle network and propose safety criteria for transmits /receivers signal consistency, latency, reliability, and technologies with it applications [1–4] (Fig. 1).

1.1 5G Use Cases and Scenario

- Amazing fast
- In a crowded environment, excellent service is provided.
- Following your line is the best result
- Ubiquitous things communications
- Real-time and reliable links

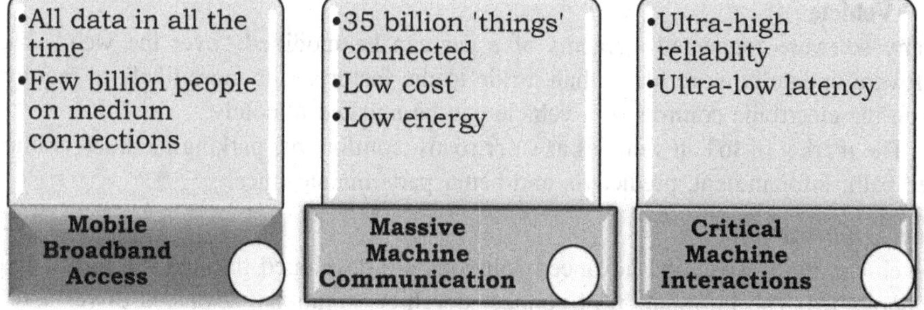

Fig. 1. A broad range of 5G service and paradigms

- Better performance: 1000fold better mobile data volumes per area and 10 to 100 times higher data ranges. It can also improve spectrum efficiency and network capacity for all users connected via heterogeneous network and vehicle applications, allowing them to use the regional resources.
- Less latency: delay is minimized as well as it takes short distances without the involvement of infrastructure
- Ultra-high performance is achieved by providing a wide range of vehicle and devices while using V2V as a reaction mechanism in the case of a network.
- To extend the coverage, it has reached ultra-high reliability and the use of V2V as a backward solution in the absence of infrastructure.
- More connectivity density: 100 times higher devices connected
- Higher mobility: up to a few km/h
- Full coverage

1.2 Internet of Things

IoT refers to the widespread use of a network to connect chips and sensing to devices. The term “automotive IoT” refers to the integration of Internet of Things (IoT) technology into automotive systems (smart home, train, and vehicle) in order to develop new technologies and solutions that can make cars faster, smarter, safer, more reliable, and more comfortable to drive [10].

The Web and cloud-based vehicles vacuum up, it transfer relay data heaps from 20 to 200 megabytes a day. Such data are then used to construct safer roads, to predict a breakdown of the equipment with functional activities, and to improve vehicle functionality. This megabyte is anticipated that the autonomous revolution will sail to the terabyte sector. In particular, these smart automotive ease lifestyles for both riders and manufacturers when it comes to technological updates even while technology is still emerging.

IoT-Vehicle

Many software-connected elements of a car can be modified “over the web.” The software update is more likely than a ride to the factory. It is more likely to require. Even the electronic controls of a vehicle can be updated remotely.

The market of IoT in vehicles as safer roads, comfortable parking facilities, traffic-free path, infotainment, predictive, and better parts maintenance.

Key Applications

In-vehicle, innovative, and advanced solutions are developed through the use of IoT technologies. The information of connected vehicle solutions, advanced driver assistance systems, in-car drivetrains, mapping and telecommunications options, and advanced predictive solutions are all available. The connection bonding of vehicles, devices, infrastructure, applications, and Vehicles-to-All (V2X) apps are all identified and maintained.

1.3 Internet of Vehicle

IoV is a new generation ICT for the development of the entire network between cars, vehicle equipment, roadside systems, buses, self-support, and service platforms. It strengthens the awareness, driving skills and can create a modern automotive and transport service model. The vehicle’s Internet definition involves intranet, cloud, and mobile vehicles. It has an integrated wireless and network knowledge sharing program [5].

Broadband Vehicle Communication (Vehicle to Everything) is the premier internet-based vehicle communication platform that allows standards for information sharing and interactivity between cars and certain entities. It includes vehicles such as buses, infrastructure, public sectors pedestrians, and networked vehicle. The most recent vision of V2X technology, in which primarily combines DSRC and cellular vehicle-to-everything (C-V2X) tools. C-V2X is a mobile networked cellular network wireless networking solution. This was launched in 2016 by the 5 G national organization. The evolution approach is transparent. 5G-V2X is the current iteration of the 5 G standard [6–8].

2 Proposed Method

Zone: Zone in the sense field-network coverage or cluster or specific formation of mesh, and it has the following things are necessary for the area.

- Cloud
  (Centralized intelligent files midpoint)
- Core Connectivity
  (QoS, Multi-cast, Link service, Mobile packet, IP)
- Edge service
  (Ground area Network, multi or hybrid connection (3G/4G/5G/Wi-Fi))
- Sensors and systems (Smart things network, embedded connections)

The zone can be formed by numerous clusters like vehicle affinity, actuator affinity, driving affinity, manufacture, and from the coverage point of view micro, pico, femto level cells are varied. Based on this criteria frequency, coverage, capacity may different for the rapid mobility in the network (Fig. 2).

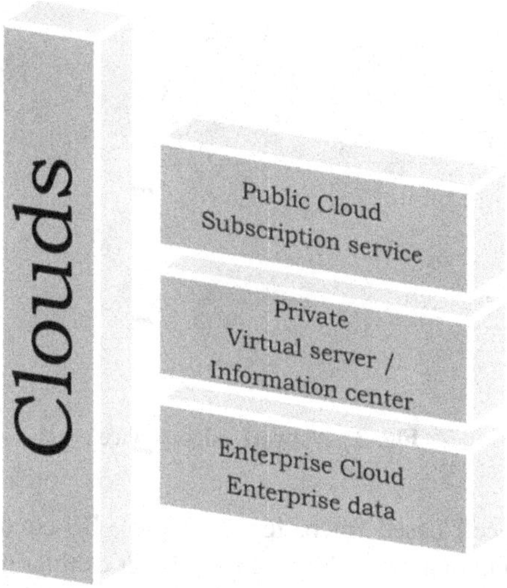

Fig. 2. Cloud data centers

2.1 Zone Localization

Our solutions rely heavily on APs and mobile as well as vehicle actuator's location information. GPS is the most common form of physical position. Nevertheless, alternative approaches are available that, in inter-zone environments and in certain other situations, may not access the GPS online tracking database via beacon data demand. Thus navigation is particularly practical with air hearing beacons and online queries based on location information of surrounding APs. The new zone Surround Sense system, which uses environmental fingerprinting (such as tone, light, and color) to locate a mobile and vehicle actuator, can also be introduced.

2.2 Zone Broadcasting and Multicasting Service (ZBMS)

The method of a vehicle device communication system to enable the mutual transfer of D2D zones efficiently in our presentation. The vehicle-zone cell broadcast, multicast technology combined more D2D Multi-Cast communication to provide ZBMS service in a small cell range via D2D transport network. In accumulation to integrating basic grid skills and improving the overall experience, these hybrids often lower demand on BSs and relieve bandwidth strain demands. Picture 1 provides a scenario for incorporating the D2D cellular network multi-cast technology. In this case, the adjacent D2D UE zone consists of a multi-cast broadcasting community (Fig. 3).

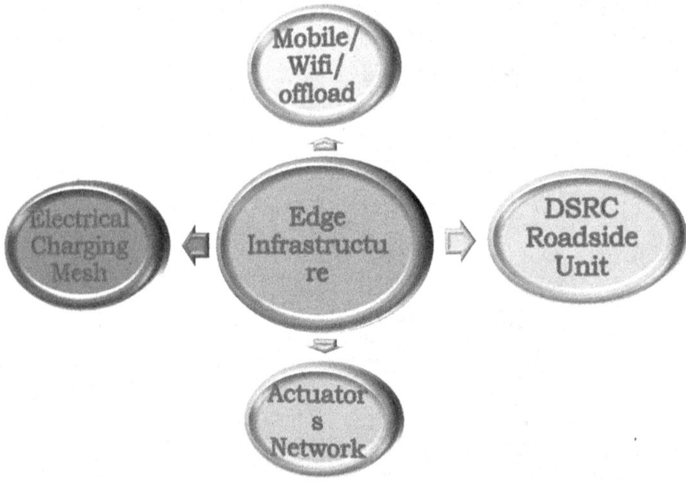

Fig. 3. Network edge service

A D2D-zone is a cell based (pico, femto, micro), BS-controlled self-organizing network that allots orthogonal or multiplexed ad hoc or cellular resources to the region in the licensed TDD, FDD bands. The cell multi-cast transmitter can typically be used as a zone heads for communication among the inner numerous zone-cell clusters of D2D user equipment and the particular cell base station. The cell-BS can relay free information to the leaders of zone, while every head of zone translates the data to further members of the zone. The administrator, however, will transmit data gathered from the D2D nodes to the BS. Due to the short distance between D2D connections, this approach achieves a maximum of the performance benefit and therefore increases the quality of appropriate cell UEs at the cell edge [9–11].

2.3 Zone Broadcast Radio Service (ZBRS) IP Level

The ZBRS has the following phase in the handoff techniques.

- Zone-data collection
- Rapid-IP obtaining
- Assistance
- Make before-break
- Route-Redirection

Each node (vehicle) broadcasts its own details as well as neighbor's node positions, location, moving speeds, and direction periodically in the information collecting process. It should also re-diffuse messages it has received to regulate the IP direction as follows the time to live (TTL) of the posts. The message must be retransmitted if the TTL of the message is significantly higher than 0. The TTL is based on the expected size of the virtual grid and on the base station's contact range. Once the nearby vehicle has obtained knowledge, a vehicle may locate, shift speed, and the direction of the surrounding vehicle, thus grouping proper vehicles into a virtual bus and selecting appropriate cooperative nodes to assist in moving the IP address at the right time [12, 17, 18].

Zone plays a significant role in only three sate of vehicles such as

- Keeps the pass(ed) IP (Vehicle receives (V_K)).
- Leaves the particular BS's (The vehicle communication region (V_L)).
- Enters the target BS's (The vehicle communication region V_E).

2.4 Zone Joining Handoff

The BS usually directly manages every unit's transfer. Besides, when sufficient single or multiple access channels and a lot of transfer devices are available, the culture approach takes advantage of low time. Several mechanisms may request a switch simultaneously into a dense network. In particular, with the internet of the objects converging into the 5 G networks, this scenario is becoming more common. It might lead to a significant shortage of channel services and a typical disruption of activity (Fig. 4).

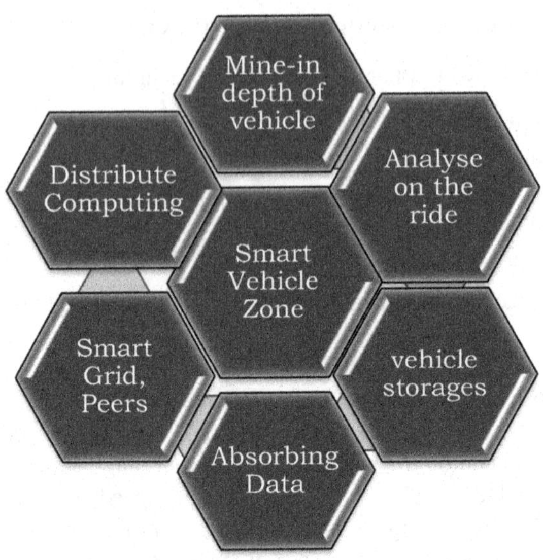

Fig. 4. Role of distributed vehicle data management

The zone displays a two-hop distribution protocol using the D2D multi-cast. It stimulates the head to collect and submit the relevant data from the D2D UE and RSS. After the transmission decisions are based on recorded information, the BS that provides the transfer data to the head. The transfer of data to D2D devices within the area is also given.

Although transmission of two-hop signals can be delayed for a more extended period, the situation can be best controlled with a broad range of nearby devices. In general, every D2D cluster is allocated an orthogonal or multiplex resource set. D2D UEs acquire a random access conflict or a zone heading schedule within a group. The channel used by the cluster head will also be delegated for resource pool information. The delivery channel used by the particular zone level articular cluster head is often assigned by the resource pool. Therefore, the multi-hop approach will reduce the blocking of access channels if a large number of devices request a joint transfer. Consequently, it is crucial to decrease the transmission delay and the risk of a cell-border interruption. Majority of Static, dynamic TDMA protocols used in actuators networks and this zone level also take a same for that [13–15].

Zone Explore the IP and Lifetime

```
Step 1: Ready to leave the BS in VL (Leaving Vehicle)
Step 2: VL sends IP packet to VE (Entering Vehicle)
Step 3: if VL receives ACK from the VE
                    VL disconnects the BS;
            Else if  VL goto the virtual bus station
                        From the TTL msg to obtain the
IP passing direction;
                        VK (Keeping passed IP) receives
and keeps the passed IP;
                        VK sends ACK to VL;
                        VL disconnects the BS;
Step 4: If VK moves target BS boundary
                    Goto step 1;
            Else
```

Zone to Zone Obtaining IP

```
                    VE sends the IP request to server
and set IP_obtainting_time (TIPO), timer = 0;
Step 5: If { TIPO + (VE reqtime from VK + VE IP
rectime)} < TServer then
                    VE broadcast IP reqmsg to VK
            Else
                    VE receives new IP from the server
Step 6: if VE has received a passed IP from VK
                     VE configure the interface
                     VE reply the IP passing ACK to VK
                     VE send a server_abort_packet to
server
            Else  if (TIPO >=(VE reqtime from VK + VE
IP rectime))
                                TIPO = TIPO + timer;
                                Set timer =0;
                                Goto step 5;
Step 7: Get a necessary details and QoS;
```

3 Result

Table 1 shows the ns2 simulation tool network setting, and the Fig. 5, 6, 7, 8 is used the handoff results. Figure 5 presents the throughput variations of proposed work and Zone cell level broadcasting handoff service, not affect the throughput in networks.

Table 1. Network settings

Parameter	Value
Network simulation tool	NS 2.35
MAC	802.11
Cell range	3–4 km
Number of vehicles	50 nodes, 100 nodes, 150 nodes
Speed	10–100 km/h
Simulation time	350 s
Protocol	DSR
Packet size	1000
Packet rate	510 p/s

Figure 6 shows the packet loss versus IP passing hops between the vehicles, and it may zone to zone, within the infrastructure, hybrid network mesh, software-defined based, intelligent based, cloud. Image 7 displays the result of network fragments versus losses in the mesh, and Picture 8 is the vehicle speed with a loss comparison of proposed work. From these results, proposed zone to zone handoff efficiently works with our simulation area.

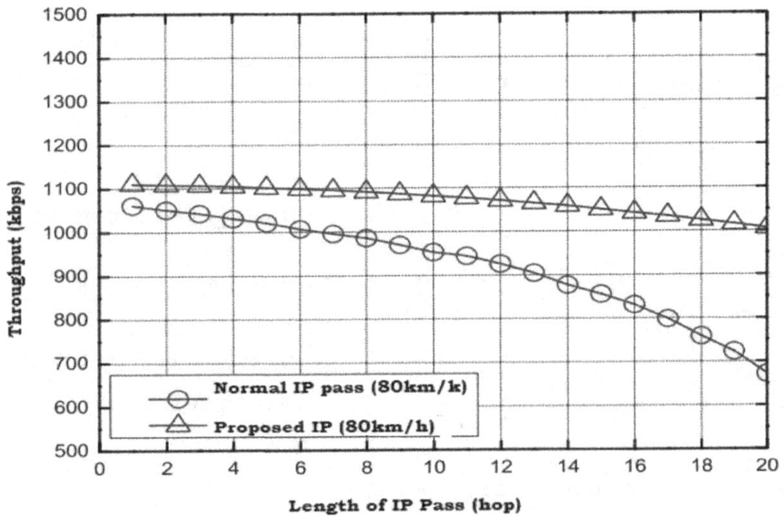

Fig. 5. Throughput levels in IP passing

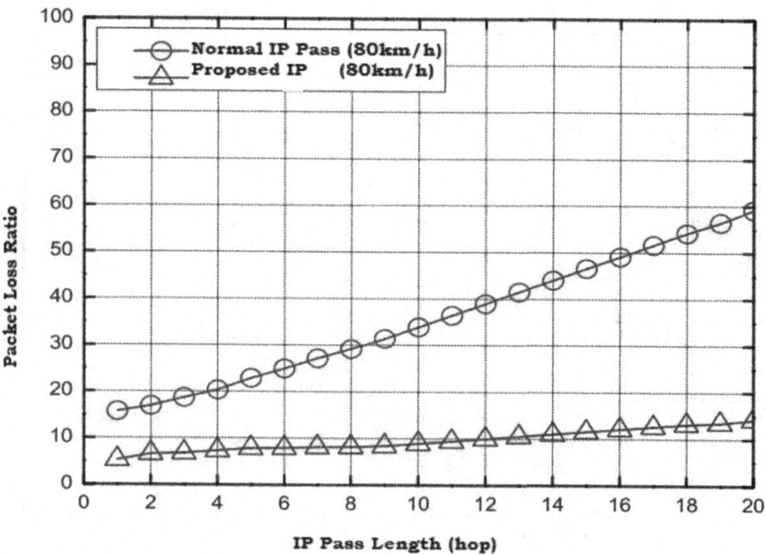

Fig. 6. Loss of packets vs. IP passing hops

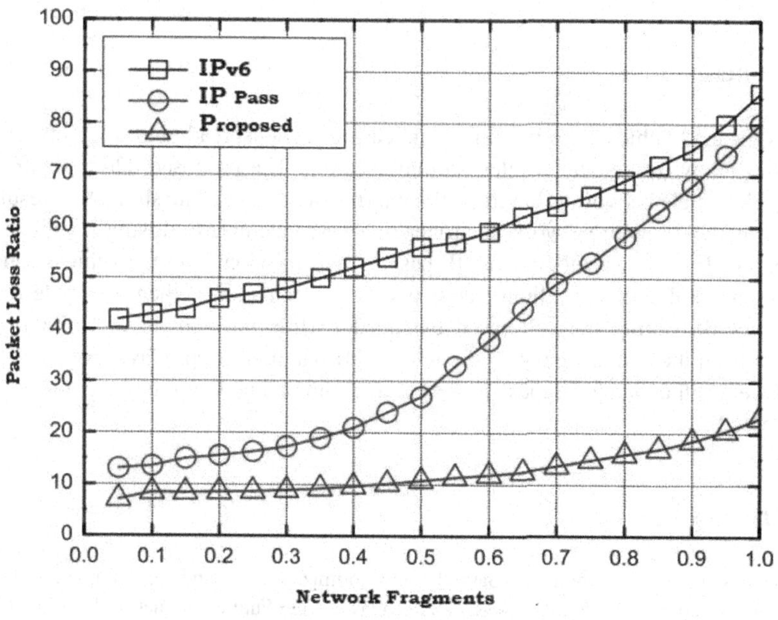

Fig. 7. Network fragmentation of proposed work

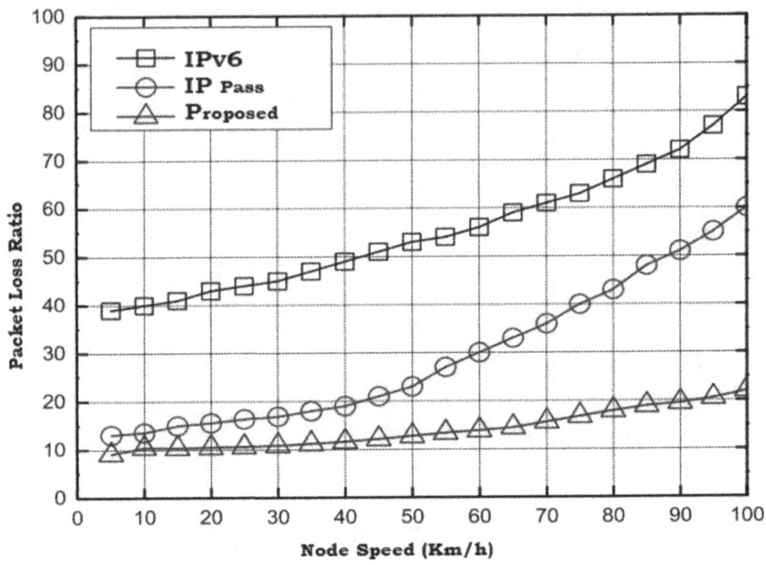

Fig. 8. Speed level of proposed work

4 Conclusion

Interconnected vehicles are becoming increasingly widespread, and a variety of technologies allow for vehicle wireless communication. The proposed d2d handoff in the zone-cell vehicle network is based on the internet of vehicles. The simulation results for vehicle networks with network heterogeneity were calculated utilising a vehicle-zone cell-based IP passing method. This IP passing transmission from the vehicle zone cell reduces handoff time and eliminates network fragmentation. When a vehicle reaches the target BS during the cell-based extended IP life, the vehicle will obtain an IP address from the vehicle carrying the released IP via multi-hop relays. As a result, the results reveal that handoff times are kept to a minimum and that Internet connectivity is maintained.

References

1. Davaasambuu, B., Keping, Y., Sato, T.: Self-optimization of handover parameters for long-term evolution with dual wireless mobile relay nodes. Future Internet **7**, 196–213 (2015). https://doi.org/10.3390/fi7020196
2. Uma, C., Jeonga, J.: On microcell-macrocell handoff queueing scheme in heterogeneous industrial networks. Procedia Comput. Sci. **134**, 169–176 (2018)

3. Kumar, K., Prakash, A., Tripathi, R.: Spectrum handoff scheme with multiple attributes decision making for optimal network selection in cognitive radio networks. Digital Commun. Netw. (2017). https://doi.org/10.1016/j.dcan.2017.01.003
4. Xie, K., Cao, J., Wang, X., Wen, J.: Pre-scheduled handoff for service-aware and seamless internet access. Comput. Netw. **110**, 324–337 (2016)
5. Aljeri, N., Boukerche, A.: A two-tier machine learning-based handover management scheme for intelligent vehicular networks. Ad Hoc Net. **94**, 101930 (2019)
6. Kaiwartya, O., et al.: Internet of Vehicles: motivation layered architecture network model challenges and future aspects. IEEE Access **4**, 5356–5373 (2016)
7. AlFarraj, O., Tolba, A., Alkhalaf, S., AlZubi, A.: Neighbor predictive adaptive handoff algorithm for improving mobility management in VANETs. Comput. Netw. **151**, 224–231 (2019)
8. Roy, P., Midya, S., Majumder, K.: Handoff schemes in vehicular ad-hoc network: a comparative study. In: Corchado Rodriguez J., Mitra S., Thampi S., El-Alfy ES. (eds.) ISTA 2016. AISC, vol. 530, pp. 421-432. Springer, Cham (2016). https://doi.org/10.1007/978-3-319-47952-1_33
9. Sivabalan, S., Rathipriya, R.: Slot scheduling Mac using energy efficiency in ad hoc wireless networks. In: 2017 International Conference on Inventive Communication and Computational Technologies (ICICCT), Coimbatore, pp. 430–434 (2017)
10. Sivabalan, S., Rathipriya, R.: Enhanced multi-hop routing for smart home network transmission. J. Anal. Comput. (2019). ICETC 2018
11. Din, S., Paul, A., Rehman, A.: 5G-enabled hierarchical architecture for software-defined intelligent transportation system. Comput. Netw. (2018)
12. Oyewobi, S.S., Hancke, G.P., Abu-Mahfouz, A.M., Onumanyi, A.J.: A delay-aware spectrum handoff scheme for prioritized time-critical industrial applications with channel selection strategy. Comput. Commun. **144**, 112–123 (2019)
13. Oyewobi, S.S., Hancke, G.P.: A survey of cognitive radio handoff schemes, challenges and issues for industrial wireless sensor networks (CR-IWSN). J. Netw. Comput. Appl. (2017). https://doi.org/10.1016/j.jnca.2017.08.016
14. Val, A., et al.: Design, analysis and implementation of a time-bounded spectrum handoff algorithm for real-time industrial wireless sensor and actuator networks. J. Netw. Comput. Appl. **125**, 1–16 (2019)
15. Zhao, Y., Li, W., Sanglu, L.: Navigation-driven handoff minimization in wireless networks. J. Netw. Comput. Appl. **74**, 11–20 (2016)
16. Chen, Y.-S., Hsu, C.-S., Yi, W.-H.: An IP passing protocol for vehicular ad hoc networks with network fragmentation. Comput. Math. Appl. **63**, 407–426 (2012)
17. Kulanthaiyappan, S., Settu, S., Chellaih, C.: Internet of Vehicle: effects of target tracking cluster routing in vehicle network. In: 2020 6th International Conference on Advanced Computing and Communication Systems (ICACCS), pp. 951–956 (2020). https://doi.org/10.1109/ICACCS48705.2020.9074454
18. Kolandaiappan, S., Chellaih, C., Settu, S.: Smart vehicles zone creation for vehicle ad hoc network. Turkish J. Comput. Math. Educ. **12**(12), 3333–3343 (2021)

Electronic Circuits for Communication Systems

Comparative Study of Photo Voltaic Panel Cooling Methods for Efficiency Enhancement

Sampurna Panda[1(✉)], Manoj Gupta[1], and C. S. Malvi[2]

[1] Poornima University, Jaipur, India
manojg@poornima.edu.in
[2] Madhav Institute of Technology and Science, Gwalior, India

Abstract. The mother of all renewable energy sources is solar-oriented technology, which is one of the many energy sources. Photovoltaic modules experience short-term and long-term corruption as a result of high temperatures. Hence Photovoltaic cooling is a major concern for enhancing the PV framework's visual appeal. Standards state that the efficiency of a PV panel decreases by 0.5% for every degree of temperature increase. To increase efficiency by reducing temperature, this paper discusses ways to improve different cooling procedures for commercial photovoltaic boards. On equal irradiance, three cooling methods using non-cooling Photo Voltaic panels were tested simultaneously. The results show that dispersing water on the module's front surface lowers the temperature by 50 °C while increasing the most extreme power and effectiveness by 2% and effectiveness.

Keywords: A photovoltaic system · A fill factor · A cooling system for the panels

1 Introduction

The only way to meet future energy demands is with clean, renewable sources of energy. PV panels, or photovoltaic systems, are the most common form of renewable energy technology on the market today. About 80% of the sun's total rays are either absorbed as heat or reflected back to space. As a result, no electricity is generated from the solar radiation that strikes the PV Panel. The Photo Voltaic panel's performance suffers greatly as a result of the excessive heat. According to research, the conversion efficiency drops by 0.4 to 0.5% for every degree of temperature increase [2]. Because of this unwelcome rise in temperature, photovoltaic efficiency has dropped precipitously.

The cooling of a photovoltaic panel is critical to keeping its temperature within the Maximum Allowed Temperature (MAT, 25 °C under STC) [3]. STC is an acronym for Standard Test Procedures. A standard range of 1000 W per sqmetre "daylight" is used in the estimation of these figures. Cooling can be accomplished in one of two ways. Active cooling refers to the use of an external energy source for cooling purposes; passive cooling refers to the use of no external energy source [3].

There are numerous active and passive cooling methods available depending on the coolant used to lower the temperature in various parts of the world.

R. S. Tomar et al. (Eds.): CNC 2020, CCIS 1502, pp. 291–300, 2021.
https://doi.org/10.1007/978-981-16-8896-6_23

This paper compares three different cooling methods with one without a cooling panel in the same geographic location with the same climatic conditions as before. The temperature was lowered with the help of three different cooling methods. Water, water mixed with dry grass, and water mixed with sand are the cooling options. For front surface cooling, only water has been used, but the other two are Methods of cooling the back surface of the object. They are all compared to a non-cooled PV panel in order to get accurate results.

1.1 Experimental Set Up

1.1.1 Geographical Location

ITM Universe in Gwalior has experimental equipment set up. The coordinates for this location are: 26.2183 °N 78.1828 °E. A look at the map reveals that there aren't any trees or shrubs nearby (Fig. 1).

Fig. 1. A satellite image of the area revealing completely shade free

1.1.2 The Intensity of the Sunlight at the Site

Direct normal irradiance, or beam radiation, is measured with a surface element parallel to the Sun at a specific location on the Earth's surface (Fig. 2).

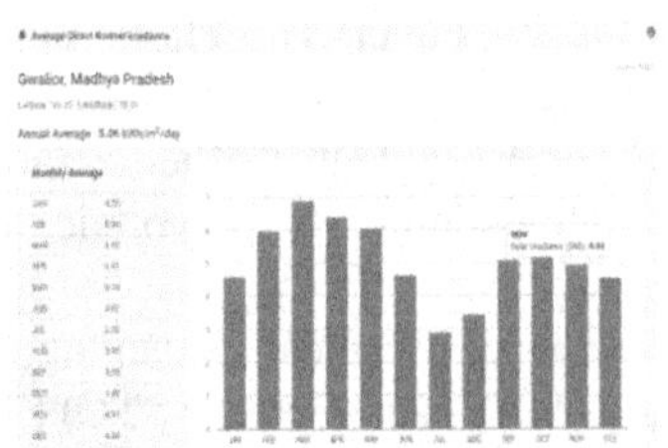

Fig. 2. NREL's Gwalior average direct normal irradiance

1.1.3 PV Panel

PV panels with a multicrystalline structure are used in this setup (Table 1).

Table 1. Manufacturer's datasheet

Brand	Ajit solar
Power Max Pmpp	15 W
Maximum system voltage	1000 V
Vmpp	18.8 V
Voc	22.6 V
Impp	8.35 A
Isc	8.95 A
Fuse rating	15 A

1.1.4 Solar Angle

An azimuth angle is the direction in which sunlight is coming from on a given day. The sun is always in the south in the Northern Hemisphere between 23 and 90 latitudes. In order to make the most of the sun's energy, the panels are oriented to face south. The polar opposite is true in the Southern Hemisphere.

South-facing roofs are best for installation because they receive the most sunlight.

Because of this, the azimuth angle selection could make up for any energy lost in the morning or afternoon.

1.1.5 Tilt Angle

For maximum output in winter, PV panels should be oriented more vertically; in summer, they should be oriented more tilted.

The declination angle (δ) is the angle formed by the sun's rays as they pass through the equator and the earth's surface. There is a 23.45° angle between the Earth's rotational angle and the orbital plane, which causes the declination angle.

Declination angle is calculated by the equation,

$$\delta = 23.45 \sin\left[360 * \frac{(284 + n)}{365}\right] \tag{1}$$

Assume that n is the number of days in the year, and begin on the 1st of January. The tilt angle () measures the inclination of the panels with respect to the horizontal.

The southern hemisphere's edge is located in the north, while the southern hemisphere's is located in the south. The tilt point varies from 0° to 180°. As long as a plane maintains a fixed east-west axis with only a single daily change, the surface's tilt will remain constant every day and be determined by the accompanying conditions [6].

$$\beta = |\varphi - \delta| \tag{2}$$

1.1.6 Pyranometer

Model SP 110 by Apogee Instruments makes it. Analog sensor with an output range of 0–400 mV that runs on its own power. The sensor has a self-cleaning sensor housing and a silicon cell photodiode (Fig. 3).

Fig. 3. Pyranometer is attached to the panel in this location.

1.1.7 Analytical Tool for Recording Data

There are 8 analogue inputs on the data logger from Everon, and it saves data at a 10 min interval for each panel, including voltage, current, temperature, and solar irradiance (Fig. 4).

Fig. 4. Everon data logger

1.1.8 Temperature Sensor

The sensor is of the RTD variety. RTD stands for Resistance Thermometer. Resistance Thermometers are another name for these instruments. Resistant thermometers are defined by ASTM as thermometers comprised of resistors, which are used to measure temperature. It is based on the idea that as the temperature changes, so does the metal's resistance.

1.1.9 Load

Nonlinear loads can be made simpler by using resistors instead of capacitors. In series with a 2, 20 W resistance, a 20, 20 W resistor is used.

2 Cooling Techniques

2.1 Water Cooling of the Front Surface

To keep things cool, water is sprayed on them. On the panel, water is made to flow naturally or gravitationally. The top of the panel has a 56-cm pipe with 10 holes in it. There are three different water flow rates available: 1 L/min, 1.5 L/min, and 2 L/min.

The panel's output is compared to three different water flow rates. The most efficient flow rate is 2 L per minute (Fig. 5).

Fig. 5. Water cooling of the front surface

2.2 Dry Grass and Water for Cooling the Back Surface

Dry common grass is spread on an iron-netted PV Panel stand. Dry grass is commonly used as a cooling agent in household appliances. The grass is watered with a 3 mm pipe that has holes spaced evenly apart. A path to the grass is also provided, which allows for proper air circulation (Fig. 6).

Fig. 6. Dry grass and water for cooling the back surface

2.3 Sand and Water Cooling of the Back Surface

In this experiment, dry grass and other expensive options for supporting surface cooling were replaced with sand. As a quick heat absorber and reliever, sand has a long and illustrious history. The back of the Photovoltaic panel is kept cool by allowing water to flow and wet the sand (Fig. 7).

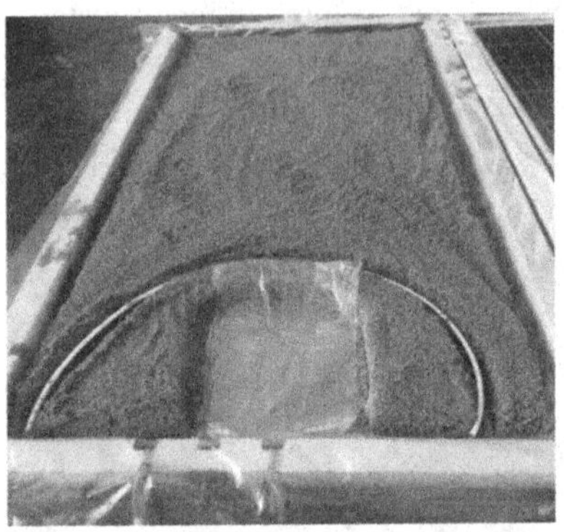

Fig. 7. Sand and water cooling of the back surface

3 Methodology

204 W/m^2 of maximum irradiance was used for this experiment on a partly sunny July day. To begin, four different cooling rates were tested with and without a cooling panel to determine the water flow rate for the cooling panels. Water flow rates of 1, 2, 3, and 4 L per minute are used on a panel for 30 min intervals on a panel. To make a comparison, the voltage, current, power, and temperature of the two systems are analysed.

Each of the four photovoltaic panels generates electricity independently at the same time. 1PV Panel with cooling on the front surface, 1PV Panel with cooling on the back surface by using common grass and water, 1PV Panel with cooling on the sand and water, and 1PV Panel with no cooling.

Water pipes with holes have been installed through the panel's back side, and a net has been spread there with dry grass and sand. All of the panels are on from 6 a.m. to 6 p.m., Monday through Friday. The data logger records voltage, temperature, and irradiation every 10 min (Fig. 8).

Fig. 8. Four panels working at a time

4 Results and Discussion

Water flow rates of 1 L/min, 2 L/min, 3 L/min, and 4 L/min are compared after a 30-min interval (Fig. 9).

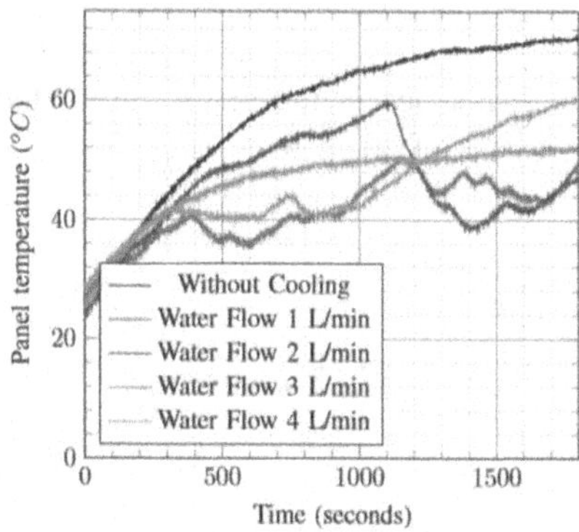

Fig. 9. Effect of water flow rate on panel temperature

The water flow rate of 1 L/min shows the lowest temperature, while a panel without cooling gives the highest temperature throughout the experiment. Water flow rate (Fig. 10).

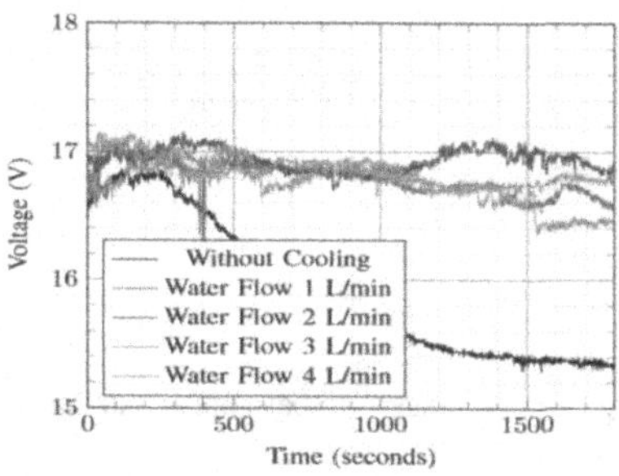

Fig. 10. Effect of water flow rate on panel voltage

Due to the high temperature, the output voltage of the PV panel with no cooling system drops dramatically. Reaching the voltage's lowest point the water flow rate of 2 L/min gives the highest output voltage among cooling types and is therefore preferred.

With a water flow rate of 2 L/min, the temperature dropped to its lowest point while the voltage reached its highest point of the day. As a result, the front panel cooling water flow rate was set to 2 L per minute (L/min) (Fig. 11).

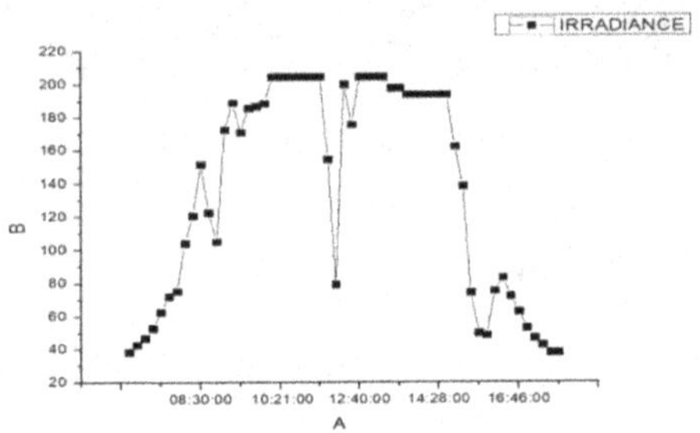

Fig. 11. Irradiation throughout the day

The day is cloudy, with notches in the graph due to the irradiation starting at 75.45 w/m^2 and reaching a peak of 204.8 w/m^2 (Fig. 12).

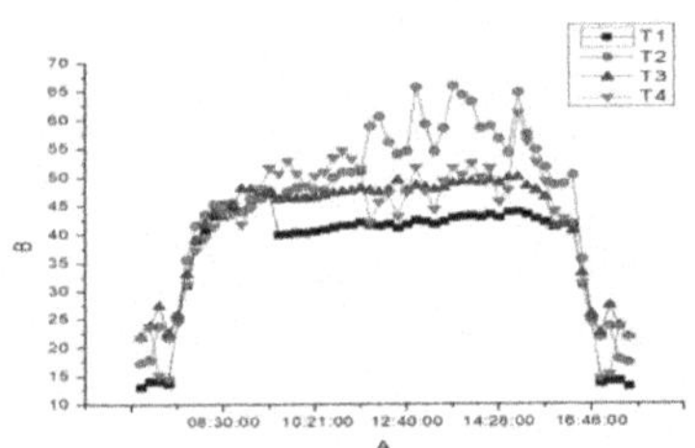

Fig. 12. Temperature comparison of our panels

Cooling on the front surface maintains a lower daytime temperature than heating without cooling (Fig. 13).

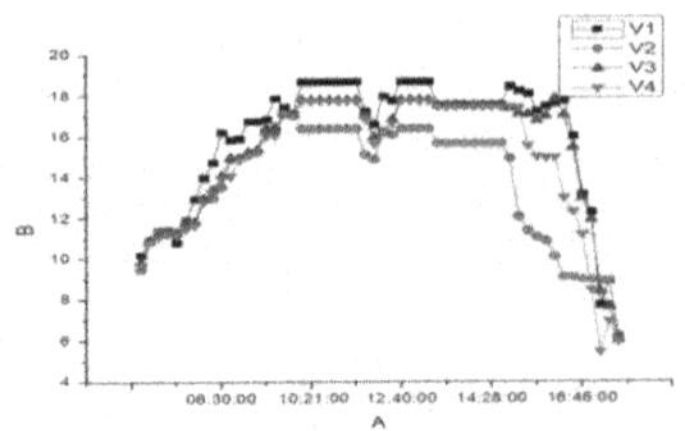

Fig. 13. Voltage comparison of our panels

When compared to other panels, the voltage of a PV panel without cooling is consistently low. There isn't much of a difference in output voltage when cooling with water and sand or water and grass. Except on cloudy days, a water-cooled front-surface panel provides the highest possible output voltage.

5 Conclusion

A 3% increase in efficiency is achieved by cooling the front surface with a water flow of 2 L per minute. In comparison to the water-cooled front surface, the dry grass and sand cooling system uses less water while increasing photovoltaic panel efficiency by 2%.

The temperature of the water dropped. When it comes to generating electricity and warm water for preheating purposes, photovoltaics have a lot of potential. Water, when used as a cooling medium, traps more heat than does air. The photoelectric conversion efficiency of a sun-based module can be viably built by lowering the temperature under cooling conditions. The above test assumes that water cooling increases both maximum power and module proficiency.

References

1. Kumra, A., Gaur, M.K., Kumar, R., Malvi, C.S., Gupta, R.B.: Sizing of standalone photovoltaic system for cottage industry in a remote rural area in India (2012)
2. Arshad, R., Tariq, S., Niaz, M.U., Jamil, M.: Improvement in solar panel efficiency using solar concentration by simple mirrors and by cooling. In: 2014 International Conference on Robotics and Emerging Allied Technologies in Engineering (iCREATE), pp. 292–295 (2014)
3. Bahaidarah, H.M., Rehman, S., Gandhidasan, P., Tanweer, B.: Experimental evaluation of the performance of a photovoltaic panel with water cooling. In: 2013 IEEE 39th Photovoltaic Specialists Conference (PVSC), pp. 2987–2991 (2013)
4. Hardy, P.K., Malvi, C.S., Gaur, M.K., Dixon-Hardy, W., Crook, R.: A low cost local level PV panel assembly process targeted at rural energy supply in developing nations. In: SWC-2011, Berlin, Germany (2011)
5. Malvi, C.S., Dixon-Hardy, D.W., Crook, R.: Energy balance model of combined photovoltaic solar-thermal system incorporating phase change material. Sol. Energy **85**(7), 1440–1446 (2011)
6. Karafil, A., Ozbay, H., Kesler, M., Parmaksiz, H.: Calculation of optimum fixed tilt angle of PV panels depending on solar angles and comparison of the results with experimental study conducted in summer in Bilecik, Turkey. In: 2015 9th International Conference on Electrical and Electronics Engineering (ELECO), pp. 971–976. IEEE (2015)
7. Augustin, D., Chacko, R., Jacob, J.: Canal top solar energy harvesting using reflector. GRD J. Eng. **1**(8), 26–31 (2016)
8. Ramkumar, R., Kesavan, M., Raguraman, C.M., Ragupathy, A.: Enhancing the performance of photovoltaic module using clay pot evaporative cooling water. In: 2016 International Conference on Energy Efficient Technologies for Sustainability (ICEETS), pp. 217–222. IEEE (2016)

9. Jianping, S.: An optimum layout scheme for photovoltaic cell arrays using PVSYST. In: 2011 International Conference on Mechatronic Science, Electric Engineering and Computer (MEC) (2011)
10. Sannasiraj, S.A., Sundar, V.: Assessment of wave energy potential and its harvesting approach along the Indian coast. Renew. Energy **99**, 398–409 (2016)
11. Suresh, V., Naviynkumar, S., Kirubakaran, V.: Improved power output of PV system by low cost evaporative cooling technology. In: 2013 International Conference on Green Computing, Communication and Conservation of Energy (ICGCE), pp. 640–643. IEEE (2013)
12. Sandhya, S., Starbell, R.N., Wessley, G.J.J.: Study on performance enhancement of PV cells by water spray cooling for the climatic conditions of Coimbatore, Tamilnadu. In: 2015 International Conference on Innovations in Information, Embedded and Communication Systems (ICIIECS), pp. 1–5 (2015)
13. Babu, B.C., Gurjar, S.: A novel simplified two-diode model of photovoltaic (PV) module. IEEE J. Photovoltaics **4**(4), 1156–1161 (2014)
14. Breitenstein, O.: An alternative one-diode model for illuminated solar cells. IEEE J. Photovoltaics **4**(3), 899–905 (2014)
15. Sridhar, Y.V.:Case study of grid connected PV plant feeding power to electrical submersible pumps. In: IEEE International Conference on Power and Renewable Energy (ICPRE), pp. 547–552. IEEE (2016)

Fisher Discriminant Ratio Based Classification of Intellectual Disability Using Acoustic Features

Gaurav Aggarwal[1,2(✉)], Neha V. Sharma[1], Kavita[1], and Atharv Sinha[1]

[1] School of Computing and Information Technology, Manipal University Jaipur, Jaipur 303007, Rajasthan, India
{nehav.sharma,kavita.jhajharia}@jaipur.manipal.edu
[2] Department of IT and Engineering, Amity University Tashkent, Tashkent, Uzbekistan
gaggarwal@amity.uz

Abstract. In human interaction, speakinghas a crucial partwhen it comes to expressing ideas and thoughts. Classification of speech disorder is considered as a motivation to the research of speech processing, recognition and analysis. In this work, we investigate whether regular speech sentences could be utilized to distinguish between typically developed (TD) children with Intellectually Disabled (ID) children aged from 8 to 15 years. An optimization technique using the Fisher Discriminant Ratio is applied to identify distinct highlights from the discourse tests of the ID children and their age-matched control group. A speech dataset containing 141 different features, consisting of Mel-Frequency Cepstral Coefficients (MFCC), Linear Predictive Coefficients (LPC) among a few, is used. Classification techniques including Support Vector Machines (SVM), Random Forest and Artificial Neural Networks (ANN) are used for classifying the two categories. The outcomes proved the efficiency of the implemented feature selection algorithm. On using the Fisher Discriminant Ratio, the total number of features get reduced to 98 from 141 with crucial improvement in the classifier's performance. The selected 98 features are used to analyze whether the individual is intellectually disabled or not. These outcomes may be helpful for the advancement of clinical tests and reducing the features to be extracted to distinguish intellectual disability.

Keywords: Fisher Discriminant Ratio · MFCC · LPCC · SVM · ANN · Random Forest

1 Introduction

Communication deficiencies disturb the method of early cognitive development, which is carried forward to adolescence and adulthood. Neurodevelopmental diseases including ID, Autism and Stuttering directly affect the development of language in children. Mentally challenged people are profoundly powerless to creating language impediment, which hurts speech advancement.

R. S. Tomar et al. (Eds.): CNC 2020, CCIS 1502, pp. 301–311, 2021.
https://doi.org/10.1007/978-981-16-8896-6_24

According to WHO (World Health Organization, 1980), individual with intellectual disability commonly develop speech impairments, which are further categorized into use and understanding of languages, inability in the linguistic function, learning disabilities and communication impairments. They additionally face hardships in creating voice, speech capacities and language content. The condition causes constraints in viable spoken correspondence which causes social ponderousness, ill-advised educational achievement or expert result, separately or inside a gathering.

An authentic clinical experiment shows that naturally developing children achieve a significantly good verbal and vocal system from their surroundings [1–5]. But for an ID child, the result is unsatisfactory for a similar age group. Speech debilitation is an ordinarily resolved issue with the kids with intellectual disability [6]. The fundamental 3–5 years of a kid's life expectancy is a profoundly significant timeframe for speech and language advancement. Generally growing kids ordinarily become familiar with the fundamental design of language by this age [7] while kids with ID acquire fractional language abilities and comprehension of few general words. Research on speech and language development is also affected due to the low number of speech pathologists and analysts who survey recorded speech samples [8–10].

Children with Intellectual disability contribute in fewer activities in and outside their schools compared to their control peer groups [11]. Participation in outdoor activities is important for developing children as it promotes physical and intellectual growth, social receptivity, mental security and also creates associations with others of similar age group [11–14]. Due to lacking participation in outdoor events, children with intellectual disability may suffer from loneliness [15] and lethargic behavior which is generally reported in the literature.

The kids with ID are also impaired in language and speech development [16, 17]. These children also have multiple articulatory restrictions [18] and often indicate inadequacy in sentence structure and language advancement, contrasted with ordinarily growing kids [19]. Research related to speech refers to acoustic-prosodic features to examine speech development [20].

In this research, a study is conducted on problems of developing a completely automatic classification system that practices verbal data from a child's usual atmosphere and categorizes the speech as **(i)** intellectually disable (ID) or **(ii)** normally developed (TD). The statistics is mined by conducting tasks including Sustained Phonation, reading and picture identification. The input undergoes noise reduction and preprocessing, and substantial acoustic-prosodic attributes are identified, and articulation is evaluated in a beneficial manner for predicting development stages and for analysing developmental disabilities. A univariate feature selection algorithm, Fisher Discriminant Ratio (FDR) is applied to identify the most useful features out of the complete dataset of 141 features. The dataset consists of Mel-Frequency Cepstral Coefficients (MFCC) and Linear Prediction (LPC, LPCC and WLPCC). After extracting features, significant characteristics from the complete dataset are selected using FDR. It is used to reduce the computation time and space. SVMs, Random Forests and ANNs are used to compute the accuracies for the classifications. In this study, a comprehensive procedure, allowing large-scale speech recordings and utilization of extracted data for the tracing of acoustic developments is described. Our method uses state-of-the-art tools and methods for classifying the children into two categories i.e. **(i)** children with intellectual disability and **(ii)** typically developed children. The architecture for the proposed method of speech disorder recognition has been described in Fig. 1.

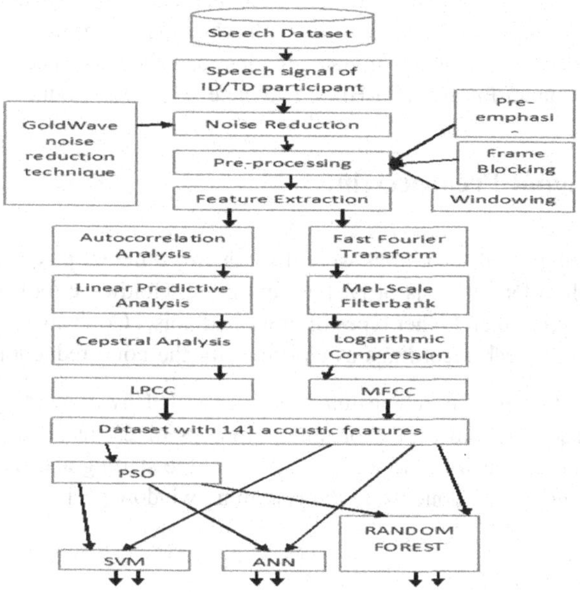

Fig. 1. Diagrammatic representation of speech disorder classification

2 Dataset and Recording Technique

The dataset contained 48 applicants, where 24 children had intellectual disability while 24 were typically developed children, as shown in Table 1. Speech recordings of the participants with ID children were comprised of an organization SIRTAR in INDIA. Each research applicant was diagnosed as per the clinical standards mentioned in the DSM-V by a group of psychologists and neuropsychiatrists. The speech sample of children belonging to the TD class wastaped from a private school in Delhi NCR region, India. The consent for each candidate was taken from the respective guardians before the candidate's participation in the research.

Table 1. Research dataset

Speech type	Mean age	Gender	
		Boy	Girl
Intellectually disabled	14.2 years	16	8
Typically developed	13.9 years	14	10

Speech for the dataset was taped in an audio-insulated room with a head-mounted voice recorder (Sony UX533F). A sampling rate of 44.1 kHz, 16 bit PCM (Pulse Code Modulation) was used for recording. Speech was recorded primarily through two tasks: continuous phonation task and imitation task. In the first task, children were asked to pronounce the two and three letter words in English and Hindi for about 30 s. They were requested to maintain a steady voice pitch while the recording is taking place. In the imitation task, the participants imitated the instructor's voice. The reading material for this task contained English and Hindi language sentences, rhymes etc.

3 Speech Signal Preprocessing

Noise Cancellation: The recordings were done at two different places for ID and TD participants with different levels of background noise. Goldwave toolbox was used to remove the background and other types of unwanted noise. Goldwave used the original sound existing in speech recordings as an origin for the noise reduction.

Frame and Windowing: Speech features were extracted by converting each sample into 33% overlapping frames of short-time windows of 25 ms. For minimizing the signal discontinuities, each frame was windowed at the starting and the ending of the frame. Windowing can be done using the Hamming window [21], as shown in Eq. (1)

$$H(z) = 1 - \alpha * z^{-1} \tag{1}$$

where α = 15/16 = 0.9, Hamming window was applied to extract the features of the signal. Details of speech parameterization has explained in the next section.

4 Speech Parameterization

4.1 Mel-Frequency Cepstral Coefficients

MFCCs are deemed as the most robust parameterizationmethodsfor classifying disordered speech. It is an illustration of the acoustic system in humans [22] and closely approximates the structure of the auditory system found in humans, using an encapsulation of the short-time power spectrum. MFCC is computed using the Fast Fourier Transform (FFT) on moving window speech signals, which divides the speech signal into smaller frames. Power spectrum density for each subframe is calculated. Further on, Mel filter bank is applied to the power spectrum through Mel-scale filter, a triangular bandpass filter [23], and its logarithm is calculated after adding the spectral energy of each filter bank. The linear auditory frequency mapped to Mel-frequency is represented using Eq. (2)

$$Mel(f) = 2595 log_{10}(1 + \frac{f}{700}) \tag{2}$$

Finally, discrete cosine transform (DCT) of logarithmic energies converts the log of Mel-spectrum into time, resulting into MFCC [24]. In speech-related studies, vocal signals can be described by convolving the vocal tract filter and source excitation. Deconvolution can be established by applying the cepstral analysis to both the above components.

Many studies related to speech processing discard the MFCC's 0th coefficients due to its frequency irregularities. Despite, in this research, the 0th coefficient is used as the mean energy of every filter bank of estimated speech signal [25, 26]. Following parameters were used to calculate MFCC: frameshift =: 20 ms, α =: 0.97, filter bank channels =: 20, lifter parameter =: 22 and frequency limit =: 300–3700 Hz. Figure 2(a) and (b) shows the representation of the MFCC features of a child with ID and an age-matched TD child.

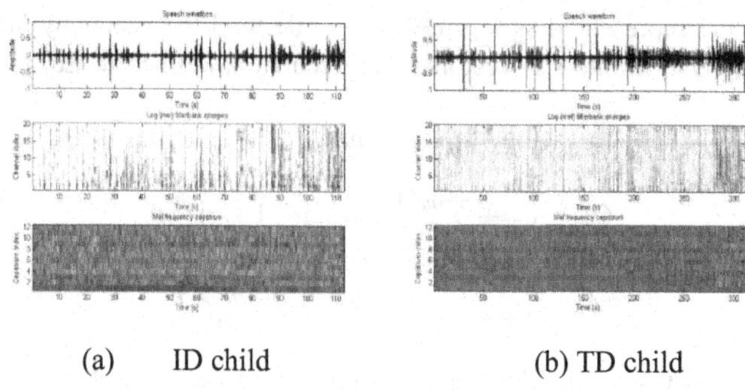

(a) ID child (b) TD child

Fig. 2. MFCC Representation of age matched ID and TD children

4.2 Linear Predictive Analysis

Linear Predictive Analysis illustrates all the individual speech signals in the time domain using a linear mix of previous 'p' samples, where p denotes the order of the LPC analysis. Here, LPC estimations use an auto-correlation function of order of p, where = 12 [27]. The error reduction of the 'p' th order of linear predictions creates the expression, defined in Eq. (3) [28].

$$\sum\nolimits_{n=1}^{N} s(n)s(n-i) = R(i) \tag{3}$$

The set of the simultaneous equations are described in the Eqs. (4) & (5).

$$\begin{aligned} &\sum\nolimits_{(k=1)}^{p} \alpha_k \sum\nolimits_{(n=1)}^{N} s(n-k)s(n-i) = R(i) = \\ &\sum\nolimits_{n=1}^{N} s(n)s(n-i) \quad for\ i = 1,2,3\ldots p \end{aligned} \tag{4}$$

$$\sum\nolimits_{k=1}^{p} \alpha_k R(k-i) = R(i)\ for\ i = 1,2,3\ldots\ldots p \tag{5}$$

R(k-i), which is the coefficient, defines an auto-correlation matrix with structures similar to the symmetric Toeplitz matrix, given in Eq. (6). In the equation, all the values along the descending diagonals from both sides are equal.

$$R = \begin{matrix} r(0) & r(1) & r(2)\ldots & \ldots & \ldots r(p-1) \\ r(1) & r(0) & r(1)\ldots & \ldots & \ldots r(p-2) \end{matrix}$$

$$\begin{matrix} r(2) & r(1) & r(0)\ldots\ldots\ldots r(p-3) \\ r(p-1) & r(p-2) & r(p-3)\ldots\ldots r(0) \end{matrix} \tag{6}$$

where R is a p*p auto-correlation matrix. LPC vector is calculated using a matrix inversion technique.

It is represented by a logarithmic magnitude spectrum, which is computed using the Fourier transform. The calculation of CC is possible after computing the LPC vector. The CC vector is represented as $(c_1c_2c_3\ldots c_p)$ while the LPC vector by $(a_1a_2a_3\ldots a_p)$. The latter is converted into CC vectors using recursion, defined in Eq. (7)–(9) [26].

$$C_0 = ln\sigma^2 \tag{7}$$

$$C_m = a_m + \sum_{k=1}^{m-1} C_k a_{m-k} \quad 1 \le m \le p \tag{8}$$

$$C_m = \sum_{k=1}^{m-1} C_k a_{m-k} \quad m > p \tag{9}$$

C_m = CC, σ^2 = Gain in LPC model, a_m = Predictor Coefficient, k = 1 < k < N–1, p = p^{th} order.

Weighted Linear Predictive Cepstral Coefficients (WLPCC) are approximated by the multiplication of LPCC and the weighted formula given in Eq. (10).

$$w_m = \left[1 + \frac{Q}{2} sin\, sin\left(\frac{m\pi}{Q}\right)\right] 1 \le m \le Q \tag{10}$$

In this research, 128 linear predictive coefficients (LPC, LPCC and WLPCC) were used with 13 MFCCs to classify the children using speech samples, into ID and TD. The following specifications were applied to extract MFCC and LPCC features: Frame Size = 25 ms, Frameshift = 20 ms, Filter Bank channels = 20, CCs = 12, α = 0.97 and order ‘p’ = 12 with a 256-point FFT. Figure 3 (a) and (b) demonstrate LPC representations for age-matched ID and TD children. The result section discusses in detail the final inferences of the analysis.

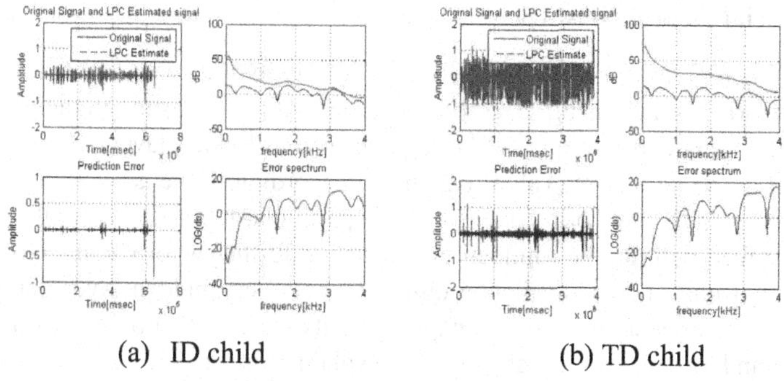

(a) ID child (b) TD child

Fig. 3. LPC representation of age matched ID and TD children

5 Feature Selection

5.1 Fisher Discriminant Ratio (FDR)

To grasp more discriminative highlights from the extricated feature set for kids with ID versus TD, important features were chosen through a Fisher Discriminant Ratio (FDR) based methodology [29]. Using FDR, the resultant features and labels relating to all individual subjects (ID and TD) by language pathologist analysis were computed to come up with a score named an FDR score, for each feature.

For instance, for the 1st feature MFCC, the notch was calculated using Eq. (11).

$$FDR_{1st} = \frac{(\mu_{1st-MR} - \mu_{1st-TD})^2}{\sigma^2{}_{1st-MR} + \sigma^2{}_{1st-TD}} \tag{11}$$

Here, μ_{1st-MR} *and* μ_{1st-TD} are the average means, $\sigma^2{}_{1st-MR}$ *and* $\sigma^2{}_{1st-TD}$ represent the variances for MFCC, calculated throughout the MR and TD dataset respectively. Each feature is classed and sorted based on the FDR score, in a descending order. For the study, 13 MFCC and the first 85 LPC features are chosen based on their FDR scores, being the most relevant features in the complete dataset. After applying FDR, the total 141 features were reduced to 98 most notable features, which are further used for classification of speech of ID and TD children.

6 Classification

This section discusses in detail, the fundamentals of ANNs, SVMs and Random Forests, used here. The dataset created using the techniques mentioned in Sect. 3, act as the inputs for the classification models. A 10-fold cross validation is implemented, where 70% of data is used for training the model while the rest is used for testing.

6.1 Artificial Neural Network

An artificial neural network (ANN) is a multi-layer, type of network. It's a feed-forward neural network trained using back-propagation with stochastic gradient decedent. Between its inputs and outputs, ANN has one or two hidden layers. An input signal compressed to the data layer; values calculated according to the activation function by the other layers of the network. ANN follows a particular topology where the input unit is entirely linked with the first hidden unit which is further wholly connected with the second hidden unit and so on till the output layer. Every hidden layer denoted by k generally uses a logistic method for mapping of its all inputs to below layer, x_k is the scalar state and y_k sends to the above layer explained in Eq. (12).

$$y_k = \text{logistic}(x_k) = \frac{1}{1+e^{-x_k}}, x_k = b_k + \sum_j \; y_j w_{jk} \tag{12}$$

Here b_k denotes the bias in the layer k, index of layers is denotes as j in the below unit, and w_{jk} is the connection weight from layer j to the layer k.

The ANN is trained using the back propagation approach, where derivative loss in the cost function is propagated back to the input layer to calculate the error between the target output and the tangible output generated for each training case [30]. Further on, the softmax output function or normalized exponential function is applied. The cross-entropy between the production of the softmax function and the target probabilities leads to the original cost function C shown in Eq. (13).

$$\mathrm{C} = -\sum_k \; d_k log\, p_k \tag{13}$$

To train ANN, information is provided, which is usually taking target probabilities values of zero or one [31].

6.2 Random Forest

It is a group learning characterization model. It assembles a coppice of decision trees for quite a long-time set. The last resulting class is the lump of the grouping of a solitary tree. A high-level adaptation of the method was created by Leo and Adele which partner packing with an irregular determination of elements that develops a gathering of choice trees with estimated fluctuation. This strategy is regularly utilized as a classifier in numerous applications like article recognizable proof [32].

6.3 Support Vector Machine

Support Vector Machine (SVM) is a classification technique that comes from the computational learning theory. The primary goal of SVM is to obtain the most optimized classification function that categorizes classes of the training dataset. It is used as a classifier and is commonly used for both linear and non-linear classifications like pattern recognition and density estimation tasks. A non-straight planning is utilized to make an interpretation of the preparation information into a higher measurement utilizing a nonlinear change ϕ and afterward apply a direct partition [31].The training dataset is categorized as Eq. (14):

$$\{x_i, y_i\}, i = 1, \ldots, l, y_i \in \{-1, 1\}, \qquad x_i \in R^d \tag{14}$$

7 Results

Three classifiers were trained to classify the speech dataset to categories the speech as impaired or normal. FDR assisted optimization technique was applied to the dataset to select the best significant features for classification. 98 features were chosen from the complete dataset of 141 features. Two different datasets were produced with and without feature selection. Table 2 and Table 3 represents the performance of the proposed system with and without FDR for SVM, random forest and ANN using MFCC and LPCC acoustic features.

Table 2. Result without FDR using 141 features

Classifiers	No. of features	Accuracy	Precision	Recall
Support vector machine	141	92.82%	90.54%	95.28%
Artificial neural network	141	86.57%	84.08%	89.66%
Random forest	141	89.35%	87.98%	91.38%

Table 3. Result with FDR using 98 selected features

Classifiers	No. of features	Accuracy	Precision	Recall
Support vector machine	98	97.57%	95.48%	100%
Artificial neural network	98	91.66%	90.02%	92.39%
Random forest	98	93.02%	91.77%	95.64%

From the experiment outcomes, it is evident that the FDR assisted optimization has better results than usual. All the algorithms performed well as compared with dataset without optimization. From the three classifiers, random forest outperformed the SVM and ANN. The accuracy of SVM classifiers is 97.57% with FDR. Therefore it is recommended to use FDR with SVM for differentiating between the speech of children with intellectual disabilities and typically developed children.

8 Conclusion

In the 1st Experiment, support vector machine, artificial neural network and, random forest classifiers are applied to speech dataset without using any feature selection algorithm. In the 2nd experiment, Fisher Discriminant Ratio, a univariate feature selection algorithm, is used to select the important features carrying maximum information from the dataset. The attributes are reduced to 98 from 144 without losing any essential characteristics. Support vector machine is performed well as compared to other classification models with selected features, and the classification accuracy has increased by 5% on using FDR.

References

1. De Villiers, J.G., De Villiers, P.A.: Competence and performance in child language: are children really competent to judge? J. Child Lang. **1**(1), 11–22 (1974)
2. Slobin, D.I.: Cognitive prerequisites for the development of grammar. In: Studies of Child Language Development, pp. 175–208. Holt, Rinehart, & Winston (1973)
3. Pinker, S.: The language instinct. How the mind creates language (1994)
4. Cutler, A., Klein, W., Levinson, S.C.: The cornerstones of twenty-first century psycholinguistics. In: Twenty-First Century Psycholinguistics: Four cornerstones, Erlbaum, pp. 1–20 (2005)
5. Kumin, L.: Early communication skills for children with Down syndrome: A guide for parents and professionals. Woodbine House, Bethesda (2003)
6. McLeod, S., van Doorn, J., Reed, V.: Normal acquisition of consonant clusters. Am. J. Speech-Lang. Pathol. **10**(2), 99–110 (2001)
7. Philofsky, A., et al.: Linguistic and cognitive functioning and autism symptoms in young children with fragile X syndrome. Am. J. Mental Retard. **109**(3), 208–218 (2004)
8. Oller, D.K.: The emergence of the sounds of speech in infancy. In: Yeni-Komshian, G., Kavanagh, J.F., Ferguson, C.A. (eds.) Child Phonology, 1: Production, pp. 93–112 (1980)
9. Sheinkopf, S.J., et al.: Vocal atypicalities of preverbal autistic children. J. Autism Dev. Disord. **30**(4), 345–354 (2000)
10. Wetherby, A.M., et al.: Early indicators of autism spectrum disorders in the second year of life. J. Autism Dev. Disord. **34**(5), 473–493 (2004)
11. Abells, D., Burbidge, J., Minnes, P.: "Involvement of adolescents with intellectual disabilities in social and recreational activities. J. Dev. Disabil. **14**(2), 88 (2008)
12. Murphy, N.A., Carbone, P.S.: Promoting the participation of children with disabilities in sports, recreation, and physical activities. Pediatrics **121**(5), 1057–1061 (2008)
13. Pratt, H.D., Greydanus, D.E.: Intellectual disability (mental retardation) in children and adolescents. Prim. Care Clin. Office Pract. **34**(2), 375–386 (2007)
14. Westendorp, M., et al.: Are gross motor skills and sports participation related in children with intellectual disabilities? Res. Dev. Disabil. **32**(3), 1147–1153 (2011). https://doi.org/10.1016/j.ridd.2011.01.009
15. Rimmer, J.H., Rowland, J.L., Yamaki, K.: Obesity and secondary conditions in adolescents with disabilities: addressing the needs of an underserved population. J. Adolesc. Health **41** (3), 224–229 (2007)
16. Cardoso-Martins, C., Mervis, C.B.: Maternal speech to prelinguistic children with Down syndrome. Am. J. Mental Def. **89**, 451–458 (1985)
17. Mervis, C.B.: Developmental relations between cognition and language: Evidence from Williams syndrome. In: Research on Communication and Language Disorders: Contributions to Theories of Language Development, pp. 75–100 (1997)
18. Stoel-Gammon, C.: Down syndrome phonology: developmental patterns and intervention strategies. Down Syndr. Res. Pract. **7**(3), 93–100 (2001)
19. Harris, N.G.S., et al.: Contrasting profiles of language development in children with Williams and Down syndromes. Dev. Neuropsychol. **13**(3), 345–370 (1997)

20. Ballard, K.J., et al.: "Developmental trajectory for production of prosody: lexical stress contrastivity in children ages 3 to 7 years and in adults. Journal of Speech, Language, and Hearing Research **55**, 1822–1835 (2012)
21. Rabiner, L., Juang, B.H.: Fundamentals of speech recognition. Prentice-Hall **1**, 993 (1993)
22. Davis, S., Mermelstein, P.: Comparison of parametric representations for monosyllabic word recognition in continuously spoken sentences. IEEE Trans. Acoust. Speech Signal Process. **28**(4), 357–366 (1980)
23. Dhanalakshmi, P., Palanivel, S., Ramalingam, V.: Classification of audio signals using SVM and RBFNN. Expert Syst. Appl. **36**(3), 6069–6075 (2009)
24. Jothilakshmi, S., Ramalingam, V., Palanivel, S.: Unsupervised speaker segmentation with residual phase and MFCC features. Expert Syst. Appl. **36**(6), 9799–9804 (2009)
25. Picone, J.W.: Signal modeling techniques in speech recognition. Proc. IEEE **81**(9), 1215–1247 (1993)
26. Aggarwal, G., Singh, L.: Classification of intellectual disability using LPC, LPCC, and WLPCC parameterization techniques. Int. J. Comput. Appl. **41**(6), 470–479 (2019)
27. Hariharan, M., et al.: Classification of speech dysfluencies using LPC based parameterization techniques. J. Med. Syst. **36**(3), 1821–1830 (2012)
28. Aggarwal, G., Singh, L.: Evaluation of supervised learning algorithms based on speech features as predictors to the diagnosis of mild to moderate intellectual disability. 3D Res. **9** (4), 55 (2018)
29. Padilla, P., et al.: NMF-SVM based CAD tool applied to functional brain images for the diagnosis of Alzheimer's disease. IEEE Trans. Med. Imaging **31**(2), 207–216 (2011)
30. Aggarwal, G., Singh, L.: Comparisons of speech parameterisation techniques for classification of intellectual disability using machine learning. Int. J. Cogn. Inf. Nat. Intell. (IJCINI) **14**(2), 16–34 (2020)
31. Bourlard, H., Wellekens, C.J.: Speech pattern discrimination and multilayer perceptrons. Comput. Speech Lang. **3**(1), 1–19 (1989)
32. Aggarwal, G., Monga, R., Gochhayat, S.P.: A novel hybrid PSO assisted optimization for classification of intellectual disability using speech signal. Wirel. Pers. Commun. **113**(4), 1955–1971 (2020)

Performance Analysis and Comparison of Low Power Various Full Adder Circuits

Ekta Jadon and Shyam Akashe(✉)

Department of Electronics and Communication,
ITM University, Gwalior, MP, India

Abstract. An adder is an integral part of many digital devices, DSPs, etc. Due to the reduction in leakage power and the location, recent VSSI circuits have been created. As the technology continuously decreases, the transistor threshold voltage is also decreased and the static power discharge is therefore high. Different fulladder (FA) were modeled in this paper and evaluated afterward. Specific full Adder circuits like 90 nm have achieved leakage power consumption. The designed Diverse FA circuits are compared in terms of leak energy consumption & surface area with Cadence instruments. We designed and compared 28T, 14T, 12T, 10T and 9T Full adder circuit, in terms of area, power.

Keywords: Beam steering · Microstrip antenna · Satellite communication

1 Introduction

The energy consumption in Very Large Scale Integrated (VLSI) circuit designs is a major performance factor. However, the explosive growth of VLSI technology leads designers to seek smaller silicon areas, longer battery life, higher speeds, lower power use and higher circuit efficiency, with demand and popularity for mobile devices. The design criteria for a complete adder cell requires the transistor counts, which greatly affect the design complexity of a large number of feature units such as multiplier and algorithmic logistic units, the optical Adder ALU) [1, 2]. Speed of design is restricted due to size of transistor, the capability of the parasitic and critical path delay. Driving power of a FA is very significant since it is used primarily in the cascade setup where one output provides the input for the other different full adder circuits for design accents such as delay, area & power have been proposed. The use of a transistor logic has been commonly used for reducing power consumption [3, 4] among the designs with less transistor numbers. Pass-transistor logic & CMOS logic [5] divided into two forms. In this paper, the development of all adherence circuits within terms of lower power consumption, higher speed & less chip size has been briefly described (Fig. 1).

R. S. Tomar et al. (Eds.): CNC 2020, CCIS 1502, pp. 312–321, 2021.
https://doi.org/10.1007/978-981-16-8896-6_25

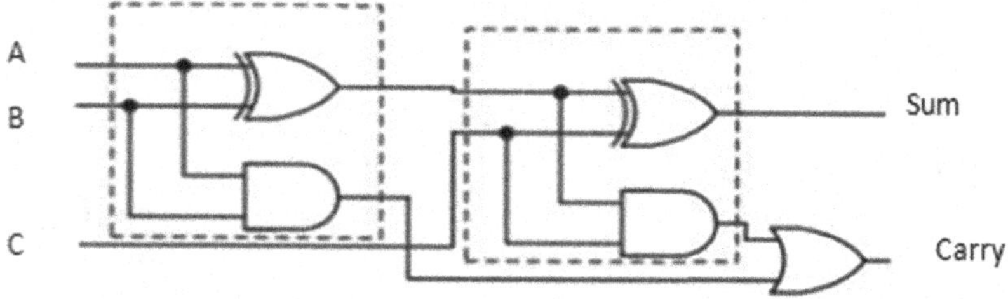

Fig. 1. Circuit diagram of full adder Circuit has three inputs A,B & C and two outputs sum and carry.

2 Techniques

Main work in electronic field is energy-efficient design of portable devices such as Desktop notebooks, mobile phones, tablets. The decrease area is one way to achieve a less efficient design. In ALU operations, binary additives play an important role. A number of adder circuits have recently been suggested. The goal of the design, however, will differ. Main focus of this paper is on power reduction [6] and the circuit field. A designer can use a large array of different techniques such as CPL, C-CMOS, DC & DC gate, GDI & 28 transistors, the complete CMOS-based adder design [7] is similar to conventional PMOS and NMOS transistors. Designer has full adder designs. By set of transistors makes full adder for bad driving ability. It covers more area, since it has a lot of transistors, another important design technique is Complementary pass transistor logic (CPL). Primary difference between complementary CMOS and CPL [8] is that pass transistor is an input from the source area. But complementary CMOS acts as source inputs on power lines. CPL logic is much better than CMOS logic due to threshold voltage drop but no more than C-CMOS. Also, this logic requires inverters at output stage to achieve sufficient instability. A transmission Gate Adder Designs Pull-up and Pull-down Transistor Complimentary Properties. There are twenty transistors. This TGA (Transmission Gate Adder) is composed of a PMOS and NMOS transistor parallel connectivity. Complementary signals control the operation of the circuit. Major drawback of TGA compared to pass-transistor logic is that it uses twice number of transistors. The primitive gates, such as the 4-transistor full adder [9] XOR gate based on the Majority function, eliminates the need for more time.

2.1 CMOS Full Adder

An adder is an electronic digital circuit used to add binary numbers. Full adder is a three-bit additional combination circuit (Fig. 2).

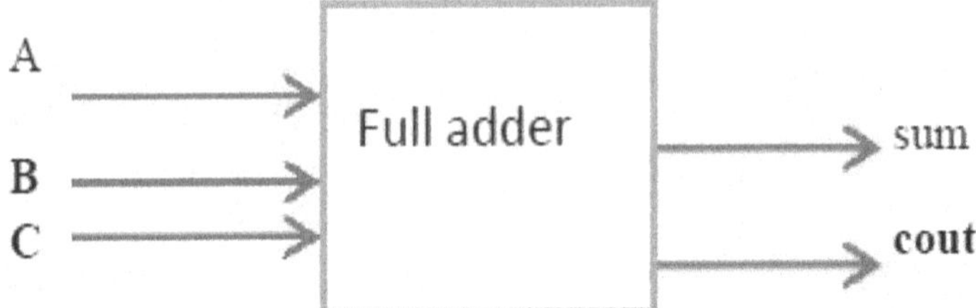

Fig. 2. Block diagram of full adder

Take a CMOS FA. This circuit consists of two operands, A & B, & an input transmission is Cin. This generates the sum

$$SUM = A \oplus B \oplus Cin$$

$$CARRY = AB + BCin + ACin$$

2.1.1 Various Full Adder Circuits Comparative Analysis

2.1.1.1 28T Full Adder Circuits

On the basis of standard CMOS topology, as exposed in Fig. 4a, traditional CMOS adder cells using 28 transistors were discussed in paper [10]. Due to the high number of transistors & PMOS transistors from pull up, its high energy consumption was defined, and this resulted in high retardation and dynamic capacity. It was based on standard CMOS structure. Therefore, the FA with 28 transistors was presented in paper. Same one as rest of the circuit & Transient waveform is shown in Fig. 3 and 4.

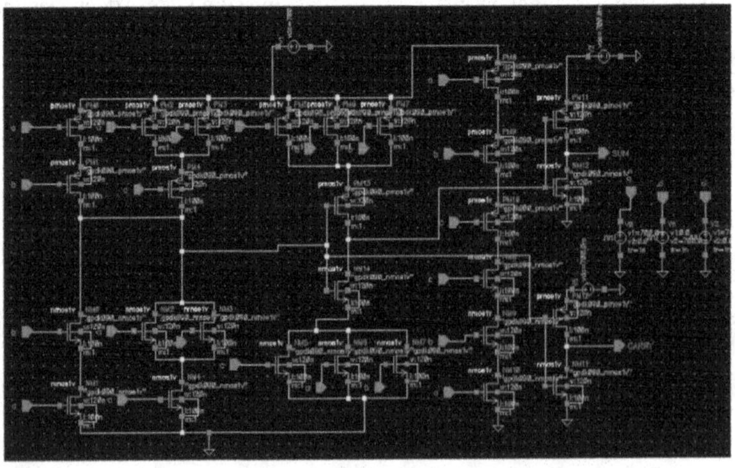

Fig. 3. Schematic of 28T full adder circuit

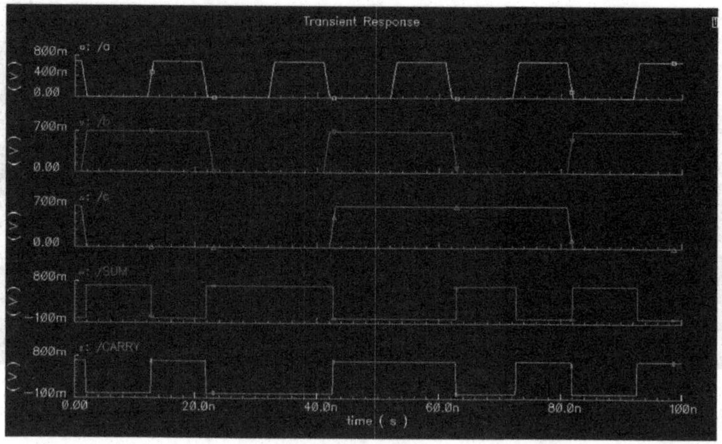

Fig. 4. Transient response of 28T full adder circuit

2.1.1.2 14T Full Adder Circuits

Paper [11], contrasts numerous current full adder circuits including many circuits such as the CMOS TG, Gate Diffusion Input (GDI), Complementary Pass transistor Logic (CPL) Low Power Full Adder, GDI-based FA, Pass Transistor Logic (PTL). Thus Fig. 5 shows 14 transistors using the full adder scheme, and Fig. 6 shows Transient Response(TR).

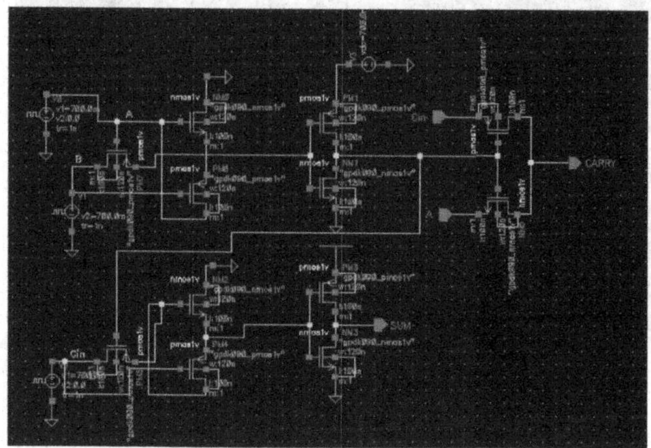

Fig. 5. Schematic of 14T full adder circuit

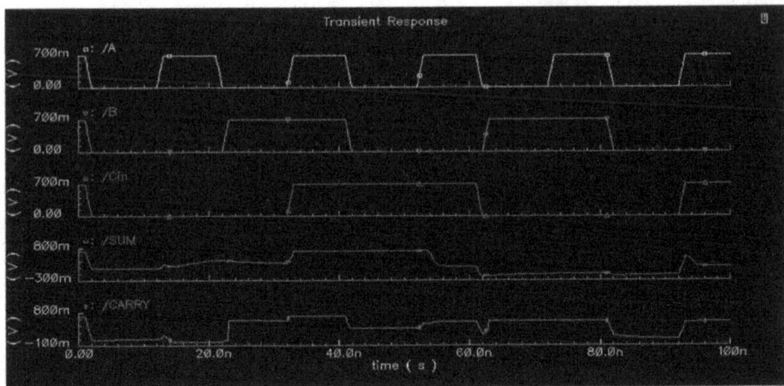

Fig. 6. Transient response of 14T full adder circuit

2.1.1.3 12T CMOS Full Adder

In the paper [12], two new designs FA for XOR transistors were added. Simulations of similar were performed at dissimilar reverse supply voltages of NMOS transistors and there was increased consumption of adder electricity. So, in that paper full adder with 12 Transistor was introduced & we choose and took the same and was compared with other circuits and the schematic 12T FA Circuit & TR is shown in Fig. 7 and 8.

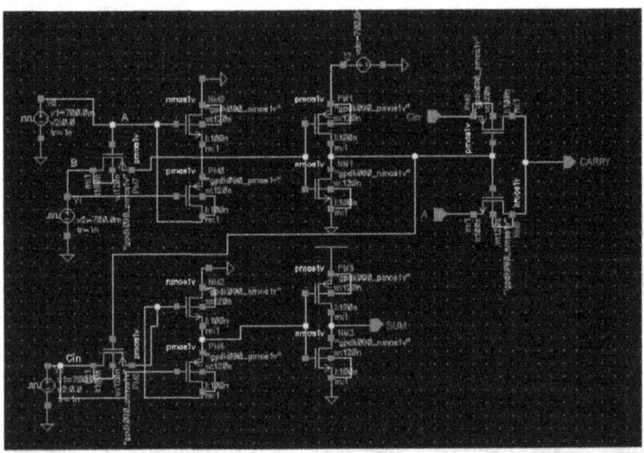

Fig. 7. Schematic of 12T full adder circuit

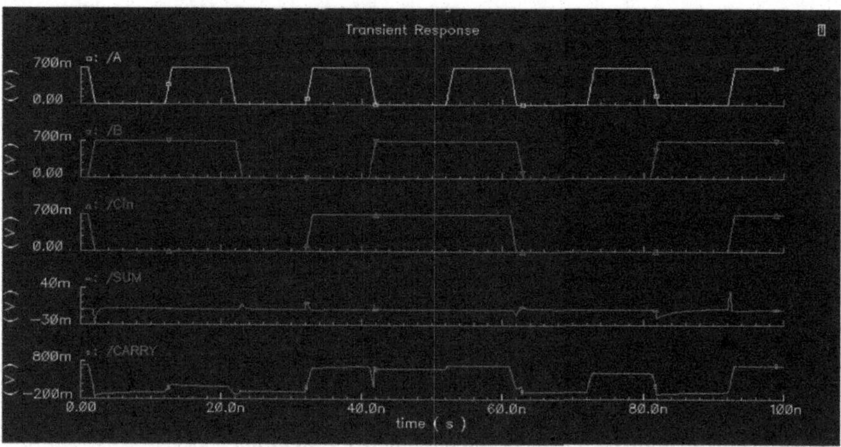

Fig. 8. Transient response of 12T full adder circuit

2.1.1.4 10T CMOS Full Adder

We required 4 Transistors XOR and XNOR circuits and 2-to-1 multiplexers to implement specific 10 CMOS full-adder transistor circuits. Figure 9 illustrations the 10T full adder schematic & Fig. 10 shows the output waveform.

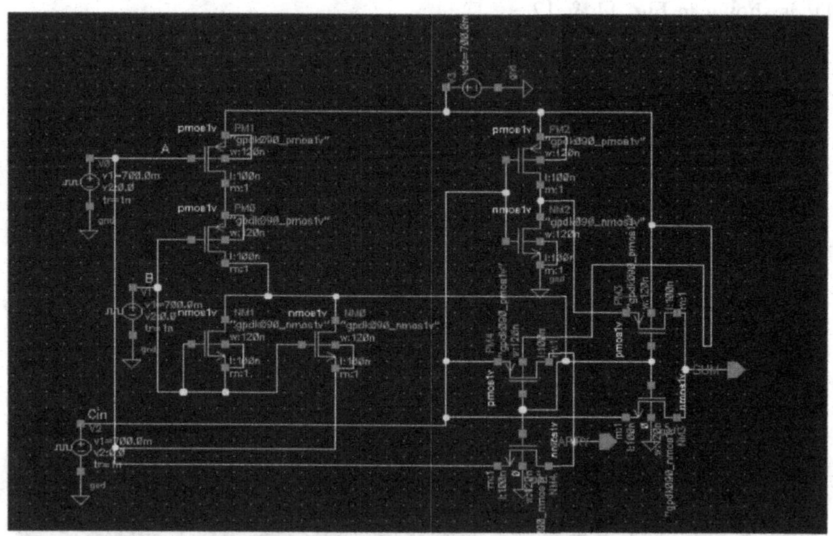

Fig. 9. Schematic of 10T full adder circuit

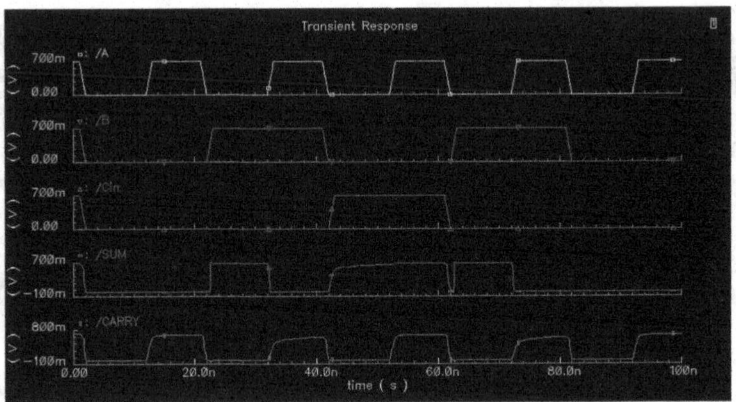

Fig. 10. Transient response of 10T CMOS full adder

2.1.1.5 9T CMOS Full Adder

New 9 T FA cell simulations at low voltages are given in paper [13]. Main aim of design was to achieve low energy consumption & total voltage swing at low supply voltage. The proposed model demonstrated its dominance in terms of energy usage, power product delays (PDP), resilience of temperatures and tolerance to noise. Therefore, in that paper, the whole adder with 9 transistors was presented and we chose the same one, which was contrasted with other circuits and the scheme 9 T Full Adder & TR is shown in Fig. 11 & 12.

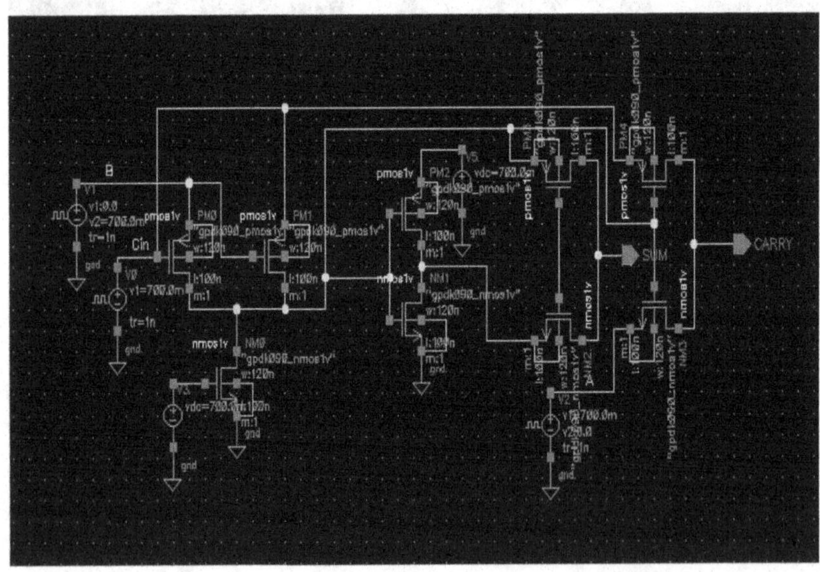

Fig. 11. Schematic of 9T CMOS full adder

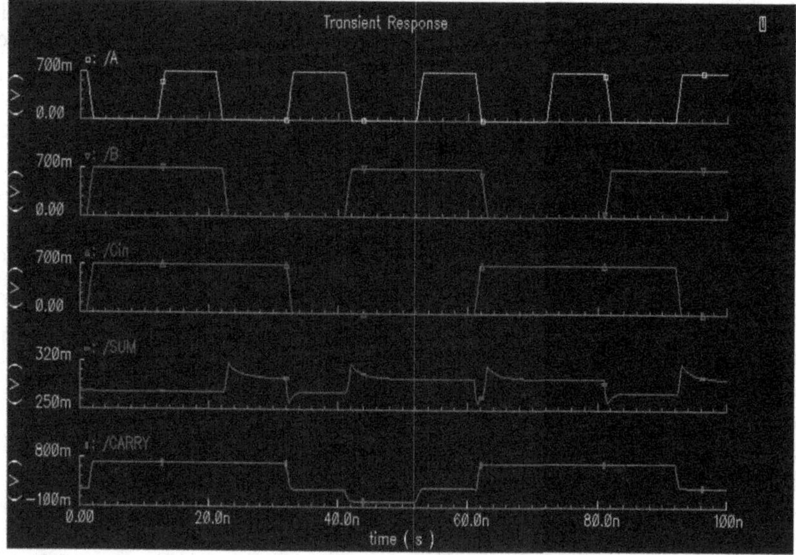

Fig. 12. Transient response of 9T CMOS full adder

3 Simulation Result

The Gate Leakage is the only main mechanism at the temperature of 27 °C. There are different techniques used to decrease power consumption and to preserve the output of the 28T, 14T, 12T, 10T and 9T Full Adder Circuit (FAC). Different Full Adder circuit

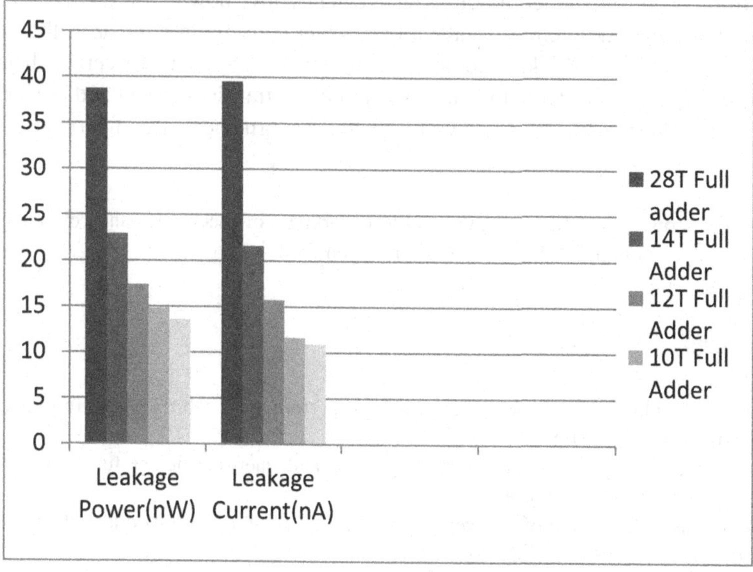

Fig. 13. Comparison graph of full adder

Simulators with 90 nm and 45 nm nominal voltage supply Vdd = 0.7 V. Its comparative analysis of Various FAC the parameter like Leakage Current and leakage power is shown in below in Graph and Table 1 respectively (Fig. 13).

3.1 Comparative Analysis Result Summary of Various FACs Shown Below Table 1

Table 1. Simulated result summary

Parameter of performance FAC	28T FAC	14T FAC	12T FAC	10T FAC	9T FAC
Technology used	90 nm	90 nm	90 nm	90 nm	90 nm
Supply voltage	0.7 V	0.7 V	0.7 V	0.7 V	0.7 V
Leakage power	38.7 nW	22.9 nW	17.4 nW	14.8 nW	
Leakage current	39.5 nA	21.6nA	15.7 nA	11.6 nA	10.9 nA
Transistor count	28	14	12	10	9
Area used	Large	Large	Large	Less	Less

4 Conclusion

Specific Full Adder circuits were planned for review in this paper. Different Full Adder designs have used leakage power and leakage current in the circuit. Different Full Adder circuits are compared with sentences of leaking capacity, leakage current and surface area. In terms of power and surface area, we built and compared 28T and 14T full adder circuit, 12T, 10T, and 9T full adder circuit. This removes problems of diving ability from other full adder modules and catches low power for use at 0.7 V. In addition, many full adder circuits have a low power consumption as far as the number of transistors needed to build a complete combination circuit is concerned from this correlation Table 1. According to Various FA circuits, transistor count and power of 9T CMOS Full Adder is less and shows the better performance in comparison to other circuits.

Acknowledgments. The authors are grateful to department of Electronics and communication, ITM University, Gwalior for providing basic research facilities.

References

1. Keivan, N., Omid, K.: Low-power and high-performance 1-bit CMOS full-adder cell. J. Comp. **3**, 48–54 (2008)
2. Tiwari, N., Shrma, R.: Implementation of area and energy efficient full adder cell. In: International of CRAIE, pp. 978–983 (2014)
3. Wei, Y., Shen, J.: Design of a novel low power 8- transistor I-bitfull adder cell. J. Zhejiang Univ. Sci. C. **12**, 604–607 (2011)

4. Jiang, Y., Al-Sheraidah, A.Y., Wang, S.E., Chung, J.: A novel multiplexer-based low-power full adder. IEEE Trans. Circuits Syst. Analog Digit. Signal Process. **51**, 345–348 (2004)
5. Wang, D., Yang, M., Guan, W.C., Zhu, Z., Yang, Y.: Novel low power full adder cells in 180 nm CMOS technology. In: 4th IEEE conference on Industry Electronics and Application, pp. 430–433 (2009)
6. Singh, R., Akashe, S.: Modelling and analysis oflow power 10T full adder with reduced groundnoise. J. Circ. Syst. Comput. **23**(14), 1–14 (2014)
7. Suguna, A., Madhu, D.: 180 nm technology basedlow power hybrid Cmos full adder. Int. J. Emerg. Trends Eng. Res. **3**, 168–172 (2015)
8. Zimmermann, R., Fichtner, W.: Low-powerlogic styles: CMOS versus pass-transistor logic. IEEE J. of Solid-State Circuits. **32**, 1079–1089 (1997)
9. Navi, K., Maeen, M., Foroutan, V., Timarchi, S., Kavehei, O.: A novel low power full-adder cell for low voltage. Integration VLSI J. **4**, 457–467 (2009)
10. Panda, S., Banerjee, A., Maji, B., Mukhopadhyay, A.K.: Power and delay comparison in between different types of full adder circuits. Int. J. Adv. Res. Electric. Electron. Inst. Eng. **1**, 168–172 (2012)
11. Kumar, P., Mishra, S., Singh, A.: Study of existing full adders and to design a LPFA (low power full adder). Int. J. Eng. Res. App **3**, 509–513 (2013)
12. Kumar, M., Arya, S.K., Pandey, S.: Low power CMOS full adder design with 12 transistors. Int. J. Inf. Tech. Conv. Serv. **2**, 11 (2012)
13. Garg, R., Nehra, S., Singh, B.P.: Low power 9T full adder using inversion logic. Int. J. VLSI Embedded Syst. (2013)

For Enhancing the Performance in Single Bit Hybrid Full Adder Circuits Using XNOR Gate

Ekta Jadon and Shyam Akashe(✉)

Department of Electronics and Communication,
ITM University, Gwalior, MP, India

Abstract. In this paper, the use of XNOR Gate was proposed for single-bit full adder hybrid circuits. Performance of single-bit full Adder hybrid circuits is completely determined by their key modules. Hybrid single bit 16, 14, 10 and 8 transistor full adder designs are proposed in this paper. Key purpose of the design is to swing full voltage at low power supply & to reduce power consumption. This results in a significantly lower leakage power, leakage current and a lower parasite capacity than the 16T design. By using Cadence tools, the designed Hybrid Full Adder circuits are compared in phrases of leakage power consumption and surface area.

Keywords: CMOS · Hybrid Full Adder · Leakage power · Leakage current · Area · Cadence

1 Introduction

Low power has now come to the fore in the electronics industry. The low power requirement has become an important factor as region and performance [1]. The full adder is a key component for all the digital circuits, so that the improvement of performance will certainly improve overall design performance [2]. The wide usage of this operation has attracted a lot of researchers in the arithmetic and logical field to develop different types of unique logic styles for the 1-bit full adder cell. Three most significant parameters of the VLSI system are speed, area & power consumption. Due to rapid growth in technology in no. of transistors, the design of low-power VLSI systems has converted a key goal to achieve any logical function has become profitable to reduce chip zone & parasite capacitance, resulting in a high speed &low power consumption [3] Exponential relationship between transistor no. and region. Therefore, low-power circuits in modern VLSI design became a top priority. To meet the increasing demands, we are now proposing a new full energy efficient adder using 14 transistor units that produce highly promising performance, In comparison to a range of current full adder with different transistor numbers of 28, 32, 16, 10 and so on for power area cover and threshold loss [4].

In today's age, we as VLSI design engineers face two main problems, i.e. Disposal of power and delay. With various technologies and techniques, we can design our circuit, but there are constraints that are not to be ignored in every design technology. The operations that are widely used are in applications including microprocessor, optical signals processing and image processing operations which are generally used

R. S. Tomar et al. (Eds.): CNC 2020, CCIS 1502, pp. 322–330, 2021.
https://doi.org/10.1007/978-981-16-8896-6_26

i.e. AND & OR, Subtraction & Extension. The viewpoint of efficiency, latencies and delays are main function of performance of addition in framework for digital signal processing. Not only does most adder systems increase the delay, they also dissipate the massive power. Our main focus in the circuit is therefore on rising power and time. But also, the scale of the circuit has to be discussed side by side, as size plays a crucial role in it in the miniature period. If the propagation delay is reduced, energy is increased and high heat dissipation in the circuit costs, so we have tried to optimize the circuit with almost the same delay values. Several strategies have been proposed, such as Full Adder Hybrid Circuit [5], Circuit XNOR 3T [6], 8T Full Adder Circuit [6], in order to decrease the transistor number and low power absorption. Certain methods are also used to absorption low power and increase circuit speed [7].

At the cost of others, different logic types tend to favor some dimension of success. The most important logic design types of traditional domain have been standard static complementary metal-oxide-semiconductor (CMOS), complementary pass-transistor logic (CPL) [8], logic transmission gate full adder (TGFA) [9–11] and dynamic CMOS [13]. For their implementation, another adder design has used more than one logic style, the hybrid-logic design style [14].

2 Single Bit Hybrid Full Adder Circuits (HFAC) Using XNOR Gate

2.1 16T Single Bit Hybrid Full Adder

Scheme of 16T full adder (FA) [4] is shown in Fig. 1 and Transient Response is illustrated in the following Fig. 2. The SUM signal module contains three modules representing XNOR logic functions, Module 1 and 2. COUT signal implement a transmission gate (TG) used in Module 3.

Module 1 & 2: These modules are responsible for most of the power dissipation throughout the circuit. This module is therefore developed to avoid power degradation deliberately removed by a transistor-based inverter P1 & N1, output of which is B. The XNOR output is created with low logic swing using transistors P2 and N2 (controlled inverters). Transistor P3 and N3 are set for added full swing of output levels. In Module 2, P4, P5 (PMOS) & N4, N5, & N6 (NMOS) are also included in Module 2.

Module 3: A carrying P6, P7, N7 & N8 (signal output) is introduced. The transistor aspect ratio was high for deficiency of COUT signal propagation delay.

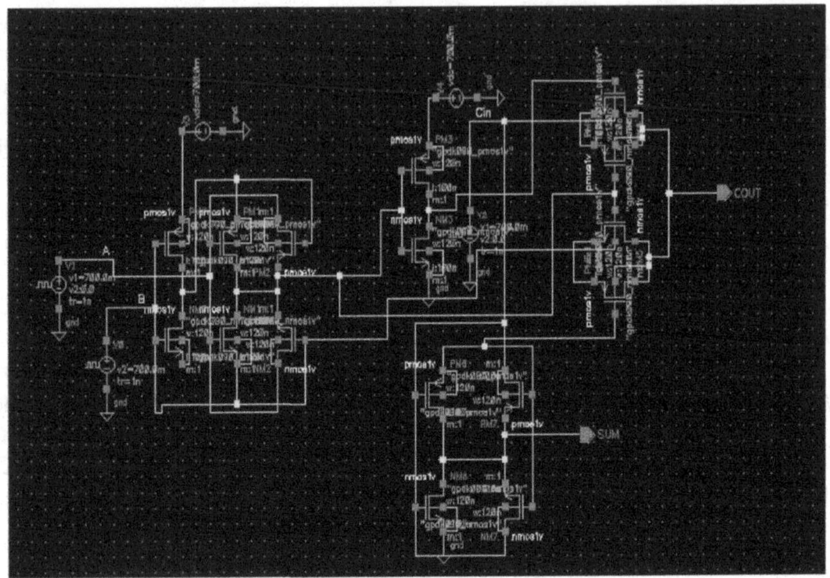

Fig. 1. Schematic of 16T Hybrid Full Adder circuit

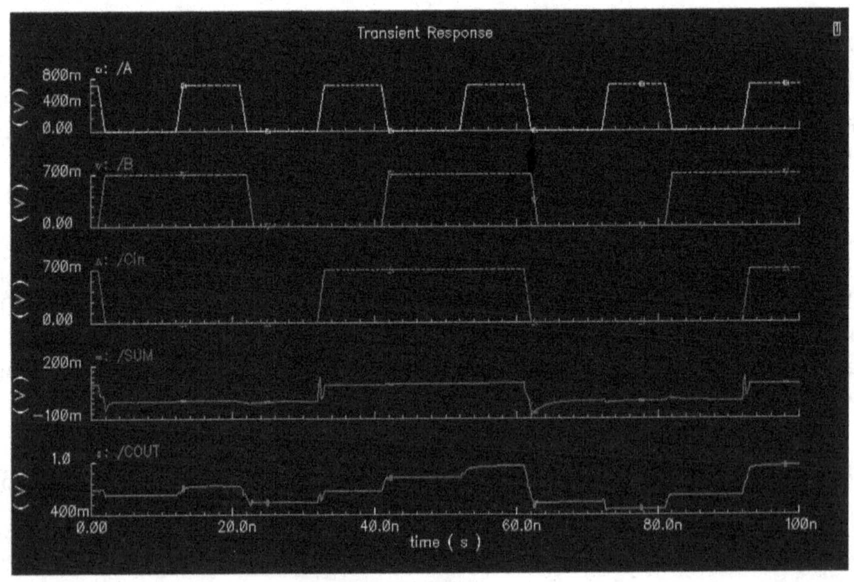

Fig. 2. Transient response of 18T Hybrid Full Adder circuit

2.2 14T Single Bit Hybrid Full Adder

This paper proposes to comply with necessities for low power electronic devices in a new design of 14 transistor FA. Diag.3 shows scheme of 14T FA and Fig. 4 shows the

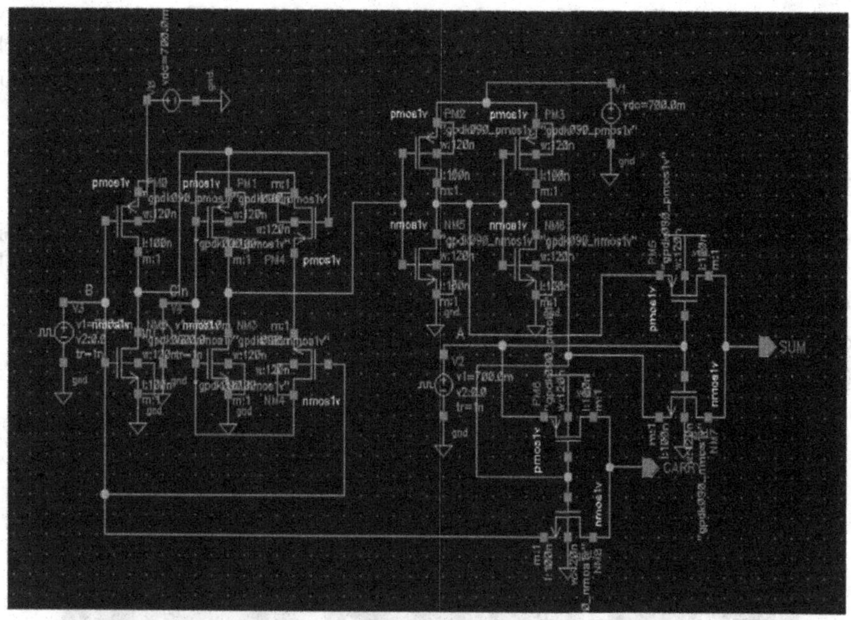

Fig. 3. Schematic of 14T Hybrid Full Adder circuit

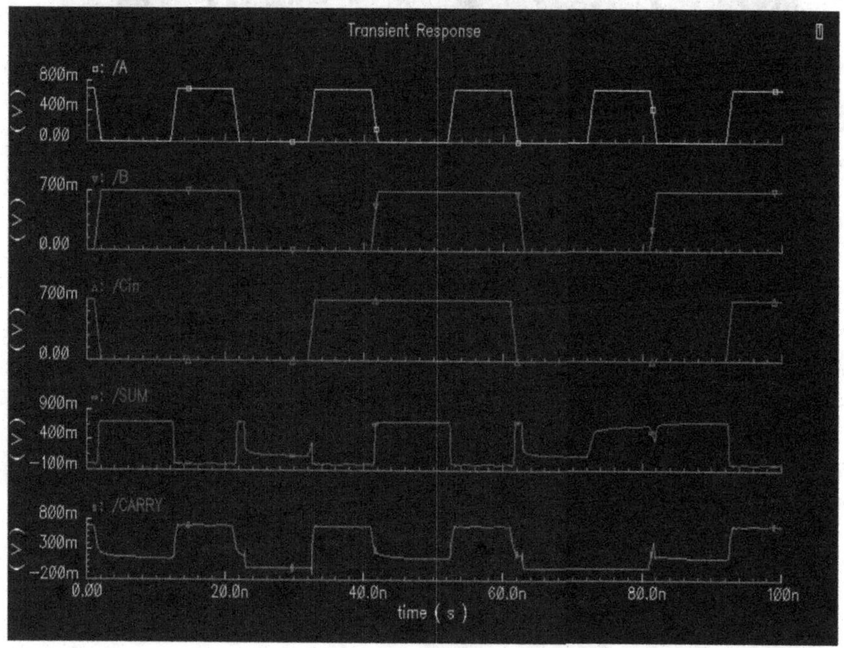

Fig. 4. Transient response of 14T Hybrid Full Adder circuit

Transient response. The P1, P2 and P3 (pMOS) & N1, N2 and N3 (nMOS) transistor are used to form XNOR gates on this circuit. Figure 3 displays the aspect ratio of each transistor (W/L). The P6 and N3 transistors are used to receive SUM signal output where P7 and N4 output signal carry is received.

2.3 10T Single Bit Hybrid Full Adder

We needed 4 transistors XNOR circuits and 2-to-1 multiplexers for the implementation of different 10 transistors of CMOS full adder circuits. Figure 5 shows the 10T full adder circuit and Fig. 6 shows the output waveform.

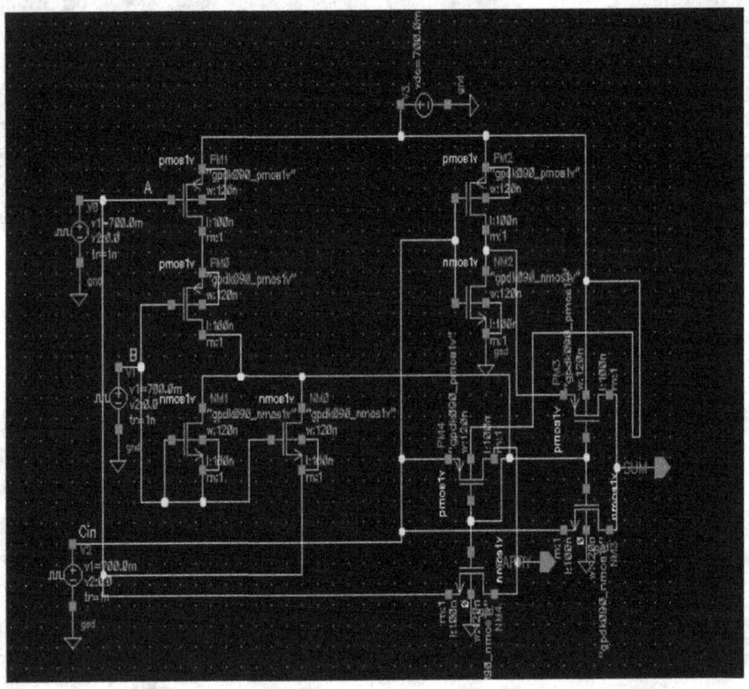

Fig. 5. Schematic of 10T Hybrid Full Adder circuit

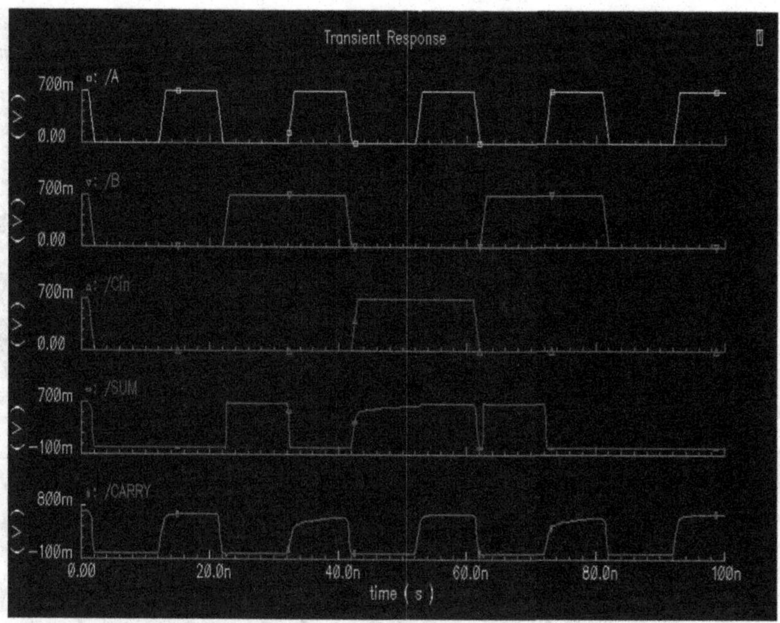

Fig. 6. Transient response of 10T Hybrid Full Adder

2.4 8T Single Bit Hybrid Full Adder

The 3T XNOR Circuit is another feature from the hybrid Full Adder. It provides the basis for phase detector compressor, arithmetic circuit, DSP architecture, parity checkers, multipliers, & code converters, microprocessor in a variety of modules. It consists of three transistors by means of the notion of hybrid CMOS FA with 8T.

The PTL is used to design the 3T XNOR circuit. In 3T XNOR circuit, NMOS transistor will turn OFF when AB = 00 & PMOS VDD develops through the transistor. NMOS transistor is turned ON and the output is set to "zero" in both cases, When AB = 10 or 01. NMOS is switched on, & at output both the PMOS and NMOS transistors are formed, When AB = 11. In this case, NMOS generates the weak "1" and PMOS generates the strong '0' at output. Another, i.e. 8T Full Adder, for low power consumption. Figure 7 shows the 8T hybrid full adder circuit, and Fig. 8 demonstrates Transient Response. Sum and FA Boolean expressions are:

$$\mathrm{Sum} = \left((\mathrm{A}+\mathrm{B})'' + \mathrm{C}\right)' \tag{1}$$

$$\mathrm{Carry} = (\mathrm{A.B}) + \left[(\mathrm{A}+\mathrm{B})' \cdot \mathrm{C}\right] \tag{2}$$

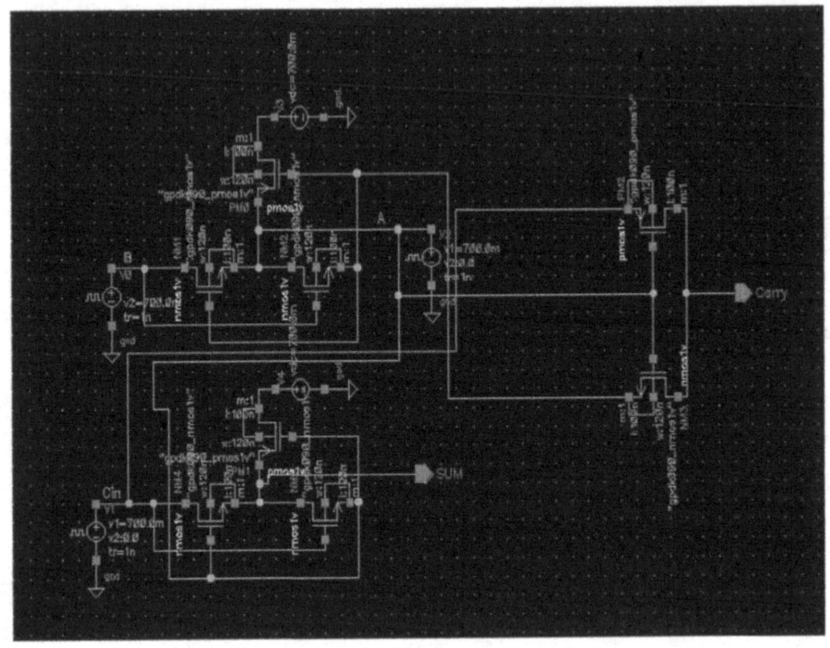

Fig. 7. Schematic of 8T Hybrid Full Adder

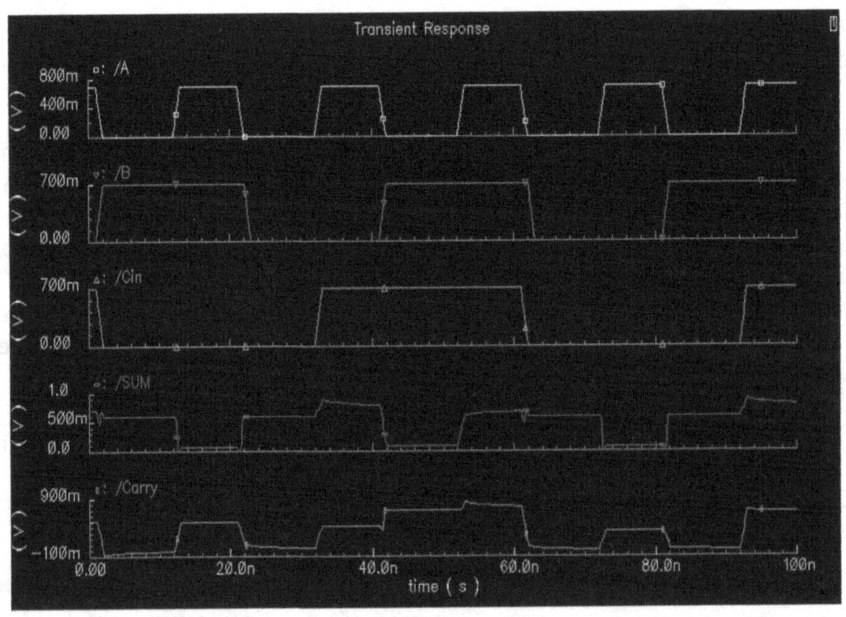

Fig 8. 8T Hybrid Full Adder transient response

3 Simulation Result

The Gate Leakage is only the dominant mechanism at room temperature at 27 °C; different methods have been used to reduce power consumption & maintain output of 16T, 14T, 10T and 8T Full Adder Circuit, which is the only mechanism to be used for the simulation of cadence tools using the 90nm technology with a nominal supply voltage Vdd = 0.7 V. Its comparative analysis of Various Full Adder Circuits the parameter like Leakage Current and leakage power is shown in below in Table 1 respectively.

Comparative Analysis Result Summary of Single bit Hybrid Full Adder Circuits shown below Table 1.

Table 1. Simulated result summary

Performance parameter	16T HFAC	14T HFAC	10T HFAC	8T HFAC
Technology used	90 nm	90 nm	90 nm	90 nm
Supply voltage	0.7 V	0.7 V	0.7 V	0.7 V
Leakage power	18.6 nW	16.9 nW	14.8 nW	7.09 nW
Leakage current	19.7 nA	14.4 nA	11.6 nA	8.01 nA
Transistor count	16	14	10	8
Area used	Large	Large	Less	Less

4 Conclusion

In this paper the XNOR Gate is a concept for single-bit FA hybrid circuits. Performance of the single bit HFAC is completely determined by the performance of its core modules. The leakage power consumption and Leakage current has been done in the circuit using Single bit HFAC. Designed HFAC are compared in phrases of leakage power, leakage current and surface area. We have designed and compared 16T, 14T, 10T and 8T Hybrid full adder circuit in terms of power & region. It eliminates the problems of diving capacity in other full adder modules and records a low power of 0.7 V in operation. According to, Various Full Adder circuits, transistor count and power of 8T Hybrid Full Adder is less and shows the better performance in comparison to other circuits of, Hybrid Full Adder.

References

1. Weste, N., Eshraghian, K.: Principles of CMOS Digital Design. A System Perspective. Addison Wesley, Massachusetts, MA, USA (1993)
2. Kang, S., Leblebici, Y.: CMOS Digital Integrated Circuit Analysis and Design, 3rd edn. McGraw-Hill (2005)
3. Roy, K., Prasad, S.C.: Low Power CMOS VLSI Circuit Design (2000). ISBN 0471-11488

4. Bhattacharyya, P., Kundu, B., Ghosh, S., Kumar, V., Dandapat, A.: Performance analysis of a low-power high-speed hybrid 1-bit full adder circuit. IEEE Trans. Very Large Scale Integr. (VLSI) Syst. **23**(10), 2001–2008 (2015)
5. Shant, K., Mahajan, R.: 1-bit hybrid full adder by GDI and PTL technique. Int. J. Innov. Res. Comput. Commun. Eng. **4** (2016)
6. Sathyabhama, B., Deepika, M., Deepthi, S.: Area and power efficient carry select adder using 8T Full Adder. In: IEEE ICCSP Conference Briefs, vol. 16 (2015)
7. Dubey, A., Dubey, S., Akashe, S.: A competent design 2:1 multiplexer and its application in 1-bit full adder cell, pp. 4673–4529 (2012)
8. Weste, N.H.E., Harris, D., Banerjee, A.: CMOS VLSI Design: A Circuits and Systems Perspective, 3rd edn. Pearson Education, Delhi, India (2006)
9. Rabaey, J.M., Chandrakasan, A., Nikolic, B.: Digital Integrated Circuits: A Design Perspective, 2nd edn. Pearson Education, Delhi, India (2003)
10. Radhakrishnan, D.: Low-voltage low-power CMOS full adder. In: IEE Proceedings on Circuits Devices and Systems, pp. 19–24 (2001)
11. Zimmermann, R., Fichtner, W.: Low-power logic styles: CMOS versus pass-transistor logic. IEEE J. Solid-State Circ. **32**, 1079–1090 (1997)
12. Chang, C.H., Gu, J.M., Zhang, M.: A review of 0.18-μm full adderperformances for tree structured arithmetic circuits. IEEE Trans. Very Large Scale Integr. (VLSI) Syst. **13**, 686–695 (2005)
13. Shams, A.M., Darwish, T.K., Bayoumi, M.A.: Performance analysis of low-power 1-bit CMOS full adder cells. IEEE Trans. Very Large Scale Integr. (VLSI) Syst. **10**(1), 20–29 (2002)
14. Aranda, M.L., Baez, R., Diaz, O.G.: Hybrid adders for high-speed arithmetic circuits: a comparison. In: Proceedings of the 7th IEEE International Conference on Electrical Engineering, Computing Science and Automatic Control (CCE), Tuxtla Gutierrez, NM, USA, pp. 546–549 (2010)

Design and Analysis of MEMS Microphone Using Helical Spring

Mayank Sharma[1(✉)], Ranjeet Singh Tomar[1], Bhupendra Dhakad[1], Sadhana Mishra[1], Prateek Jain[2], and Shailendra Singh Ojha[1]

[1] Electronics and Communication, ITM University, Gwalior, India
{mayanksharma.ec, ranjeetsingh, bhupendradhakad.ece, sadhanamishra.ece, shailendraojha.ece}@itmuniversity.ac.in

[2] VIT-AP University, Andhra Pradesh, India

Abstract. This paper shows an improved version of microphone that is having good sensitivity towards sound pressure, so that any small sound pressure can be observed and converted to useful signal. It uses a very emerging technology in the field of electronics i.e. MEMS (Micro Electro Mechanical Systems).It also feasible to fabricate these microphones because they can be fabricated in the same manner as the integrated circuit (ICs) are. The sensitivity improvement is established using helical spring type structures connected with its diaphragms that is made of steel which have good tensile strength and resistant to break on applying high frequency or pressure of sound signals. It shows quite good improvement over other microphones made by other conventional method.

Keywords: Microphone · Diaphragm · Pressure · Sensitivity

1 Introduction

The research and development of MEMS in the last 20–25 years have been grown dramatically, in the universities, research labs and in the industry also. Micro electro mechanical system are integrated circuit with tiny mechanical structures fabricated by robust integrated circuits (ICs) fabrication process, and because our semiconductor industry is quite mature they have very less chance to failure. Basically all the MEMS devices are based on silicon and other semiconductor materials like Ge, SiO2 etc. Moreover nowadays due to continues advancement in fabrication technology people are going in smaller dimensions lot of MEMS devices like pressure sensors, ion sensors, smart dust are now fabricating at nano scale and called as nano electro mechanical devices. Compare to other macro structures MEMS devices are more reliable, smaller and smarter. Silicon is a good material, it consist excellent physical properties such as, Young's module, higher strength, and compatibility with integrated circuit process. The later one is very vital as it makes the integration of ICs and micro electro mechanical devices [1].

R. S. Tomar et al. (Eds.): CNC 2020, CCIS 1502, pp. 331–342, 2021.
https://doi.org/10.1007/978-981-16-8896-6_27

A transducer that converted acoustic energy into electrical energy is known as microphone. These electrical signals can be transmitted to larger distance in order to do voice communications. So these microphones are used in communication devices, surveillance, military aims,, hearing aids, acoustic distinction under water ultrasonic and ultrasonic noise and vibration control [1]. In MEMS technology Micromachining has been used in designing and fabrication various silicon microphones. Variety of microphones are there like capacitive, condenser based and perforated. Among all these varieties of microphone capacitive pressure microphones is widely used of smaller size, integration, bulk fabrication, practicability, long stability and high achievable [1]. Capacitive microphone uses the property of a variable capacitor i.e. capacitance will change when the gap between its two plates changes.

2 Design of MEMS Microphone

Generally capacitive microphones consist of a diaphragm, a back plate and air gap. When waves of acoustic pressure impinge upon that diaphragm it vibrates. A diaphragm is stretched over a conductor plate in such a way that there remain a gap between the black plate and the membrane. The Capacitance value is inversely proportional to the gap between the diaphragm and conductive plate and it is directly proportional to the diaphragm area. Due to the movement of black plate and electrically charged membrane voltage variation take place and this voltage variation is the electrical sensitivity of microphone.

2.1 Design

Comsol multiphysics software version 4.4b, is used to conduct all multiphysics finite elements analysis, because it reduce cost and time. Figure 1 shows that structure of mems microphone whereas Fig. 1 shows that one fourth structure model in which physical properties and boundary condition for analysis multiphysics were configured. Residual stress that occur in the SINX membrane process is the simulation condition that provides tensile stress of 77 Mpa, sound pressure 1.0 pa in frequency range, bias voltage 12 V.

2.2 Mathematical Analysis and Designing Parameter of Mems Helical Microphone

A Theoretical model of resonant frequency and lateral displacement of this structure is expressed Free Deformation.

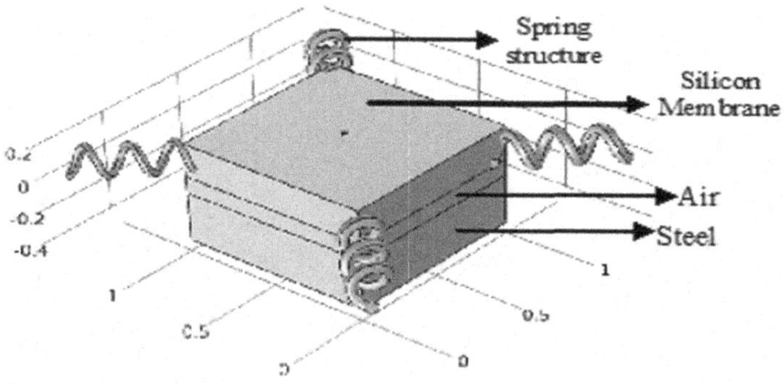

Fig. 1. Helical MEMS microphone design

Parameter

Name	Expression	Description
P0	20 [kPa]	Max pressure
T0	20 [degC]	Operating temp
Tref	70 [degC]	Die bonding temp
V0	20 [mV]	Potential generated
C	100 [pF]	Capacitance

2.3 Material Coating on MEMS Helical Microphone

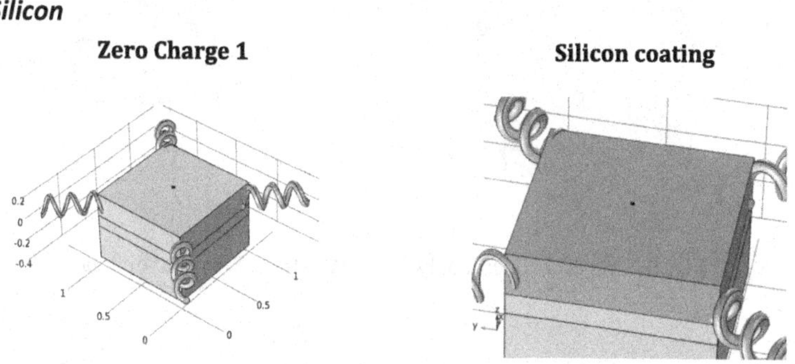

Fig. 2. Zero charge and Silicon coating

Above Fig. 2 shows that zero charge and Silicon coating respectively (Figs. 4, 5, 6, 7 and 8).

Above Fig. 3 shows that Steel AISI 4340 coating and air filled respectively (Figs. 9, 10, 11, 12, 13 and 14)

Air

Fig. 3. Steel AISI 4340 coating and airfilled respectively

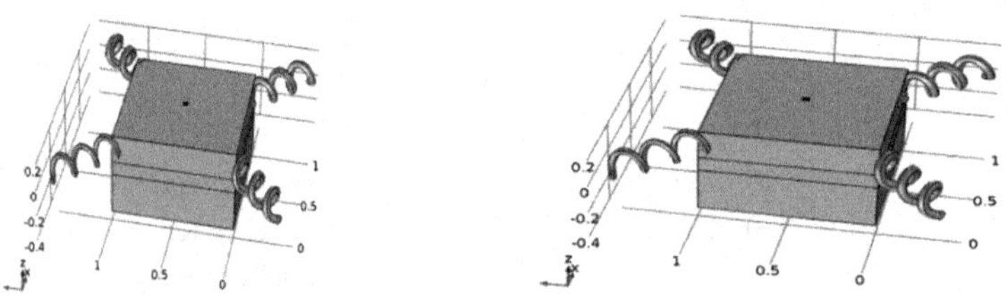

Fig. 4. Shows that material coating in mems helical microphone

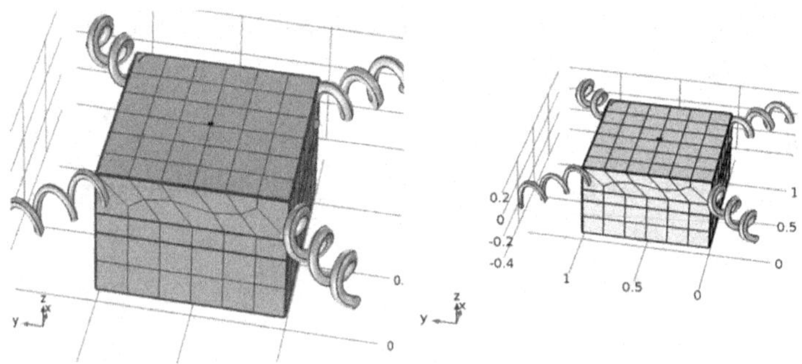

Fig. 5. Mesh mapped analysis of MEMS helical Microphone

3 Results

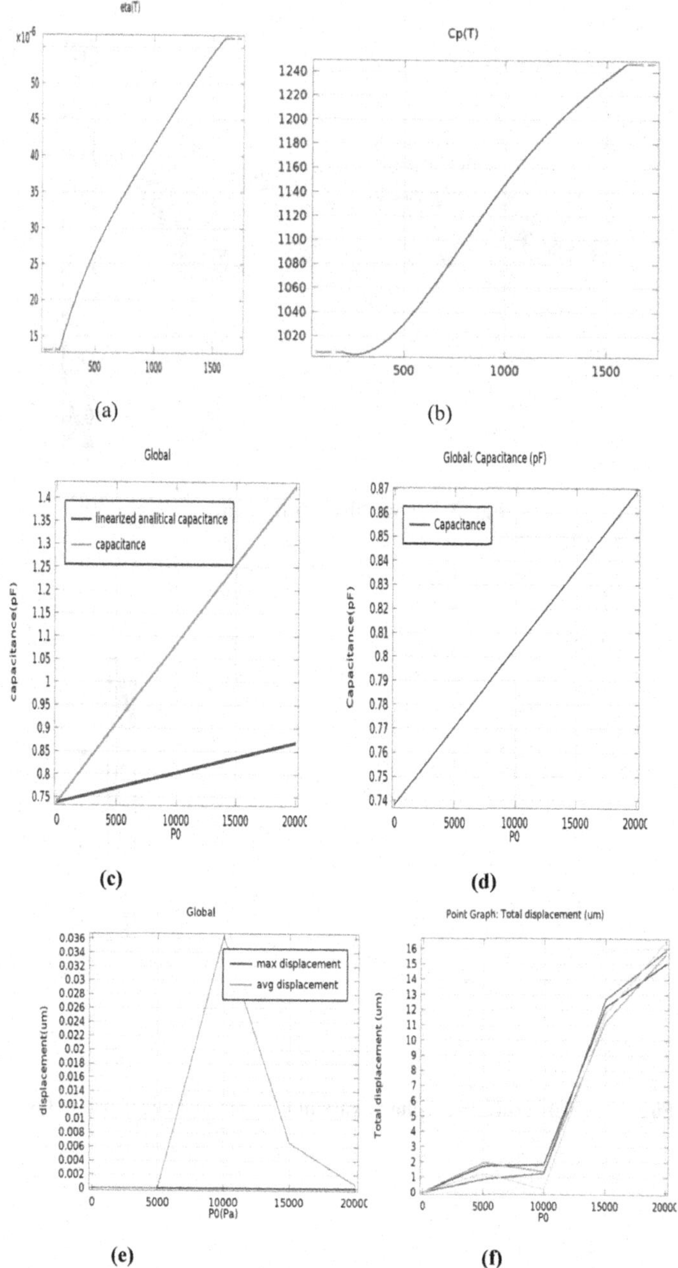

Fig. 6. (a, b, c, d, e) shows that capacitance variation with pressure and (f) represent total displacement of mems helical microphone

3.1 Comparative Analysis Mems Microphone and Helical Microphone

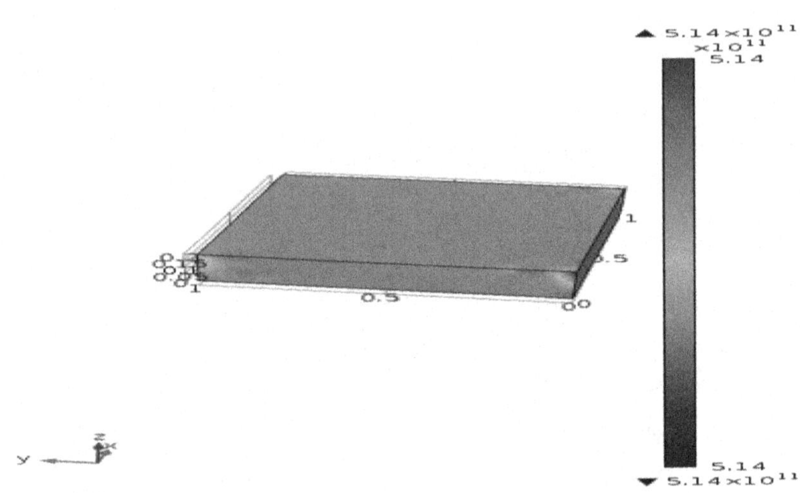

Fig. 7. Shows that Surface stress

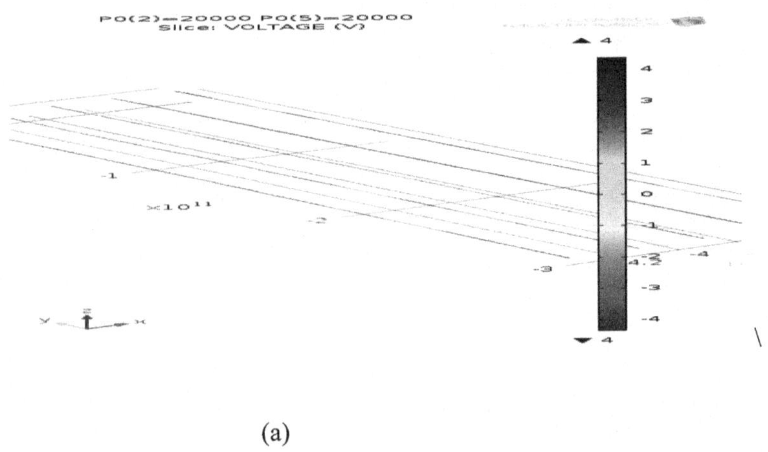

(a)

Fig. 8. (a, b) shows that voltage variation of mems helical microphon

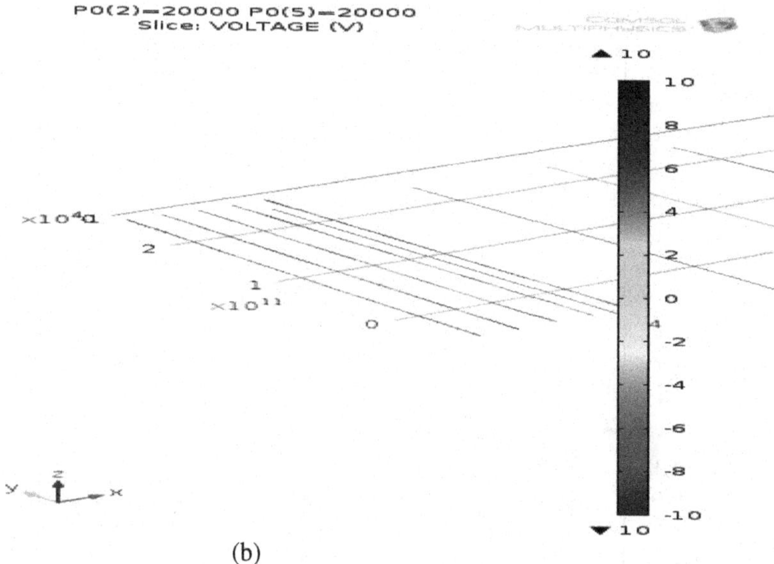

(b)

Fig. 8. (*continued*)

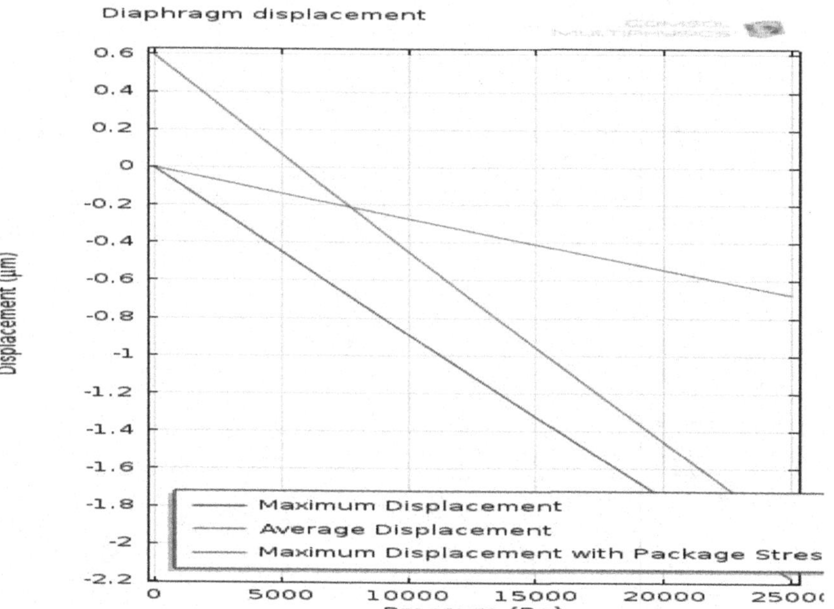

Fig. 9. Shows that diaphram displacement of mems helical microphone

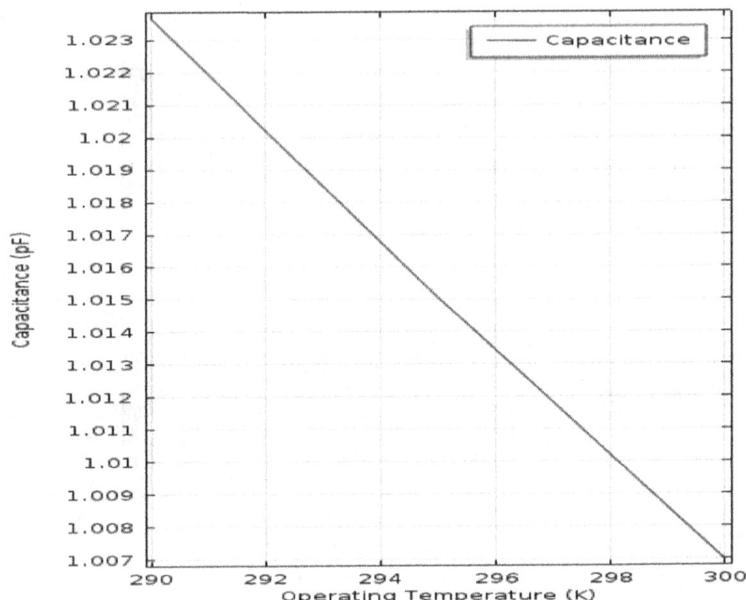

Fig. 10. Shows that capacitance variation with temperature

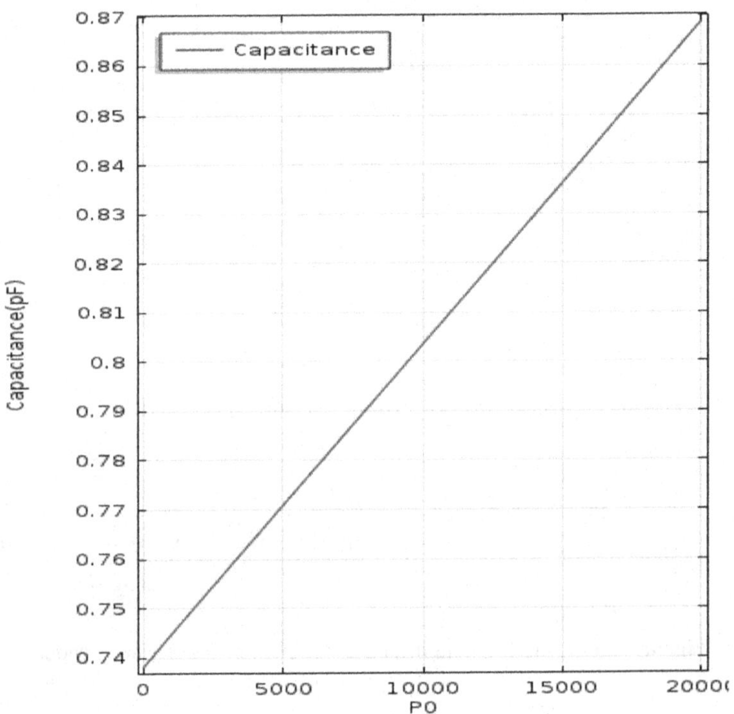

Fig. 11. Capacitance change with pressure

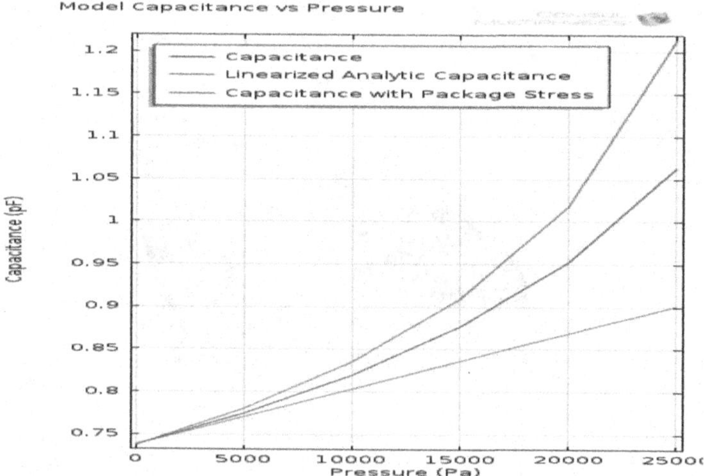

Fig. 12. Capacitance change with Pressure of helical microphone

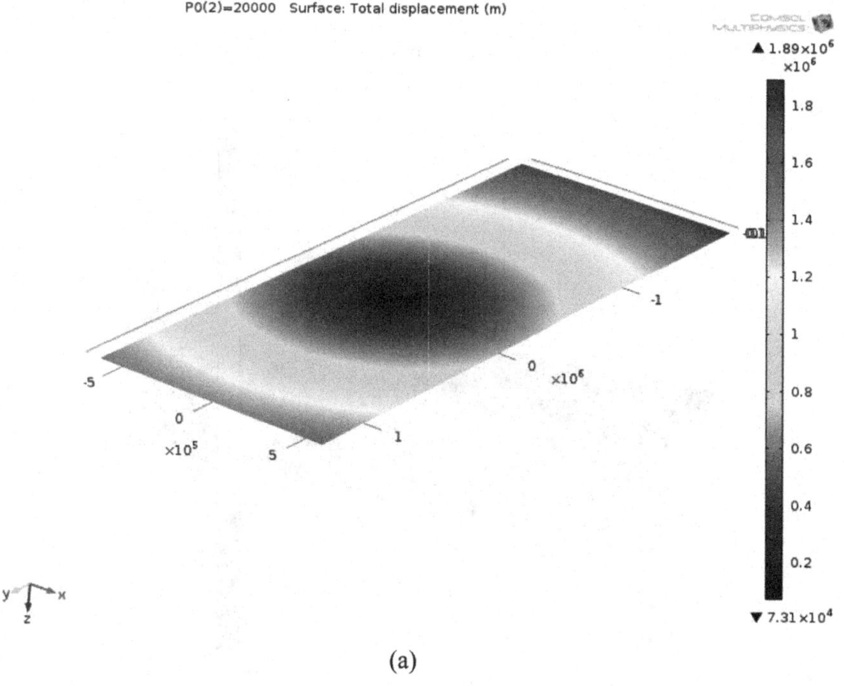

(a)

Fig. 13. (a, b, c) shows that total displacement variation with different pressure in Mems helicalmicrophone

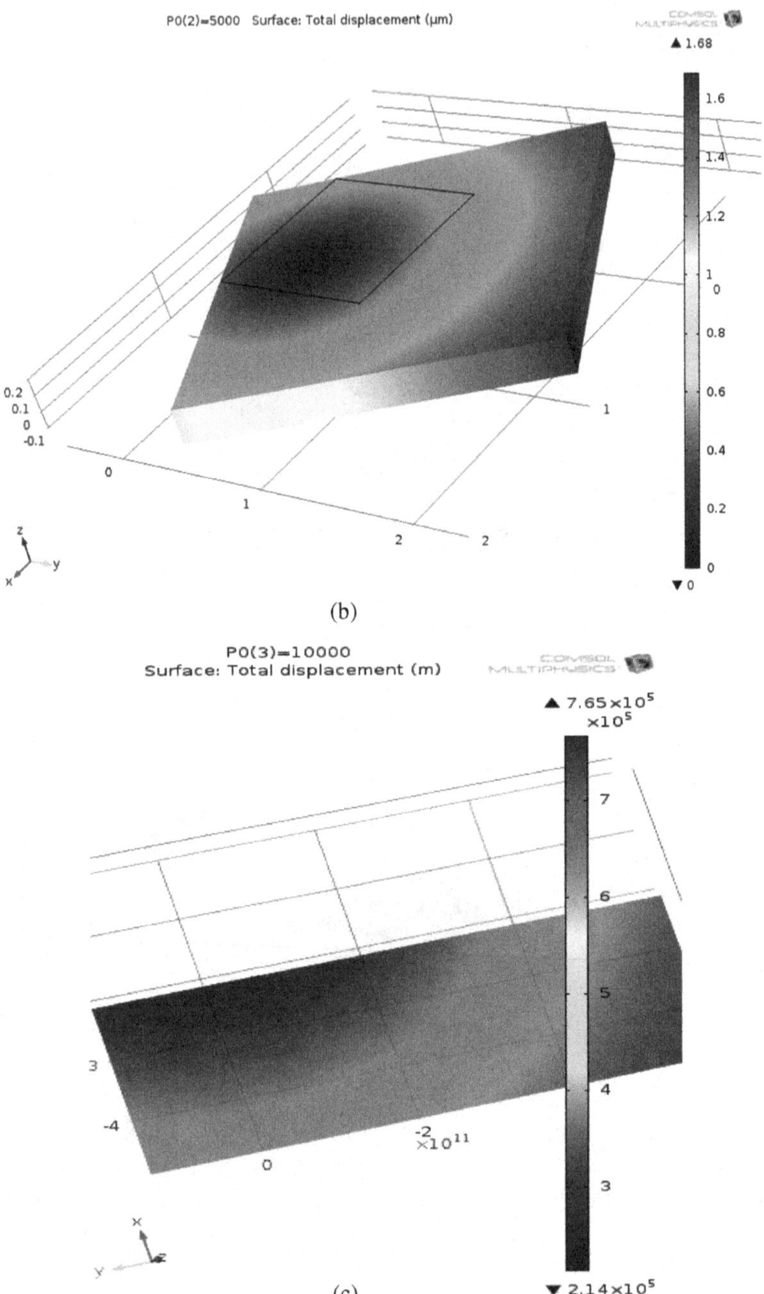

Fig. 13. (*continued*)

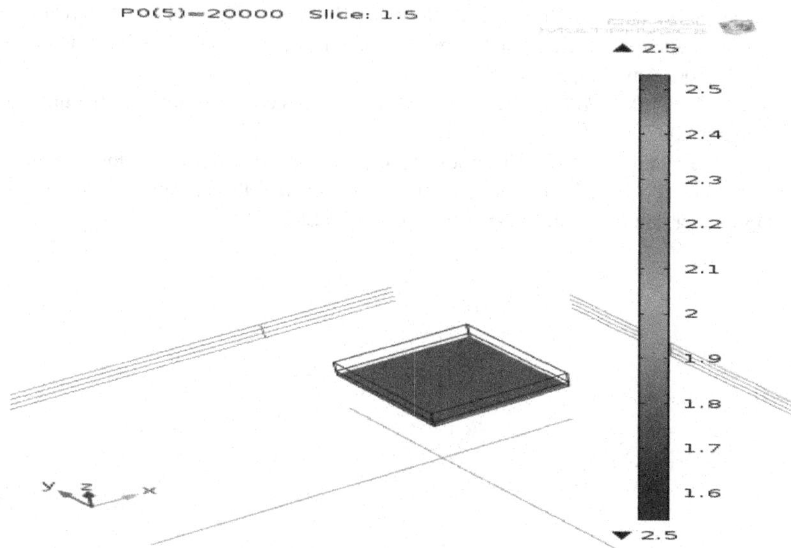

Fig. 14. Pressure variation

Conclusion

In this paper we have studied MEMS helical microphone, Result shows that Sensitivity has increased compare to normal microphone, we have also simulated capacitance response with modification on the helical microphone geometry was conducted. we have observed that COMSOL can give reliable result compare to theoretical models. In this paper we have simulated all parameter of MEMS helical microphone with different parameter such as temperature, pressure, voltage.

References

1. Hur, S., Jung, Y.-D., Lee, Y.-H., Song, W.-J., Kim, W.-D.: Fabrication of biomimetic MEMS acoustic sensor and analysis of its frequency characteristics. J. Korean Soc. Nondestructive Test. **31**(5), 522–528 (2011)
2. Scheeper, P.R., van der Donk, A.G.H., Olthuis, W., Bergveld, P.: Fabrication of silicon condenser microphone using single wafertechnology". J. Microelectromech. Syst. **1**(3), 147–154 (1992)
3. Yang, C.-T.: The sensitivity analysis of a mems microphone with different membrane diameters. J. Mar. Sci. Technol. **18**(6), 790–796 (2010)
4. Shivok, T.J.: MEMS PolyMUMPs-based miniature microphonefor directional sound sensing. Master's thesis Monterey, California, September 2007
5. Harrison, S.C.W.: Free field modeling of a MEMS-based pressure gradient microphone. Master's thesis Monterey, California, December 2009
6. Marshall Leatch, Jr., W.: Introduction to Electroacoustics and Audio Amplifier Design, 3rd edn., Kendall/Hunt Publishing Company (2003)

7. Lavergne, T., Durand, S., Bruneau, M., Joly, N., Rodrigues, D.: Dynamic behaviuor of the circular membrane of an electrostatics microphone: Effect of holes in the backing electrode. J. Acoust. Soc. Am. **128**, 3459 (2010)
8. MEMSCAP: PolyMUMPS (2003). http://www.memsrus.com/nc-mumps.poly.html. Accessed 30 Aug 2007
9. Griffiths, D.J.: Introduction to Electrodynamics, 3rd edn., Pearson Education (2008)
10. Hur, S., Jung, Y., Lee, Y.H., Kwak, J.-H.: Two-chip MEMS capacitive microphone with CMOS analog amplifier. In: SENSORS, pp. 1–4. IEEE (2012)

An NLP Based Sentimental Analysis and Prediction: A Dynamic Approach

Chandramohan Dhasarathan[1(✉)] and Hewan Shrestha[2]

[1] Computer Science & Engineering Department, Thapar Institute of Engineering & Technology, Patiala, Punjab, India
[2] Department of Computer Science and Engineering, Madanapalle Institute of Technology and Science, Madanapalle, India

Abstract. Natural language processing is an contemporary research field in which ample of work carried towards Speech processing, reorganization, intrusion, communication, emotional activity, voice over robot interaction, travel navigation, automatic car/pilot, smart appliances and many more tremendous novel community pinpointing towards machine learning and deep learning. It is an attempt to apply and process any language for an efficient Sentimental analysis and would be an alternative for applications which uses Natural Language Processing (NLP).

Keywords: Sentimental analysis · Natural Language Processing (NLP) · Naïve Bayes Classifier (NBC) · Decision Tree Classifier (DTC)

1 Introduction

The Natural Language Processing (NLP), is a subfield of linguistics. Most high impact research works have been identified in fields like computer science and synthetic aptitude troubled with connections concerning computers and hominid languages. NLP plays a major role in text and speech application with the support of machine learning algorithms. It also supports automatic systems like schmaltzy analysis, vocalizations recognition, article summarization, contraption translation, unwanted user detection, named individual recognition, subject answering, auto complete, prophetic typing, material removal, and the list keeps growing. In contemporary research era, NLP would improve the power of auto search engines; by filtering unwanted spam moreover it helps to obtain analytics in a debauched and climbable method. Sentimental analysis is the initial NLP chore that each data scientist requirements, accomplish to realize the occupied appliance and obligation of data in NLP. The article is planned with several sections it deliberates a summary of sentimental analysis and its unorthodoxies by diverse authors is shown under Sect. 2. Core logic of NLP built analysis tactic conversed and it is higher in Sect. 3 with various mock familiarity and tokenization. In Sect. 4 Practical Approach for the Sentiment Analysis evaluation is illustrated. At Sect. 5 consists of discussion about the necessity of the proposed approach and its advantages. Finally, the paper is resolved with satisfactory and addressable borders in sentimental analysis.

R. S. Tomar et al. (Eds.): CNC 2020, CCIS 1502, pp. 343–353, 2021.
https://doi.org/10.1007/978-981-16-8896-6_28

2 Literature Study

Speech enhancement and its attention to the research, academic community get increased on all regions. The intelligibility of noise filtering and improving the quality of speech signals would be necessary in this communication advancement era. A well skilled classical is desirable to citation the spotless dialogue fields. Simple Recurring unit (SRU) is proposed in 2020, Xingyue et al. [1]. Recurring neural network (RNN) for language development is used by utmost scholars. Natural language duty is fingered by SRU for outstanding parallelized divisions.

J.A. Domínguez-Jiménez et al. [2], fascinated the physiological indicators to strainer the reactions of hominoid feedbacks and behaviours intermittently. Wearable device announcement for witnessing the atypical bustle and it is castoff to diagnose the behaviour of a specific in all context. Photoplethymography is espoused for relentless distinctions in responsive happenings. Moreover, a accidental plantation recursive algorithm is charity for unremitting checking and a piece variety backing trajectory contraption to catalogue and analysing the happenings. The galvanic coating rejoinder appearances suitable comeback with beset passionate accomplishments.

Humberto Perez-Espinosa et al. [3], to ascertain the children's sensitive communication by relating with two changed machines using Wizard of Oz (WoZ). The verified voice is segmented physically grounded on excitement and assertiveness for a recovering child mainframe interface. Paralinguistic evidence is presented to the study communal for numerous tongue shakeup study activities. The current rejoinder to a families' excitement might be apprehended established on their ordinary terminologies seasoned in cooperating passionate children's communication quantity.

Bikmukhametov. T et al. [4], the heaviness and malaise assessment of multiphase stream tariffs in construction have a near drift metering structure to diminish the affluent policies to the trade. Ground amounts of burden and illness which is voluntarily offered would be functional in algebraic mock-ups are charity to envisage the course frequency. Machine learning systems theoretically functional to recognize the insecurity and combine the hearty Virtual Flow Meter system.

Ali Bou Nassif et al. [5], Speech related application issues are resolved using deep learning approach by statistical analysis of specific information. It shed light on research focus to current trends in voice reorganization. Speech signal mitigation in health care system to lead a normal life for the betterment of gifted child for emotional activities identification. Supervised, unconfirmed, semi-supervised, strengthening education and bottomless erudition strategies are adopted for speech recognition.

Zebang Shen et al. [6], a Long short term memory (LSTM) and Mel-Frequency cepstral coefficient (MFCC) approach to categorize the vocalist of a melody retime by segregating the background instrumental music separately.

Li et al. [7], the discernibility of Information systems and decision systems redundant features appears in different webpage classification, speech recognition, and text categorization is identified using the neighbourhood rough set model. Partially labelled data is tested by semi supervised algorithms and it is applied to several data sets to verify the effectiveness of feature selection.

Ihm et al. [8], deep learning algorithm is used for fixed length word embedding by Skip-gram-KR and a Korean affix tokenizer. Neural network based approach for speech and pattern reorganization it pays the way for digitizing the Korean word to identify the low dimensional dense vector.

Yoo et al. [9], there is need for hand free interface to operate devices which are in need for controlling through voice based input. A convolutional neural network constructed yawning knowledge algorithm for monitoring the devices without keyboard and mouse, a gaze-writing for the manoeuvre of crucial devices functionality. The classification technique for speech interaction interface with a gaze-tracking technology.

Shrestha et al. [10], designed SAH focusing on script based optimization approach to analyse and identify the appropriate specification for describing human languages in a structured way. It shows the adoption of two different machine learning classifiers for the purpose of text extraction from any given text pattern.

Naseem et al. [11], proposed a transfomer-based method for sentimental analysis including transformer representations and deep intelligent contextual embeddings as a result to enhance the quality of sentiments and semantics of any given context. Morever, it proposes bi-directional LSTM (Long and Short Term Memory) network for determing sentiment of a given text.

Alamoodi et al. [12], shows a systematic review of articles related to text extraction and sentimental analysis in different scientific disciplines ranging from social, medical health and technology services. Past research articles on sentiment analysis domain have been reviewed over a span of 10 years including articles from Web of Science, Scopus, PubMed, IEEEXplore and so on. It reflects that common patterns have been identified among the reviewed articles.

Dahooie et al. [13], proposes an integrated system that joins sentiment analysis and multi criteria decision making (MCDM) techniques on fuzzy sets. Precisely, it shows sentiment analysis of products and services available through various possible accesses using expert based systems as well. Moreover, effective features have been detemined using sensitivity analysis.

Wang et al. [14], proposed a sentence-to-sentence attention network (S2SAN) using multihead attention and conducting domain-specific and multi-domain sentiment analysis experiments on multiple datasets. Results verified that S2SAN outperfomed other best methods available out there including regular CNNs, RNNs, and LSTMs.

Zhao et al. [15], proposed Local Search Improvised Bat Algorithm based Elman Neural Network (LSIBA-ENN) for performing sentiment analysis on online product reviews. The proposed model undergoes various stages for proper sentiment classifications. Additionally, Long-Term Frequency based Modified Inverse Class Frequency (LTF-MICF) and Hybrid Mutation based Earth Warm Algorithm (HMEWA) have been used through the classification process.

Park et al. [16], introduces a semi-supervised sentiment analysis approach using partial sentiment information of any content. It also preserves local information generated form original representation of the content. It has been validated by using various sentiment visualization and classification tasks upon some real-world datasets. Proposed approach enhanced sentiment class separation on Amaon review datasets when compared to other approaches.

Zhang et al. [17], introduces an interactive long short term memory (LSTM) network for sentiment analysis to facilitate interactions amongst speakers. It also proposes a new conversational dataset named ScenarioSA and investigates interaction dynamics associated with the conversations amongst the users.

Yanxia et al. [18], proposed a new context and aspect memory network (CAMN) method to resolve the issue of sentiment analysis on aspect level products and services. It uses bi-directional long short term memory(LSTM) and multi-attention mechanisms for better capturing of sentimental features in short length documents. Also, it makes use of encoder-decoder architecutre for calculating context and aspect relevance of the text.

Mohammad et al. [19], proposed a hybrid sentiment analysis algorithm combining two feature selection techniques using the ReliefF and Multi-Verse Optimizer (MVO) algorithms. Results show that the proposed method outperforms other techniques and classifiers in terms of accuracy. Precisely, the proposed method is dependent on three classes: positive, negative and neutral using Support Vector Machines algorithms.

Song et al. [20], introduced a novel text representation model named Word2PLTS for short text sentiment analysis using probabilistic linguistic terms sets (PLTSs). These sets are later used by Support Vector Machines for finding polarity and thus a novel framework called SACPC is obtained. It is observed that the proposed technique has better improvement in results compared to lexicon-based approaches.

3 NLP Dynamic Approach for Voice Prediction and Recognition

Sentiment analysis approach for a guesstimate of emotion by a text based milieu. The opinion of numerous unstructured texts might have a value that dealt various situations with an expected opinion of either optimistic or undesirable result. Consuming the systems from NLP, dynamic system considers the input from all possible ways by observing human emotions significantly high observation. Mawkishness scrutiny has developed crucial element to analytically cutting, categorize, and enumerate the data.

Sentiment Analysis for any language script is scarcely create which has gigantic promises it inclines to modernize the examinations and analysis assemblages in various amid its nascent employers want to a commodious diversity of tenders in expected lifespan from CPU investigation to promotion. Language Sentiment Analysis commonly comprises of trial language data assemblage, data dispensation, feature withdrawal, and arrangement. It acts as a outfit for detecting the appropriate context matching to the expected users result would be extracted from all possible sources. Moreover, it concludes valid meaning for the given input Hindi-Contextual-Data in appropriate block. The extracted information helps to identify, segregate and classify the data more reliable and scheduling with various identification marks with true positive, false negative or true and false neutral class.

4 NLP Sentiment Analysis Augmentation in Languages

Each and every language has their unique way of transformation to convey the original meaning of text or speech and it is well recognized by all analysis databases. The basic difference between any languages is the core structure; it gets varied in all human languages broadly in practice. Notable, the world communication language has

```
Dynamic Analysis of any language text process:
Step 1: Initializing the Unknown Tokenization
Step 2: Filtering and Scrubbing the data
Step 3: Identify and delete unwanted Stop Words
Step 4: Utilizing the best Classifier
Step 5: Modeling the process and Calculating the prediction
```

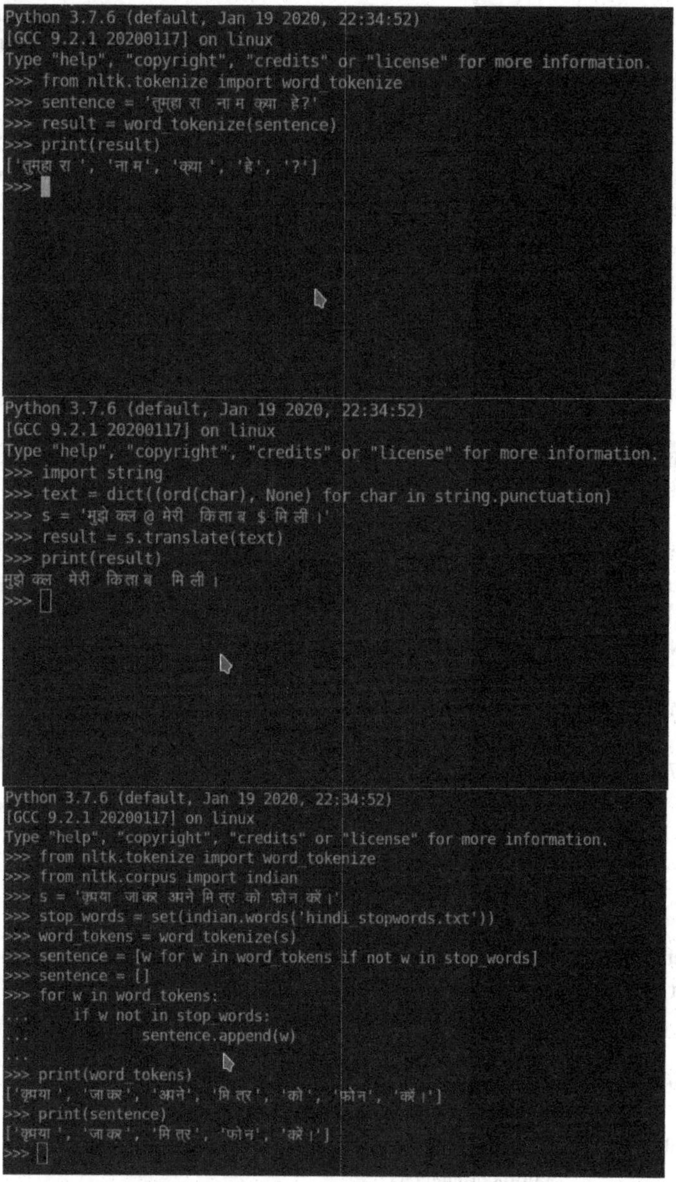

```
Python 3.7.6 (default, Jan 19 2020, 22:34:52)
[GCC 9.2.1 20200117] on linux
Type "help", "copyright", "credits" or "license" for more information.
>>> from nltk.tokenize import word_tokenize
>>> sentence = 'तुमहा रा  ना म क्या  है?'
>>> result = word_tokenize(sentence)
>>> print(result)
['तुमहा रा ', 'ना म', 'क्या ', 'है', '?']
>>>
```

```
Python 3.7.6 (default, Jan 19 2020, 22:34:52)
[GCC 9.2.1 20200117] on linux
Type "help", "copyright", "credits" or "license" for more information.
>>> import string
>>> text = dict((ord(char), None) for char in string.punctuation)
>>> s = 'मुझे कल @ मेरी  किता ब $ मि ली ।'
>>> result = s.translate(text)
>>> print(result)
मुझे कल  मेरी  किता ब  मि ली ।
>>>
```

```
Python 3.7.6 (default, Jan 19 2020, 22:34:52)
[GCC 9.2.1 20200117] on linux
Type "help", "copyright", "credits" or "license" for more information.
>>> from nltk.tokenize import word_tokenize
>>> from nltk.corpus import indian
>>> s = 'कृपया  जा कर  अपने मि तर को फोन करें ।'
>>> stop_words = set(indian.words('hindi_stopwords.txt'))
>>> word_tokens = word_tokenize(s)
>>> sentence = [w for w in word_tokens if not w in stop_words]
>>> sentence = []
>>> for w in word_tokens:
...     if w not in stop_words:
...             sentence.append(w)
...
>>> print(word_tokens)
['कृपया ', 'जा कर', 'अपने', 'मि तर', 'को', 'फोन', 'करें ।']
>>> print(sentence)
['कृपया ', 'जा कर', 'मि तर', 'फोन', 'करें ।']
>>>
```

Fig.1. SVO and SOV design and empathy

Subject_Verb_Object (SVO) erection, while all language follows Subject_Object_Verb (SOV) arrangement. Polarity of Hindi text is getting unchanged and moreover it is not mapping with the English language. If the system attempts to give wrong interruption for the same word by changing its order level would affect entire sentence phrase and leads to change in the meaning. The dynamic approach pays a way for a deeper linguistic analysis would help in production with languages to quiz, validate and accomplish the romanticism scrutiny. The proposed system is tested for various sentences with SVO and SOV of English and Hindi data sets for validating the performance. The results gives a clear identification of considering NLP based dynamic approach shows increasingly high demand in sentimental analysis.

The sentence illustration of SVO and SOV under various criteria have been tested and shown in Fig. 1. It demonstrates the real scenario of meaning getting effected in normal case itself. The result indicates abnormality in structure of language is effecting and the core linguistics changes have been identified.

Table 1. Research identified as notable contribution in Speech Recognition

Researchers	Methodology proposed	Year	Publisher
Xingyue et al. [1],	Simple recurrent unit (SRU) & Recurrent neural network (RNN)	2020	Elsevier
J.A. Domínguez-Jiménez et al. [2],	Photoplethymography by random forest recursive algorithm	2020	Elsevier
Humberto Perez-Espinosa et al. [3],	Paralinguistic based Wizard of Oz (WoZ)	2020	Elsevier
Bikmukhametov. T et al. [4],	Machine learning for virtual flow metering (VFM)	2019	Elsevier
Ali Bou Nassif et al. [5],	Deep learning approach by statistical analysis	2019	IEEE
Zebang Shen et al. [6],	Long short term memory (LSTM) and Mel-Frequency cepstral coefficient (MFCC)	2019	IEEE
Li et al. [7],	neighbourhood rough set model and semi supervised algorithms	2019	IEEE
Ihm et al. [8],	Skip-gram-KR, Korean affix tokenizer, Neural network & deep learning approach	2019	IEEE
Yoo et al. [9],	A convolutional neural network based deep learning algorithm	2019	IEEE
Shrestha et al. [10]	NLP based Sentimental analysis	2020	Springer
Naseem et al. [11]	Transformer-based context embedding	2020	Elsevier
Alamoodi et al. [12]	Systematic review on vaccine hesitancy	2021	Elsevier
Dahooie et al. [13]	Multi criteria decision making (MCDM) techniques on fuzzy sets	2021	Elsevier
Wang et al. [14]	Sentence-to-sentence attention network for sentiment analysis	2021	Elsevier

(*continued*)

Table 1. (*continued*)

Researchers	Methodology proposed	Year	Publisher
Zhao et al. [15]	Local Search Improvised Bat Algorithm based Elman Neural Network (LSIBA-ENN) for sentiment analysis on online product reviews	2021	Elsevier
Park et al. [16]	Semi-supervised sentiment analysis approach of a given content	2019	Elsevier
Zhang et al. [17]	Interactive long-short term memory (LSTM) network for sentiment analysis	2021	Elsevier
Yanxia et al. [18]	Context and aspect memory network (CAMN) for aspect level sentiment analysis	2021	Elsevier
Mohammad et al. [19]	Hybrid sentiment analysis approach combining ReliefF and Multi-Verse Optimizer (MVO) algorithms	2020	Elsevier
Song et al. [20]	Novel text representation model named Word2PLTS for short text sentiment analysis	2020	Elsevier

The issues of speech/voice prediction might be addressed by various research novelties and it is approached by deep learning, machine learning, neural network, optimization algorithm, natural language processing, Healthcare management etc. Authors from various domains came forward collaboratively to solve the issues noted in this area and it is shown in Table 1.

Table 2. Research Community working under voice prediction/recognition around the world

Research addressed in	No. of articles	IEEE	Elsevier
China	18	7	11
USA	7	3	4
India	5	1	4
South Korea	4	4	–
Pakistan	3	2	1
France	2	1	1
Saudi Arabia	2	–	2
Germany	2	2	–
Colombia	1	–	1
Mexico	1	–	1
Norway	1	–	1
UAE	1	1	–
Lanzhou	1	1	–
Italy	1	1	–
U.K	1	1	–
Iran	1	–	1

(*continued*)

Table 2. (*continued*)

Research addressed in	No. of articles	IEEE	Elsevier
Morocco	1	–	1
New Zealand	1	–	1
Japan	1	1	–
Spain	1	–	1
Canada	1	–	1
Denmark	1	–	1
Taiwan	1	–	1

Research community working periodically on voice/speech recognition, modelling, prediction, noise reduction, extraction and it is not limited. The issues and challenges of current trends in speech using machine learning is vigorously improving in the research arena, it reflects as research article published in peer reviewed reputed international journals and it is illustrated in Table 2. In Table 2 it is considered only IEEE and Elsevier for illustrating the comparison, there are similar and even more reputed journal also there and those are yet to be illustrated to the research world.

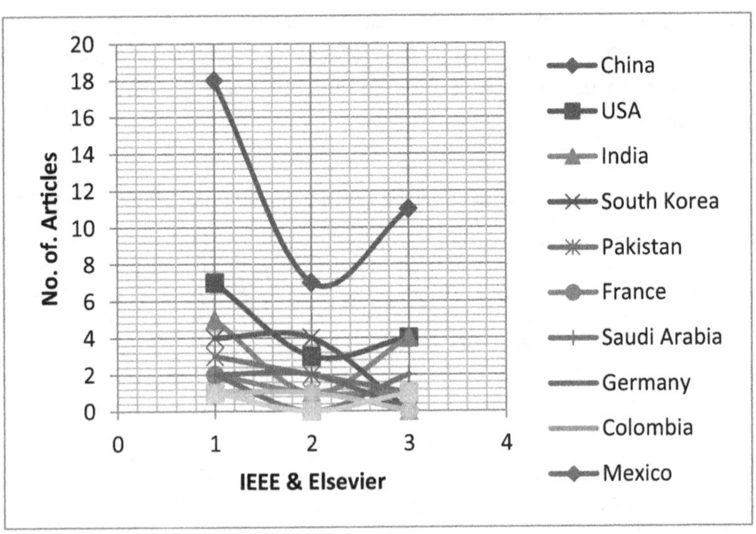

Fig. 2. Country contributed for voice prediction/recognition & its research challenges

Illustration of various research activity carried around the world in specifically speech reorganization is plotted in Fig. 2. The figure indicated the importance of NLP under various circumstances.

Table 3. True Positive and False Negative testing for Prediction

No. of testbeds	Naïve Bayes classifier		Decision tree classifier	
	+ve	−ve	+ve	−ve
4	0.3333	0.6666	0.6666	0.3333
8	0.14285	0.85714	0.57142	0.428571
12	0.10	.9	0.5	0.5
16	0.0769	0.92307	0.53846	0.461538
20	0.1875	0.8125	0.5625	0.4375

The structure of true positive and false negative sentences testing and illustration has been carried out under various decision classifiers as shown in Table 3. Identified result shows the increasing benefit of dynamic approach illustrating the structure of any sentence with positive and negative testing.

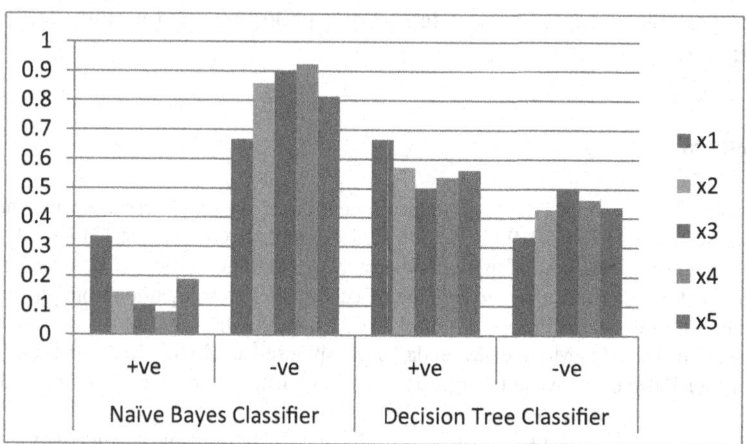

Fig. 3. Prediction of True Positive and False Negative Sentences testing and illustration

In Fig. 3 Value of true positive and false negative sentences testing with various linguistic approaches is illustrated. The research is carried out under various language decision classifiers as shown in Table 3. Its output shows an improvement in decision making in SOV and SVO and its benefit by applying a dynamic approach for testing. For the romanticism examination of languages ruling and evaluations, this paper used a dataset of hindi stop words. The dataset is fashioned with united of optimistic and undesirable dictionaries as showed in countless tables. To test the data composed is experienced and advanced using the NLTK (Natural Language Toolkit) library which is voluntarily offered for Python indoctrination philological. By trafficking all essential occupations and skins from NLTK library, the anticipated analyzer efficacious confirmed to get the prerequisite scrutiny which is explained in the result section. Moreover, the proficient datasets are categorized by using Naïve Bayes Classifier and

Decision Tree Classifier which is corroborated for the breakdown of optimistic and undesirable disputes to ghettoize the correct represention.

5 Conclusion

The article ensures the necessity of NLP based sentimental analysis importance and a dynamic approach role in analysis of various test by highlighting a traditional language. In current technological era, social media and twitter news provender are collective with customary dialects and writing as sound and it would convert challenging in perilous positions for the populaces who are unversed to the corresponding lingoes. Most scientists are engrossed concerning material extraction from individual's writings offered terminated the internet. Everywhere the ecosphere sundry scientists and academician's involvement and recommending their attitude towards evaluating soppiness from customary languages and text. However, in this article it is verified by on condition that a concrete methodology for evaluating the sentiment of customary morphological and text. It might help for an open research problem and cheer the scholars who are agreeable to exploration on Indo-Aryan philosophy and writings for analysis and prediction.

References

1. Cui, X., Chen, Z., Yin, F.: Speech enhancement based on simple recurrent unit network. Appl. Acoustics **157**, 107019 (2020). https://doi.org/10.1016/j.apacoust.2019.107019
2. Domínguez-Jiménez, J.A., Campo-Landines, K.C., Martínez-Santos, J.C., Delahoz, E.J., Contreras-Ortiz, S.H.: A machine learning model for emotion recognition from physiological signals. Biomed. Signal Process. Control **55**, 101646 (2020)
3. Perez-Espinosa, H., Martinez-Miranda, J., Espinosa-Curiel, I., Rodriguez-Jacobo, J., Villasenor-Pineda, L., Avila-George, H.: IESC-child: an interactive emotional children's speech corpus. Comput. Speech Lang. **59**, 55–74 (2020)
4. Bikmukhametov, T., Jäschke, J.: First principles and machine learning virtual flow metering: a literature review. J. Petrol. Sci. Eng. (2019). https://doi.org/10.1016/j.petrol.2019.106487
5. Nassif, A.B., Shahin, I., Attili, I., Azzeh, M., Shaalan, K.: Speech Recognition Using Deep Neural Networks: A Systematic Review. https://doi.org/10.1109/ACCESS.2019.2896880
6. Shen, Z., Yong, B., Zhang, G., Zhou, R., Zhou, Q.: A deep learning method for Chinese singer identification. Tsinghua Sci. Technol. **24**(4), 371–378 (2019)
7. Li, B., Xiao, J., Wang, X.: Feature selection for partially labeled data based on neighborhood granulation measures. IEEE Access, 1 (2019). https://doi.org/10.1109/ACCESS.2019.2903845
8. Ihm, S.-Y., Lee, J.-H., Park, Y.-H.: Skip-gram-KR: Korean word embedding for semantic clustering. IEEE Access, 1 (2019). https://doi.org/10.1109/ACCESS.2019.2905252
9. Yoo, S., Jeong, D., Jang, Y.: The study of a classification technique for numeric gaze-writing entry in hands-free interface. IEEE Access. **7**, 49125–49134 (2019). https://doi.org/10.1109/ACCESS.2019.2909573
10. Shrestha, H., Dhasarathan, C., Munisamy, S., Jayavel, A.: Natural language processing based sentimental analysis of Hindi (SAH) script an optimization approach. Int. J. Speech Technol. **23**(4), 757–766 (2020). https://doi.org/10.1007/s10772-020-09730-x

11. Naseem, U., Razzak, I., Musial, K., Imran, M.: Transformer based deep intelligent contextual embedding for Twitter sentiment analysis. Future Gener. Comput. Syst. **113**, 58–69 (2020). https://doi.org/10.1016/j.future.2020.06.050, ISSN 0167-739X
12. Alamoodi, A.H., et al.: Multi-perspectives systematic review on the applications of sentiment analysis for vaccine hesitancy. Comput. Biol. Med. (2021). https://doi.org/10.1016/j.compbiomed.2021.104957
13. Dahooie, J.H., Raafat, R., Qorbani, A.R., Daim, T.: An intuitionistic fuzzy data-driven product ranking model using sentiment analysis and multi-criteria decision-making. Technol. Forecasting Soc. Change **173**, 121158 (2021). https://doi.org/10.1016/j.techfore.2021.121158, ISSN 0040-1625
14. Wang, P., Li, J., Hou, J.: S2SAN: a sentence-to-sentence attention network for sentiment analysis of online reviews. Decision Support Syst. **149**, 113603 (2021). https://doi.org/10.1016/j.dss.2021.113603, ISSN 0167-9236
15. Zhao, H., Liu, Z., Yao, X., Yang, Q.: A machine learning-based sentiment analysis of online product reviews with a novel term weighting and feature selection approach. Inf. Process. Manag. **58**(5), 102656 (2021). https://doi.org/10.1016/j.ipm.2021.102656, ISSN 0306-4573
16. Park, S., Lee, J., Kim, K.: Semi-supervised distributed representations of documents for sentiment analysis. Neural Networks **119**, 39–150 (2019), https://doi.org/10.1016/j.neunet.2019.08.001, ISSN 0893-6080
17. Zhang, Y., et al.: Learning interaction dynamics with an interactive LSTM for conversational sentiment analysis. Neural Networks **133**, 40–56 (2021). https://doi.org/10.1016/j.neunet.2020.10.001, ISSN 0893-6080
18. Lv, Y., et al.: Aspect-level sentiment analysis using context and aspect memory network. Neurocomputing **428**, 195–205 (2021). https://doi.org/10.1016/j.neucom.2020.11.049, ISSN 0925-2312
19. Hassonah, M.A., Al-Sayyed, R., Rodan, A., Al-Zoubi, A.M., Aljarah, I., Faris, H.: An efficient hybrid filter and evolutionary wrapper approach for sentiment analysis of various topics on Twitter. Knowl. Based Syst. **192**, 105353 (2020). https://doi.org/10.1016/j.knosys.2019.105353, ISSN 0950-7051
20. Song, C., Wang, X.-K., Cheng, P., Wang, J., Li, L.: SACPC: a framework based on probabilistic linguistic terms for short text sentiment analysis. Knowl. Based Syst. **194**, 105572 (2020). https://doi.org/10.1016/j.knosys.2020.105572, ISSN 0950-7051

Hand Gesture Image Enhancement for Improved Recognition and Subsequent Analysis

Jatinder Kaur[1], Nitin Mittal[1(✉)], and Sarabpreet Kaur[2]

[1] Department of Electronics and Communication Engineering, Chandigarh University, Mohali 140413, India
jatinder.j230@cgc.ac.in, nitinmittal.me@cumail.in

[2] Department of Electronics and Communication Engineering, Chandigarh Engineering College, Mohali 140413, India
sarabpreet.kaur@cgc.ac.in

Abstract. This manuscript entails the preprocessing of hand gesture images for subsequent gesture recognition and cognitive communication. From this detailed analysis, it is obvious that the preprocessing stage is important for hand gesture recognition and its enhancement. Key to achieving the system design goal is optimizing this stage's performance. Through the techniques that are described in this stage, the quality of the image for the subsequent stages will be assured. The techniques discussed in literature are rarely successful when they seek to retain the image quality and provide a low noise result. At the segmentation stage, the image is filtered to include only the Region of Interest, which is a clear visual representation of the hand portion, separated from the rest of the information. These techniques are implemented on the images acquired from the dataset and various pre-processing techniques are compared and identified which technique yields the best possible results for optimizing the preprocessing of hand sign images.

Keywords: Peak signal to noise ratio · Pre-processing · Contrast enhancement · Mean square error · Natural image quality evaluator · Normalized factor

1 Introduction

Pre-processing is an area of major significance in digital image processing, with an enormous number of image processing areas, such as pattern identification and image analysis relying heavily on the quality upgrading of contaminated images. The main objective of pre-processing involves upgrading the visual quality of an input image [1]. Image contrast enhancement, ghost artifacts removal, and noise reduction are some of the elementary level operations performed at this stage.

1.1 Noise Removal

Pre-processing is benchmark dataset dependent algorithm. The research highlighted that filtering of redundant pixel values is needed for improving the visual quality of an image. To smooth the contour area for example of hand region different filters are

R. S. Tomar et al. (Eds.): CNC 2020, CCIS 1502, pp. 354–365, 2021.
https://doi.org/10.1007/978-981-16-8896-6_29

applied on the image captured through camera or the sample image taken from validated dataset. Filtering may help to alleviate the noisy information from the image. Noise can occur through different causes such as defective sensors, during image capture, poor lighting conditions, during transmission and many more. Among the most common varieties of unwanted information are Gaussian noise, salt & pepper noise, Impulsive noise, and a combination of these [2]. In general, noise reduction has a significant impact on the visual quality of image processing output. Various image noise filtering algorithms are already well established in the image processing field. The sort of noise distorting the image determines the nature of the image filtering challenge. Special strategies that aid in the preparation of grayscale images are discussed in. The basic goal of these strategies is to detect the presence of contaminated pixels and suppress them using an appropriate manner, while processing the remaining picture pixels with an algorithm designed to reduce Gaussian noise. Another series of strategies for color image noise removal is based on digital methods. To reduce the combination of noises in grayscale photographs, devised an efficient filter approach known as the trilateral filter (TF).

A technique for suppressing noise from an image distorted by impulse and Gaussian noise was proposed. This hybrid algorithm incorporates a Bayesian classification alongside the kernel regression framework. This technique was created for grayscale and color image filtration. Regularization methods founded on partial differential equations are another significant family of filters. As improved test statistics were developed, an important class of noise filtration methods was established. A denoising algorithm for video signals called FAST DENOISING is described in [3] and an adaptive noise suppression algorithm is proposed for X-ray images. Entropy concept was used for noise reduction in X-ray images. The method described involves weighted averaging to handle hybridized noises in color plane digital images. This process consists of summing up the pixel values within the filtering window and then calculating a weighted average. The nonlocal means filter (NLM) developed [4], which is notable for its ease of use and outstanding ability to effectively reduce white noise by preserving the edges details at the same time, has sparked a significant improvement in image processing area. To remove AWGN, researchers use a variety of NLM filter based approaches, as well as other types of noise such signal-dependent nonadditive speckle noise, additive mixed noise, and salt and pepper noise. It has also been demonstrated that existing NLM-based iterative techniques outperform their predecessors. The denoising methods of MR image was demonstrated in.

1.2 Contrast Enhancement

Pre-processing Contrast depicts the pixel intensity that will help to distinguish one object from the other object or distinguish between foreground and background of an image. In gray-scale images, contrast is calculated by finding the difference between the object brightness and its external environment (Surroundings). Contrast enhancement is one of the essential steps in image analysis that is significantly used in various areas such as processing of an image, pattern identification, and many more fields. Contrast enhancement sharpens the edges details in an image, making it very easier to extract objects and other information from the quality improved image. In actual, the main motive of image contrast improvement is to make an image suitable for a particular application by improving the quality of it.

In the literature, several approaches for contrast enhancement have been proposed. This section discusses the evolutionary level of development in the field contrast enhancement of 2-D images. The contrast of the source sample image was greatly increased using histogram equalization techniques [5]. This input is obtained under various environmental conditions. Image enhancement is primarily concerned with upgrading the visual quality of images, with the goal of focusing on required attributes and making them less obscured. Sometimes due to this the quality of image degraded. Various image enhancement techniques are developed in the field of digital image enhancement. Contrast enhancement is a common example of image enhancement. The frequency domain enhancement methods named as Tang's algorithm [6], works in the discrete cosine transform (DCT) domain, and wavelet-based approaches, such as Jin's method, which applies LAHE to individual frequency bands. Algorithms rely on multi-scale decompositions are also available. These include Toet's [7] method, which employs a low-pass pyramid ratio, and Mukhopadhyay and Chanda's method, which employs morphological top-hat transformations.

Iqbal et al. [8] presented image enhancement using Dual-Tree Complex Wavelet Transform and Nonlocal Means (DT-CWT-NLM) in 2013. The dual-tree complex wavelet transforms (DT-CWT principal)'s role is to find the high-frequency sub-bands and process them separately. In addition, the Lanczos interpolator was used to interpolate the input images. They recommend employing resolution enhancement if they want to prevent losing high-frequency components.

1.3 Ghost Artifacts

Ghost artifacts represents blurred information of an image. They occur due to the presence of dynamic objects while acquiring image. These blurry objects are known as ghosts. Several deghosting strategies for eliminating fuzzy elements from HDR images have been proposed throughout the last decade. These algorithms may attempt to detect moving things and improve the localization of objects move accurately. Depending on the approach used, the resulting image may contain broken/incomplete objects or noise. Deghosting methods are frequently computationally demanding; yet a simplistic deghosting strategy that is computationally cheap may give adequate results. As a result of this inspiration, a simple deghosting method based on the spectrum angle mapper (SAM) metric is offered.

Deghosting is a topic that has been focus by many researchers in the last decade. Tursun et al. divided HDR image deghosting approaches into four categories in a recent study: global registration, moving object, selection, and registration. Ward suggested a multiple stage resolution-based algorithm for correcting translational misalignment among acquired input images using pixel values rely on median system, based on the global exposure registration methodology. Cerman et al. [9] suggested applying frequency domain correlation to minimize misalignment caused by both translation and rotation. Because CIFT system have not required any support system such as photometric registration as a requirement for geometric registration, Gevrekci et al. [10] used it for geometric registration of multi-exposure photos. Tomaszewska et al. [11]

demonstrated spatial attribute extraction using special feature transform named as scale invariant with the estimation of a planar homograph. Im et al. [12] proposed estimating transformation method for reducing the sum of square errors. In 2011, Akyuz et al. [13] introduced a method for testing pixel order relations that was inspired by Ward's method. It was discovered that pixels with a lower intensity than their bottom neighbour and a higher intensity than their right neighbour should have the same relationship across exposures. They discovered a link between these types of relationships and reduced the hamming distance between correlation maps for alignment. Ghosting artifact is a systemic problem that is generated by the instability of the primary magnetic field B0 and timing error connected with the scanner hardware. These ghost artifacts appear as shadows of the original object in DTI acquisitions in various diffusion gradient directions. This can make it harder to see the true anatomy of the spinal cord and make the true position of the cord more ambiguous. In the literature, several approaches for solving echo misalignment problem have been investigated. Reference scan-based approaches are now employed primarily on clinical MRI scanners. These strategies use modest gradients to align echoes after performing a calibration scan to estimate the on-axis gradient/data collection time delay. Reference scans, on the other hand, are susceptible to time changes such as object mobility, which complicates MRI pulse sequence design. Parallel imaging techniques are another option to reduce ghosting phenomenon.

Despite the good performance of the various spatial filters for upgrading image quality, there is need of hybrid denoising, contrast enhancement and removal of ghost artifacts with improved metric values. This stage is dedicated to identifying and reducing impulses, the approach can be significantly enhanced. To do this, we combined the stage of image denoising with the NLM filter, which was specifically designed to provide the best noise suppression outcomes. The experiments will show the performance of filters in terms of metrics peak signal to noise ratio (PSNR), the mean square error (MSE), and (SSIM), the NIQE attributes and other state-of-the-art filters. Then, in this work, a new hybrid method called Modified Yanowitz and Bruckstein's binarization (MYBB) has been utilized to tackle ghosting effects of an image. There are two stages to the suggested hybrid technique. A two-step approach based on NLM, and top hat filtering is used in the first stage of the complete model to reduce the effect of noise and improve image contrast. Then, a hybrid technique based on the Yanowitz and Bruckstein's binarization filter is utilised to enhance the metric values of pre-processed stage.

2 Methodology

The objectives of this manuscript have been identified as to implement a pre-processing stage for removal of noise, ghost artifacts and contrast enhancement along with improved objective metric values such as MSE, PSNR, SSIM etc.

For the minimization of noise, contrast enhancement, removal of ghost artifacts and for the improvement of various metric values, different algorithms are utilized to achieve adequate results and at final point hybrid algorithm is used to yield adequate results. Table 1 lists the details of the above-said Pre-processing objectives.

Table 1. Objectives for the Image Quality improvement

Name of the objective	Description
Image filtering	To minimize the noise effect from input image
Contrast improvement	To improve the contrast of filtered image
Deghosting	To reduce the interference contributed by the capturing system
Peak signal to noise ratio	To maximize the peak signal to noise ration through adequate filter
MSE	To reduce the mean square error

Algorithmic Steps

Hybrid algorithm approaches to upgrading the pre-processing stage with improved objective metric values based on Fig. 1 divided into three sections:

Step 1: Noise Reduction

Nonlocal mean filter

- Read red, green, and blue plane of input sign image.
- contaminated RGB image converted into the L*a*b color space, after the conversion the non-local means filter smooths perceptually similar colors.
- Draw out a homogeneous L*a*b patch from the noisy background to calculate the noise standard deviation.
- After the calculation of standard deviation, next step involves the computation of Euclidean distance from the origin from the L*a*b patch. Then, estimate the noise using the standard deviation of the Euclidean distance.
- Use a high 'Degree of Smoothing' value and set it above the standard deviation of the patch. Applying non-local means to the L*a*b* image's helps reduce the image's noise.
- Convert the filtered L*a*b image to the RGB color space. Display the filtered RGB image.

One of the best image suppression methods named as nonlocal means (NLM) algorithms is used in RS image preprocessing because of its capability to retain texture details.

Non-local filters are unlike "local mean" filters, which smooth an image by averaging the values of pixels around a target pixel. Image detail is preserved by using a local mean algorithm post-filtering.

Let us suppose A be the area of an image, and x and y are two points within that image. Then Filtered image at point x,

$$\mathrm{F(x)} = \frac{1}{N(x)}\int_A n(y)\omega(x,y)dy \tag{1}$$

F is the filtered image at point x.

n(y): noisy image at poiny y.

w(x, y): weighted function.
N(x): normalized factor. Given as:

$$N(\mathrm{x}) = \int_{A} \omega(x,y)dy \tag{2}$$

Weight computed the similarity of weighted function between a neighborhood of x and y points. Neighborhood of *x* and a neighborhood of *y*.

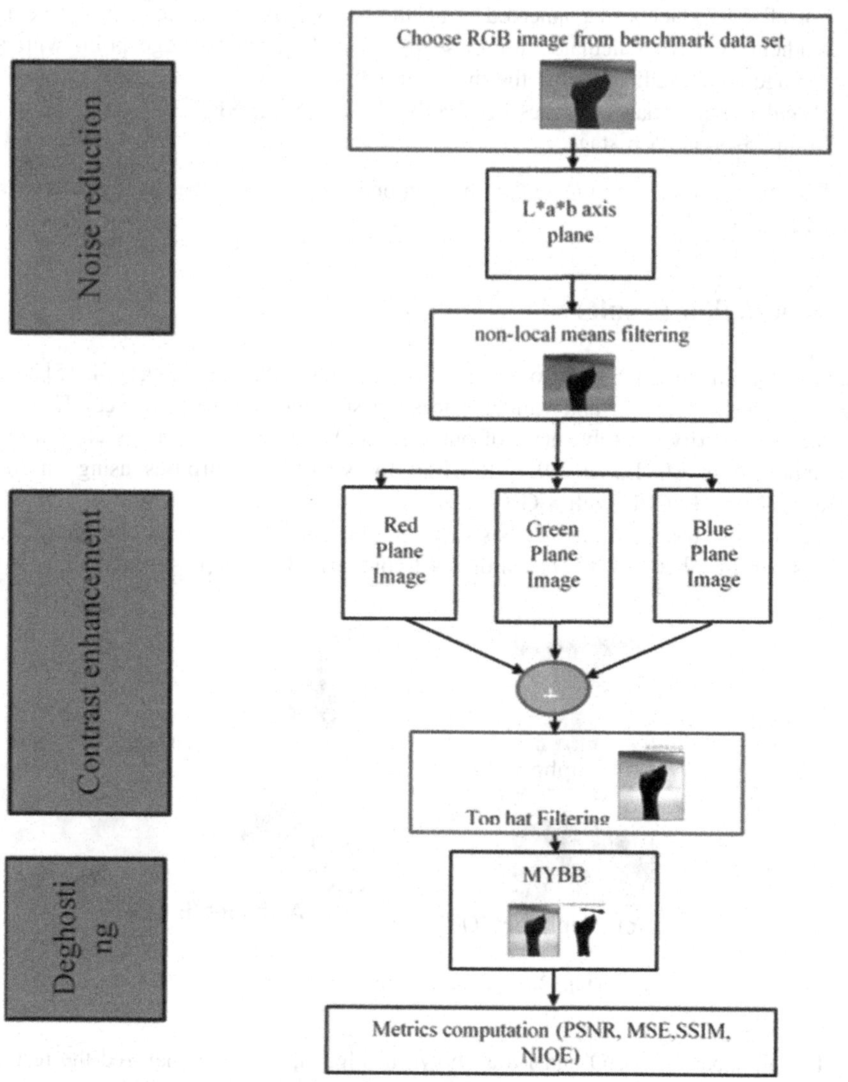

Fig. 1. Hybrid pre-processing stage design

Step 2: Contrast Enhancement
Top hat filtering for contrast enhancement

- Create the structuring element.
- Perform the top-hat filtering and display the image.

Steps 3: Deghosting of artifacts using Yanowitz and Bruckstein's binarization method

- Evaluate the gradient of the contrast enhanced image, using, e.g., Sobel's edge operator.
- Select threshold point value.
- For all components of connected print, the focus is on the edge pixels. Average gradient is to be calculated for these print pixels. Remove edge point with an average edge gradient below the threshold point.
- Calculate performance metrics i.e., PSNR, MSE, SSIM, NIQE.
- Comparison at each stage.

The main aim is to minimize the noise on one hand and on other hand preserve the signal quality.

3 Simulation Results

Sample input images are used from the two types of dataset references as [14, 15] based on ASL and ISL to test and validate the suggested model's performance. This will enable us to verify the robustness of our system. The proposed model's algorithm is implemented in MATLAB V9.4 (R2018a) for simulation purposes using an Intel Core I i5-1035G1 CPU with 8 GB RAM.

The dataset based on ASL consists of 26 Alphabets and 3 special character, 3000 images per alphabet and ISL based data set contains 1320 samples in overall.

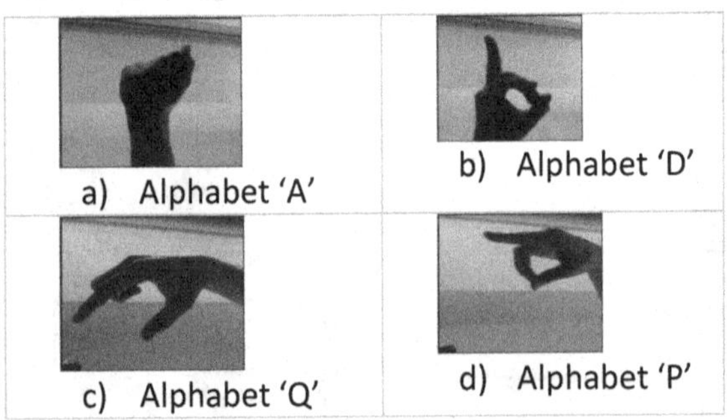

Fig. 2. The Sample input Alphabets.

For alphabets A, D, Q and P (as shown in Fig. 2), we have analyzed the results. Various noise minimization and ghost removal algorithms are used at the preprocessing stage. Figure 3 and Fig. 4 depicts the outputs of hybridized algorithm and various other filtering methods for alphabet A. The comparative analysis of proposed method with state of art is shown below in Table 2 in terms of various metric values.

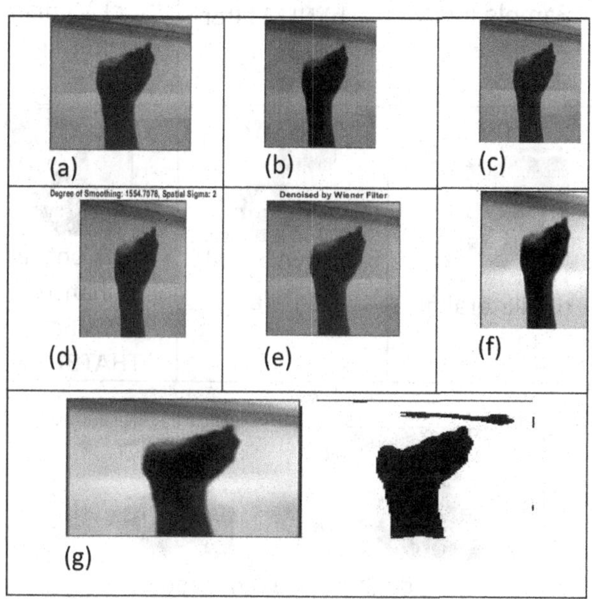

Fig. 3. The Proposed Model outputs for Alphabet 'A' (a) Input image (b) Denoised with NLM filter (c) Denoised with Median filter (d) Denoised with bilateral filter (e) Denoised with weiner filter (f) Contrast enhanced using THATBHAT (g) Deghost and binarized. Table 3 and Fig. 4 showed the preprocessing results for sample input of alphabet D.

Table 2. Comparative Analysis of proposed method with state of art in terms of Quality Metrics for Alphabet 'A'

Metric	Proposed	Median filter	Weiner filter	Gaussian bilateral filter
PSNR	**32.1432**	20.17	19.22	19.07
MSE	**2.361**	4.563	9.29	9.94
NIQE	**18.85**	6.17	5.78	6.99
SSIM	**0.9978**	0.9903	0.967	0.969

Table 3. Metric Evaluation of different filters for input image 1 (Alphabet 'D')

Metric	Proposed	Median	Weiner filter	Gaussian bilateral filter
PSNR	**31.3414**	20.19	18.51	18.460
MSE	**3.897**	5.95	12.89	13.2
NIQE	**18.86**	6.212	5.52	7.22
SSIM	**0.9980**	0.9893	0.96	0.96

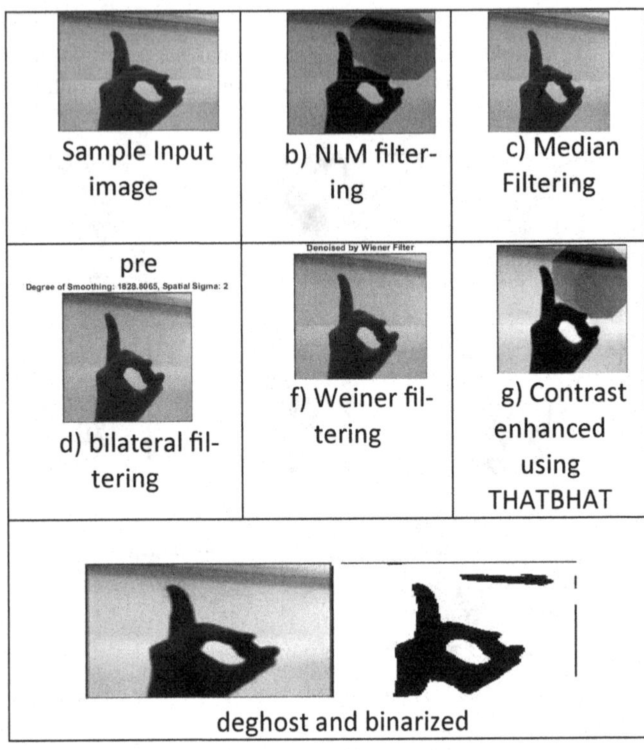

Fig. 4. The proposed model outputs for Alphabet 'D'

Table 4 and Fig. 5 showed the preprocessing results for sample input of alphabet Q and Table 5 and Fig. 6 showed the preprocessing results for sample input of alphabet P.

Table 4. Metric Evaluation of different filters for input image 1 (Alphabet 'Q')

Metric	Proposed	Median	Weiner Filter	Gaussian Bilateral Filter
PSNR	**32.5701**	21.31	19.20	15.35
MSE	**1.416**	3.55	9.38	15.23
NIQE	**18.86**	6.9	5.590	7.79
SSIM	**0.9977**	0.9911	0.972	0.933

Table 5. Metric Evaluation of different filters for input image 1 (Alphabet 'P').

Metric	Proposed	Median	Weiner	Gaussian bilateral filter
PSNR	**31.4380**	21.63	19.10	17.52
MSE	**1.879**	3.063	9.83	14.234
NIQE	**18.85**	5.0378	4.41	6.60
SSIM	**0.9979**	0.993	0.97	0.96

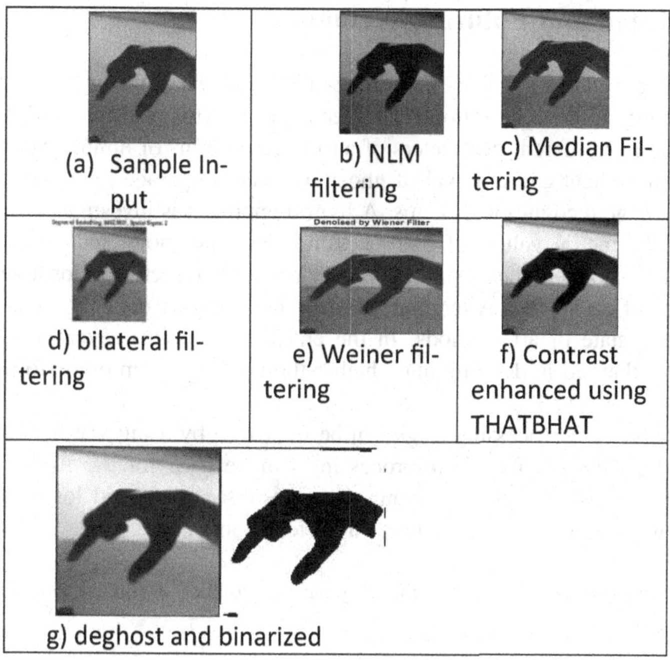

1(Alphabet ‘P’)

Fig. 5. The proposed model outputs for Alphabet ‘Q’

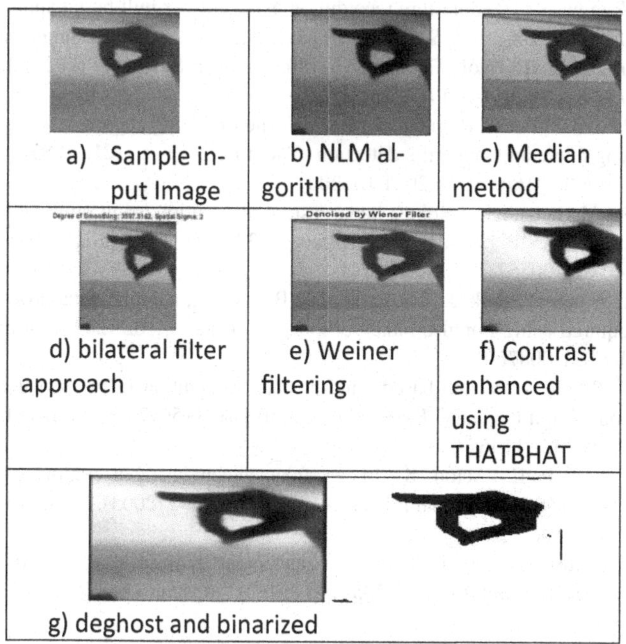

Fig. 6. The proposed model outputs for Alphabet ‘P’

4 Conclusion and Future Directions

Pre-processing could be a viable option for dealing with the challenges of improvement of image quality in the applications of image analysis. This research work focused on the adequation of different parameters of an image in terms of minimization of noise, contrast enhancement and removal of ghost artifacts to upgrade the overall results of the sign language recognition systems. A hybrid approach is investigated in this work to improve the metric values of preprocessing stage. For noise reduction, nonlinear mean filter helps to yield the required output. Then top hat filtering helps to upgrade the visual effect of an image. After that comparative analysis done between proposed algorithm and state of art methods. In the end tabular results revealed a variety of metric values that aid in determining whether the new algorithm outperforms existing methods.

In future, the pre-processing stage can be improved by using various optimization techniques then the results of pre-processing can be used for the further stages of recognition systems. The preprocessing stages results can be used for recognition of sign language system based on contact-based technology.

Conflicts of Interest. Authors declare that they have no conflicts of interest to report regarding the present study.

References

1. Wani, K., Ramya, S.: Hand gesture recognition using convex hull-based approach. In: Dhar, S., Mukhopadhyay, S.C., Sur, S.N., Liu, C.-M. (eds.) Advances in Communication, Devices and Networking. LNEE, vol. 776, pp. 161–170. Springer, Singapore (2022). https://doi.org/10.1007/978-981-16-2911-2_17
2. Alam, M.M., Islam, M.T., Rahman, S.M.M.: Unified learning approach for egocentric hand gesture recognition and fingertip detection. Pattern Recognit. **121**, 108200 (2022). Doi: https://doi.org/10.1016/j.patcog.2021.108200
3. Bakheet, S., Al-Hamadi, A.: Robust hand gesture recognition using multiple shape-oriented visual cues. EURASIP J. Image Video Process. **2021**(1), 1–18 (2021). https://doi.org/10.1186/s13640-021-00567-1
4. Ahmed, S., Wang, D., Park, J., Cho, S.H.: UWB-gestures, a public dataset of dynamic hand gestures acquired using impulse radar sensors. Sci. Data. **8**, 102 (2021). https://doi.org/10.1038/s41597-021-00876-0
5. Sharma, S., Singh, S.: Vision-based hand gesture recognition using deep learning for the interpretation of sign language. Expert Syst. Appl. **182**, 115657 (2021). Doi: https://doi.org/10.1016/j.eswa.2021.115657
6. Jinshan Tang, Peli, E., Acton, S.: Image enhancement using a contrast measure in the compressed domain. IEEE Signal Process. Lett. **10**, 289–292 (2003). https://doi.org/10.1109/LSP.2003.817178
7. Toet, A.: Adaptive multi-scale contrast enhancement through non-linear pyramid recombination. Pattern Recognit. Lett. **11**, 735–742 (1990). https://doi.org/10.1016/0167-8655(90)90092-G

8. Iqbal, M.Z., Ghafoor, A., Siddiqui, A.M.: satellite image resolution enhancement using dual-tree complex wavelet transform and nonlocal means. IEEE Geosci. Remote Sens. Lett. **10**, 451–455 (2013). https://doi.org/10.1109/LGRS.2012.2208616
9. Gevrekci, M., Gunturk, B.K.: On Geometric and Photometric Registration of Images. In: 2007 IEEE International Conference on Acoustics, Speech and Signal Processing - ICASSP 2007, pp. I-1261-I–1264. IEEE (2007). https://doi.org/10.1109/ICASSP.2007.366144
10. Im, J., Jang, S., Lee, S., Paik, J.: Geometrical transformation-based ghost artifacts removing for high dynamic range image. In: 2011 18th IEEE International Conference on Image Processing, pp. 357–360. IEEE (2011). https://doi.org/10.1109/ICIP.2011.6116490
11. Republic, C.: Exposure time estimation for high dynamic range imaging with hand held camera. Pattern Recognit. 1–6 (2006)
12. Chen, L.C., et al.: Applying a web-based integrated radiation oncology information platform to enhance working efficiency and increase patient safety. Int. J. Radiat. Oncol. **99**, E549 (2017). Doi: https://doi.org/10.1016/j.ijrobp.2017.06.1920
13. Akyuz, A.O.: Photographically guided alignment for HDR images. https://doi.org/10.2312/EG2011/areas/073-074.
14. https://www.kaggle.com/grassknoted/asl-alphabet
15. https://lttm.dei.unipd.it/downloads/gesture/#senz3d

Beam Steering Antenna Design with High Gain for Satellite Communication

Akinola Segun[1(✉)], Ghanshyam Singh[1], Prabahat Thukur[1], and Mayank Sharma[2]

[1] Centre for Smart Information and Communication Systems, Department of Electrical and Electronic Engineering Science, Auckland Park Kingsway Campus, University of Johannesburg, Johannesburg 2006, South Africa
akinolaa@uj.ac.za
[2] Department Electronics and Communication Engineering, School of Engineering and Technology, ITM University Gwalior, A43 Bypass, Gwalior, India

Abstract. This article presents an in-depth design of advanced beam steering inner ring structure (ABS-INS) with high gain for satellite communication systems. This design consists of a novel forty-two elements of a unit-cell compacted with the composite system. As the antennas are essential components for various applications specifically, in communication systems, therefore, several antennas have been designed for this purpose. For future generation communication systems, there is a need for beam steering antennas to solve high path loss challenges, low gain, attenuation of objects, and misalignment of antennas. We have designed an antenna array to feed on a dielectrics image line with a movable reflector plate. Moreover, unlike other reported antenna designs, which feed on image lines only, the serial beam gets more signals with coupling to dielectric image line from the waveguide with the transition to allow proper propagation and desired frequency range. The radiation beam angle steer when the propagation is remain unchanged with distance. The array's beam direction is controlled by the change in perturbation distance in the dielectric image line and the movable plate. We have modelled the proposed antenna with the help of 3D electromagnetic Computer Simulation Technology (CST) studio suite a commercial simulator based on finite integration techniques and optimization of the structure parameters are performed with a time-domain solver of microwave studio. Further, the validation of the proposed model has been performed with the ANSYS HFSS simulator.

Keywords: Beam steering · Microstrip antenna · Satellite communication

1 Introduction

This advanced communication system is paramount to meet the demand of modern global communication. The wireless communication system's rapid growth relies on beam steering because it is an essential antenna with high gain and directivity capability [1–3]. The use of beam steering antenna increases rapidly because of a good

R. S. Tomar et al. (Eds.): CNC 2020, CCIS 1502, pp. 366–379, 2021.
https://doi.org/10.1007/978-981-16-8896-6_30

factor from its provision of widespread viewpoint beam steering work on the higher frequency regime of the spectrum [4, 5]. The satellite communication system expansion increases microwave and millimeter-wave frequency, bringing about the beam steering antenna with an aperture coupled microstrip antenna as good and recommended for these applications [6]. Satellite communication and cellular communication are now using several methods such as electronically steerable passive array radiator, phase shifter, and servo-motor system to control the antenna system's radiation patterns to meet the demand and get the best output [7–9]. The steering of the beam of a high gain antenna is essential but most challenging in terms of requirement due to the variable nature of wireless communication link/channel. The high gain antenna is very impressive for the communication system that makes beam steering necessary for the antenna when receiving or transmitting in the mobile. Moreover, traditionally high gain is achieving by using a discharged reflector or rather with planar antenna arrays.

Furthermore, to steer the beam, the reflector is physically moved around multiple axes, but the phased array antenna use shifter in the steering beam electronically [10, 11]. The other tradition is the phased array uses a solid-state with a ferrite phase shifter at the back of the antenna element. The beam-steering array is complicating and expensive. The traditionally beam-steering antenna is typically based on a phased array with electronics scanning techniques [12]. Now focusing on these papers, beam and dielectric image feed line is the travel wave structure [13]. The signal in electromagnetic travels majorly in the dielectric image line. Those mentioned above can be perturbing in several ways and methods. The propagation change is constant in the electromagnetic field dielectric image line and can be applied to steer radiation beam angles in the patch antenna arrays. In enhancing gain, dielectric lenses, reflectors, electromagnetic bandgap, frequency selective surface, the metamaterial, and superstrate or array techniques are all traditionally used. Furthermore, the phased array system can scan very fast by integrating many circuits that include a solid-state phase shifter with the beamforming networks. This system is complex, lossy, bulky, and expensive. Some of the conventional arrays have been work on by researchers with several publications [14–17]. Meanwhile, it is expensive to use, which makes phase array limited and sophisticated military with space system to overcome this type of problem, so there is a need to develop need methods or approach to beam steering. We model a beam-steering antenna that covers the problem of complexity, lossy, bulky, high cost, our model beam steering reduces the interference, low cost, save power, increase gain, directivity, directional beams, relatively low side lobes, and ability to steer towards the target. Also, the relevance of this research is to have an antenna with a compact-sized, low profile with planner structure, low cost has an antenna that is gain and steers radiation patterns. Besides phase, the array requires more elements like more circuit components such as phase shifters with power dividers. Therefore, many techniques will minimize the complexity required for electronic beam steering. One strategy has been in terming electronically steerable passive array radiator, which can work with the phase shifter. Moreover, a passive radiator is excited with the driven antenna through mutual coupling. Therefore, a patch antenna requires additional patches for steering a beam opposing a single patch antenna, although the patch has a narrow bandwidth. In another part, the phase shifter employs the use of solid-state devices like the micro electrochemical system structure, photo conducting switches, or ferrite materials, which is utilizing for antenna beam [18]. Meanwhile, the cost of the phase shifter is still high in applying to practice. Some components increase the insertion loss between the radio frequency source with the radiating elements achievable without the phase shifters [19]. The number of beam steering directions depends on the number of passive radiators. Furthermore, many different techniques point to the main antenna radiation beam in a particular direction. First, some antennas are move by hand. [20] show in a recent publication on techniques to increase gain, such as the dielectric substrate earlier mention. The model process of a steerable antenna comprises electromagnetic beam theory with beam steering methods. The beam theory explains using mathematical properties of the angular spectrum of a plane wave. Meanwhile, beamforming is the combination of signals from array elements in high directional beam radiation. This theory exhibits the amplitude distribution over any average plan direction of the propagation called a spherical wave. The beamforming uses precisely to align the received indicator phase from parts of the array forming beam. Therefore, this is realized by executing the time delay on the element signal, which originated from the pencil beam's spatial filters.

The signal receiving in an exact location meddling from added locations originate several wireless sonar communications, radar biomedicine, and acoustic applications. The beam steerable antenna is essential in electronics, microwave engineering, radar, telecommunication, and mitigation interference channels. The antenna radiation is direct to the interest area, with so many beam steering techniques been used over the years. In this paper, we focus on ABS-INS design with high gain for international space station communication. This design consists of a novel 42 compacted network elements in a composite structure. The antenna array feeds on a dielectric. The serial beam gets more signal with coupling to dielectric image line from the waveguide with the transition to allow proper propagation and desire frequency range. The radiation beam angle steers when the propagation is constant. The array's beam direction is controlled by the change in perturbation distance in the dielectric image line and the movable plate. This design was done by the computer simulation technology. The simulating were done with the validation for international space station communication. Presenting results with a comparison shows excellent. The demand increases rapidly for low profile requirements and a small antenna for wireless communication to gain more popularity in microstrip patch antennas. The antenna has an excellent complete application in the commercial area, military, and etc. [21]. The microstrip geometry can be arbitrary. Therefore, beam steering design involves change the track in the primary lobe of the antenna's radiation pattern. Furthermore, beam steering provides productive and destructive interference to steer the beam for a desire direction, comparing beam steering methods with microstrip antennas, this paper investigates the beam steering profoundly to get high gain. Several techniques researching before choosing the best to get adequate and desire results such as: (1) antenna phased arrays beam steering; the beam steering is comprehended via array arrangement in the antenna elements, 4×4 mm^2, 8×8 mm^2, and more dimensions. The beam steering operates to perform with the change in phase in the feed signal element used in the antenna structure [22], it is showing that a Ka-band slot was a couple with a microstrip feed patch antenna of 4 × 4. It shows that the structure was able to give 15.6 dBi with good % bandwidth. The control phase more shift with the integration to produce beam steering with the 30° as maximum. It was design validated to get the accuracy of its application. (2) The superstrate refractive beam steering: the high refractive superstrate is for the control in the radiating wave above the radiator. The superstrate parameters, gain, and directivity of the microstrip antenna is managed through the full-wave simulation. The beam shows the antenna deflect in the plane simultaneously superstrate. There was displacement beside E Plane, where the central beam is tilting in the E plane and H plane [23]. The antenna is enclosed quarterly by the superstrate. The beaming shows the defecting in both the antenna's principal plane's advanced angle of rebound with a phase shift observed by high-refractive-index superstrate. Antenna in [24], the an main beam experimentally found deflecting at a high angle as the superstrate's refractive index increases. It implies a novel mechanism in controlling the microstrip antenna's gain and direction, mainly on the beam's radiation is rebounded in E plane with H plane and the superstrate's position in XY plane. Furthermore, it shows that the antenna's core beam deflected in the portion's path to the patch covered partially, subjected to the superstrate's refractive index be condensed to 33° and sophisticated directivity. (3) The phase shifter beam steering: the researcher has done some work on beam steering using a phased shifter, another suitable technique. In this case, the beam steering is contingent upon the phase stay. Furthermore, the phase delays are accomplished using a phase shifter to switch meanderlines or other techniques. Using the switch will make the steering angle realized. Moreover, the steering angle is realized using a specific phase delay offered by phase shift [25]. (4) The parasitic array beam steering: this type of beam steering method has been recycled a lot. The beam titling is recognized via the antenna configuration's parasitic element, positioned at the matching layer or beyond radiating layer. The parasitic number depends on the design, but the objective goal is to activate or deactivate the parasitic elements using a shorting pin referred to as the switch. The construction of a pin diode is used as the switch along. Furthermore, the antenna can maintain the gain of 4 dBi from the angle of 53 with the parameter spacing. Meanwhile, the length of the parasitic elements is influenced via the tilt angle [19]. (5) Switching pin diodes beam steering research shows that beam steering in a microstrip antenna realizes through switches among the fed with the radiating patch. Furthermore, the steering angle or a route of foremost controls with a different artificial switch state, a sole beam steering broad-band microstrip is fabricated with measurement. This performs by steering the pin diode connecting stubs with the application on health care's [26]. (6) Leaky-wave beam steering: leaky-wave beam steering, the antenna's main beam route is controlling by altering the interrupted reactive filling of the microstrip line. Furthermore, the reactive loading provides the periodic patch couple to the stubs in the microstrip line. Meanwhile, the patches are associated with the ground through PIN diodes, with an individually irregular patch coupled to the ground via the switch to steer the main beam. The design is a reconfigurable antenna steering man since 40° to 64° at 6.2 GHz [27, 28]. The author's contributions are that a prospective novel framework is projected on ABS-INS design with high international space station communication gain. A novel concept of sequential beam steering network techniques is used to enhance the gain and improve the directivity with all results presented. The advanced design will signal the coupling dielectric image line with the transition, allowing propagation to get the desired frequency range (Ku-band). Furthermore, the radiation angle steers when the propagation is constant. The array's beam direction is controlled by the change in perturbation distance in the dielectric image line and the movable plate. Validation of results ANSYS adaptive mesh algorithm methods to reduce the cost of experimental fabrication of the prototype. The remainder of this paper is structured as follow, Sect. 2 investigates the antenna material, methods, modeling with configuration, in Sect. 3 details the results and discussion with the presentation of figures or images, state of the arc comparison with the table, finally, Sect. 4 is the conclusion.

2 Techniques

Beam steering antenna deals with the change in the direction of the radiation pattern's main lobe, which is accomplished with different techniques. How can the problems mention earlier, such as low cost, low gain, sophistication to manage, and small directivity, be solved in this research, how can the analysis be carried out, and the assumption on parameters to use to all this effect, we model a novel 42 compacted network elements in a composite structure, this design's goal (beam steering) is to increase the gain, improve the antenna's directivity and efficiency for a specific application and increase the already design microstrip antenna model's performance.

With its influence on the beam, the stub was investigated, importantly lengh and width are paramters when simulation is carry on. Serial compacted network elements of forty-two in beam-steering antennas with successive excitation are model to perform. The explaination in [19, 23–33], reveal that rotating in antenna array improve the beam polarization voltage. The impedance matching in the required frequency range of the elements in the form of the transmission line is used. In [34], the relative dielectric is constant, this was adopted with the frequency of the substrate, Fig. 1 shows the design model process, the calculation assumption is regularised with optimization, and this model procedure of the projected 3D image antenna in Fig. 2 from CST, the process of designing methods comprises of the rectangular patch using RogersRT5880 substrate feeding by 50 Ω microstrip. Inserting the ring with simulating parameters by optimizing to get the targeted frequency with the parameter, the ring is to shift impedance bandwidth, adding two arcs improved the already bandwidth to get the targeted results. The simulation was done and validated with results in an agreement, the validation with another simulator reduces the cost of fabrication.

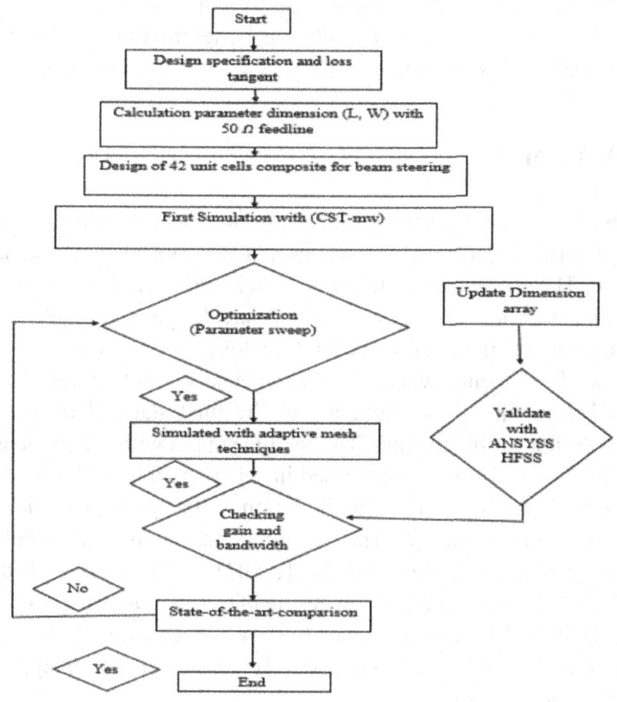

Fig. 1. Design procedures of the proposed array antenna system.

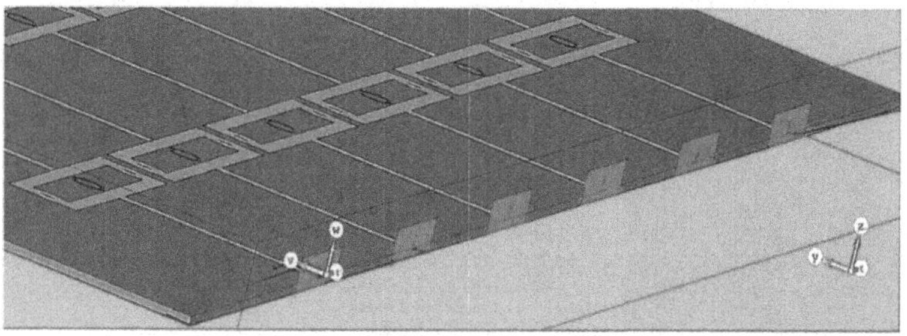

Fig. 2. 3D image of the proposed antenna array.

Feeding techniques are hybrid feed (corporate and serial feed), joining together with forty-two elements with the final implementation stage. Further explanation further on the connection design cosist of the dielectric, movable plate, aperture couple in the waveguide which propagation [35, 36]. One important property is when the right hand and left hand exhibit the same contribution in which the line is balanced and occurs when shunting with series resonance with an expression like [37]. The approaches used to steer the antenna array radiation pattern, the radiation beams are scanned with the targeted frequency, the beam steering angle can be controlled easily.

The techniques used are very low in cost, easy to fabricate, reliable, recommendable, and improve knowledge. This model limitation is deformation of the beam steering while on deflection and low-frequency agility.

3 Research Results

This design presents an ABS-INS with high gain for international space station communication, consisting of a novel 42 compacted network elements in a composite-handed structure. The antenna array feeds on a dielectric. Serial beam gets more signal with the transition to allow propagation and desire frequency range. In this design, some factors contribute to the simulated return loss. The accuracy of the forty-two compacted network elements with other parameters is putting together to get the desired results before this work could get to the final stage. The first stage is the conception and design of the antenna. The feed is simple with the numeral of antenna elements, which can be effortlessly increased in achieving a higher gain, therefore, it is organized in a tile formation. The configuration is the general brick methodology forming the active phased array. The scientific and numerical simulation in the impedance dependencies was presented for 12 GHz and 18 GHz with design beam-steering. Figure 3 after the optimization result of simulation return loss in red, this model was validated on Ku-band frequency to show agreement in the works. This is the black dotted line and on Ku-band frequency. This curve shows analysis numerically that the proposed model agrees.

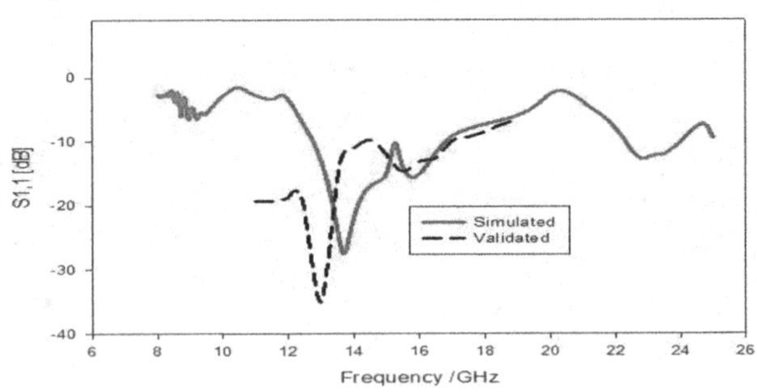

Fig. 3. Simulated and validate return loss of the proposed antenna.

The Fairfield gain at curve 12 GHz, 13 GHz, 17 GHz, and 18 GHz in Fig. 4 shows an increase in the techniques with this design, the blue line is 12 GHz, the red is 13 GHz, the green is 17 GHz, and the purple is 18 GHz. There is an increase in gain performance for 12 GHz, and 18 GHz, and it is best to know each port's signals, so the result is satisfactory after the simulation and validation.

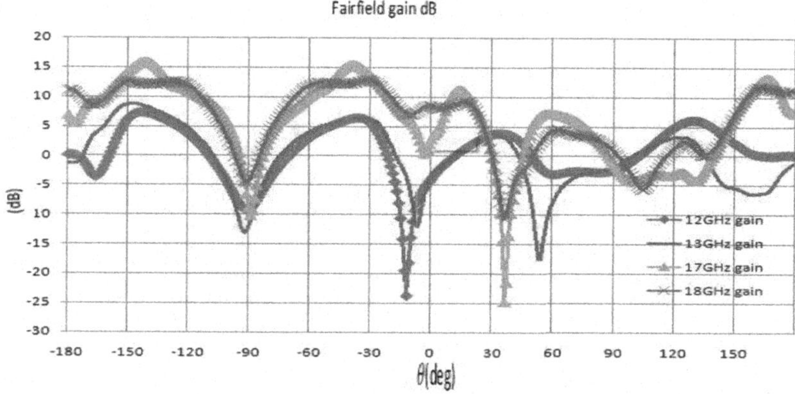

Fig. 4. Gain at each GHz

The power is accepted concerning the frequency was interesting, the integration of the antenna produced advance directional that is satisfactory both the E and H plane with the extra supremacy confined in main lobes and minus power in rear lobes in Fig. 5 Polar Plot radiation patter H plane and E plane at 12 GHz and 18 GHz. Increases in gain and directivity presented with 3D image Fig. 6, the gain of the antenna 3d view Fairfield result on gain 12 GHz, 13 GHz, 17 GHz, and 18 GHz proposed presented to show the model improved the gain and improve the directivity of the antenna. Gain and directivity increase is shown in Table 1 show performance is excellent in terms of the 12 GHz and 18 GHz. The value of the proposed axial ratio is accurate with the indication that the antenna has linear polarization. The regularized impedance of the fundamentals was determined to accomplish a required combination aperture was decided to see results. The antenna array with the forty-two elements was simulated and validated, it shows a match, high gain, wide operating range, large scanning angle., low cross-polarization, and low sidelobe with good antenna efficiency. Outcome of the design is good with and agreed with validating result with is conducted via microwave studio's and validation done ANSYS HFSS simulator, with the numerical analysis.

Table 1. Performance of the proposed

Frequency (GHz)	Gain ordinary	Directivity ordinary	The gain in Beam steering dBi	Directivity Beam steering dBi
12	3.74	4.09	7.24	8.69
18	3.61	3.78	12.9	13.4

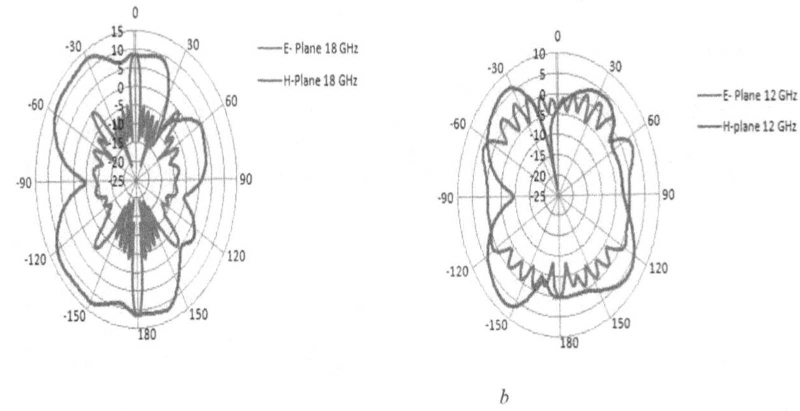

a *b*

Fig. 5. Radiation pattern: *a* – 18 GHz; *b* – 12 GHz

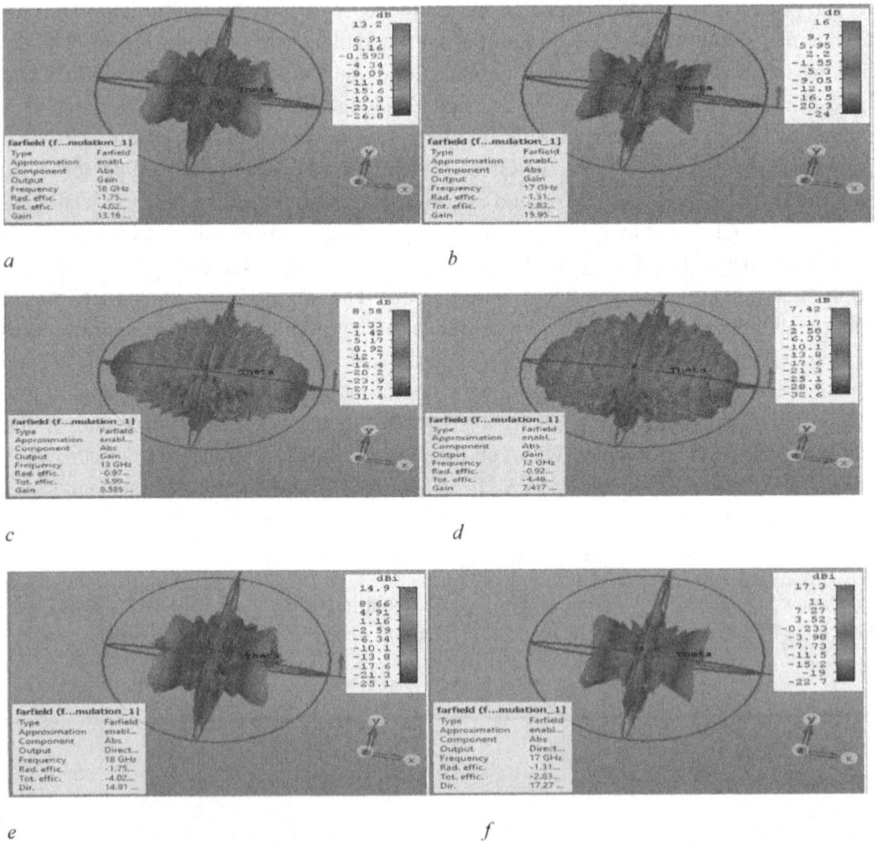

a *b*

c *d*

e *f*

Fig. 6. 3D image of a; gain at 18 GHz; b gains at 17 GHz; c gain at 13 GHz; d gain at 12 GHz; e directivity at 18 GHz and f directivity at 17 GHz

The state of the arc comparison with the literature on beam steering compared, in this study wide range of literature was conducted with depth inside on beam steering to get good gain. The comparison considers characteristics such as the techniques, beam steering angle, realized gain enchantment, the number of elements supported, and the frequency in Table 2.

Table 2. Start-of-the-art comparison

S/N	Technique's	Beam Steering angle (deg)	Realized gain enhancement (dBi)	Number of Element supported	Frequencies GHz	Ref
1	SIW-based	25	10.9	4	8–8.5	39
2	Varicap diode changing	50	12.4	32	22	40
3	Hybrid metasurface	18	7.30	6	10	41
4	GIMS lens	51	7.40	5	11	42
5	10 Element array antenna	No	10.3	10	1.72	43
6	10 Element array antenna	No	9.3	10	1.30	44
7	Double layer SIW leaky-wave	15	8.2	2	15	45
8	GIMS lens	48	11.5	2	10	46
9	Fabry perot Cavity	20	3	2	5.2	47
10	Cylindrical transformation	12	6	4	2.5	48
11	Sequential beam steering network	45	8.36–13.13	42	12–18	This work

The proposed novelty is that sequential beam steering network techniques enhance and realize beam steering with stable higher gain variation only in this work.

This frequency range of operation in the Ku band is 12 GHz to 18 GHz with a gain of 8.36 dBi to 13.13 dBi, respectively. It is also well understood that the arrays presented in this article are more compact with comparable gain.

4 Discussion of Result and Research Validation

In getting an antenna with high gain, a model antenna was designed with the forty-two compacted network unit cell serially presented in the paper. The main aim is to increase or enhance the gain of existing antenna n T shape, the feed is simple with the number of antenna elements which can be easily increased in achieving higher gain, therefore, it is arranged in tile configuration, the formation is the general brick approach, the transmitting and receiving module connected forming the active phased array. The simulating carried out via computer simulation technology microwave studio, with the ANSYSS HFSS simulator's validation. This will be correlated with measurement result and reduce the cost of experimental verification with fabricating a prototype, the design covers an interesting frequency range of 12 GHz to 18 GHz Ku-band, the gain increased at 12 GHz from 3.74 dB to 7.24 dB and at 18 GHz the gain increase from 3.61 dB to 12.9 dB. The proposed method and results obtained comparing with existing techniques show this proposed technique is better and advantageous in terms of Low cost, Normal medium size, very low insertion loss, less complexity, unlike other techniques that have the opposite of the attributes. The limitation of this study is the matching layers, the number of beam steering methods is also limited by the reduction in gain and cross-polarization generation, further, in future fast-wave structures, artificial dielectric material with constant less one can be fabricated, which will bring solutions to previous techniques.

5 Conclusions

This article's primary attention is developing a beam-steering antenna, the beam will consist of 42 network elements, unlike other antennas, in fulfilling the objectives, this model compared serially, gets more signal with coupling to dielectric image line from the waveguide with the transition to allow proper propagation and desire frequency range. They are explaining the systematic or scientific radiation beam angle steer when the propagation is constant. The array's beam direction is controlled by the change in perturbation distance in the dielectric image line and the movable plate. The model novelty advantages with this development method include the low cost, simple operating mechanism, excellent performance, high power efficiency, and good height accuracy with the design results covering an interesting frequency range of 12 GHz to 18 GHz Ku-band, the gain increased at 12 GHz from 3.74 dB to 7.24 dB and at 18 GHz the gain enhanced from 3.61 dB to 12.9 dB. Validation of results numerically presented on the estimate show results in agreement. This model uses an ANSYS simulator with adaptive mesh algorithm techniques to reduce the prototype's fabrication cost, and the results are in agreement.

References

1. Tomov, B.G., Stuart, M.B.: 3-D synthetic aperture high volume rate tensor velocity imaging using 1024 element matrix probe. In: Proceeding of the IEEE International Ultrasonics Symposium (IUS), pp. 1–4 (2020)
2. Ghasempour, Y., Knightly, E.W.: Decoupling beam steering and user selection for scaling multi-user 60 GHz WLANs. In: Proceedings of the 18th ACM International Symposium on Mobile Ad Hoc Networking and Computing, pp. 1–10 (2017)

3. Guo, W., Wang, G., Li, T., Li, H., Zhuang, Y., Hou, H.: Ultra-thin anisotropic metasurface for polarized beam splitting and reflected beam steering applications. J. Phys. D Appl. Phys. **49**(42), 425305 (2016)
4. Ayach, O.E., Rajagopal, S., Abu-Surra, S., Pi, Z.: Combining baseband processing and radio frequency beam steering in wireless communication systems, U.S. Patent8, 929, 473, 1–6 (2015)
5. Rojanski, V., Starovolski, A.: Phased array antenna, U.S. Patent Application 14/ 385, 360, pp. 3–6 (2013)
6. Vadlamudi, R., Sriram Kumar, D.: Design of a circular slot antenna with broadband dual CP bi-directional radiation pattern. In: 2020 IEEE International Students' Conference on Electrical, Electronics and Computer Science (SCEECS), pp. 1–4. IEEE (2020)
7. Panagamuwa, C.J., Chauraya, A., Vardaxoglou, J.C.: Frequency and beam reconfigurable antenna using photoconducting switches. IEEE Trans. Antennas Propag. **54**(2), 449–454 (2006)
8. Kawakami, H., Ohira, T.: Electrically steerable passive array radiator (ESPAR) antennas. IEEE Antennas Propag. Mag. **47**(2), 43–50 (2005)
9. Han, Q., Hanna, B., Inagaki, K., Ohira, T.: Mutual impedance extraction and varactor calibration technique for ESPAR antenna characterization. IEEE Trans. Antennas Propag. **54** (12), 3713–3720 (2006)
10. Deng, W., Wu, R., Chen, Z., Ding, M., Jia, H., Chi, B.: A 35-GHz TX and RX front end with high TX output power for Kaband FMCW phased-array radar transceivers in CMOS technology. IEEE Trans. Very Large Scale Integr. (VLSI) Syst. **28**(10), 2089–2098 (2020)
11. Kedar, A.: Some studies on sparse antenna arrays with the aid of exact expression of directivity. In: 2019 IEEE Indian Conference on Antennas and Propagation (InCAP), pp. 1–4. IEEE (2019)
12. Alibakhshikenari, M., et al.: Beam-scanning leaky-wave antenna based on CRLH-metamaterial for millimeter-wave applications. IET Microwaves Antennas Propag. **13**(8), 1129–1133 (2019)
13. Nissanov, U., Singh, G.: mmWave/THz reconfigurable ultra-wideband (UWB) microstrip antenna. Prog. Electromagnet. Res. C **111**, 207–224 (2021)
14. Skobelev, S.P.: Comments on "overlapped phased array antenna for avalanche radar". IEEE Trans. Antennas Propagation **68**(5), 4163–4163 (2020)
15. Malhotra, I., Singh, G.: Beam-Steering characteristics of highly directive photoconductive dipole phased array antenna. In: Terahertz Antenna Technology for Imaging and Sensing Applications, pp. 203–215. Springer, Cham (2021). https://doi.org/10.1007/978-3-030-68960-5_8
16. Gu, X., et al.: Development, implementation, and characterization of a 64element dual-polarized phased-array antenna module for 28GHz high-speed data communications. IEEE Trans. Microwave Theory Techn. **67**(7), 2975–2984 (2019)
17. Zhang, J., Björnson, E., Matthaiou, M., Ng, D.W.K., Yang, H., Love, D.J.: Guest editorial special issue on multiple antenna technologies for beyond 5G-Part II. IEEE J. Sel. Areas Commun. **38**(9), 1941–1944 (2020)
18. Won, C., Lee, M., Li, G.P., De Flaviis, F.: Reconfigurable beam scan single-arm spiral antenna with integrated with RFMEMS switches. IEEE Trans. Antennas Propag. **54**(2), 455–463 (2006)
19. Chen, S., Hirata, A., Ohira, T., Karmakar, N.C.: Fast beamforming of electronically steerable parasitic array radiator antennas: theory and experiment. IEEE Trans. Antennas Propag. **52** (7), 1819–1832 (2004)

20. Akinola, S., Hasimu, I., Singh, G.: Gain and bandwidth enhancement techniques in Microstrip Antenna; A technical Review. In: International Conference on computational intelligence and Knowledge Economy (ICCIKE), Dubai, United Arab Emirate, pp. 175–180 (2019)
21. Uchendu, Y., Kelly, J.: Survey of beam steering techniques available for millimetre wave applications "Progress InElectromagnetics Research B, vol. 68, pp. 35–54 (2016)
22. Faisal Abedin, M., Ali, M.: Effects of EBG reflection phase profiles on the input impedance and bandwidth of ultrathin directional dipoles. IEEE Trans. Antennas Propag. **53**(11), November 2005
23. Mittra, R., Li, Y., Yoo, K.: A comparative study of directivity enhancement of microstrip patch antenna using three different superstrates. Microw. Opt. Technol. Lett. **52**(2), 327–331 (2010)
24. Siddiqui, O., Attia, H., Ramahi, O.M.: Antenna beam control using high refractive index superstrates. In: Proceeding of the 9th International Symposium on Antenna, Propagation, and EM Theory, Guangzhou, China, Nov. 29–Dec. 2 (2010)
25. Ji, T., Yoon, H., Abraham, K., Varadan, V.K.: Ku-band antenna array feed distribution network with ferroelectric phase shifters on silicon. IEEE Trans. Microwave Theory Techn. **54**(3), 1131–1138 (2006)
26. Attia, H., Yousefi, L., Bait-Suwailam, M.M., Said Boybay, M., Ramahi, O.M.: Analytical model for calculating the radiation field of Microstrip antenna with artificial magnetic superstrates: theory and Experiment. IEEE Trans. Antennas Propag. **59,** 1438–1445 (2011)
27. Fallahpur, M., Ghasr, M.T., Zoughi, R.: Miniaturized reconfigurable multiband antenna for multiradio wireless communication. IEEE Trans. Antennas Propag. **62**(12), 6049–6059 (2014)
28. Olivares, I.E., Carrazana, P.: Mie scattering revisited: study of bichromatic Mie scattering of electromagnetic waves by a distribution of spherical particles. Rev. Sci. Instr. **91**(8), 083112 (2020)
29. Gambár, K., Rocca, M.C., Márkus, F.: A repulsive interaction in classical electrodynamics. Acta Polytechnica Hungarica **17**(1), 175–189 (2020)
30. Liu, Q., Zhen, W., Gao, M., Deng, D.: Goos-Hänchen and Imbert-Fedorov shifts for the rotating elliptical Gaussian beams. Results Phys. **18**, 103297/1–5 (2020)
31. Ogurtsov, S., Koziel, S.: Design and architecture selection of corporate feeds comprising EqualSplit power dividers for low-sidelobe arrays. In: Proceeding of the 23rd International Microwave and Radar Conference (MIKON), pp. 49–52 (2020)
32. Li, C., Zhu, X.-W., Liu, P., Chao, Y., Hong, W.: A metasurface-based multilayer wideband circularly polarized patch antenna array with a parallel feeding network for Q-Band. IEEE Antennas Wirel. Propag. Lett. **18**(6), 1208–1212 (2019)
33. Shookooh, B.R., Monajati, A., Khodabakhshi, H.: Ultra-wideband metamaterial-loaded microstrip array antennas using fibonacci & fractal geometric patterns, design and modelling. Europ. J. Electr. Eng. Comput. Sci. **4**(5) (2020)
34. Wilbert, D.S., Hokmabadi, M.P., Kung, P., Kim, S.M.: Equivalent-circuit interpretation of the insensitive polarization performance of THz metamaterial absobers. IEEE Trans. Terahertz Sci. Technol. **3**, 846–850 (2013)
35. Li, Y., Wang, J.: Dual-band leaky-wave antenna based on dual-mode composite microstrip line for microwave and millimeter-wave applications. IEEE Trans. Antennas Propag. **66**(4), 16601668 (2018)
36. Maquet, V., Messiaen, A., Ragona, R.: Study of the ohmic losses of a traveling wave antenna section in view of the application on DEMO. In: AIP Conference Proceedings, vol. 2254, pp. 070001/1–5 (2020)

37. Wu, P.-C., Chen, L., Luo, Y.-L.: Miniaturized wideband filtering antenna by employing CRLHTL and simplified feeding structure. Electron. Lett. **51**(7), 548–550 (2015)
38. Jung, E.-Y., Lee, J.W., Lee, T.K., Lee, W.-K.: SIW-based array antennas with sequential feeding for X-band satellite communication. IEEE Trans. Antennas Propag. **60**(8), 3632–3639 (2012)
39. Habaebi, M.H., Janat, M., Rafiqul, I.Md.: Beam steering antenna array for 5G telecommunication systems applications. Progress in Electromagnetics Research M, vol. 67, pp. 197–207 (2018)
40. Katare, K.K., Biswas, A., Akhtar, M.J.: Microwave beam steering of planar antennas by hybrid phase gradient metasurface structure under spherical wave illumination. J. Appl. Phys. **122**(23) (2017)
41. Afzal, M.U., Esselle, K.P.: Steering the beam of medium-to high gain antennas using near-field phase transformation. IEEE Trans. Antennas. Propag. **65**(4), 1680–1690 (2017)
42. Zhou, H.-J., Huang, Y.-H., Sun, B.-H., Liu, Q.-Z.: Design and realization of a flat-top shaped-beam antenna array. Prog. Electromagn. Res. **5**(5), 159–166 (2008)
43. Zhang, Z.-Y., Liu, N.-W., Zuo, S., Li, Y., Fu, G.: Wideband circularly polarized array antenna with flat-top beam pattern. Microw. AntennasPropag. **9**(8), 755–761 (2015)
44. Monavar, F.M., Shamsinejad, S., Mirzavand, R., Melzer, J., Mousavi, P.: Beam-steering SIW leaky-wave subarray with flat-topped footprint for 5G applications. IEEE Trans. Antennas Propag. **65**(3), 1108–1120 (2017)
45. Singh, A.K., Abegaonkar, M.P., Koul, S.K.: Wide angle beam steerable high gain flat top beam antenna using graded index metasurface lens. IEEE Trans. Antenna Propag. **67**(10), 6334–6343 (2019)
46. Ji, L.Y., et al.: A reconfigurable partially reflective surface (PRS) antenna for beam steering. IEEE Trans. Antennas Propag. **63**(6), 2387–2395 (2015)
47. Liang, B., Izquierdo, B.S., Parker, E.A., Batchelor, J.C.: Cylindrical slot FSS configuration for beam-switching applications. IEEE Trans. Antennas Propag. **63**(1), 166–173 (2015)
48. Reis, J.R., et al.: Electronically reconfigurable FSS-inspired transmit array for two-dimensional beam steering. IEEE Trans. Antennas Propag. **65**(9), 4880–4885 (2017)

Author Index

Printed in the United States
by Baker & Taylor Publisher Services

Printed in the United States
by Baker & Taylor Publisher Services